A Synopsis of American History

Volume II: Since the Civil War

D1300910

A Synopsis
of American
History

Volume II: Since the Civil War

Sixth Edition

CHARLES SELLERS
HENRY MAY

University of California at Berkeley

NEIL R. McMILLEN

University of Southern Mississippi

HOUGHTON MIFFLIN COMPANY   BOSTON

Dallas   Geneva, Illinois   Lawrenceville, New Jersey   Palo Alto

Printed in the U.S.A.
Library of Congress Catalog Card Number: 84-81347
ISBN: 0-395-36195-8

Cover: Thomas Hart Benton (1889–1975): "Threshing
Wheat" (detail), 1939, tempera on panel, 26 × 42 in.,
unframed.
Permanent Collection, The Sheldon Swope Art Gallery,
Terre Haute, Indiana.

EFGHIJ-A-93210

CONTENTS

CONFLICTING HISTORICAL
VIEWPOINTS

SPECIAL TABLES

MAPS

PREFACE

A *Synopsis of American History,* now in its sixth edition, provides students with a brief introduction to a complex subject. Our object in writing this comparatively slender volume is not to reduce the amount that students read, but to liberate them from the traditional, oversize textbook so that they may pursue their own historical inquiries in primary sources and specialized accounts. By design, then, the *Synopsis* is concise, but chronologically inclusive.

This edition of a textbook first published more than twenty years ago emphasizes political history, which in our opinion affords the clearest organization of the nation's past. Yet we have defined *politics* broadly, and have endeavored to link it to the larger environment in which it functioned. Thus, our focus is political, but the sixth edition also analyzes the social, cultural, economic, and intellectual currents of American life. In chapters like "A New Society, 1600s–1700s," for example, varied topics — such as colonial women, the Enlightenment, and the Great Awakening — give added dimensions to political events; a new chapter, "People of Plenty, 1946–1961," deals with post–World War II society and developments like the baby boom, suburban expansion, and consumerism.

In reducing a long and complicated story to a relatively few pages, we have found it neither possible nor desirable to avoid a point of view. While we have tried to be fair and judicious, we have not been reluctant to offer historical judgments. Appropriate reading in other books — the whole purpose of our synoptic approach — should enable students to accept or reject our interpretative statements. "For Further Reading" sections at the ends of chapters, though generally restricted to books that are readily available in college libraries, introduce students to the literature of each period. The sixteen essays called "Conflicting Historical Viewpoints" supplement the text and remind students of the subjectivity of the historian's craft; the Viewpoints highlight enduring scholarly controversies and suggest the development of scholarly thought through the years. Other pedagogical aids include nineteen time charts, which give a chronological summary of political and other important events. Three new photo essays cover the Republic's early days, the Civil War and Reconstruction, and the Depression and New Deal era. The maps have been revised and clarified, and new maps have been added.

This sixth edition has been thoroughly revised and updated. The two chapters on Progressivism in the previous edition have been combined in Chapter 22, "The Progressive Era, 1901–1917." The chapters from 28 on have been rewritten, with two new chapters: Chapter 29, "People of Plenty," mentioned earlier, and Chapter 32, "New Directions: Federal Policy in the 1980s," which covers the Reagan administration. In addition, new material on women and minorities, judicial decisions, and economic and cultural trends has been added to chapters throughout the text.

The text is also available in a two-volume edition. *Volume I: Through Reconstruction* contains Chapters 1–16, and *Volume II: Since the Civil War* covers Chapters 15–32.

We wish to thank a number of colleagues who, in one edition or another, read all or parts of this book and made many valuable suggestions. The sixth edition, like its predecessors, rests heavily on the scholarship of others, an indebtedness reflected on every page. We express particular gratitude to those generous colleagues who offered meticulous and thoughtful suggestions for this revision:

Carol M. Petillo, Boston College
Alan Jones, Grinnell College
Ellery Schalk, University of Texas — El Paso
Robert M. Calhoon, University of North Carolina —
   Greensboro
Robert E. Hooper, David Lipscomb College
Ralph E. Shaffer, California State Polytechnic University,
   Pomona
Sam Ross, California State University — Sacramento

We tried to follow their suggestions insofar as they were consistent with the philosophy of the book.

In its first two editions, the *Synopsis* was the work of Charles Sellers and Henry May. Neil R. McMillen joined the enterprise in 1974 and has assumed full responsibility for all subsequent editions.

N.R.M.

A Synopsis
of American
History

Volume II: Since the Civil War

15

★ ★ ★ ★ ★ ★

The Civil War, 1861–1865

WHEN Abraham Lincoln arose to deliver his inaugural address on March 4, 1861, few people had any very clear idea of how the secession problem should be handled. Some voices in the North counseled letting the "erring sisters depart in peace." The abolitionist minority called for a holy war to free the slaves. Majority opinion in the North was increasingly convinced that the Union must somehow be preserved, but there was no clear mandate for military coercion of the seceded states. The war that finally came, like most wars, came not because anyone deliberately willed it, but out of a chain of circumstances whose result reflected only imperfectly the conscious collective will of North or South. Insofar as a guiding will affected the outcome, it was the will of Abraham Lincoln.

LINCOLN AND THE SECESSION CRISIS

The new president was known to the country only as a tall, homely, and apparently uncultivated lawyer-politician from the prairies of Illinois. He had won brief notice years earlier when his opposition to the Mexican War caused Illinois voters to repudiate him after a single term in Congress. Not until his debates with Douglas in the senatorial campaign of 1858 had he attracted national attention. Elected president by a minority of the voters, he had given little public indication of his policy in the months between the election and the inauguration. Actually he had blocked all efforts at compromise by privately opposing any arrangement that left the slightest room for the expansion of slavery. But this position could be put down to political expediency — compromise on the territorial question would have left the infant Republican party little reason for existence — and gave no clue as to what he would do when he assumed office.

Certainly Lincoln was not prepared to lead a crusade to free the slaves. He had insisted that slavery was wrong and that its expansion should be

TABLE 8. PRESIDENTIAL ELECTIONS AND MAJOR POLITICAL EVENTS, 1860–1865

1860	**Abraham Lincoln** (Republican) elected over Stephen A. Douglas (Northern Democrat), John C. Breckinridge (Southern Democrat), and John Bell (Constitutional Unionist).
1860–1861	Seven states of the lower South secede and organize the Confederate States of America.
1861	Confederates bombard Fort Sumter, beginning the Civil War.
	Virginia, North Carolina, Tennessee, and Arkansas secede and join the Confederacy.
	Morrill Tariff. Substantial upward revision of duties, beginning a long period of high protection.
	Trent affair. Union naval officer seized two Confederate diplomats from a British vessel.
1862	Homestead Act provides free farms of 160 acres to actual settlers.
	Morrill Land Grand Act grants land to the states for agricultural and mechanical colleges.
	Pacific Railroad Act. Federal subsidies for a railroad from Omaha to California.
	Slavery abolished in the territories and the District of Columbia.
	Second Confiscation Act. Freeing escaped or captured slaves of Confederates.
1863	Lincoln's Emancipation Proclamation. Declaring free all slaves in Confederate areas.
	National Bank Act, with a supplementary act of 1864, establishes a system of banks issuing a uniform paper currency based on holdings of federal bonds.
	Turning point of the war in July, when Union forces capture Vicksburg on the Mississippi and stop Lee's invasion at Gettysburg.
	Lincoln announces his "10 percent plan" for the easy restoration of the seceded states to the Union.
1864	Lincoln vetoes the Wade-Davis bill, containing a harsher congressional plan for restoration of the seceded states to the Union.
	Abraham Lincoln (Republican) re-elected over George B. McClellan (Democrat).
1865	Lee surrenders to Grant at Appomattox Courthouse.
	Lincoln assassinated.
	The Thirteenth Amendment abolishes slavery throughout the United States.

stopped so that the country might look forward to its eventual peaceful extinction. But he had repeatedly denied any disposition, "directly or indirectly," to interfere with slavery where it already existed. Nor were his social values notably advanced. In his debates with Douglas the lanky Republican denied that he was "in favor of bringing about in any way the social and political equality of the white and black races." A "physical difference" would prevent the two races from ever living together on equal terms, he had said, and, therefore, "I, as much as any other man, am in favor of having the superior position assigned to the white race." He wanted slavery excluded from the territories so that "white men may find a home — may find some spot where they can . . . settle upon new soil and better their condition in life . . . as an outlet for *free white people everywhere.*"

The inaugural address revealed both a leader of unsuspected stature and a position around which northern opinion could rally. With an eloquence that no president since Jefferson had attained, Lincoln pleaded for preservation of the Union. "The mystic chords of memory," he said, "stretching from every battlefield and every patriot grave to every living heart and hearthstone all over this broad land, will yet swell the chorus of the Union, when again touched, as surely they will be, by the better angels of our nature." In trying to touch these chords, he reassured the South in the most positive terms that he would countenance no act against slavery in the states where it already existed.

But the address also had a vein of iron. The Union, said Lincoln, was perpetual, any violent acts against the authority of the United States were "insurrectionary or revolutionary," and these statements were to be taken "as the declared purpose of the Union that it *will* constitutionally defend and maintain itself." Though the federal government would not initiate hostilities, the president told the South, it would "hold, occupy, and possess" the federal forts and other property in the seceded states and collect the import duties there.

In retrospect, Lincoln clearly committed himself to a course that led directly to one of the bloodiest wars in history. But war was not his purpose. Eight of the 15 slave states were still in the Union. By refusing to recognize secession while at the same time declining to proceed forcibly against the secessionists, Lincoln was seeking to reinforce the manifest Unionist sentiment in the upper South. He wanted to keep the upper South from seceding, hoping that latent Unionism would eventually overcome secessionism in the seven seceded states of the lower South.

There were weaknesses in this union-saving strategy. One was that Lincoln exaggerated the strength of Unionist sentiment in the lower South. Another was the likelihood that the effort to hold the federal forts in the seceded states would lead to armed conflict. Armed conflict was the more likely because the more fiery secessionists were ready to provoke a crisis that would force the upper South to choose sides.

The issue of peace or war reached a crisis at Charleston, South Carolina. Practically all the federal forts and other property in the lower South had been taken over by the seceding states before Lincoln's inauguration. Of the few posts remaining in federal hands, the unfinished and lightly garrisoned Fort Sumter, located in the entrance to Charleston's harbor, had become the symbolic focus of the whole controversy over federal property. Sumter had sufficient supplies to hold out only six weeks, and a decision about its future could not be postponed. Lincoln finally informed the Confederate authorities that he was sending a naval expedition to reprovision Sumter. They in turn ordered their general at Charleston to demand the fort's immediate evacuation and, in case of refusal, to bombard it. The demand was made and refused, and on April 12, 1861, the Confederate shore batteries opened fire.

Lincoln responded by calling on the states for 75,000 troops. Rather than make war on their fellow Southerners, four states of the upper South — Virginia, North Carolina, Tennessee, and Arkansas — reluctantly followed the lower South out of the Union. The four slave states of Delaware, Maryland, Kentucky, and Missouri remained with the Union, though the last two had strong secessionist movements and furnished many soldiers to the Confederacy. The tables were turned on the secessionists when the strongly Unionist western section of Virginia seceded from Virginia and laid the basis for the new state of West Virginia under the aegis of the Union. Meanwhile the Confederacy acted to consolidate the adhesion of the upper southern states by moving its capital from Montgomery to Richmond, Virginia.

THE WAR BEGINS

A spirit of martial ardor swept over both sections in the spring of 1861. Northerners expected a short and easy war, while Southerners seemed oblivious to the overwhelming superiority in human and material resources against which they would have to contend. The 5.5 million free people of the 11 Confederate states faced a population of 22 million in the 23 Union states. The North had a four-to-one advantage in free males of fighting age and would muster twice as many soldiers. Even if one southern soldier was worth two Yankees — as Southerners loudly proclaimed — how were southern armies to be supplied and transported? The North had 80 percent of the country's factories and most of the coal and iron. Approximately 22,000 miles of railroad traversed the North compared to 9,000 in the South, and the North's rail network included a series of vital trunk lines between its eastern and western areas, whereas the sprawling southern regions lacked such efficient rail connections.

Not least of all, the North had Abraham Lincoln. Lincoln was never a very popular president, yet he was a consummate politician, an eloquent and inspired statesman, the symbol of an enduring Union, and an astute war leader whose military judgments were often better than those of his generals. The Confederacy, on the other hand, was less effectively led. For all his humanity, courage, and dignity, Jefferson Davis possessed neither the political nor the military gifts of his Yankee counterpart.

At the war's outset, however, the Union's advantages were not obvious. The South made a remarkable military showing, and some seasoned international observers thought it would prevail. In part, the South's initial successes were due to the strategic advantage of fighting a defensive war. The North was compelled to attack and not only to invade but to occupy the South. Southern commanders had the logistical advantage of shorter supply lines. Moreover, Jefferson Davis had at his command several outstanding generals: Albert Sidney Johnston, Joseph E. Johnston, Thomas J. ("Stonewall") Jackson, and pre-eminently Robert E. Lee. After much soul-searching, these officers had left the United States Army and had taken up arms for a new nation against the country they had once sworn to defend. Secession stripped the Union of many of its more talented officers, and Lincoln was several years in finding a truly able commander.

The Appalachian highlands, thrusting deep into the South, divided the war theater into two zones. Throughout the conflict, the greatest public attention was focused on the East, where the rival armies menaced each other's capitals, which were only 100 miles apart. The Confederate armies, magnificently led by Joseph E. Johnston and then by Robert E. Lee, repeatedly repelled Union invasions aimed at Richmond. In the first major battle of the war in July 1861, Union General Irvin McDowell's army of 30,000 was turned back by a smaller Confederate force at Bull Run in northern Virginia. Lincoln's next commander, 34-year-old General George B. McClellan, was a brilliant military administrator but not an able field commander. The cocky "Little Mack" ferried an enormous, well-trained invasion force down Chesapeake Bay and up the York River to the eastern outskirts of Richmond. But his troops were driven back by Lee and Stonewall Jackson in the series of hard fought battles that constituted the Peninsula Campaign of May–June 1862. Later that summer (August 29–30), Lee trounced another Union army led by John Pope in the second battle at Bull Run. Lee followed up this victory with an audacious advance across the Potomac River into Maryland; McClellan's army caught up with Lee's at Antietam Creek, some 50 miles northwest of Washington, in September 1862. In one of the war's crucial battles, the much larger Union army (70,000 Northerners to the 40,000 Confederates) inflicted so much damage that Lee had to withdraw to Virginia. In a single day of fighting, each side sustained some 12,000 casualties. Typically, the cautious McClellan failed to press his advantage and lost the opportunity to defeat Lee decisively.

Back on his home ground, Lee was again invincible. He defeated the blundering General Ambrose E. Burnside, McClellan's replacement, at Fredericksburg, Virginia, in December. In May 1863, Lee and Stonewall Jackson's forces repelled a Union army of more than double their numbers, led by Major General Joseph E. ("Fighting Joe") Hooker, Burnside's replacement, at Chancellorsville, Virginia. In the latter encounter, Jackson was killed accidentally by his own troops. Seeking to capitalize on the victory at Chancellorsville, Lee risked everything in a June invasion of the North, hoping to cut the east-west trunk railroads in Maryland and Pennsylvania, to imperil Washington, and to persuade the Union to make peace before the North's superiority in arms and materiel became irresistible. On July 1, 1863, Lee's 70,000 men and the 90,000 Union soldiers of George G. ("Old

Snapping Turtle") Meade, Hooker's replacement, assembled on opposing ridges outside the southern Pennsylvania town of Gettysburg. For three days during the greatest battle of the war, wave after wave of gray-clad Confederates swept against the entrenched Union position. On the hot, dry afternoon of July 3, Lee committed the costliest blunder of his career. In a last desperate charge against the center of the Union line, he sent General George Pickett with three divisions (15,000 troops) across the valley and up the Union-held Cemetery Ridge. The Confederates were cut down by withering Union fire. Casualties on both sides were staggering: the Confederates sustained more than 28,000 killed, wounded, or missing; the Union losses were slightly fewer. Repulsed at fearful cost, the South's last hope of victory gone, Lee had no recourse but retreat to Virginia.

While Lee's gamble was failing in the East, the Confederacy's military doom was being more plainly spelled out in the West. At long last Lincoln found a winning general, Ulysses S. Grant — an obscure, former junior officer in the Mexican war who had come out of retirement to join the Union cause. Using the Mississippi, Tennessee, and Cumberland rivers, which offered natural invasion routes for Union gunboats and armies, Grant drove steadily, from Cairo, Illinois, into the South. Forts Henry and Donelson, guarding the Tennessee and Cumberland rivers, fell to him in February 1862. Pressing southward on the Tennessee River, Grant inflicted a severe blow to the main Confederate army in the west during the bloody two-day battle at Shiloh (April 6–7). Both sides suffered severe losses; the outnumbered Confederates lost one-quarter of their forces, 11,000 troops compared to the 13,000 Union casualties. Also, Confederate General Albert Sidney Johnston, like many others in this era of primitive medical care, died of a minor wound. The southern troops retreated to Mississippi. Meanwhile, Union gunboats steamed up the Mississippi River from the Gulf of Mexico to take New Orleans, and others came down the Mississippi from the north to destroy a Confederate fleet at Memphis, Tennessee. The last stronghold on the river, Vicksburg, Mississippi, fell to Grant in July 1863, following a six-week siege, which exhausted Confederate forces and reduced the civilian population to eating rats and mules. With the surrender of General John C. Pemberton and 30,000 troops at Vicksburg, Grant had cut the Confederacy in two.

THE CONFEDERACY AT WAR

The burden of directing the Confederate war effort fell almost wholly on the shoulders of Jefferson Davis. Lacking able subordinates in his cabinet and in the Confederate Congress, Davis perhaps took on too much of the burden of detailed administration and sometimes made poor decisions concerning military strategy and commanding officers. But only an able and conscientious executive could have kept the Confederacy operating and its armies fighting, given the staggering difficulties that he faced.

At the beginning of the war, Davis had high hopes of aid from Europe. France's Napoleon III was openly sympathetic as were the ruling upper classes in Great Britain, and both of these countries went so far as to recognize the Confederacy's belligerent status. But Davis was counting on the economic power of the South's cotton to produce more substantial aid — full diplomatic recognition, financial assistance, and perhaps even military intervention. The South might have built up large credits for the purchase of supplies in Europe by shipping its cotton abroad. Instead, the Confederate authorities placed an embargo on cotton exports, expecting that this would force British cotton mills to close and thus bring pressure on the British government to intervene more openly on behalf of the Confederacy. Unfortunately for the Southerners, the British mills had a year's surplus of raw cotton on hand, some alternative sources of supply were available, and although some of the cotton mills eventually shut down, their unemployed workers remained sympathetic to the more democratic North and exerted their influence against any aid to the South.

The South's best chance to drive a wedge between Great Britain and the North came in November 1861 when a United States naval vessel stopped the British ship *Trent* on the high seas and took off the Confederate diplomats James M. Mason and John Slidell. But the United States promptly released Mason and Slidell, and Lincoln's skillful minister in London, Charles Francis Adams, was increasingly successful in preventing the British from aiding the Confederacy either directly or indirectly. And France refused to act without British support.

Meanwhile Lincoln had ordered the Union navy to blockade southern ports; by the time the Confederacy decided to ship cotton to Europe in exchange for supplies, this was no longer possible. Cut off from all outside goods (except a trickle brought in by swift blockade runners), the Confederacy was increasingly hard put to supply its armies with munitions or its people with the ordinary necessities of life.

As the struggle wore on and as the Confederacy's prospects expired under mounting Union industrial and military strength, the South's early optimism was replaced by growing discouragement, apathy, and disaffection. Secessionist sentiment was anything but universal in the Upper South and mountain regions. In the hill counties, the Confederate conscription law, which exempted overseers and owners of 20 or more slaves, was especially resented. Having no direct interest in slavery, some poor Southerners came to view the struggle as "a rich man's war and a poor man's fight." The disparity in materiel was also a factor. Union soldiers were adequately provisioned; sometimes encumbered federal soldiers jettisoned their unwanted articles. Often Confederate troops, on the other hand, lacked food and clothing and depended on captured Union supplies for arms. Draft evasion in the South increased following the Union victories of July 1863, and desertion became so widespread that by the end of 1863 one-third of the Confederate army was absent without leave — clearly, the morale of poorly paid Confederate soldiers was at low ebb. Desperate for manpower, the Confederacy in 1864 reached out to "the cradle and the grave," drafting men from 17 to 50 years of age; by war's end, it had resolved to draft slaves.

The South's enthusiasm for the war was probably less than wholehearted from the beginning. Its tradition of localism bred dissention. Fractious governors in some states and even Vice President Alexander Stephens resisted the inevitable centralizing policies necessary to the conduct of the war and defied the Richmond government. Raging inflation, transportation short-ages, and a federal blockade brought extreme civilian privation and unrest; in 1863 bread riots broke out in several cities, including Richmond where President Davis helped restore order. The Confederacy's most serious prob-lem, however, lay in the growing indifference of many wealthy and powerful Southerners. Never unreservedly committed to a separate southern nation, substantial portions of the planter class resented the "usurpations" of the Richmond government, particularly policies that hurt their financial inter-ests. A growing disenchantment with the Confederate cause was thus a ma-jor factor in the South's military collapse.

LINCOLN AND THE WAR

Like Davis, Lincoln also faced troubles, for wartime dissent was not con-fined to the South. In the border states (slave states that remained in the Union), anti-Union sentiment was widespread, and in the non-slave North, support for the war was not universal. As civil strife dragged on unsuccess-fully for the North, "Copperheads" — allegedly disloyal Democrats who were as dangerous as poisonous snakes — stepped up their demands for a negotiated settlement. Led by such spokesmen as Clement L. Vallandig-ham, former congressman from Ohio, and supported by Old Northwestern newspapers, these "Peace Democrats" found their greatest strength in Illi-nois, Indiana, and Ohio. Unlike the "War Democrats," who despite their differences with a Republican administration followed Stephen A. Douglas in supporting the war effort, the Peace Democrats opposed Lincoln's gov-ernment at every turn. A diverse group, they included some southern sym-pathizers, but most were loyal Unionists who for varied reasons decried "King Abraham's" leadership and thought the war to be ill-advised, unnec-essary, and even unconstitutional.

Much opposition centered on conscription, a novel wartime expedient that ran counter to the nation's tradition of voluntary military service. The draft law of 1863 exempted not only the unfit, but also those wealthy enough to hire a substitute or to pay $300. Since conscription fell disproportionately on the urban poor and immigrants, the law was widely resented. Riots oc-curred in a number of cities. The bloodiest riot took place in New York City, where for three days predominantly Irish working-class gangs vented their anger on blacks until federal troops arrived to end the looting and lynching. Not the least of Lincoln's problems was this unwillingness of whites to risk life and limb in what they viewed as a black cause.

Problems were also created by those strongly opposed to slavery. Lincoln was hounded by a group of "radical" Republicans who wanted to make the war an antislavery crusade and who advocated a punitive policy toward the South. Under the leadership of people like Senator Charles Sumner of Mas-sachusetts and Representative Thaddeus Stevens of Pennsylvania, the Rad-icals gained great power in Congress. They set up a joint congressional Committee on the Conduct of the War, which constantly criticized and interfered with the president's conduct of military operations.

The split between radical Republicans and moderate or administration Republicans did not affect cooperation on common interests, and a series of major laws was passed by the wartime Congresses. The Morrill Tariff Act of 1861 marked a turn toward higher protective duties, and subsequent legislation of 1862 and 1864 pushed duties to unprecedented levels, inaugurating an era of extravagant protectionism that would last into the twentieth century. The long fight for free land culminated in the Homestead Act of 1862, granting 160 acres to any family that wished to settle on the public domain. The Morrill Land Grant Act of 1862 donated public lands to the states for support of agricultural and mechanical colleges. In the same year Congress finally authorized the long projected transcontinental railroad, granting 30 million acres and millions in federal bonds to the Union Pacific and Central Pacific railroad companies to build a line from Omaha to the Sacramento River. By an act of 1863, Congress established a national banking system, with member banks issuing a stable currency of uniform national bank notes on the basis of their holdings of federal bonds. In passing these important measures to serve the interests of northern farmers and business enterprise, the Congress was simply legislating the Republican platform since Southerners were no longer there to oppose it.

No measures aroused the controversy in the Republican party that the subject of slavery created. Anxious to mollify the loyal slave states of Delaware, Maryland, Kentucky, and Missouri, Lincoln stoutly resisted doing anything to suggest that abolition of slavery was a northern war aim. In the fall of 1861, he removed the Radicals' favorite general, John C. Frémont, from command in Missouri for declaring that the slaves of rebels were free. Meanwhile he sought unsuccessfully to interest Congress and the loyal slave states in a plan of gradual, compensated emancipation with the federal government footing the bill. His constitutional amendment would have granted states up to 37 years to abolish slavery.

The Radicals were determined to force the issue, and in 1862 pushed through Congress legislation abolishing slavery in the territories and in the District of Columbia. More important was the Second Confiscation Act of 1862, declaring forfeit the property of all persons supporting the rebellion and proclaiming escaped or captured slaves to be "forever free." By this time, Lincoln was becoming aware that an emancipation policy would be of value in helping to win the war, especially by gaining friends for the Union in Europe. Finally, on January 1, 1863, he issued his Emancipation Proclamation. This famous proclamation was not the universal measure it has often been said to be. It freed only those slaves living in rebel areas — those who were at the moment beyond the reach of Union law — and justified even this largely rhetorical gesture on the grounds of "military necessity." Only as the Union armies advanced did the freedom proclaimed by Lincoln's document become an actuality for the slaves. Not until 1865 did the Thirteenth Amendment, forbidding slavery throughout the country, become a part of the Constitution.

The Emancipation Proclamation did not allay the Radicals' suspicion of Lincoln, but they failed to block his renomination for president in 1864. In this wartime election, the Lincoln Republicans ran as the Union party, appealing to War Democrats by nominating for vice president Andrew Johnson, the Tennessee Senator who had remained loyal to the Union. The regular Democratic nomination went to General McClellan, many of whose supporters were calling for peace negotiations. The long string of Union defeats in the East has so strengthened antiwar sentiment that Lincoln might have been defeated but for some timely military successes in the West on the eve of the election.

Despite his political difficulties, the war so changed the structure of American government and society that Lincoln wielded presidential power that his predecessors could never have dreamed of. Commanding vast land and naval forces, initially without benefit of competent professional military leadership, he intruded more often into day-to-day military operations than he wanted. A civil libertarian, he nevertheless stretched executive authority in the name of national security by ordering the arrest of disloyal and disruptive citizens. Under his direction, the government tampered with private mail, closed several dissident newspapers, suspended in "extreme" cases the writ of habeas corpus (traditional safeguard against arbitrary arrest), and incarcerated without trial thousands of men for draft evasion or suspected disloyalty.

The government's role, moreover, was greatly expanded. To ensure efficient transportation and communication, the government subsidized a transcontinental railroad, built additional track, and assumed the direction of telegraph and rail lines. To finance a war that required daily expenditures of up to $2 million, Congress taxed and borrowed heavily; at war's end, the national debt was $2.6 billion. Congress created a Bureau of Internal Revenue and imposed the first income tax. It doubled the protective tariff, reformed the banking and monetary system, and fostered scientific agriculture. During the war the federal bureaucracy necessarily burgeoned, and afterward, federal expenditures never again fell to prewar levels.

TOWARD APPOMATTOX

The fall of Vicksburg to Grant and Lee's failure at Gettysburg, both in July 1863, doomed the Confederacy. And Lincoln had finally found a successful general. Before leaving the West, Grant consolidated Union control of Tennessee with a victory at Chattanooga. In the spring of 1864, Grant was made general-in-chief of all the Union armies. Now his grand strategy was a two-pronged final offensive against the South, with General William T. Sherman leading one great Union army south from Chattanooga into Georgia and with Grant himself leading another army from Washington toward Richmond.

The twin offensives were launched simultaneously in May 1864. The two Union armies of around 100,000 each pressed back Confederate armies of around 60,000. In the West, Sherman steadily pushed the Confederates south and by September won the important rail center of Atlanta. He made an audacious decision to abandon his line of supply and wage a war of destruction between Atlanta and the sea. Devastating the countryside as he went, he was in Savannah by December, and the Confederacy was further segmented. Turning north, Sherman reached Columbia, South Carolina, in February 1865 and by March was in east-central North Carolina.

By demoralizing the Confederate areas south of Virginia, Sherman greatly facilitated Grant's advance on Richmond. In the Spotsylvania Wilderness and at Spotsylvania Courthouse in May 1864, Lee inflicted heavy casualties on the invading Union troops as he had so often done in the past. But this Union general did not withdraw to lick his wounds as had all his predecessors. By flanking movements, he kept pressing south toward Richmond. At Cold Harbor, Lee again inflicted frightful losses on the Union army, but still Grant pushed inexorably south, passing just east of Richmond and crossing the James River. Lee managed to shield Richmond as Grant moved around it to the south and southwest toward Petersburg. By June, the two armies were entrenched facing each other in a long line bending from Richmond southward around the southern side of Petersburg.

Grant would not let go, and as the siege went on through the summer and fall and winter, his superiority in numbers began to tell. Remorselessly he kept extending his line to the west, and Lee's line became steadily thinner and more vulnerable. By April, Lee could extend his line no more and had to pull out of his entrenchments, abandoning Richmond and Petersburg. But by this time Grant had cut off all the roads leading south over which Lee might effect a junction with the only remaining Confederate army of any strength. On April 9, 1865, at Appomattox Courthouse, Lee bowed to the inevitable and surrendered. One month later the fleeing Jefferson Davis was captured in disguise in Georgia and imprisoned at Fortress Monroe. The Confederacy was dead — and so were some 260,000 Confederate and 360,000 Union soldiers. In blood, if not in dollars, it was the costliest war in American history.

LINCOLN AND THE SOUTH

The treatment of the vanquished South was a point of contention between Lincoln and the Radicals. Lincoln wished to bring the rebellious states back into full membership in the Union as rapidly and painlessly as possible. By the time Union forces occupied Arkansas in December 1863, the president was ready with his "10 percent plan" of reconstruction. Under this plan he proposed to extend amnesty and restore confiscated property to all Confederates who would take a simple loyalty oath, excluding only high civil and military officers of the Confederacy or its states. As soon as 10 percent of a state's 1860 electorate had taken the oath, the state could write a new constitution and rejoin the Union.

The Radicals, however, feared with considerable reason that if the southern states were reconstructed on this basis, the old ruling class would return

MAP 5: THE CIVIL WAR

MINN.

WIS.

MICH.

ME.

VT.

N.H.

N.Y.

MASS.

CONN.

R.I.

IOWA

PA.

N.J.

ILL.

IND.

OHIO

Gettysburg

DEL.

MO.

Potomac R.
Bull Run 1861
1862
W. VA.
1863

MD.

Washington

Fredericksburg
Spotsylvania
Chancellorsville VA.
Richmond Cold Harbor
Petersburg

Chesapeake Bay

KY.

Cumberland R.

Appomattox

Fort Donelson
Fort Henry

N.C.

ARK.

Memphis

TENN.

Chattanooga

Shiloh

Mississippi R.

Tennessee R.

Columbia

S.C.

ATLANTIC
OCEAN

MISS.

ALA.

GA.

Atlanta

TEXAS

Vicksburg

LA.

Savannah

New Orleans

FLA.

GULF OF MEXICO

Union states
Confederate slave states
Union slave states

0   200   400 miles
0   200   400 kilometers

to power and the freed blacks would be little better off than they had been under slavery. Anxious for a thorough reconstruction of southern society, they insisted that black men be given the ballot and that the old rebel leadership be effectively excluded from political life. As a counter to Lincoln's plan they secured the passage in 1864 of the Wade-Davis bill. This measure required a majority, rather than 10 percent, of the 1860 voters to take a loyalty oath before reconstruction could begin and further insisted on disfranchisement of ex-Confederate leaders.

Lincoln allowed the Wade-Davis bill to die by pocket veto, but the Radicals had one tactical advantage. A state would not be fully restored to the Union until its representatives were seated in Congress, and the Radical-controlled Congress had full power over the admission of members. The Radicals used this power to deny admission to the first southern representatives who appeared under Lincoln's 10 percent plan. In March 1865, as the war drew to a close, the Radicals gave a further indication of their objectives by creating the Freedmen's Bureau to assist the ex-slaves in adjusting to freedom and to protect their rights.

The sharpening struggle between Lincoln and the Radicals was suddenly cut short on Good Friday, April 14, 1865, five days after Lee's surrender at Appomattox. As Lincoln sat in a box at Ford's Theater in Washington, John Wilkes Booth, an actor and Confederate sympathizer, fired a fatal bullet into the president's head, crying "*Sic semper tyrannis!* The South is avenged!"

A grieving nation suddenly discovered a tragic hero. To Lincoln's strength, humility, eloquence, and magnanimity was added the quality of martyrdom. He had presided over the bloodiest war in the American experience, preserving the Union as the land of liberty and last best hope of humanity. Hesitantly and grudgingly, but in the end unmistakably, he had also made the war a struggle to enlarge the sphere of American liberty. Yet the Emancipation Proclamation and the Thirteenth Amendment were only a beginning. It was Lincoln's Radical critics who saw most clearly that the task of completing emancipation still lay ahead, and even his great talents could hardly have been equal to this Herculean task. Perhaps it was a timely martyrdom that translated Abraham Lincoln — a man groping toward an ideal only dimly perceptible in his society and age — into the Great Emancipator. For a century and more to come, Lincoln, the symbol, would remind his fellow Americans that the egalitarian dream was still unfulfilled.

FOR FURTHER READING

The standard work on the Civil War era is Allan Nevins's *The War for the Union* (4 vols., 1959–1971), but James G. Randall and David Donald's *The Civil War and Reconstruction* (1961) and Peter J. Parish's *The American Civil War* (1975) are both important. Divergent interpretations of the North's reaction to secession are presented by David M. Potter in *Lincoln and His Party in the Secession Crisis* (1950), and by Kenneth M. Stampp in *And the War Came* (1950). The northern conduct of the war is best followed through the biographies of Lincoln. Benjamin P. Thomas's *Abraham Lincoln* (1952) is generally considered the best one-volume study, but see also *With Malice Toward None* (1977) by Stephen B. Oates. For greater detail, see Albert J. Beveridge's *Abraham Lincoln, 1809–1858* (2 vols., 1928) and the chronologically successive volumes by James G. Randall (completed by Richard N. Current) on *Lincoln the President* (4 vols., 1945–1955). Current has also written a fine interpretive essay on *The Lincoln Nobody Knows* (1958), while Peyton McCary analyzes *Abraham Lincoln and Reconstruction* (1978). Special aspects of the North during the war are treated in John Hope Franklin's *The Emancipation Proclamation* (1963), George Frederickson's *The Inner Civil War* (1965), James McPherson's *The Struggle for Equality* (1964), and Hans Trefousse's *The Radical Republicans* (1968). The blacks' role in the struggle is analyzed in Dudley Cornish's *The Sable Arm* (1956) and Benjamin Quarles's *The Negro in the Civil War* (1953). Emory Thomas surveys *The Confederate Nation* (1979); Frank E. Vandiver's *Their Tattered Flags* (1970) is a political and military history of the secession regime; Rembert Patrick describes *Jefferson Davis and His Cabinet* (1944). The Confederacy's *King Cotton Diplomacy* (1931) is the subject of Frank L. Owsley, while D. P. Crook's *Diplomacy* (1975) examines the maneuverings of both sides. The military history of the war from the viewpoint of the northern armies may be followed in the vivid volumes by Bruce Catton: *Mr. Lincoln's Army* (1951), *Glory Road* (1952), and *A Stillness at Appomattox* (1954). A more detailed and professional evaluation of the northern military effort through 1863, with greater attention to the western campaigns, is Kenneth P. Williams's *Lincoln Finds a General: A Military Study of the Civil War* (5 vols., 1949–1959). *The Gettysburg Campaign* (1968) is examined by Edwin B. Coddington. The fighting as viewed from the southern side is best followed in the distinguished studies by Douglas Southall Freeman: *R. E. Lee, a Biography* (4 vols., 1934–1935) and *Lee's Lieutenants* (3 vols., 1942–1944). Thomas L. Connelly in *The Marble Man* (1977) critically examines the life and legend of Robert E. Lee. Tom Henderson Wells has written an excellent history of *The Confederate Navy* (1971). Also outstanding are two works by Frank E. Vandiver: *Rebel Brass* (1956) and *Mighty Stonewall* (1957). Bell Wiley has described *The Plain People of the Confederacy* (1943), *Confederate Women* (1975), and the common soldiers of both sides in *The Life of Johnny Reb* (1943) and *The Life of Billy Yank* (1952). Edmund Wilson's *Patriotic Gore* (1962) brilliantly portrays the human and literary dimensions of the era. Of the multitude of personal accounts of contemporaries, three very different ones may be singled out as having special interest: the *Personal Memoirs* (2 vols., 1885–1886) of General Grant; *A Diary from Dixie* (1905) by Mary Boykin Chesnut; and *The Diary of Edmund Ruffin* (2 vols., 1972–1976), edited by William K. Scarborough.

The Civil War and Reconstruction

President Lincoln issued the Proclamation of Emancipation in 1863 before the end of hostilities. This lithograph of the proclamation made in 1865 by J. Mayer & Co. shows "before and after" scenes of a slavery sale and free blacks. (*Library of Congress*)

Lincoln, as Commander-in-Chief, is shown with General George B. McClellan and a group of officers at the headquarters of the Army of the Potomac. Photograph by Matthew Brady. (*Library of Congress*)

Union troops — the
96th Pennsylvania
Infantry — at Camp
Northumberland
near Washington.
Photograph by
Matthew Brady.
*(Library of
Congress)*

With the aggressive
leadership of
Generals Grant and
Sherman, Union
victories wrought
destruction on
southern cities and
countryside. The
ruins of Richmond,
Virginia, on the
James River, were
photographed by
Matthew Brady.
(*Library of
Congress*)

Confederate troops often lacked uniforms and other supplies, as this photograph of an army camp reveals. The Union army was generally better equipped. *(Library of Congress)*

Often unsuccessful in its early encounters with Confederate forces, the Union Army sustained many deaths and casualties. In June 1862, Matthew Brady photographed the wounded at a Union field hospital at Savage Station, Virginia. *(Library of Congress)*

Blacks fought on both sides of the conflict. This black gun crew participated in the battle of Nashville. *(Chicago Historical Society)*

FROM THE PLANTATION TO THE SENATE.

During Reconstruction, blacks were elected to the U.S. Congress. This poster shows, from left to right: Senator Hiram R. Revels, Representative Benjamin S. Turner, the Reverend Richard Allen, Frederick Douglass, Representatives Josiah T. Walls and Joseph H. Rainy, and the writer William Wells Brown. *(Library of Congress)*

Black sharecroppers
in the South often
found conditions
after Reconstruction
little better than
slavery. Victims of
white discrimination
and the crop lien
system, they lived in
poverty and too often
in virtual peonage.
(Brown Brothers)

16

★ ★ ★ ★ ★ ★

Reconstructing the Union, 1865–1890

IN THE GENERATION after the Civil War, economic expansion absorbed most of the nation's energies. The people's attention, however, centered at first on the Reconstruction of the Union and the new order in the defeated South. They faced difficult questions involving the rights of the freed slaves.

THE PROBLEM

The problems of Reconstruction were numerous. The most obvious and easiest problem was the physical rebuilding of shelled cities and ruined railroads. Harder to reconstruct was the defeated section's economic life. The South's industry was at a standstill; much of its farming land was lying idle. Its labor system was destroyed, investment capital was lacking, the savings of many people were wiped out by the collapse of Confederate currency and bonds. Beneath every other problem lay that of a new relationship between the South's two races. All that was clear about the country's 4,500,000 blacks was that none of them remained a slave. Some 286,000 were Union soldiers; a few were settled on confiscated plantations in the sea islands off the Carolinas; and many were simply wandering, drifting from Union army camps to southern cities with great hopes and no means of support. Nearly everybody assumed that they were to continue to work on the land. A few radicals had suggested that they would become landowners, and the sea islands experiment raised some hopes. White Southerners assumed that blacks would work as laborers for white landowners.

By 1865 three southern states were already reconstructed under the easy terms offered by President Lincoln, which demanded only that 10 percent of the citizens take an oath of future loyalty and recognize that slavery was ended. Once this was done, elections were held for both state governments and federal Congress. But Congress refused to admit these delegates.

To settle this difficulty, Americans turned to the Constitution. What was the status of a sovereign state that had seceded and been forced to return to the Union? Was it still a state or was it, as Thaddeus Stevens insisted, merely a conquered province? Who would decide: Congress or the president? The president was commander-in-chief of the armed forces and had the power to pardon. But Congress had the right to admit new states, to make rules for territories, and to judge the qualifications of its own members. Long before Lincoln's death, the executive and congressional branches of government had been at loggerheads over these issues. In this unprecedented situation, the Constitution offered few unambiguous answers to these questions.

More important in the long run than the constitutional question was the state of mind of three main groups: the ex-slaves, the defeated white Southerners, and the victorious Northerners. Though able black leaders soon appeared, most of the ex-slaves were not only illiterate but inexperienced, both in participating in politics and in dealing with such economic institutions as wages and rent. Many pathetic stories are told about the strange hopes and fears of these displaced people. Yet the basic desires of the freed blacks were clear. What they wanted was real freedom, and the signs of that freedom were the right to move around the country, access to education, and ownership of land.

Right after the war, according to northern travelers in the South, shock rather than bitterness was the most common state of mind among southern whites. With their institutions destroyed, what was to become of them? Most pressing of all, without slavery, how was the cotton going to be picked and planted? At first, many looked northward for their answers.

Northern whites comprised the third and largest group, which was by no means a united body. Nearly half were Democrats. Only a few Democrats had been willing to accept the breakup of the Union, but many had sharply criticized the conduct of the war and had opposed emancipation. The sole purpose of the fighting, the party's leaders had insisted, should have been the restoration of "the Union as it was." In the 1864 elections, the Democrats had lost some ground, yet they still mustered a formidable 45 percent of the votes. Not even the Republicans were sure of what they wanted. The group called "Radicals" agreed that Lincoln had been too weak, too lenient on the South, but they agreed on little else. Republicans were also divided on such matters as the tariff and finance, and few had thought through the future status of the blacks.

Two paradoxes made constructive action inordinately difficult. First, slavery had been abolished and the ex-slaves armed by a nation that believed overwhelmingly in the inherent inferiority of the black race. Even among the abolitionists, only a few had accepted blacks as intellectual and political equals.

Second, during Reconstruction the government had to undertake a program of drastic, even revolutionary measures. Yet nearly all nineteenth-century Americans had been taught that government action should be sharply limited. This had been said by Jefferson, Jackson, and Lincoln. Schools and colleges taught as gospel truth the maxims of *laissez-faire* political economy, that is, minimum governmental interference in the economy.

The choice faced by the North, in its simplest terms, was the choice offered to every victor: occupation or conciliation. Most Northerners preferred the latter, but they wanted conciliation on northern terms: the South must recognize its errors and govern itself — according to northern ideas.

Yet to whom in the South could government be confided? To the ex-rebels who were, many Northerners believed, still rebels at heart? To the ex-slaves whom most Northerners regarded as members of an inferior race? Even if they were given the vote, the freedmen, inexperienced in politics and a minority in all but two states, could hardly govern alone. They would have to have the support either of a substantial number of southern whites or of sufficient occupying forces. With or without black suffrage, the same choice existed: conciliation or occupation.

PRESIDENTIAL RECONSTRUCTION

The first alternative, conciliation, was attempted under the authority of Presidents Lincoln and Johnson and is often referred to as Presidential Reconstruction. It is hard to tell how Lincoln's "10 percent plan" might have worked if it had been continued. This plan had already been sharply challenged by Congress, and Lincoln himself had said that it was only one of many possible approaches. The Wade-Davis bill, the most extreme congressional substitute, had been left unsigned by Lincoln.

Like Lincoln, President Andrew Johnson embodied the log-cabin tradition of humble origins. He was a tailor by trade and learned to read only as an adult. A resident of eastern Tennessee where slaves were few, and a former Jacksonian Democrat, he had been an outspoken opponent of secession and a lifelong enemy of the southern planter class. Yet he was not committed to either rights of blacks or the Republican party. Though honest and able, Johnson lacked Lincoln's gifts of patience and political realism. Soon the very Republicans who had hailed his remarks about the infamy of treason and the punishment of traitors found him to be too soft on the former Confederates and too eager to forget and forgive.

Like his predecessor, Johnson offered amnesty to those who would sign an oath of allegiance. Exceptions included important Confederate officials and Confederates who owned more than $20,000 worth of property, seemingly the leaders of the Old South. Those who took the oath were to vote for constitutional conventions for each state, which were, in turn, to repeal the ordinances of secession, to abolish slavery, and to repudiate Confederate war debts. The state thus reconstructed could then elect a new government and send representatives to Washington. By the end of 1865, all the states had actually passed through either the Lincoln or the Johnson version of this process, and in conservative and southern eyes, Reconstruction was over. Southern government was functioning, and the people, black and white, were returning to work.

Much in the new order was deeply disturbing to northern opinion. Some reconstituted states elected prominent Confederates to state and federal office. Most enacted special "Black Codes" to regulate the conduct of freed blacks. To former slaveholders, such rules seemed natural and necessary; to freed blacks and many Northerners, the rules looked much like the slave codes of the antebellum period. In some states, blacks were not allowed to assemble, to intermarry with whites, to possess alcohol or firearms, or to pursue a skilled trade. In others, the labor of petty offenders could be sold at auction; in some, black children could be apprenticed to white men without the consent of indigent parents. Most codes provided for strictly enforced compulsory labor contracts, and for the binding out (forced apprenticing) of unemployed blacks declared vagrant. In South Carolina, the code spelled out the intent of such contracts: blacks were to engage only in agricultural labor or in domestic service. In Mississippi, blacks could work, but not own, agricultural land. Even some white Southerners found these measures to be unduly provocative of Yankee sensibilities.

In 1865–1866, northern opinion was further affronted by outbreaks of racial violence in the South. Responsibility for race riots was of course disputed, but the victims nearly always turned out to be blacks or pro-black whites. To Radical Republicans, it seemed that life was not safe in the South for those who supported a change in southern society, and this change the Radicals were determined to bring about. To some this was a moral duty; to others, a political necessity.

In the spring of 1866, Congress extended the life of the Freedmen's Bureau, a wartime organization designed to supervise and aid the ex-slaves, and passed a Civil Rights Act prohibiting many kinds of discriminatory legislation. Congress also refused to admit the representatives of the new southern state governments, among them former Confederate officials: the vice president, six cabinet officers, four generals, and numerous other high-ranking civilian and military leaders of the secessionist government.

Johnson could not expect to carry forward his policy without regard for such formidable congressional opposition. Yet the imprudent Johnson, like other presidents in other battles with Congress, seemed to grow steadily less flexible and more defiant. He blamed southern race riots on the Radicals, minimized southern denial of black rights, and pardoned thousands of southern leaders. In the spring of 1866, he vetoed both the Freedmen's Bureau bill and the Civil Rights Act, arguing that such measures were unconstitutional and that blacks were not ready for full citizenship. When the Fourteenth Amendment was proposed to guarantee blacks equality before the law, he condemned it on similar grounds.

By this time, Johnson had gained the support of Democrats and solidified the Republican party against him. In the fall, he toured the country and violently denounced his opponents as traitors, particularly Thaddeus Stevens and Charles Sumner. In the November congressional election, Johnson was repudiated at the polls. The Republicans won two-thirds of both Houses, and the Radical leadership moved into key positions of power. The pendulum of power had swung to the congressional side; a new phase of Reconstruction was at hand.

CONGRESSIONAL RECONSTRUCTION

During congressional, or Radical Reconstruction, the alternative to conciliation, military occupation, was finally given a trial. The purpose behind this move was still reform; the South was to be occupied only until her society could be altered and a new electorate formed. This meant attempting something like social revolution, and it was clear that in this revolution blacks must play a major part.

The Freedmen's Bureau and Civil Rights bills, both repassed over the president's veto, established that the former slaves were to be protected by the federal government during a transitional stage. They were not, however, to be given land; in this property-loving age only a few suggested such an extreme measure, and local experiments in this direction (including one in Mississippi on land owned by Jefferson Davis) were abandoned. Ultimately, the failure to attempt some form of land redistribution and provide some measure of economic security for former slaves assured their continued dependence on their former masters.

Federal protection for blacks already implied a change in the relationship between the federal government and the states, and this change was spelled out in the Fourteenth Amendment submitted to Congress in June 1866. The first section of this amendment provided that no state should infringe any citizen's "privileges or immunities," nor "deprive any person of life, liberty or property, without due process of law," nor deny to any person "the equal protection of the laws." Thus individuals were guaranteed by the *Union* against oppression by the *states*. (The Bill of Rights already protected individual liberties from the federal government.)

The second section of the amendment edged toward black suffrage. It provided that if a state denied the vote of any of its male citizens, its representation should be reduced accordingly. The third and fourth sections barred leading Confederates from Congress or federal office and forbade states to repudiate the federal or recognize the rebel debt. Obviously this all-important amendment could not be ratified by three-fourths of the states without some southern support. As President Johnson urged southern states not to ratify, Congress moved on to still more drastic reconstruction action.

The First Reconstruction Act, passed in March 1867, divided the South into five military districts, wiping out the existing state governments. Under military supervision, each state was to elect a constitutional convention. Delegates to these conventions would be chosen by vote of the whole male population, including the freed blacks and excluding leading Confederates.

Each constitution was to be ratified by a majority of the state's new electorate and approved by Congress. When the new state had ratified the Fourteenth Amendment, its representatives might be admitted to Congress. This act was clarified and tightened by further legislation, and in 1870 Radical Reconstruction was completed by the ratification of the Fifteenth Amendment, once and for all forbidding suffrage discrimination on the basis of "race, color, or previous condition of servitude."

All these actions were taken against the firm opposition of the president and in the face of the nearly certain disapproval of the Supreme Court. To safeguard Radical Reconstruction, Congress made the most drastic attempt in American history to establish the dominance of a single branch of government. To disarm the court, Congress simply withdrew certain kinds of cases from Supreme Court jurisdiction, and the court prudently refrained from challenging this action. Johnson, however, could be rendered powerless only by impeachment and conviction for "treason, bribery, or other high crimes or misdemeanors." Failing after much effort to find serious evidence of "crimes," Congress saw its best chance for impeachment in the Tenure of Office Act passed in 1867. This act, of dubious constitutionality, forbade the removal of cabinet officers without congressional sanction. Johnson challenged it by trying to remove Secretary of War Edwin Stanton, an appointee of Lincoln. In the spring of 1868, the House of Representatives impeached the president in a long, confused, and shaky set of charges. Anger ran so high that his accusers failed by only one vote to secure the two-thirds of the Senate votes necessary for conviction.

RADICAL RECONSTRUCTION IN ACTION

How did the Radical program actually work in the South? To this crucial question, historians have developed two opposite answers. A generation ago, most accounts said that Radical Reconstruction had been a dreadful mistake. According to this traditional view, southern state governments, dominated by ignorant blacks, self-seeking carpetbaggers, and despicable southern "scalawags" (that is, collaborationists) had imposed a reign of terror, extravagance, and corruption. Finally the South, supported by a revival of moderate opinion in the North, had risen in revolt and thrown off the yoke. The very name given to those who overthrew Reconstruction, *redeemers*, speaks to the conclusions of this perspective.

More recently this version has been challenged by an opposite one. According to this second, neo-Radical view, Radical Reconstruction was a long overdue attempt to bring justice and progress to the South. It was sustained in the South not only by federal forces but by determined black support. Its defeat was brought about by brutal terrorism and northern betrayal.

The truth about this abortive social revolution is various and complex. It is clear that some Radical governments were indeed both extravagant and blatantly corrupt. Yet the redeemer governments that followed were not notable for political or fiscal probity, and both extravagance and corruption were common in both the North and South. Moreover, the Radical governments scored some accomplishments, bringing to the South broader suffrage for whites as well as blacks, relief for the poor, and the beginnings of free, popular education. Taxes did go up (though not to northern levels), but tax monies were put to valid social uses.

Could Radical Reconstruction have effected a permanent change in southern institutions and customs? Successful Reconstruction would have demanded either prolonged northern occupation, repeated federal intervention, or some degree of cooperation between southern whites and blacks. For the first two alternatives, Northerners proved to have no enduring appetite. The third — white-black cooperation — seemed initially more promising. Many southern whites did make an effort to accept the new situation, though many did not. Contrary to legend, some scalawags were well intentioned, just as many carpetbaggers were honest and many black leaders were well informed and moderate. But any permanent alliance among these elements faced great difficulties. The cooperating southern whites were willing to accept black voting only under white leadership; the blacks demanded political equality. Predictably, the necessary coalition failed.

Conservative whites quickly regained power. With this shift in power, violence against blacks and their political allies continued to escalate; at first determined to suppress the Ku Klux Klan and other secret terrorist organizations, Congress grew weary of the attempt. In one state after another, with differing degrees of fraudulent and forcible action, conservative southern whites achieved victory at the polls. In 1877 when President Hayes withdrew the last federal troops, the cycle was complete: the South was "redeemed" and restored to native white rule. At first, the new "lily-white" governments, mostly led by the prewar planter class, allowed blacks some token participation in politics. Then in the 1890s, governments claiming to represent poor whites came to power. Denouncing the alleged political "fusion" of aristocrats and blacks, these governments effectively nullifed the Fifteenth Amendment (universal manhood suffrage) and drove southern blacks out of politics. These acts were accomplished partly by violence and intimidation and partly by the discriminatory application of such legal sophistries as the grandfather clause, the literacy test, and the poll tax. Faced with the most flagrant violations of federal law, the federal government and northern public opinion looked the other way. White Northerners, including some former abolitionists, came to value national harmony more than equal rights.

SOCIAL RECONSTRUCTION

Since blacks never received the "40 acres and a mule" for which they had longed in 1865, they had to work for white landowners. As money to pay them was lacking, the only possible solution was some form of tenantry. The result was the sharecrop and the crop-lien systems. Throughout the South, sharecroppers, both white and black, received their seed, tools, and staple necessities from landlords to whom they turned over a third or a half of their produce. Most, and often all, of the remaining produce went to pay long-standing debts accumulated by the tenants at country stores or plantation commissaries with high monopoly prices and exorbitant rates of interest. The system was not slavery, and it got the crops planted and harvested. Yet the black farmer — forever in debt and unable to move, without education or political privileges, subject to white courts and terrorism — could hardly be called free. Indeed, recent research suggests that the shadow of slavery still darkened southern race relations as *peonage* (the use of laborers bound in servitude because of debt) was fairly widespread. To make matters worse, planter-class paternalism was supplanted by an increasingly virulent race hatred among whites who feared their inability to control their former slaves.

In the 1880s, the white-ruled South put on a spectacular drive for industry. Heavy inducements were offered to attract capital, and much was accomplished in developing steel, lumbering, tobacco, and, especially, textile industries. However, by the turn of the century, the region had barely held its own; the South's percentage of the nation's industry was about that of 1860. Even this, in a rapidly expanding economy, was a considerable achievement. But the price was heavy. In southern mill towns, disease and child labor were endemic. Most industry profits were flowing out of the section. Until World War II, the South remained both poor and overwhelmingly agrarian.

Perhaps the saddest chapter in all American history is the general acceptance in the North of the failure of so much effort. Thirty years after the war, most people took for granted a southern system that included not only disfranchisement, economic dependence, and rigid social segregation of blacks, but also recurrent violence. In 1892 and 1893, for example, more than 150 blacks were lynched each year; they were often sadistically tortured, and virtually always the crimes went unpunished. If Reconstruction was a tragedy, it was because it heightened interregional tensions without either lessening racial hatred or securing a place in the national mainstream for the former slaves.

How could the people who had defied the Fugitive Slave Act, fought the war, and voted for Radical Reconstruction accept this situation? First, it was easy to emphasize the seamy side of Radical Reconstruction, the greed and corruption with which the process was sometimes executed. Next, most white Northerners shared the white southern assessment of black worth. White supremacist assumptions were reinforced by turn-of-the-century American imperialism. If the "little brown" Filipino was a lesser breed of man in need of the firm, guiding hand of a superior white American nation, should not the Afro-American be left to the direction of his southern white betters? Moreover, the conventional wisdom of the age argued that stateways could not change folkways, that government was powerless to change customs or alter social mores. Thus a failure of northern resolve partly explains the failure of Reconstruction. The courts, Congress, the White House, and a popular majority all came, in time, to accept the view that white Southerners knew best how to handle the race problem. It also seems likely that failure was built into the system itself. Federalism, whatever its

TABLE 9. EVENTS OF RECONSTRUCTION, 1863–1877

Date	General tendency	National events	State events
1863	**Presidential Reconstruction**	Lincoln Plan announced.	Governments set up in Louisiana, Arkansas.
1864		Wade-Davis Plan pocket-vetoed by Lincoln.	
1865		Lee surrenders. Lincoln shot. Johnson Plan announced.	Governments partly functioning in Virginia, Tennessee.
1866		Freedman's Bureau bill and Civil Rights bill vetoed. Fourteenth Amendment submitted to states. Congressional elections: Radical gains.	All remaining states reorganized under Johnson Plan. Tennessee readmitted.
1867	**Height of Radical Reconstruction**	Reconstruction Acts. Tenure of Office Act.	Military Rule in effect.
1868		Impeachment of Johnson. Fourteenth Amendment in effect. Grant elected.	North Carolina, South Carolina, Florida, Alabama, Louisiana, Arkansas readmitted under Radical governments.
1869	**Conflict**	Fifteenth Amendment in effect. First Enforcement Act.	Conservative government restored in Tennessee. Virginia readmitted under moderate government.
1870		Congressional elections: Republican majorities reduced.	Moderate government restored in North Carolina. Mississippi, Texas, Georgia readmitted under radical government.
1871		Second and third Enforcement Acts.	Conservative government restored in Georgia.
1872		Grant re-elected.	
1873			
1874	**Restoration of White Rule**	Congressional elections: Democrats gain control of House.	Conservative government restored in Arkansas, Alabama, Texas.
1875		Civil Rights Act (declared invalid 1883).	Conservative government restored in Mississippi.
1876		Hayes-Tilden disputed election.	Federal troops removed from Louisiana, South Carolina.
1877			Conservative government restored in Florida, South Carolina, Louisiana.

other advantages, proved to be an imperfect instrument for the protection of black rights. As the experience of the post–World War II civil rights struggles suggests, the Fourteenth and Fifteenth Amendments were often unenforceable in the face of adamant white opposition. The traditions of federalism, which required wide-ranging deference to local, state, and regional customs, seemed to deny effective enforcement of a colorblind Constitution. In the last analysis, the left wing of the Republican party, for all its apparent radicalism, accepted prevailing constitutional conservatism. The Radicals created a formal structure of racial equality — and in the process no doubt promised much more than most northern whites would willingly see the nation deliver — but they did not challenge a federal system that permitted intransigent southern whites to sabotage congressional intent. Still "old republican" in their fear of the centralized national power necessary to reconstruct the South, the Radicals returned to the old federal balance of national and state power, a position sustained by the Supreme Court in a series of cases beginning in the 1870s.

In the Slaughterhouse Cases (1873) the court found that the Fourteenth Amendment conferred no new privileges or immunities that would protect blacks from state power. In the Civil Rights Cases (1883), it decided that the Fourteenth Amendment did not prevent *individuals*, as opposed to states, from practicing discrimination. In *Plessy* vs. *Ferguson* (1896), the court held that "separate but equal" accommodations for blacks in trains (and by implication in restaurants, schools, hotels, and the like) did not violate their rights. Few inquired very carefully into whether accommodations were indeed equal.

If blacks found the promises of Reconstruction largely empty, the period had a brighter side for whites. A great Civil War had been settled on remarkably magnanimous terms, without the postwar blood-letting, executions, confiscations, and mass incarcerations that have characterized internecine struggles in other times and places. As the two sides inched toward reconciliation, it was all too easy to forget that Afro-America was paying most of the bill for the intersectional accord.

The upshot, then, of the greatest struggle in American history seemed to be a tragic failure. Yet the story had not ended. Blacks had gained a few rights and a great many hopes. And in neither the North nor the South was the national conscience really at ease.

CONFLICTING HISTORICAL VIEWPOINTS: NO. 7

Was Reconstruction a Tragic Era?

Until the 1930s, historians generally agreed that Reconstruction was a period characterized by sordid motives and human depravity. It was the "Age of Hate," "The Blackout of Honest Government," "The Dreadful Decade," and "The Tragic Era." In 1939, however, Francis Butler Simkins, a distinguished southern scholar, urged his fellow historians to adopt "a more critical, creative, and tolerant attitude" toward the period. In a notable essay

(*Journal of Southern History, 1939*), *Simkins suggested that the traditional interpretation of Reconstruction was rooted in "the conviction that the Negro belongs to an innately inferior race."*

Until Simkins's time, most white students of Reconstruction did in fact approach their work with decidedly racist views. In the first serious history of the era, James Ford Rhodes's enormously influential History of the United States from the Compromise of 1850 *(7 vols., 1839–1906), blacks were described as "the most inferior race." Similarly, in John W. Burgess's* Reconstruction and the Constitution *(1902), blacks were characterized as inherently inferior beings incapable of "subjecting passion to reason." Although Rhodes and Burgess were sharply critical of the motives and actions of congressional Radicals, the traditional interpretation of Reconstruction is best identified with the work of William A. Dunning. A Columbia University scholar and the author of* Reconstruction, Political and Economic *(1907), Dunning and his many students uncovered a wealth of factual information about the period. But their work was seriously marred by their pro-southern and anti-black biases. They portrayed the postbellum scene in darkly tragic hues of unrelieved brutality, scandal, corruption, and licentiousness. According to the Dunningites, Reconstruction was not only unnecessary but harshly cruel to the prostrate South and ruthlessly exploitive of the ignorant ex-slaves.*

Black scholars — most notably W. E. B. Du Bois, author of Black Reconstruction *(1935) — vigorously disputed Dunning School conclusions. But in an age of virtually unchallenged white supremacy, few Caucasians thought to question simplistic characterizations of vindictive Radicals, venal carpetbaggers, reprobate scalawags, and barbarous blacks. A shift in the climate of racial opinion, however, ushered in a new era of Reconstruction historiography. Reflecting a growing national sensitivity to civil rights, historians since the 1930s have turned Dunning's conclusions inside out. First in a series of monographs and biographies, then later in such sweeping syntheses as John Hope Franklin's* Reconstruction After the Civil War *(1961) and Kenneth Stampp's* The Era of Reconstruction *(1965), revisionists discarded racial stereotypes and viewed the postbellum period in a generally favorable light. According to these modern scholars, traditional studies grossly exaggerated not only the extent of corruption, fraud, and black rule, but even the length of Radical control. To both Franklin and Stampp, Reconstruction was a tragic era only in that it failed to ensure blacks economic, political, and social equality.*

At present the revisionists are clearly in the ascendancy. But as Stampp has written, revisionism's "ultimate and inevitable fate is one day to have its own revisions revised."

FOR FURTHER READING

Leon Litwack's *Been in the Storm So Long* (1980) lyrically describes the transition from slavery to freedom. Both Herman Belz's *Reconstructing the*

Union (1969) and John and LaWanda Cox's *Politics, Principle, and Prejudice* (1963) analyze presidential Reconstruction. Howard Beale in *The Critical Year* (1930) and E. L. McKitrick in *Andrew Johnson and Reconstruction* (1965) offer conflicting views of Lincoln's successor. David Donald's *The Politics of Reconstruction* (1965) and W. R. Brock's *An American Crisis* (1963) are noteworthy revisionist works. Janet Herman's *Pursuit of a Dream* (1981) and Willie Lee Rose's *Rehearsal for Reconstruction* (1964) examine land redistribution experiments that failed. William Gillette traces the *Retreat from Reconstruction* (1979); Phillip Paludan's *A Covenant with Death* (1975) considers the failure of Reconstruction within a framework of law and tradition; and James McPherson's subject is *The Abolitionist Legacy* (1975). Robert Cruden examines *The Negro in Reconstruction* (1969), and Hans L. Trefousse sympathetically analyzes *The Radical Republicans* (1969). There are numerous state studies, but among the best are: F. B. Simkins and R. H. Woody's *South Carolina During Reconstruction* (1932); Joel Williamson's *After Slavery* (1965); and V. L. Wharton's *The Negro in Mississippi, 1865–1890* (1947). James L. Roark's *Masters Without Slaves* (1977) examines planter life and thought during war and reconstruction. C. Vann Woodward's justly celebrated trilogy *(Reunion and Reaction* [1951], *Origins of the New South* [1951], and *The Strange Career of Jim Crow* [1955]*)*, Paul Gaston's *New South Creed* (1970), and George Tindall's *The Persistent Tradition in New South Politics* (1975) are valuable for understanding the South during the post-Reconstruction period. Stephan DeCanio in *Agriculture in the Postbellum South* (1974) and Robert Ransom and Richard Sutch in *One Kind of Freedom* (1977) offer strikingly different conclusions about the nature of the southern economy.

17

★ ★ ★ ★ ★ ★

The Triumph of American Industry, 1865–1893

LIKE A VAST and bloody wound, the Civil War seems to divide nineteenth-century American history into two parts. Yet America's industrial expansion, the most important development of the postwar years, was under way before the war and continued during it. This immense process would have taken place if slavery or secession had never been heard of and still would have transformed world history. American industrial growth was not unique: England had gone through a similar transformation earlier, Germany experienced an industrial transformation about the same time as the United States, and such transformations were taking place before the end of the century in Japan and other countries. But American industrialization was larger in scale than that of any other country and perhaps transformed the national culture more profoundly. The American tendency to overstate the nation's economic miracles should be checked at the outset, however, by the realization that the United States trailed other industrial nations in important respects. By 1900 its impressive gross national product (GNP) may have made it "the prime industrial power of the planet." But its product per capita — the per capita value of its industrial production, which is a more valid measure of individual welfare than the GNP — was exceeded by Germany, France, and Sweden.

"THE SECOND AMERICAN REVOLUTION"

Many historians have credited America's industrial surge specifically to the Civil War. In their influential *The Rise of American Civilization* (1927) Charles and Mary Beard, for example, argued that the war was in reality a Second American Revolution, a social and economic conflict in which the nation's once-dominant agricultural interests were deliberately driven from their places of power and privilege by the expanding industrial forces of the North and East. In their view, war production, the system of wartime finance, and such wartime business achievements as the high protective tariff, banking and currency stabilization, and the construction of a transcontinental railroad were instrumental in the growth of an industrialized economy. Indeed, even Reconstruction, in the Beards' interpretation, was designed largely by industrial interests to keep the agricultural South away from the corridors of power while their program was perfected and entrenched.

More recent research has cast doubt on the thesis of the Second American Revolution. Industrialists and business people were by no means united on the issues of the Civil War or Reconstruction. Nor were they in accord on the economic programs presumably executed for their private interests under cover of a great national tragedy. In the eyes of most Americans, including industrialists, the war and its aftermath were political, not economic, struggles. The triumph of industry was not a planned and masterful capture of the government by powerful insiders.

Recent scholarship, moreover, has also challenged the economic importance of the war. According to one index, *the value added by manufacturing* — the difference between the value of raw materials before and after manufacturing — the century's largest percentage gains took place in prewar decades, most notably in the 1840s and 1850s. Though the war created certain demands: shoes, blankets, weapons, and woolen cloth for uniforms, many scholars argue that these necessities diverted productive resources and that the rate of technological improvement slowed during the crisis. Indeed, one of America's great economic advantages in the nineteenth century was that *except* in the 1860s economic growth did not have to be shaped for military ends.

It remains true, however, that industry did receive unprecedented governmental support during the war, reached new production heights in wartime, and continued this rise, with few interruptions, for the rest of the century. Though industrialization and the modern factory system antedated the Civil War, the year 1860 (if not the war itself) represents a turning point in American economic life. The antebellum period produced no giant conglomerations of wealth and influence to compare with the great postwar railroad, manufacturing, and banking empires. Even in the 1850s, the largest industrial operations were relatively small-scale and possessed few big-business characteristics, such as huge capital requirements, high fixed costs, separation of ownership and control, diversity and multiplicity of function, geographically scattered operations, and political and economic might. Thus, the "Lords of Creation," as Frederick Lewis Allen aptly called them — the Carnegies, Dukes, Hills, Morgans, Rockefellers, Swifts, and Vanderbilts — and the astonishing riches and power they amassed belong to the half century after 1860, the Age of Enterprise.

PRECONDITIONS OF GROWTH

In many areas outside of politics, postwar conditions were even more favorable to industrial expansion than those that had brought about the 1850s boom. The production demands of the transportation revolution were creating a foundation for America's heavy industry. The railroad lines were the nation's pioneer big businesses, its first large-scale companies. The railroad promoters led the way to business consolidation, to the accumulation of vast pools of capital, and to the corporate form of business organization. Railroad enterprises seemed to nurture the nation's economy; they consumed the lion's share of its finished and natural products, its coal, iron, steel, and timber. Railroads changed American life by linking raw materials to processing centers and agricultural produce to urban consumers, by standardizing time and work habits, by connecting the far-flung points of the national market, and by speeding the development and population of the West.

In addition, the railroads' need for governmental largesse, particularly in the inhospitable reaches of the trans-Mississippi region, helped create a sympathetic climate for business development. Because railroads were generally recognized as the key to economic growth and therefore often as essentially public projects, they were given substantial public support. Though private investors, primarily British, provided much of the construction costs, state and federal interest-free loans and outright gifts of land were lavish. Land grants approached 200 million acres, roughly an area the size of Belgium, the United Kingdom, and Spain combined. This generosity and such innovations as steel rails, a standard gauge, automatic and uniform coupling devices, and air brakes assured phenomenal growth. By 1900 the United States accounted for one-third of the world's railroad tracks, some 200,000 miles of steel rails that included five east-west transcontinental lines.

Preceding and accompanying the transportation revolution was a revolution in agriculture, which was characterized by mechanization, dramatic increases in production, and a vast expansion of cultivated land. The wheat crop illustrates this revolution. On the prairies of Illinois and Indiana, in the new and booming spring wheat belt of Minnesota and North Dakota, in the great valley of California, and in good years even on the dry plains of Montana, new varieties of wheat produced ever-bigger crops. By 1896 one farmer, equipped with such mechanized marvels as the harvester, twine binder, and steam thresher, could reap more wheat than 18 men six decades before had reaped. Transformed into flour in the new American rolling mills, this crop became the mainstay of industrial populations at home and abroad.

The story was much the same for other basic food commodities: geographical expansion, advancing mechanization, and development of widening markets. After 1870 these and parallel developments in Russia, Canada, Argentina, and elsewhere glutted the world market. Farm prices fell, farm problems proliferated, and agricultural distress became a major political and economic headache. But to those interested primarily in increased industrial production, more and cheaper food was an unalloyed blessing.

America's natural resources turned out to be even more plentiful than anybody had suspected. Deposits of coal and iron, the main essentials for heavy industry, were found within transportable range in many places from the Appalachians to the Great Lakes. The center of copper production moved from Michigan to Montana and Arizona. Like the minerals, the timber of Wisconsin and the far Northwest seemed inexhaustible. The problem was not to save resources, but to multiply methods of using them ever faster.

Americans also seemed to possess a large share of inventive talent. Though much of the nation's industrial progress came on borrowed European technology, some crucial improvements in basic industry, such as the Bessemer and open-hearth processes of steel production, were of combined European and American origin. Perhaps because of the needs of a continent-sized democracy, Americans excelled in the field of communication and business machines. They produced the telephone, the typewriter, the stock-market ticker tape, the linotype, the cash register, and the adding machine. Urban needs brought further American adaptations of worldwide scientific development. In the 1870s electricity was introduced as a source of light and power; by the 1890s electric street railways, incandescent light, and the phonograph had become common fixtures of urban life. The public was inclined to credit this "American ingenuity" to the romantic figure of the lone inventor — to the likes of Thomas Alva Edison, one of the most popular men of his time. Remarkable as Edison's achievements were, industrial capitalism was sustained not by the occasional dramatic inventive breakthrough but by the steady increments of technological improvements from anonymous scientists and engineers, the new university-trained technologists of the machine age.

Another precondition to growth was people. They were needed to operate the factories and to swell the markets, and they came. In the half century after 1870, 26 million immigrants arrived from Europe and Asia, and 20 million of them stayed. Between 1870 and 1900, the population of the United States grew from nearly 40 million to some 76 million, swelled by the immigrants. They were not always welcome. Many Americans, particularly those of "old-immigrant" (Anglo-Saxon) stock, looked askance at these often ragged and seemingly ignorant peasants. Organized labor feared and resented the tide of cheap and docile immigrant workers. But the demands of industry prevailed. Except for Orientals who were excluded early, the cries of alarmed nativists went unheeded until the passage of restrictive and pointedly discriminatory immigration legislation during and following World War I. (See Chapter 20.)

The immigrant influx affected the occupational and social progress of the native population unevenly. It is ironic that old-stock whites, usually the group most resentful of "New Immigrants," often discovered that these new workers pushed them out of menial labor jobs into clerical and white-collar positions. On the other hand, the relatively small number of blacks in the industrial centers found that increased European immigration limited their own occupational opportunities, because white foreigners, even those who could speak no English, were more acceptable to both industry and white labor than native-born Afro-Americans. The immigrants themselves generally lacked career mobility. Rarely organized in labor unions and often stigmatized by differences of language, custom, and religion, they supplied industry's demand for a cheap and stable work force.

Like people, capital flowed westward across the Atlantic. At the turn of the century, about a third of all American railroad securities was owned by

Europeans, who were mostly British. Much capital investment came, however, from Americans. Between 1869 and 1898, some 13 percent of the national income went into industrial expansion. This high figure reflects, in part, profitable and competitive innovation; in part, it reflects the ability of the period's industrial capitalists, the most constructive of whom used their money to expand their enterprises rather than to live lavishly. The great capital investment certainly reflects the rise of the modern investment banking houses; centered on Wall Street in New York City, they marketed industrial securities and ultimately promoted consolidation in a once-competitive economy.

THE CONSOLIDATION MOVEMENT

Nearly all conditions in the United States seemed to favor large-scale enterprise. Demand at first seemed inexhaustible. New urban populations needed consumer goods, while expanding agriculture, transportation, and industry itself needed machines. In some industries, particularly steel and oil, technology became so expensive that only very large units could meet the staggering fixed costs of production. Mounting competition caused prices to decline during the last half of the century, putting a premium on economic efficiency and large-scale production. Depressions squeezed out weak competitors, underlining the disadvantages of cutthroat competition and pointing to the desirability of merging rival operations into single units. The direction throughout the period was toward monopoly, although in most cases the process stopped short at *oligopoly,* a term economists use to describe control of a market by relatively few sellers. Theoretically, competition may have been the life of trade, but in the free enterprise jungle, consolidation was a surer way to profit.

In the consolidation movement, as in other areas, the railroads led. The industry was immersed in the ruinous competition of rate wars because it had expanded more rapidly than the demand for rail services, and it was desperate to meet its high costs. Seeking order and profits in what they saw as a destructive and chaotic marketplace, some railroad barons tried cooperation. Initially reaching gentlemen's agreements and then entering into written pooling agreements, they formed cartels or loose associations to limit competition and to share profits. Voluntary measures without standing in court, these devices were generally short-lived. Moreover, they amounted to price fixing, and such collusion raised eyebrows, if not legal questions. Thus the railroads became early targets of public indignation, political scrutiny, and finally government regulation. In time the agreement and the pool gave way to more formal combinations in railroading and in other industries.

Bigness could take several forms. A large firm might expand or *integrate horizontally,* attempting to monopolize a single product by buying out competitors. Or a diverse empire might *vertically integrate* by tying together many related but not identical enterprises at several levels of production and distribution. John D. Rockefeller and his associates built the first trust in 1882, when the stockholders of the nation's largest refineries abandoned a loosely structured cartel arrangement and exchanged their voting shares for certificates of the Standard Oil Trust. In the process, the management of some 90 percent of the industry's refining capacity was transferred to a single board of trustees. Having consolidated horizontally, Standard Oil then moved vertically, from crude oil wells to barrel factories to pipelines — all the way to the markets at home and abroad. Until its dissolution under the Sherman Anti-Trust Act in 1911, Standard Oil dominated the industry in the United States and much of the world.

Other prime examples of horizontal and vertical consolidations include Gustavus Swift's meat-processing empire and Andrew Carnegie's iron and steel operations. Building a huge integrated organization that encompassed stockyards, slaughterhouses, refrigerated railroad cars, and marketing operations, Swift left other packers, Armour and Morris among them, with no choice but imitation. By 1890 the meat-packing industry was dominated by a handful of firms. Carnegie likewise moved from raw supply to marketing. After honing his business skills in railroading, he opened a Pennsylvania steelworks in 1873 and eventually controlled ore and coal fields, Great Lakes carriers and railroads, coke ovens, pig iron and steel converting plants, and rolling mills. Although he never monopolized his industry, he did command annual earnings of $25 million and control 25 percent of the nation's steel. In 1901 Carnegie sold his massive operations to the master consolidator and finance capitalist J. P. Morgan. Morgan made the Carnegie Company (along with his own Federal Steel Company) the centerpiece of the United States Steel Corporation, which became the first billion-dollar corporation and the controller of at least 60 percent of the American steel business.

The consolidation process in steel, oil, meatpacking, and railroads was repeated in many other industries: tobacco, cottonseed oil, sugar, explosives, whiskey, nonferrous metals, flour, sewing machines, and rubber and electrical goods. In finance, too, the process occurred. The House of Morgan and its closest rival, Kuhn, Loeb, and Company, overshadowed all investment banking houses. They controlled much of the nation's capital and credit supply, and played midwives at the birth of many industrial giants.

In some areas, competition survived, among them labor-intensive, low-technology industries like furniture, food, and clothing. Relatively modest production costs encouraged the development of new firms in these industries. In other areas, market forces were restored. This happened in the low-technology salt industry: the monopoly power of the National Salt Company was broken after 1900 by the re-entry of rival sellers.

In the more technologically advanced industries where economies of scale (cheaper per unit production of large factories) were critical, the consolidators generally had their way. Whether by trusts, holding companies, or the creation of huge corporations, industrial consolidation grew rapidly in the United States. From 1888 to 1905, 328 giant combinations or consolidated businesses (representing 40 percent, or $7 billion, of the nation's manufacturing capital) were formed; half of them possessed monopoly power in their industries.

Born of changing technology and the quest for market dominance, the consolidation movement marked the end of highly competitive capitalism and the beginning of "price leadership." Explicit price-fixing was rarely necessary in the new order. Wary of federal anti-trust proceedings and comfortable with profits assured by tacitly accepted "standard" prices, oligopolistic industries competed in areas other than price: advertising, design variation, or bureaucratic efficiency. Small businesses failed by the thousands, and the social costs of this narrow concentration of economic power were incalculable.

The consumer did not invariably lose under consolidation. Large enterprises could often deliver goods more cheaply than smaller ones. Some industries that were typified by extraordinarily high fixed costs were "natural" monopolies. Until its recent court-ordered divestiture, American Telephone and Telegraph was an obvious example. Checked by state and federal regulatory agencies, this giant holding company (owner of Bell Telephone and Western Electric) managed consistently handsome profits and yet provided the most efficient and very likely the cheapest mass communication system in the world.

THE ACHIEVEMENT AND ITS CONSEQUENCES

There was reason for widespread public admiration of the industrial accomplishment. Before the end of the century, industrial growth had built factories from Michigan to Georgia, had drawn workers for them from the farms and villages of the world, had linked factories to mines, forests, and ports, and as a result had made the United States one of Earth's great producers of wealth.

The most spectacular accomplishment may have been the American railroads, by 1900 the largest and finest system in the world. But there was also steel, a luxury product at midcentury that became the mainstay of the industrial age, the stuff of rails, oil drilling equipment, steam turbines, ships, and skyscrapers. By 1900 the United States produced as much steel as its two closest competitors (England and Germany) combined. Oil, a once-worthless by-product of the salt industry, became almost overnight the chief illuminant and lubricant of the machine age. By 1900, Americans produced and used more oil than any other people.

The benefits of large-scale industrial development were not uniformly distributed. Though much of the wealth created by industry was plowed back into the productive process, a great deal of it made life easier, more efficient, and pleasanter for some workers including the expanding clerical class. By the 1890s, the rising popularity of sports, the sharp increase in the numbers of high school students, the flood of magazines and popular novels, and even the bicycle craze testified to the presence of a substantial, growing, and relatively leisured middle class. Industrial workers (see Chapter 20) fared less well, and the national economy was marked by gross disparities in wealth. In the three decades after 1865, however, real wages may have risen by as much as half, due to stable hourly rates and falling living costs.

The expansiveness of industrialization also invaded the nation's cities, "the supreme achievement of the new industrialism." By 1900, 40 percent of the American people lived in urban places having a population of 2,500 or more, compared to only 15 percent in 1850. The trend was not universal, for the South and the western mountain and plains states were hardly touched by urbanization. Though more people earned their living on farms than in factories as late as 1900, cities in the regions of the Great Lakes, the Pacific Coast, and the East burgeoned as rural Europeans and Americans made their way to the nation's industrial and business centers. Much of this astonishing growth came in the 1880s, when the populations of more than 100 cities doubled. By 1890 there were 26 cities with more than 100,000 people, and a decade later, six of those cities had populations of over 1 million.

The city was both an irresistible magnet and a profound disappointment. It promised economic opportunity and amenities like the incandescent light, the telephone, indoor plumbing, and the trolley. But too often the newcomers exchanged one form of drudgery and poverty for another. Haphazardly built, the late nineteenth-century American city suffered from growth that was unplanned and unregulated. The poor were packed into barracks-like tenements; provisions for recreation, sanitation, fire and police protection, education, and water supply were inadequate for the multiplying population.

To the confident promoters of the new order, urban blight, not unlike poverty itself, was the inevitable by-product of human progress. They believed the benefits of headlong industrialization and urbanization far outweighed their costs. Yet in nineteenth-century America, as elsewhere in the industrial world, costs were largely met by those who could least afford them. In a shocking portrait of the other half of the urban-industrial world, immigrant-journalist Jacob Riis portrayed the victims of economic progress: the sallow, joyless factory child, the shoemaker displaced by mechanization, the uprooted and often despised immigrant, the seasonally and cyclically unemployed worker. These submerged Americans knew that the moral, social, and psychological costs of industrialization were as tangible as its rewards.

The nation was generally of two minds about the new industrialism: it applauded the material promise of a mature economy, and it feared the darker implications of concentrated power and wealth. Given the American devotion to property rights, the political influence of business, and the conservatism of the American polity, regulation appeared to be the most acceptable answer to monopoly power. State regulatory commissions and federal regulatory agencies, such as the Interstate Commerce Commission (1887), the Federal Trade Commission (1913), and the Federal Communication Commission (1934), were appointed. Regulatory agencies were designed to protect the unorganized buying public from highly organized sellers, and sometimes they did. Yet government regulators have not been noticeably hostile to private profits, and the business community, despite its initial fears, recognized the benefits accruing from the stability of a regulated market.

Perhaps because industrial consolidation threatened to narrow the channels of economic opportunity, Americans clung to their traditional notions of upward mobility. The 119 popular novels of Horatio Alger, expressions of post–Civil War American materialism and optimism, underscored the faith in unlimited opportunities awaiting the virtuous and industrious. The rags-to-riches theme was an axiom of the Age of Enterprise, and was reiterated in speeches, sermons, textbooks, newspapers, and literature. Skeptics had only to look at Andrew Carnegie, that former bobbin boy of immigrant, working-class stock, or to the humble origins of E. H. Harriman, who rose from railroad office boy to master of the Union Pacific Railroad. Despite these individual success stories, the captains of industry typically were not poor immigrant or farm boys who made good. Nearly all were native-born, and the majority emerged from advantaged circumstances. The literature on the period also is ambivalent about the new industrialism. The nineteenth-century poet Walt Whitman lamented "the depravity of the business classes" of his time. His judgment was widely shared by historians. In the best known critique, written during the Great Depression, Matthew Josephson likened the industrialists to "robber barons," the rapacious predators of medieval Europe who cheated, swindled, and robbed without compunction. Later scholars, however, have often been less interested in the industrialists' moral character than in analysis of the structure and nature of the industrial achievement. Influenced, no doubt, by the politically conservative climate of Cold War America, these historians characterized the "industrial states-men" as innovative, venturesome risk-takers who brought order to a chaotic industrial scene and economic progress to the nation.

In a sense, both views of the nineteenth-century industrialists are right, and in fact they address different issues. The best among these bold and colorful moguls were constructive builders who left behind not only baronial palaces and immense fortunes but legacies of achievement and of long-range benefit to a developing industrial nation. But they could be contemptuous of the public welfare. Their attitude is suggested by John D. Rockefeller's declaration: "God gave me my money." The disregard for legal canon and popular concerns is plain in the remarks attributed to railroad baron Cornelius Vanderbilt ("What do I care about the law? Hain't I got the power?") and to his son, William ("The public be damned!"). At their worst, the industrialists were corporate scavengers, as lawless, exploitative, and avaricious as any medieval knight gone bad.

Thus, the Age of Enterprise is viewed with ambivalence: the deeds of these new Lords of Creation inspired confidence in some quarters and dismay in others, and their machines churned out both abundance and poverty. But there is no uncertainty about the outcome: the revolution was irreversible. A new and increasingly centralized order had arrived, sweeping away landmarks, destroying traditional patterns, and raising but not answering difficult questions.

FOR FURTHER READING

Douglass North's nontechnical synthesis, *Growth and Welfare in the American Past* (1966) is a good point of departure for studying economic development, and so is Daniel Boorstin's *The Americans: The Democratic Experience* (1973). Perhaps the best brief account of *The Rise of Big Business* (1972) is by Glenn Porter. It should be supplemented by more detailed accounts: T. C. Cochran's *Business in American Life* (1972), E. C. Kirkland's *Industry Comes of Age* (1961), W. W. Rostow's *The Stages of Economic Growth* (1960), and Alan Trachtenberg's *The Incorporation of America* (1982). Comparing Matthew Josephson's *The Robber Barons* (1934) or Gabriel Kolko's *Railroads and Regulation* (1975) with Alfred Chandler's *The Visible Hand* (1977) would be beneficial. Valuable biographies from the period include Harold Livesay's *Andrew Carnegie and the Rise of Big Business* (1975), Joseph Wall's *Andrew Carnegie* (1970), Allan Nevins's admiring *John D. Rockefeller* (1940), and Frederick Lewis Allen's *The Great Pierpont Morgan* (1949). Important histories of selected subjects include Peter Temin's *Iron and Steel in Nineteenth-Century America* (1964), Lee Benson's *Merchants, Farmers, and Railroads* (1955), Constance Green's *The Rise of Urban America* (1965), Thomas Bender's *Toward an Urban Vision* (1975), Edward Kirland's *Dream and Thought in the Business Community* (1956), and John Cawelti's, *Apostles of Success in America* (1965).

18

★ ★ ★ ★ ★ ★

The Last West, 1860–1890

WHILE the United States was struggling with the tragic heritage of an old region, it was also confronting the problems of a new one. Between 1860 and 1880, half the present area of the country was occupied and exploited. By 1860, settlers were fast filling up the eastern parts of Kansas and Nebraska. San Francisco and Sacramento were bustling towns, and farming was well established in the Willamette Valley of Oregon. Between these two distant borders — the Pacific settlements and the states just west of the Mississippi — lay a vast region of plains and mountains barely penetrated by European civilization.

Two things make this last and greatest West different from all earlier frontier regions. First, far more than ever before, this West was the frontier of an urban and industrial country. Second, its geography made it much less hospitable to settlers than any earlier American frontier.

PLAINS AND MOUNTAINS

From Jamestown to the Mississippi River, though the conditions of frontier life might have been hard, there had normally been enough rainfall for farming. Long accustomed to forest, pioneers of the last generation had encountered from northeastern Illinois to eastern Kansas rich prairies covered with tall grass and had learned to overcome their suspicion of treeless land. This was a lesson they were going to have to unlearn a little farther west.

Beyond the prairies lay the Great Plains, which begin at an invisible line of semiaridity that runs a wavering course, more or less close to the 98th meridian, from eastern North Dakota to the Texas Panhandle. Some of the area west of this line, particularly in its northeastern parts, could be profitably farmed by those who knew how. Westward toward the Rockies, however, the Plains grow steadily higher, drier, and less fertile. In 1860 nothing grew there but the short native grass, and aside from the soldiers who

TABLE 10. WESTERN HISTORY, 1860–1895

Year	Mining rushes	Indian wars	Miscellaneous events	States (in capitals) and territories
1858			Butterfield-Overland Express (transcontinental stage route).	
1859	Nevada (gold and silver). Colorado (gold).		Pony Express.	1859 OREGON
1860	1860–1866 Idaho (gold).			
1861			Pacific Telegraph.	1861 KANSAS, Colorado, Nevada, Dakota
1862	Arizona (gold). 1862–1864 Montana (gold).	1862 Massacre of whites, Minnesota.	Homestead Act.	
1863				1863 Arizona, Idaho
1864		1864 Arapaho-Cheyenne War Massacre of Indians, Sand Creek, Colorado.		1864 NEVADA, Montana
1865		1865–1867 War with Western Sioux.		
1866			Long Drive to Sedalia, Missouri.	
1867	Wyoming (gold).	1867 Indian Peace Commission.		1867 NEBRASKA
1868		1868 War on Southern Plains.		1868 Wyoming
1869			Union Pacific Railroad completed.	
1871		1871 War in Texas Panhandle.		

Year	Mining rushes	Indian wars	Miscellaneous events	States (in capitals) and territories
1873	Deeper portion of Comstock Lode, Nevada (richest strike ever).		Timber Culture Act.	
1874		Red River War.		
1876	Black Hills, Dakota (gold).	1875–1876 War in Black Hills.	Barbed wire patented.	1876 COLORADO.
1877	Leadville, Colorado (silver, lead).	Nez Percé uprising, Idaho.	Desert Land Act.	
1878			Timber and Stone Act.	
1879	Tombstone, Arizona (silver).			
1882	Butte, Montana (copper).		1882–1883 Santa Fe, Southern Pacific, and Northern Pacific routes completed.	
1885		Capture of Geronimo and end of Apache War.	1885–1886 Disastrous winters, end of range cattle industry.	
1887		Dawes Act.	Drought and western farm crisis.	
1889		1889–1890 Ghost Dance, Battle of Wounded Knee.	First Oklahoma rush.	1889 NORTH DAKOTA, SOUTH DAKOTA, MONTANA, WASHINGTON
1890				1890 WYOMING, IDAHO
1893			Great Northern Railroad completed.	

guarded the wagon trails at a few forts, it remained in the possession of its ancient inhabitants. These included the jackrabbit, antelope, coyote, and buffalo (all biologically adapted to live in arid country), along with the Plains Indians, who were culturally adapted to live on the buffalo.

Beyond the Plains lay the Rockies, rich in minerals and long penetrated by fur trappers, and beyond them the intermountain plateaus, made up mostly of sage brush desert, jagged mountain ranges, and, in the Southwest, true desert dotted with cactus and mesquite. Some of the land in this forbidding province could be irrigated and used, as had been demonstrated by Spaniards on the Mexican borderlands and Mormons near the Great Salt Lake. Beyond these plateaus lay the Pacific mountain chains: first the Sierra Nevada and the Cascades and then the Coast Ranges, with rich valleys between.

The whole region had been given the bad name of the Great American Desert. Only the strongest motives could draw settlers into it. These motives were the same as those that had first drawn Europeans across the Atlantic: religious freedom (in the case of the Mormons), adventure, independence from one's neighbors, and most common of all, desire for land and gold.

THE MINERS

Between 1859 and 1864, gold rushes occurred at scattered points in what later became the states of Nevada, Colorado, Idaho, Montana, and Arizona. One more major rush, to the Black Hills of South Dakota, took place in 1876. In each case, the boom went through nearly identical stages. First, as the fever spread following word of a promising strike, hundreds, perhaps several thousand restless opportunists converged on the spot; they included greenhorn prospectors, veterans of other mining booms, and such camp followers as merchants, prostitutes, gamblers, and more ordinary bandits. The rough-and-ready gold town itself seemed to appear overnight, a jumble of ramshackle rooming houses, shops, and whiskey mills. Women were rare, commonly outnumbered by men by three to one. Although the lawlessness of the West has probably been exaggerated, justice was often informal. An association of miners arbitrated claim disputes, and a rough semblance of law and order was maintained by citizens' vigilance committees. More settled communities appointed sheriffs, who were themselves not always models of civic probity.

When the easy pickings available through placer (surface) mining gave out, mining towns often became ghost towns. Sometimes a second metal was found and a second rush occurred, as in the cases of Colorado silver or Montana copper. Occasionally, as in Nevada in 1873, deeper digging uncovered a major lode and another bonanza. Often, after the raw surface metal was gone, organized exploitation with expensive machinery and deeper drilling produced richer results. Meanwhile, the impecunious "sour doughs," the original pick-and-basin miners, found work with the new mining companies or moved on to the next likely wilderness in the United States, Canada, Alaska, or beyond.

This haphazard but intense exploration of mineral resources doubled the world's gold supply, with important results for American political history. Silver production also increased sharply and created in a few western states a special economic interest that provided political power for more than half a century. In many cases, towns created to serve the needs of miners found other means of livelihood and survived when the mines closed. These new populations, scattered throughout the West, raised new problems, particularly those of transportation and protection against Indians.

TRANSPORTATION

The earlier Oregon migrants and California gold seekers traveled either around Cape Horn, across the Isthmus of Panama, or over the American plains. Beginning in the late 1850s, stage lines (notably Wells, Fargo, and Company) and wagon trains reached across the country. At the end of the 1850s, the enterprising firm of Russell, Majors, and Waddell developed the short-lived but spectacular pony express, which transported letters (initially at five dollars per half-ounce) from Independence, Missouri, to San Francisco in 10 days of fast relay riding. In 1861 this system was displaced by a coast-to-coast telegraph line.

Meantime, the secession of the South had settled the old arguments about the route for a railway, and in 1862 work was started under heavy government subsidy. The Central Pacific climbed painfully east through the Sierra from Sacramento, while the Union Pacific drove west along the wagon train route from Omaha via Cheyenne to South Pass. In 1869, while the nation celebrated, top-hatted dignitaries met at Promontory, Utah, to watch the driving (and retrieval) of the golden spike linking the two roads. For the next decade and a half, mostly a time of depression, the Union Pacific–Central Pacific remained the only coast-to-coast route. Then in the prosperous early 1880s, three more lines were completed: the Southern Pacific and the Santa Fe systems through the Southwest, and the Northern Pacific from St. Paul to Portland, Oregon. In 1893, a fourth road, the Great Northern, connected St. Paul and Seattle by a route still farther north. This last railroad, unlike its competitors, was developed without government subsidy by the public-spirited James J. Hill, chiefly by promoting development of the surrounding region.

THE INDIAN TRAGEDY

Penetration of the plains and mountains by miners, migrants, and stage coaches had made Indian troubles inevitable. The long and bloody struggle for the last West is one of the least pleasant stories in American history. A peaceful solution of this conflict between an aggressive, expanding nineteenth-century civilization and a nomadic, stone-age culture dependent on vast hunting spaces was probably not possible. Yet, mistakes made a hard problem worse. Part of the fault lay with divided councils, civilian administrators squabbling with soldiers, soldiers disagreeing among themselves, and settlers arguing with eastern humanitarians. Part of the long tragedy arose from inevitable anger over traditional Indian methods of war. Yet no Indian atrocity was more grisly than such white actions as the Sand Creek massacre of 1864, when several hundred men, women, and children of a tribe trying to surrender were exterminated and their bodies mutilated by a detachment of U.S. troops.

Many Native Americans, from the Utes of the Great Basin and the Nez Percés of Idaho to the Modocs of northern California, fought the whites at one time or another. But the most serious opponents of frontier advance were the Sioux of the Northern Plains and the Apache of the Southwest. Divided into small, efficient war bands led by such resourceful leaders as Red Cloud and Crazy Horse, the Sioux proved remarkably adept at high-speed, mounted warfare. On their swift ponies, they were expert with the short bow and later with rifles, and they provided their white enemies with little more target than a heel and a hand. The Apaches, who had been fighting Mexicans for years, were equally dangerous and still more elusive in their own country of desert and rocky canyon.

The long struggle with the Plains Indians began with a Sioux massacre of whites in Minnesota in 1862. Fierce fighting with Sioux and many other tribes continued through the Civil War years and sporadically in the 1870s. The last serious Sioux war broke out in 1876 when the Dakota gold rush penetrated the Black Hills, recently guaranteed to the Indians. But as late as 1890, a messianic ghost dance ritual on the Northern Sioux reservation led to an uprising and one last tragic slaughter at Wounded Knee, South Dakota. Long before this, the Plains Indian's way of life had been destroyed with the slaughter of the buffalo. These animals, once among the most numerous in the world, were almost exterminated in the decade after 1870 by railroad hunters, sport shooters, and professionals catering to the eastern demand for hides. Meantime the Apache wars in the Southwest dragged on until Geronimo, the last important chief, was captured in 1885.

Since the Monroe administration, the government's official policy had been to move the Indians beyond the reach of the white frontier. Once not only Oklahoma but the whole plains area had been talked about as permanent Indian country. Inevitably, reservations had become smaller and more crowded with the advance of the settlers, and forced Indian resettlement had to be supplemented with doles of beef, staples, and clothing.

In time, foolish and cruel government policies toward native Americans produced protest campaigns, all of them well-intentioned and some helpful. As the Indian menace ebbed, idealistic eastern sympathizers, many of them members of the Philadelphia-based Indian Rights Association, argued that a policy amounting to conquest, pauperization, and in some cases virtual genocide, was intolerable. Helen Hunt Jackson, an Easterner living in the West, became the most effective critic of federal Indian policy. Her best-selling books, *A Century of Dishonor* (1881) and *Ramona* (1884), dramatized the Native American's plight and stirred the nation's conscience. The Indian, most reformers believed, should be extended the benefits of white civilization and assimilated into the dominant culture, rather than maintained in primitive tribal condition. This proposal sat well with nineteenth-century ethnocentrism and also with the wish of land-hungry whites for reservation land. After a number of minor reforms, the Dawes Act of 1887 reversed Indian policy. Tribal authority and ownership of land was gradually to be extinguished, and reservation land was to be parceled out to individual Indians, each head of family receiving 160 acres. Such allotments were to be held in trust pending complete ownership after 25 years. Indians living in nontribal fashion were to become citizens. Land not so parceled out could be sold by the government to individual settlers with the proceeds of the sale going toward Indian education.

This well-intentioned statute proved disastrous to the Indians. Most of the reservation land, particularly the most desirable, went to white settlers. Tribal authority was destroyed and individual Indians were often victimized by white neighbors. Some received allotments too soon; others were deprived of incentive by the waiting period. In 1934 this misguided policy was reversed by the Indian Reorganization Act, which attempted to protect what remained of tribal life.

THE OPEN RANGE

Before the Indians and buffaloes had quite vanished, the plains began to be occupied by cattle, the advance guard of the expanding American economy. The range cattle industry, so much the staple of legend that the reality is hard to see, was actually a boom-and-bust episode typical of the period's economic history.

Longhorn cattle were developed in Texas, and from Hispanic sources there, the Anglo-American (and sometimes Afro-American) cowboy got his distinctive dress, his high-backed saddle, and some of his colorful vocabulary. Forage was free on the unoccupied grassland, and the buffalo was no longer abundant enough to compete for the grass. A market for cattle was provided when railroads reached Kansas in the 1860s. Thereafter, huge herds of 2,000 to 3,000 steers were driven 1,500 miles across the Texas plains to the cow towns of Sedalia, Missouri, and Abilene and Dodge City, Kansas. The drive north from Texas at about 15 miles a day was a dangerous, lonely, and difficult business beset by Indians, angry homesteaders, diseases, drought, and stampedes. From these towns, cattle went by rail to the packing centers of Chicago and Kansas City for slaughter, and then by refrigerated railroad car to the industrial markets of the East. Some 10 million cattle were driven across the plains in the two decades after 1866.

Texas longhorns were tough, wiry beasts, and it soon proved more profitable to drive them still farther and fatten them up en route through the open grasslands of western Kansas and Nebraska, the Dakotas, Wyoming, and even Montana. For a while, free grass, cheap cattle, and rising demand brought about boom conditions. Romance attracted such eastern dudes as Theodore Roosevelt, who had his fling as a rancher in South Dakota; 30 percent dividends attracted English syndicates. Soon, inevitably, even the vast plains became overcrowded. As in the mining camps, competition was regulated by semilegal codes. Cattle rancher associations divided up the government-owned unfenced range, regulated the annual roundup when new calves were separated and branded, and dealt summarily with rustlers.

By the early 1880s, two new enemies of the cattle industry appeared. The first of these was the prairie farmer advancing hopefully onto the dry plains and fencing the land. The second enemy was sheep. The sheep industry had spread from the New Mexico plateaus via the Colorado parks and Utah tablelands to the western plains. According to cattle owners, sheep cropped the range too closely, destroyed turf with their hooves, and drove away the cattle, which were superior and had arrived first.

The end of the open-range cattle industry and thus of the classical age of the American cowboy came with the disastrous blizzards of 1885–86 and 1886–87 when millions of cattle froze and starved. From this point on, successful ranchers abandoned traditional ways, enclosed the range, scientifically improved their herds, and put the once-independent "saddle tramp" to mending fences and growing fodder. The legendary cowboy, however, would be reincarnated, first in the fiction of writers like Zane Grey, then in motion pictures, and finally on television.

THE FARMERS

In the 30 years after the Civil War, more land was settled than in the whole of American history before that time. This great movement of population belonged only in part to the history of the Great Plains. Much of the new population completed the job of settling the fertile prairies. However, once the farmers solidly occupied eastern Kansas, Nebraska, and the Dakotas up to the line of semiaridity, they inevitably spilled over it into the plains. Some tried their luck as far west as Wyoming and Montana. In many ways, the experience of these western settlers was like that of prairie farmers in the past generation. In other ways, both the new environment and the changing national economy made this last chapter of frontier farming different.

This was the first migration of farmers to take place since that great farmer victory, the passage of the Homestead Act of 1862. Under this law any head of family who lived on and cultivated his claim for five years could get title to 160 acres free. This amount of land seemed generous to legislators familiar with conditions farther east, but on the Great Plains, where farming cost more and was more risky, it was not enough to make a profitable venture. Later legislation made some attempt to adapt to western realities. The Timber Culture Act of 1873 allowed a homesteader another 160 acres if the homesteader planted at least a quarter of it in trees. The Desert Land Act of 1877, lobbied through by cattle ranchers, allowed a prospective irrigator of dry lands to buy 640 acres for 25 cents an acre down. These irrigators would get title in three years on payment of the balance, provided they could prove they had irrigated a portion of the land. The Timber and Stone Act permitted the purchase of western lands not suitable for farming but valuable — sometimes very valuable — for timber or stone at the absurdly low price of $2.50 an acre.

All these laws, like many earlier American land laws, played into the hands of speculators; many of the laws invited fraud. Cattle, lumber, and land companies used their employees as false homesteaders and hired new immigrants for the same purpose. The country was too big for careful government scrutiny, so all but a small part of the land settled by farmers in this period was acquired, contrary to congressional intent, not from the federal government but from speculators and other intermediaries. Some land was acquired from land companies and some from western states that had received land under the Morrill Act for the purpose of promoting education.

The biggest of all the land sellers, however, were the railroads. The first transcontinentals and some other railroads had received enormous grants along their rights of way. Their main interest was not in revenue from direct sale of this land but in building the population in the areas they served. Thus railroads offered favorable terms, free inspection trips, agricultural information and demonstrations, credit, and even prize bulls. They also advertised. In their promotions, the Great Plains seemed to be a new Canaan. Railroad agents together with state immigration bureaus and steamship-line employees attracted newcomers by flooding Europe with leaflets about the low prices, bountiful yields, and easy profits of western farming. In 1882, the peak year for this kind of migration, 105,000 Scandinavians and 250,000 Germans crossed the ocean, many heading for agricultural life in the Midwest and beyond.

As farmers moved farther west, they confronted new problems: frequent tornadoes, prairie fires, swarming grasshoppers, torrid summer heat and searing winds, and killer blizzards and subzero winter temperatures. Where there were no trees, farmers spent their first winters in dugouts or sod houses. For heat they burned animal chips (dried buffalo or cattle dung), corncobs, or hay. Fencing presented a problem until the invention of barbed wire in 1874. To make wells, the settlers had to dig down hundreds of feet in the drier areas. To save what surface moisture there was, they learned to plow deeply and to harrow the surface to make a dust mulch. Finally, the farmers needed machines to harvest crops quickly in a region where the weather could change rapidly and ruin a season's work.

For fencing, for expensive well-drilling machinery and windmills to pump the water, for steel or chilled-iron plows to break the heavy prairie sod, for harvesters, threshers, and binders, as well as for the land itself, farmers needed credit. In the good harvest years of the early 1880s, credit was plentiful at high interest rates. In the Red River Valley of Dakota and the San Joaquin Valley of California, wheat ranches of scores of thousands of acres gave an early foretaste of industrialized agriculture. Elsewhere in the new areas, a more modest prosperity prevailed. Farmers built better houses; farming towns paved their streets and improved their schools. The price of land skyrocketed.

To many, it seemed that the Great American Desert (as the relatively arid West was often called) had at last been conquered. Advances had been made in techniques of "dry farming" and in the use of new varieties of drought- and cold-resistant wheat. Farmers, of course, hoped that good times would continue indefinitely. Cooperative experts frequently testified that the climate of the plains was changing and that tree planting, irrigation, and even the building of railroads and telegraphs somehow brought more rain. In fact, the Great Plains were nearing the end of a cycle of relative humidity. In 1887 the first of a series of rainless summers withered the crops in the fields. When credit also quickly dried up, the boom collapsed. Many who had moved beyond the line of semiaridity hastened eastward in despair. Half the population of western Kansas disappeared in four years; whole towns were deserted. The American farmer was learning that nature could fix the limits of agriculture.

THE HERITAGE OF THE FRONTIER

In 1893, historian Frederick Jackson Turner said that a period in American history had closed in 1890 with the end of the frontier. Until its passing, the frontier had molded American character and institutions. It had also, Turner and his followers believed, served as a safety valve for urban discontents. Without the frontier, the Wisconsin historian argued, this would be a very different country.

Much of this "frontier thesis" has been disputed. More government land was disposed of in the decade after 1890 than in the decade before. "Free land," moreover, had always been something of a delusion, for much had gone to speculators rather than directly to small farmers. And city workers without training, equipment, savings, or credit experienced special difficulties when they tried to "go west." In fact, since the Civil War at least, most people seeking to escape poverty had moved in the opposite direction, from the farm to the city.

Yet it was true, as Turner said, that the 1890 census for the first time found no continuous border beyond which the country was unsettled. It was true also that a great many people in the 1890s *felt* that a period was ending with the filling up of the West and that American problems in the future would be different and perhaps more difficult. While few historians agree with Turner that American individualism, egalitarianism, and nationalism come entirely from the ever-retreating West, few would deny that the American temperament owes something to both the reality and the legend of the frontier.

One obvious legacy of the West, and of this last West in particular, was a habit of violence. From vigilantes, frontier sheriffs, and cattle rancher associations, the West drew a tradition of rough justice. From mining camps and cowtowns and end-of-track railroad settlements came the western custom of roughhouse. And in the twentieth century, violence sometimes hung on in still less attractive forms such as the bloody labor wars of Colorado, which also had their class dimensions, and the persistently high homicide rates of some western states. Perhaps violence was inseparable from some of the more attractive traits of the frontier legend — the devotion to individual freedom and equality thought of as western.

In politics, the West has shown certain consistent traits. Sometimes the western liking for innovation has made easterners think it radical. Four far-western states pioneered in women's suffrage. The Initiative and Referendum came from the West and so did that last extreme of egalitarianism, the popular recall of judicial decisions. Yet the West has given the nation such vigorous conservatives as Senator Barry Goldwater and Presidents Richard Nixon and Ronald Reagan. Sometimes western radicalism and western conservatism are inextricably blended in the same people. What Westerners have in common, perhaps, is a fierce devotion to individual independence, a contempt for tradition, a willingness to try something new, and a delight above all in defying whatever mysterious forces are currently meant by the term "the East."

FOR FURTHER READING

R. A. Billington's *Westward Expansion* (1949) is a usable general history of the West; his *America's Frontier Heritage* (1966) offers a reappraisal of the Turner hypothesis; and his *Frederick Jackson Turner* (1973) is a magisterial biography. L. R. Hafen and C. C. Rister in *Western America* (1941) give a detailed account of the trans-Mississippi region. Walter P. Webb's *The Great Plains* (1931) is a fascinating and controversial interpretation of the region by a devoted native. Rodman Paul's *Mining Frontiers of the Far West, 1848–1880* (1963) is the most scholarly overview of the subject but it does not supplant Mark Twain's *Roughing It* (1872). J. D. W. Guice in *The Rocky Mountain Bench* (1972) comments on the quality of frontier justice. Summaries of United States Indian policy in the period are: L. B. Priest's *Uncle Sam's Stepchildren* (1942); Wilcomb E. Washburn's *Red Man's Land — White Man's Law: A Study of the Past and Present Status of the American Indian* (1971); and Francis Paul Prucha's *American Indian Policy in Crisis* (1976). Angie Debo's *A History of the Indians in the United States* (1970) and her *Geronimo* (1976) are both excellent; Dee Brown's *Bury My Heart at Wounded Knee* (1971) is a passionate account of the Indian wars; Stephen E. Ambrose's *Crazy Horse and Custer* (1975) is a study of the clash of cultures on the far western frontier; and Brian W. Dippie's *Custer's Last Stand* (1976) studies the anatomy of a great American myth. Among the many books on the cattle kingdom are: E. S. Osgood's *The Day of the Cattleman* (1929); E. E. Dale's *The Range Cattle Industry* (1930); and Louis Pelzer's *The Cattleman's Frontier* (1936). Studies by Joe B. Frantz and Julian E. Choate, Jr., *The American Cowboy* (1955), Philip Durham and Everett L.

Jones, *The Negro Cowboys* (1965), and Charles W. Harris and Buck Raincy, eds., *The Cowboy* (1976) examine aspects of the much fabled western drover. The problems of the plains farmer are authoritatively discussed by F. A. Shannon in *The Farmer's Last Frontier* (1945) and effectively portrayed in the works of Hamlin Garland, especially *Main Travelled Roads* (1891). The social history of the northern plains is discussed by Everett Dick in *The Sod-House Frontier* (1937), and the special problems of the Scandinavian immigrant are depicted in Ole Rolvaag's *Giants in the Earth* (1927). R. M. Robbins in *Our Landed Heritage* (1942) surveys public land policy. Henry Nash Smith's *Virgin Land: The American West as Symbol and Myth* (1950) is an important and highly sophisticated interpretation of the effect of the West on American thought and emotion.

MAP 6:   THE AMERICAN WEST, 1860–1890

PACIFIC OCEAN

Mining centers

Gold

Silver

Copper

Indian reservations, 1890

Railroad routes

Cattle trails

X   Indian battles

TABLE 11. AMERICAN POLITICS, 1868–1896

Year	President	Presidential vote (in thousands)		Control of House of Representatives			Major tariff legislation	Financial and other important legislation	Business conditions
		R	D	R	D	Other			
1867							Reduction narrowly beaten.		To 1869 Moderate prosperity for agriculture. Moderate depression for industry.
1868	Grant R	3 013	2,707	149	63				
1869								Resolution to pay bonds in coin.	1869 Collapse of farm prices.
1870				134	104	5	Slight reductions.	Bonds refunded at lower rates.	
1871									1869–1873 Moderate prosperity for industry.
1872	Grant R	3,597	2,843	194	92	14	10 percent off protected articles. Coffee, tea, free.	Most remaining internal taxes repealed.	
1873								End of silver coinage. Greenback expansion vetoed.	1873 Panic.
1874				109	169	14			
1875							10 percent cut restored.	Resumption Act (greenbacks to be convertible 1879).	Depression →

Year	President						Tariff	Legislation	Economic conditions
1876	Hayes *R*	4,037	4,284	140	153			Bland-Allison Act. Resumption (greenbacks convertible).	
1878				130	149				
1879						14			1879 Recovery.
									Prosperity
1880	Garfield *R*	4,453	4,414	147	135	11			
1882				118	199	10			
1883							"Mongrel Tariff."	Pendleton Act.	Panic and depression.
1884	Cleveland *D*	4,850	4,880	140	183	2			
1885									1885 Partial recovery.
1886				152					
1887					169	4	Cleveland Tariff Message.	Interstate Commerce Act.	1887 Collapse of farm prices. Uneven prosperity
1888	Harrison *R*	5,447	5,538	166	159		Mills bill (reduction) passes House.		
1889								Omnibus bill (4 western states).	
1890				88	235	9	McKinley Tariff (increase).	Sherman Anti-Trust Act and Sherman Silver Purchase Act.	Minor panic.
1892	Cleveland *D*	5,183	5,555	127	218	11			
1893								Repeal of Sherman Silver Purchase Act.	1893 Major panic.
1894				244	105	7	Wilson-Gorman Tariff (slight reduction).		
1895									
1896	McKinley *R*	7,102	6,493	204	113	40			Depression

19

★ ★ ★ ★ ★ ★

The Political Parade, 1868–1892

THE POLITICS of the generation after the Civil War is generally considered to be one of the least important and most sordid topics in American history. During this period, the American people were concentrating on industrial development. Politics, it is said, became a meaningless sideshow in which second-rate politicians made pompous speeches while special interests maneuvered for advantage behind the scenes. This picture has much truth in it, but it is not complete. Much was at stake politically, though the campaign slogans did not always reflect the real issues.

THE STAKES OF THE GAME

Political affairs were, for instance, deeply affected by the period's three depressions: the major one of 1873–1879, the minor one of the mid-1880s, and the collapse initiated by the panic of 1893. These depressions and related events, such as the fall of farm prices in 1869 and 1887, greatly influenced people's political behavior. They did not, however, produce effective governmental action. Only in the depression of the mid-1890s did demands for relief and remedy absorb political argument briefly, and even then the call for action was temporarily rejected. Throughout the period after 1868, depressions affected people mainly by motivating them to vote for the party out of power. They also influenced people's attitudes toward the two big economic arguments of the period, those over the tariff and over the currency.

According to the period's dominant economic theory, it was not part of the government's duty to interfere with the business cycle. Distress would always be remedied in the long run by the action of the invisible, all-powerful laws of political economy. The government's role in the economic sphere was simple: (1) it should raise enough money for its own modest wants by equitable means; (2) it should provide a sound currency; and (3) perhaps (there was disagreement on this point) it should seek to advance the national products in the international market. But the Civil War had thrown these traditional economic functions way out of kilter. In its great need, the government had raised huge sums by any means available. It had placed internal taxes on everything in sight, from coal and iron to billiard tables. It had, for the first time, taxed incomes. Partly to make up for these taxes, it had increased the moderate prewar protective tariff. It had issued $450 million worth of fiat money, or greenbacks not backed by gold, and floated immense loans. Most people agreed that the problem was to get rid of these burdens and go back to the simple old ways. These actions proved harder than they sounded.

Removing the income tax and other internal taxes was easy enough to do, and this was largely accomplished by 1872. It seemed obvious that the tariff came next. Many people thought that the high wartime rates constituted unfair favors to special interests and placed a heavy burden on consumers. At first, most politicians took it for granted that the rates must go down. Somehow, though, tariff reduction bills that passed one house tended to be amended piecemeal in the other house and again in conference committee until they were no longer reduction bills.

Part of the difficulty lay in the nature of Congress, in which each member represented certain constituents and, consequently, very often a geographical and economic special interest. Each commodity was likely to have its own powerful advocate. It soon developed that the easiest way to compromise between two conflicting interests, such as raw wool and woolen textiles or raw sugar and refined sugar, was to do some kind of favor for each. Thus, despite many attempts, wartime rates were never substantially and permanently lowered. By 1890 the Republican party and a minority of the Democrats were openly committed to raising protection still higher, though the opposition continued to be both sizable and fervent. Certainly this issue was a real one; the rates on steel rails or woolens mattered a great deal to some people and the price of sugar to others.

A problem that accompanied the high tariff — and one unknown to modern readers — was the treasury surplus. Governmental functions were so comparatively simple that increased revenues could not easily be spent. Consequently too much of the limited supply of money accumulated in the treasury. One way to handle this problem was suggested by Grover Cleveland in 1888: lower the protective tariff. Other suggestions, however, proved more politically appealing. One could, for instance, lower the nonprotective tariff rates on articles like coffee, tea, or sugar that were not made in this country. This was done in 1872 and again in 1890. It had the advantage of reducing the income of the government only and not of private interests. And money could always be spent on veterans' pensions, river and harbor improvements, and subsidies to silver miners, railroad builders, and other powerful groups.

The other main economic argument arising from Civil War finance centered upon inflation. Right after the war, businesses were deeply divided on this matter and so were the still prosperous farmers. Gradually, however, as farm prices sank in the 1870s and then again in the late 1880s and 1890s, farm opinion turned toward inflation. At the same time, bankers, eastern editors, and some businesses became more and more convinced that tampering with the value of money was dishonest and invited disaster. Many economists today would agree that the country's money supply during the whole period was insufficient and inflexible. Certainly many who lived in that era believed this because of their own bitter experiences.

Three main methods of encouraging inflation attracted widespread support. The first was the suggestion, sometimes called the Ohio Idea and incorporated in the Democratic platform in 1868, that the government bonds be paid in the fluctuating greenback currency instead of in gold. Congress turned down this suggestion decidedly in 1869, resolving to pay bondholders in "coin or its equivalent." It proved possible, however, to refund the bonds at lower than original rates of interest.

The next method of encouraging inflation centered upon the greenbacks, toward which there were different attitudes. One group said that more of the "money of the people" should be issued to relieve financial tightness. Another said that the existing greenbacks should be retired as fast as possible. A third, the group that won the argument, said that existing greenbacks should remain in circulation but no more should be issued. In 1875, Congress resolved that $300 million in greenbacks should be left in circulation, but that on January 1, 1879, greenbacks should be made redeemable in gold. Despite a rise, during the depression of the late 1870s, of angry demands for more greenbacks, this policy was carried out on time. In the good times of the early 1880s, agitation against this accomplished fact gradually declined.

The third inflationary proposal to get a big following was the demand for "free" coinage of silver. Traditionally, gold and silver had been the basis of American money, and since 1834 the official ratio between the value of the two metals had been sixteen to one. Since this undervalued silver in terms of world prices, people had hoarded the silver dollars, which gradually disappeared. In 1873, the coinage of silver was quietly ended, an act later known to farmers and other debtors as the "crime of 1873." In the 1880s, however, the huge silver strikes of the Far West greatly increased the supply of silver. If the silver dollar were to be coined at the old ratio, it would be the cheaper, and therefore the dominant coin. This would expand the currency and also help the silver-mining interests, strategically located in underpopulated western states and therefore disproportionately strong in the Senate.

The gold standard, the money of imperial Britain and of international bankers, was blamed for all the farmer's troubles. Pressure to go back to free coinage of silver at sixteen to one became almost irresistible, and twice Congress was forced to make a half-hearted concession to the silver forces. In 1878 the Bland-Allison Act directed the Treasury to purchase $2–4 million worth of silver bullion a month at market prices and to coin it into dollars. In 1890 the Sherman Silver Purchase Act required the purchase of the whole output of the silver mines and the issuance thereon of treasury notes. However, by action of the Secretary of the Treasury, these notes, like the silver dollars coined under the previous legislation, remained convertible into gold on demand; thus the gold standard was still intact.

Aside from the tariff and money, the main recurrent issue was political reform. From the late 1870s on, it became painfully clear that the government did not, as standard theory said it should, stay out of economic competition. Its favors in terms of tariffs and tax remissions and subsidies were bought by influence and even money. Some members of the well-established eastern middle class became deeply aroused on moral grounds. Perhaps they were alarmed also by the power of the new rich, who did not share their own traditions of public service. In any case, these essentially conservative reformers, Republican by normal allegiance but independent by conviction, became a surprisingly powerful influence. As parties were evenly balanced, professional politicians might hate the reforming Mugwumps but could not ignore them.

The chief proposal of these reformers was the development of a federal civil service. This would end bribery and corruption, take the power of appointment away from unscrupulous politicians, and perhaps create a class of devoted, impartial public servants like those said to exist in England and Germany.

"Snivel service," as the indignant professional politicians called the movement, never achieved its ideal of completely just, impartial administration. It did, however, make it harder to get away with outright fraud and theft. Some of the most powerful politicians of the day were kept out of the presidency because their records were not pure enough to satisfy the reform element. And after many frustrations, the civil service movement did finally secure, in 1883, the passage of the Pendleton Act. Under this, certain federal offices were filled by competitive examination, rather than by the cruder forms of patronage that exchanged government jobs for political support. Since that time, presidents have frequently added to the number of offices under civil service, especially when the opposing party has been about to come to power. The increase of federal employees has, however, prevented reform from destroying traditional political methods.

Tariff, money, and civil service reform were the most important of the obvious political issues, and, underlying these, business depressions played a big part in politics. On the surface, however, campaigns were fought over whatever false issue lent itself best to emotional slogans, torchlight parades, and bitter hatreds more or less forgotten between elections. The first of these false issues, sadly enough, was Reconstruction — a real and tragic problem subordinated to the political battle. While people lost interest in the fate of southern blacks, Republican politicians "waved the bloody shirt," blaming their opponents for all the horrors of war. Conversely, Southerners and Democrats dwelt on the alleged horrors of black rule.

After attacks on rebels, blacks, and carpetbaggers began to pall, there were always Catholics, immigrants, and foreigners in general to be assailed. One big section of the population could be counted on to respond to fear of the Pope, and another always cheered an attack on Great Britain. Finally, the war records, drinking habits, appearance, and marital life of leading candidates could be raised as political issues.

THE RULES AND THE PLAYERS

The character of post–Civil War politics can partly be explained by two political facts: the overwhelming power of Congress and the remarkably even division between the two great parties. In Reconstruction, Congress effectively broke the power of the executive branch. Real power in the period after 1870 was centered in the Senate, which was so business-oriented and so flush with wealthy members that it became known as the Millionaires' Club. Powerful and arrogant, some leading senators — Rhode Island's Nelson W. Aldrich and Ohio's Mark Hanna among them — created nearly unbeatable personal political machines in their home states. Appointed at their behest, both state and federal officeholders could be assessed for campaign contributions. When this was theoretically outlawed by the 1883 Pendleton Act, local business interests could still be heavily tapped. Thus the "right kind" of governors and members of Congress would be elected, and subservient legislatures would send the real rulers of their states back again and again to the Senate. With the presidency weakened, there was no powerful advocate for general national needs, and politics took such forms as *spoilsmanship* (the distribution and seeking of patronage) and *logrolling* (the trading of political favors).

The Civil War and Reconstruction demoralized the Democratic party but by no means destroyed it. Though the Republicans held the presidency during all but Grover Cleveland's two terms, 1884–1888 and 1892–1896, the Democrats won a popular plurality more often and controlled the House of Representatives more than half the time. National elections frequently depended on a few thousand well-distributed votes.

Since no single interest group commanded a majority, each party had to appeal to many elements. The Republicans could count on the Union veterans and the blacks, when and where they could vote. Those business people who favored the high protective tariff voted Republican and so, usually, did believers in the gold standard (though many western Republicans were inflationists). In good times, midwestern farmers could be counted on for Republican votes. To a large group of respectable middle-class Protestants, it was unthinkable to vote Democratic. The clergyman who said in the abusive campaign of 1884 that the Democrats were the party of "Rum, Romanism, and Rebellion" went too far and may have helped Cleveland more than the Republican candidate, James G. Blaine of Maine. But he voiced a stereotype that many took for granted.

After Reconstruction, the Democrats started with the Solid South. Most immigrants in the coastal cities, neglected by Anglo-Saxon Republicans and helped by efficient Democratic bosses, were also safely Democratic. Western farmers and much of labor tended to vote Democratic when times were bad. Thus the Democrats were potentially a party of moderate protest, of agitation for low tariffs, and of cheap money. Yet in the East and Midwest as well as the South, some party leaders were ultrarespectable lawyers and business executives. This kind of conservative Democrat (Cleveland was a prime example) might favor foreign trade and a lower tariff, but oppose any other kind of change as vigorously as the staunchest Republican.

Each party was thus divided. The Republicans had three factions. The Stalwarts, led by Senator Roscoe Conkling of New York, were all-out believers in party regularity and the bloody shirt. They even favored a third presidential term for Grant in 1880. At the opposite pole were the liberal or independent Republicans, the Mugwumps, who joined civil service reformer Carl Schurz in deserting their party for Cleveland in 1884. Between these extremes were the Half-Breeds led by the "Plumed Knight," Senator James G. Blaine; they were much like the Stalwarts, but less blatantly partisan. Rivalry between these factions was such that in 1884 when Senator Conkling was asked whether he would support the party's candidate, Senator Blaine, he replied, "No, thank you, I don't engage in criminal practice." In the Democratic party, the factions included Bourbons (reactionaries) and near radicals, supporters of the corrupt New York City machine (Tammany Hall), and reformers.

With such party divisions, it is not surprising that the two parties tended to select colorless, compromise presidential candidates and to write meaningless platforms. Because the parties needed to play down divisive issues, it was necessary to play up personalities, scandals, and party regularity. In crucial states in tightly contested campaigns, bribery and violence were not rare.

The system seemed to work in spite of itself. The nation's industry expanded; its presidents and some other politicians were honest and often reasonably competent. Party discipline, growing stronger through the period, accomplished the government's business and usually kept the most divisive issues out of politics. Interest groups were able to influence government but seldom dominated it altogether. Stable rather than innovative, the political order of the Gilded Age served business better than popular interests. Yet in relatively peaceful and prosperous times the political system seemed to satisfy Americans. When widespread popular discontent raised its head in the 1890s, political habits necessarily, if reluctantly, changed.

THE GRANT ERA

When Ulysses S. Grant was elected in 1868, many people expected a dignified, masterly administration in the Washington tradition. Naturally, the chief national hero of the Civil War was flattered by politicians and big business. Equally naturally, Grant, who before the war had had little interest in politics and no experience of success, enjoyed the flattery. Originally inclined toward a lenient Reconstruction policy, he was skillfully maneuvered by the Radicals into their camp. His appointments dismayed his admirers.

Though he chose real leaders like Hamilton Fish, the New York aristocrat who became Secretary of State, the appointees also included routine politicians, incompetents, seedy relatives of the Grants, military men out of jobs, and crooks. Grant's personal integrity made his muddling political naiveté all the more tragic.

In financial matters Grant was moderately conservative, vetoing a measure to increase the greenbacks but battling the Supreme Court to defend the validity of those in circulation. Secretary Fish handled foreign affairs with surprising effectiveness. In 1871 the difficult issues arising out of England's wartime friendliness to the Confederacy were sensibly settled by arbitration. To placate reformers, the Civil Service Commission was set up, but it was not allowed initially to interfere with the serious matter of patronage.

By 1872 the reformers were tired of Radical Reconstruction, irritated by the failure of tariff reduction, and disgusted by the administration's moral laxity. Determined to block Grant's re-election and "turn the rascals out," they held a separate Liberal Republican convention and nominated for the presidency the vain and thin-skinned veteran reformer and editor Horace Greeley of the *New York Tribune*. Hoping to make a "new departure" and end the constant attacks on their patriotism, the Democrats nominated Greeley also. Greeley, a former Whig, Republican, abolitionist, and relic of the antebellum past, was an odd Democratic candidate. Vulnerable to ridicule as a utopian for his many causes (including vegetarianism, spiritualism, and Fourierism) he was disastrously beaten.

With Grant re-elected and reformers momentarily discredited, the way seemed clear for Stalwart domination. However, the Democrats captured the House of Representatives in the depression year of 1874 and used their victory to investigate the Republican administration. A sinister pattern was revealed in department after department: the purchase of political favors for money. This corruption, known as "Grantism," tarred great causes like the building of the Union Pacific. Corruption honeycombed the Indian Service, the Freedmen's Bureau, and the collection of internal revenue; it touched ambassadors, cabinet members, and even the president's private secretary. In the face of investigation, the hero of Appomattox realized that something was the matter and apologized on the grounds of his own political inexperience.

THE DISPUTED ELECTION

In 1876, Republican regimes remained in power in only three southern states. With the South back on the Democratic side and many Northerners hostile to the administration, it seemed likely that the Democrats would return to power. To prevent this unthinkable disaster, the Republicans nominated the honest and able, though rather uninspiring, Rutherford B. Hayes of Ohio. The Democrats also bid for the reformers by nominating Samuel J.

Tilden, who as governor of New York had destroyed the grafting Boss Tweed ring in New York City.

Tilden won a sizable popular plurality, capturing New York and several other northern states in addition to the South. It seemed clear that he had won the election. The Republicans, however, claimed the votes of the three southern states still under carpetbagger rule: Florida, South Carolina, and Louisiana. In each of these states, the Democrats had intimidated blacks, and both parties had been guilty of other dubious practices. After a long and bitter dispute, the conflicting returns from these states were referred to an electoral commission; acting on strictly party lines, it gave the election to Hayes by one vote.

Certain Republicans had approached certain Democrats in advance to make sure this result would be accepted. The Compromise of 1877, as this has been called, somewhat resembles the prewar compromises. Like them, it was made by conservatives for the purpose of preventing trouble. Southern Democratic leaders were assured that, if they accepted Hayes's election, he would remove the troops from the remaining southern states and that the South would receive its share of railroad subsidies and similar federal favors. Conservative southern Democrats, many of them former Whigs who believed in supporting industry, had no love for the agrarian Democrats of the Northwest. The Republican conservatives, on the other hand, hoped to build up their party in the southern states. This hope did not mature, however, and by the next election, the bloody shirt was again waving in the breeze. One result of the compromise stood: the North was through intervening on behalf of the southern black. Once again, conservative white Southerners controlled the South, and the stage was set for the disfranchisement and segregation of the former slaves.

THE PRESIDENTIAL SEESAW

Hayes made a serious effort to reform the federal bureaucracy, an effort that involved him in a bitter fight with the Stalwarts of his party. But that did not go far enough to please the reformers. A financial conservative, he stood firm against inflation. A believer in the principle of a single presidential term, Hayes made too many enemies to be renominated even if he had changed his mind. After a stalemate between the Stalwart backers of a third term for Grant and the partisans of James G. Blaine, the oratorically gifted but somewhat tarnished "Plumed Knight" of the Half-Breeds, the nomination went to the moderately reform-minded James A. Garfield of Ohio. To placate the defeated Stalwarts, the Republicans gave the second place on the ticket to Chester A. Arthur of the New York Custom House, a perfect representative of machine politics. Garfield won a close election against General Winfield Scott Hancock and, like his predecessor, began struggling with the Stalwarts over patronage. On July 2, 1881, this promising president was shot by a psychotic office-seeker, who cried out, "I am a Stalwart and

Arthur is President now." After lingering in pain for several weeks, Garfield died on September 19 — a martyr, many thought, to the spoils system.

To the surprise of most public-spirited citizens and to the dismay of some friends, the handsome, genial Arthur made an honest and able executive. Turning against his old cronies, he fought against corruption in the post office and machine politics in his own bailiwick. He backed the Pendleton Act, the first real civil service law, and even attempted to put through a thorough revision of the tariff. In this he failed, and the so-called Mongrel Tariff of 1883 was amended out of all reform meaning.

In 1884 the Half-Breeds finally pushed through the nomination of their hero, Blaine. The Democrats nominated Grover Cleveland, the stout and solid governor of New York, who had a reputation for honesty and independence. In a campaign that reached a peak of scandal-mongering on both sides, Cleveland won.

To the horror of many Republicans, a Democrat was in power — the first since 1860. No disaster ensued, however. Cleveland dealt effectively with the most obvious and immediate problems facing the government. One of these was the rising treasury surplus. Instead of dissipating this surplus through continually bigger pensions for veterans, a move that he courageously opposed, Cleveland insisted on tariff reduction. In 1887, using the most forthright language employed by any president since the war, he attacked the high tariff as the creator of oppressive monopolies and managed to push a tariff reform bill through the House of Representatives, though not through the Senate.

The protective tariff, therefore, was the one national issue that played a big part in the campaign of 1888. The Republicans nominated the cold and correct Benjamin Harrison of Indiana, grandson of Old Tippecanoe. Since it was clear what was at stake, they were able to go farther than usual in "frying the fat," that is, wringing campaign contributions out of protected industries. Despite these and less savory tactics, Cleveland won a popular plurality; however, Harrison secured a majority of the electoral votes.

For some reason, the Harrison administration took this doubtful mandate as a green light for an extreme program along Stalwart lines. With liberal pension acts and rich pork-barrel appropriations for rivers and harbors, post offices, and the like, the new Congress launched a successful assault on the surplus in the old-fashioned manner. The administration leaders gave their cordial support to the complex and ultraprotectionist McKinley Tariff of 1890. To put this across, it was necessary to make several accommodating gestures toward the western critics of the administration. For the first time, the tariff offered protection to farm products as well as to manufactures. The administration supported both the Sherman Silver Purchase Act and antimonopoly legislation. The admission of six western states and an unsuccessful attempt to give Congress power to control southern elections completed the strategy of the administration high command.

In 1890 the Republicans were repudiated overwhelmingly in Congress, and in 1892, Cleveland was vindicated by re-election. Despite the reappearance, however, of his corpulent and familiar figure, there were signs that the conventional pattern of politics was changing. In the heavily Democratic Congress there were several members of a new third party calling itself the People's party and demanding a whole list of radical reforms. Shortly after Cleveland's inauguration, a severe financial panic alarmed businessmen. This was only the beginning; the second Cleveland administration was to face a host of new problems at home and abroad. Or, more accurately, it would encounter old problems that could no longer be ignored.

FOR FURTHER READING

Any serious study of the period should include James Bryce's classic, *The American Commonwealth*, 2 vols. (1888). Matthew Josephson's *The Politicos* (1938) is dated but still fascinating. The best overview of the period is John A. Garraty's *The New Commonwealth* (1968). H. Wayne Morgan's *From Hayes to McKinley* (1969) is a synthesis of party politics; Robert Marcus describes the *Grand Old Party* (1971); J. Rogers Hollingsworth's *Whirligig of Politics* (1963) looks at the Democracy from Cleveland to Bryan; and Daniel Rothman's *Politics and Power* (1966) studies the Senate closely. Irwin Unger in *The Greenback Era* (1964) relates financial controversy to political ideological divisions, and Ari Hooginboom in *Outlawing the Spoils* (1961) examines civil service reform. For the Grant administration, see: William Hesseltine, *Ulysses S. Grant, Politician* (1935), and Allan Nevins, *Hamilton Fish* (1936). Other biographies of note include Kenneth Davison's *The Presidency of Rutherford B. Hayes* (1972) and Nevins's *Grover Cleveland* (1932). The disputed Hayes-Tilden election is interpreted by C. Vann Woodward in *Reunion and Reaction* (1951); and both Vincent Desantis in *Republicans Face the Southern Question* (1959) and Stanley Hirshson in *Farewell to the Bloody Shirt* (1962) review Republican efforts to woo the white South.

20

★ ★ ★ ★ ★ ★

The Ripening of Protest, 1870–1896

IN THE 1890s, sharp criticism of industrial and urban conditions roiled the calm political waters of the United States. Once confident that serious unrest was impossible in America, conservatives became alarmed by strident social criticism and class resentments and began to talk of a revolutionary menace. Though dissent was widespread and originated in part from radicals, the mass of the discontented generally sought redress through reform rather than revolution. Much discord could be traced to the painful adjustments required of a nation that, as Richard Hofstadter wrote, "was born in the country, but has moved to the city."

One important challenge to the new socio-economic order was the force of tradition and the reluctance of native-born farm people and foreign-born peasants to accept the rule of clock and machine. Though industrial capitalism ultimately brought a rising standard of living, abundant goods and services, and wider opportunities, initially its long-range benefits were not appreciated by workers and farmers, who had experienced its uncertain, boom-bust cycles. Those who endorsed industrial capitalism were also committed to traditional values, demanding the loyalty and dedication of workers under radically altered circumstances. And these unfolding ideological struggles of the Gilded Age colored the nation's political arguments for much of the twentieth century.

DEFENDERS OF LAISSEZ FAIRE

Many educated people of the nineteenth century believed, in the tradition of competitive individualism, that human affairs were ruled by immutable natural law. According to the central law of political economy, the general good was best served by the unrestrained pursuit of individual self-interest.

If such competition caused social suffering, this was an unfortunate but necessary spur to greater effort. Rewards went to those who earned them through hard work and right living, whereas poverty was almost always a punishment for vice and sloth. People believed it to be foolish and immoral for the state or any private organization to intervene in economic affairs. As formal economic theory, this argument is known as classical economics.

Late in the nineteenth century, classical economic theory was attacked by a new generation of reform-minded scholars associated with the American Economic Association (AEA). Until then, however, laissez faire was not only the test of economic orthodoxy, but as the first president of the AEA observed, "It was used to decide whether a man were an economist at all." Laissez-faire economists in the United States borrowed heavily from Adam Smith (*Wealth of Nations*, 1776). Like Smith's disciples on both sides of the Atlantic, they taught that economic competition unchecked by the state assured human progress. Laissez faire, as one Harvard professor explained, means " 'things run themselves'. . . which means, of course, that God regulates them by his general laws, which always, in the long run, work to good."

Leading ministers also argued that laissez faire was the law of both science and God. The Reverend Henry Ward Beecher of Brooklyn's Plymouth Church (whose annual salary was over $20,000) took an extreme view when he said that any sober, nonsmoking laborer could feed a family of six on a dollar a day: "Water costs nothing; and a man who cannot live on bread is not fit to live." Some Protestant churchmen, influenced by the Calvinist ethic of individual achievement and responsibility, justified unbridled competition on ethical and religious grounds; they found no conflict between God and Mammon and were confident that, as the Episcopal Bishop of Massachusetts said, "Godliness is in league with riches." Commanded by the tenets of this "gospel of wealth" to be their brothers' keepers, the rich did have an obligation to the poor. But the yawning disparities in worldly goods between the industrialists and their workers were the proper concerns, in Andrew Carnegie's words, of "the man of wealth . . . the mere trustee and agent of his poorer brethren," and not of the state.

The Protestant establishment also took to the social applications of Darwinian science. Initially troubled by the theory of evolution, toward the end of the 1800s the nation's prominent churchmen discovered its "providential purposes" and, as readily as others of their social class, accepted Social Darwinism. According to the English philosopher Herbert Spencer and his American disciple William Graham Sumner of Yale University, the unimpeded struggle for existence was the means by which the human race had reached its present high development; social action or state regulation of any kind would disrupt the natural design, encourage the unfit, fetter the strong, and thereby slow progress. In the "survival of the fittest," Spencer's adaptation of Darwinian natural selection, apologists for the status quo found scientific confirmation of the values of competitive individualism.

Taught by political economists and preached by the clergy, the doctrines of laissez faire and Social Darwinism were also invoked by jurists. During

the 1880s and 1890s, the Supreme Court gradually worked out an interpretation of the Fourteenth Amendment that made it, too, a bastion of
business. To protect the former slaves, the amendment prohibited states
from depriving "any person of life, liberty, or property, without due process
of law." The court, however, interpreted the amendment to mean that no
state could deprive any corporation of liberty or property. "Liberty" was
read as liberty of contract, and "person" could mean corporation. "Without
due process" covered any sort of unreasonable regulation of, say, hours of
labor or railway rates. What was reasonable depended on the tenets of laissez-faire capitalism. By such logic, the court employed federal law (the Sherman Anti-Trust Act) to limit labor strikes but not to limit the growth of big
business.

The conservative Supreme Court Justices, like most other defenders of
laissez faire, seemed oblivious to the fact that the doctrine of competitive
individualism, however useful as an ideology for the propertied class, was
out of date in an age of large-scale enterprise. The dominant economic tendency of the industrial revolution, as Chapter 17 illustrates, was away from
competition toward monopoly.

REVIVAL OF REFORM

Not all Americans were agreed with Social Darwinism, though up to the
1890s, classical economics and Darwinian individualism were in the ascen-
dant. But the growing inequities caused by the industrial revolution stirred
reformers to challenge the social and economic utility of unrestricted
competition.

Some evils of the period, like recurrent corruption in government and
fraud in business, raised no new moral problems; these were recognizable
evils requiring punishment. Under the new economic order, however, the
line between legitimate action and wrong-doing was less clearly drawn.
Bribery was wrong, but were investment tips to helpful public officials and
special prices for favored insiders wrong, or merely questionable?

Monopoly was a closely related problem. From the early days of the Republic, Americans had feared concentrated power. Increasingly, the nation's
industrial experience suggested that giant concerns threatened opportunity,
perhaps competitive individualism itself. Railroads drew the first fire. By
the mid-1880s, when the Supreme Court began to overturn state regulatory
laws, demand for national railroad legislation became overwhelming. In
1887 the Interstate Commerce Act forbade certain unfair practices, required
that rates be published and "reasonable," and set up a commission to investigate abuses and to appeal to the courts for redress.

In 1890, mounting demand for general antimonopoly legislation was met
by the Sherman Anti-Trust Act, which nominally prohibited all contracts,
combinations (monopolies), or conspiracies that restrained interstate or foreign trade. Like the Interstate Commerce Act, this measure was not enforced for many years. Both acts presented an interesting paradox: govern-

ment intrusion in the name of laissez faire by regulating to preserve free competition.

Another major area for reform was the exploding American cities. The process of suburbanization enabled by new forms of public transit tended to insulate the advantaged classes from the problems of innercity life. Yet even those who believed the poor deserved to be poor could not ignore the social impact of rapid, unregulated industrial and urban growth. Though not new on the urban scene, the slums with their crime, disease, overcrowding, decaying housing, poverty, and unemployment had expanded and their conditions had rapidly worsened.

Among the first to show concern for the urban poor was a new breed of Protestant clergy, who could not square the cramped ethics of laissez faire with the Golden Rule. This Social Gospel movement owed much to the example of the Salvation Army (the so-called slum angels imported from England in the 1870s) and to clerical concern with the erosion of metropolitan church attendance. Advised by the conservative Protestant clergy to accept their lot, the alienated working class stayed away from organized religion in droves. In contrast, Washington Gladden and other reform-minded ministers urged their parishioners to apply the law of love to labor relations and to the relief of poverty. Christian socialist clergy, notably Baptist Walter Rauschenbusch, went beyond these injunctions to advocate a radical restructuring of society. The Social Gospel movement's mainstream, however, saw no inherent conflict between capitalism and Christianity and sought to make social conditions better by applying their religious beliefs to their actions.

Somewhat more readily than Protestants, the Roman Catholic Church — with its large following among working-class immigrants — also linked religion to reform. Scarcely touched by the Calvinist alliance between business and faith and certainly influenced in 1891 by Pope Leo XIII (*Rerum Novarum*), the Roman Catholic Church in America officially favored "the equality of rich and poor" and recognized "the employers' moral obligation to pay fair wages." At about the same time, Reform Judaism moved that wing of the Jewish faith in much the same direction.

Until the late nineteenth century, relief to the poor had been administered through individual handouts or crowded and inadequate poorhouses. Proponents of laissez faire endeavored to deny charity to the "undeserving poor" and to severely limit it to the "deserving poor" lest their characters be spoiled. By 1890, however, distinctions between the deserving and undeserving poor were fading due to shocking descriptions of slum life, such as Jacob Riis's *How the Other Half Lives*, and to the development of the social work movement. About 100 settlement houses, all modeled after London's Toynbee Hall, were formed as "neighbors to the poor." Jane Addams's Hull House in Chicago and Lillian Wald's Henry Street Settlement in New York are outstanding examples of settlement houses, which provided health, education, welfare, and recreation services in congested tenement districts.

Thus, their consciousness raised, many Americans found it impossible to accept the theories of laissez faire. Among the most radical were Daniel De Leon of the faction-ridden Socialist Labor party and the less doctrinaire Eugene V. Debs of the Socialist Party of America, who were Marxist. Others, including Edward Bellamy, author of the enormously popular *Looking Backward* (1888), sought to supplant competition and private ownership with a utopian socialist order of cooperation and collectivism. Henry George, perhaps the most influential American social theorist of the period, targeted land monopoly for extinction. The author of the best-selling *Progress and Poverty* (1879), George traced all social evil to private gain from increased land values. A confiscatory *single tax* on that "unearned increment," he believed, could reduce the contrast between "the House of Have and the House of Want." George's assault on laissez faire helped lead to a more critical appraisal of the nation's social problems.

Less radical than George were many academic theorists, including such social reformers as Lester Frank Ward and Richard T. Ely. They accepted the broader contours of the free enterprise system, but denied that unrestrained competition assured either equity or progress. A pioneer sociologist, Ward challenged Social Darwinist assumptions about the social development of the human animal with a reform Darwinism that preferred cooperation to conflict, rational choice to natural selection, purposeful intelligence to blind struggle. Although he did not deny the validity of evolutionary theory, Ward argued in *Dynamic Sociology* (1883) and *Applied Sociology* (1906) that human beings, by virtue of thought and will and through social planning and positive social action, could direct the process of nature and alter their environment in beneficial ways. The "New School" economist Richard T. Ely, one of an emerging group of European-educated American critics of laissez-faire capitalism also embraced the state as an instrument for social progress. An unabashed meliorist, Ely never doubted that human beings, through government, could correct the worst ills of an urban and industrial society.

A dark side to the attack on laissez faire involved immigrants. In the best tradition of the free market, the United States was open to all who sought liberty and opportunity. During the 100 years after 1820, some 38 million immigrants came — 5,250,000 of them in the 1880s alone. Old-stock Americans were alarmed by the influx of Asians during the middle of the century and, after 1870, of Italians, Greeks, Russians, Poles, and other southern and eastern Europeans. Most of these people were Roman or Orthodox Catholics, and some were Jews. The new immigrants became the objects of fear and prejudice in a hitherto largely Anglo-Saxon and Protestant nation. These prejudices found expression in the Nordicism of Madison Grant, author of *The Passing of the Great Race* (1916). Added to an ugly mix of anti-Semitism, anti-Catholicism, nativism, and xenophobia were the concerns of organized labor, which was always less hospitable than management to the seemingly endless stream of job-hungry newcomers. Often destitute, not speaking English, and disoriented by the swift transition from their villages to the unsavory environment of city slums, the immigrants seemed to resist Americanization. In many cities they organized their own communities and cultural societies, maintained their native languages, religious customs, and newspapers, and clung to Old World customs. Some foreign born, moreover, became mainstays of urban political machines, trading votes for badly needed assistance from corrupt city bosses. To many middle-class Americans, then, sections of New York, Chicago, and San Francisco were as alien as Naples, Prague, and Shanghai.

Whether demand for immigration restriction came from reformers, conservatives, or both, the result was a series of government actions. In 1882, Congress excluded Chinese, a group especially resented by organized labor. In the same year, convicts, paupers, and criminals were banned, and this list was later amended to include anarchists and other "undesirables." In 1885, the importation of contract labor was forbidden. In 1907 by executive agreement, the Japanese were effectively excluded. A decade later, over Woodrow Wilson's veto, Congress imposed literacy requirements for immigrants. Then, during 1921–1927, Congress passed laws limiting immigration according to nationality quotas designed to restrict Latins and Slavs.

LABOR MOVEMENT

An effective workers' response to industrialism, despite the hardships they endured, developed more slowly in the United States than in most other industrialized nations. Earnings did increase between 1860 and 1890 by about half, largely because of falling food prices, but wages were exceedingly low. Unskilled workers earned $1.00 to $1.50 a day, enough to live on but not enough to tide them over illness, accident, and unemployment, nor to provide for old age. By 1900 the average work week was 60 hours long, and the average worker earned $400 to $500 annually, less than the minimum ($600) required for a "subsistence-plus" standard of living. In addition to low pay, workers faced unhealthy and unsafe conditions in mines and factories, which had high mortality and accident rates. Some workers lost jobs due to technological advances, while many more were cyclically unemployed.

Would-be labor organizers experienced great difficulties. Management was generally hostile to workers' organizations, and in fact organized itself (the General Managers' Association and the National Association of Manufacturers) to keep labor from doing the same. Large sections of the press and the public shared this antiunion sentiment, and government could nearly always be counted on to side with owners against their employees. Frequent economic depressions, industrial spies, and "goon squads" made pro-union sentiment dangerous. Workers were aware that thousands of the unemployed and the new immigrants eagerly waited to replace those fired and blacklisted for union activity. Finally, a heterogeneous work force, composed of many nationalities, lacked the working-class solidarity that effective labor organization seems to require.

The first post–Civil War unions attacked these problems with prewar idealism. The National Labor Union (NLU) and the Knights of Labor, for example, were broadly reformist, industrial unions that sought to unite all segments of the work force (agricultural and industrial, skilled and unskilled) and to supplant the wage system with worker-owned "producer cooperatives." The NLU survived only until the depression of the 1870s. The Knights flourished briefly in the late 1870s and early 1880s and had 750,000 members at peak strength, but like the NLU, its energies were scattered. In 1886 at a labor rally in Chicago's Haymarket Square, a bomb killed and injured police; the Knights were unjustly associated with the incident in the public mind. The union lost members and perished in the depression of the 1890s. Its major competitor and successor was the American Federation of Labor (AFL).

Samuel Gompers, who founded the AFL in the 1880s, was a tough-minded cigar maker who had absorbed the craft tradition of his trade. He blamed the Knight's defeat on loose organization, naive idealism, and polit-ical involvement, and thus organized the AFL along craft rather than indus-try-wide lines. Gompers called for "pure and simple unionism," by which he meant the pursuit of such issues as higher wages, shorter hours, and union protection, including if possible the *closed shop* (one that employed only union members). To reach these goals, Gompers avoided politics and employed such traditional tools as the strike and the boycott. His organiza-tion had no quarrel with the existing capitalist system, and Gompers (al-though once sympathetic to socialism) attempted to deny socialists influen-tial positions within the AFL. Under his leadership the AFL stood apart from radical organizations like the Molly Maguires and, somewhat later, the Industrial Workers of the World. These two organizations represented some of the most oppressed workers and were targets of industrial and govern-ment suppression. In the essentially conservative American labor move-ment, they did not enjoy the appeal that the pragmatic AFL did.

By adapting to existing conditions rather than fighting them, the AFL survived in the hostile world of the nineteenth century. It weathered the depression of the 1890s and by 1900 had half a million members and a lim-ited measure of public recognition. It proved unable, however, to organize the large groups of immigrant workers in heavy industry. Many members of the labor movement, including a strong minority within the AFL itself, wanted to change the organization's nature — to add political activity to trade union methods, to abandon craft for industrial unions, and, above all, to "organize the unorganized." In the disturbed mid-1890s, this opposition got so strong that Gompers lost the leadership of the AFL for a year.

The mainstream of the American labor movement did not evince the anti-capitalist rhetoric and radical ideology of some of its European counterparts, but this did not mean that nineteenth-century workers were contented or that no industrial strife existed. History of the period bristles with accounts of violent labor-management struggles — the most violent, thought the young Winston Churchill at the turn of the century, of any western industrial nation. In the two decades after 1880 there were some 23,000 strikes in-volving more than 6.5 million workers. Sometimes, as in the railroad strikes of 1877 or the Pullman Strike of 1894, the turmoil spanned much of the continent. In other cases, as in the Chicago Haymarket riot or in the steel strike at Carnegie's Homestead, Pennsylvania, plant in 1892, the violence was localized. Whatever their scope, some encounters were marked by pitched gunfire-and-dynamite battles between workers and industrial guards. In the great interstate railroad convulsion of 1877 workers fought militia in Baltimore, Buffalo, Chicago, Pittsburgh, and San Francisco until order was restored by federal troops. More than 100 workers were killed in some two weeks of turmoil that paralyzed rail traffic from West Virginia to California. Incredibly, only 3 Pinkerton strikebreakers and 10 workers died in an exchange of rifle and cannon fire at Homestead 15 years later, but some 8,000 state militia were used to crush the strike of some 4,000 steel workers. In these and in the great majority of the period's work stoppages, the workers' grievances were legitimate and their objectives were limited. But management routinely portrayed all strikes as revolutionary activity, and government (local, state, and federal) usually intervened at management's request.

Although strikes generally centered on such bread-and-butter issues as wages and hours, much of the period's unrest can also be traced to worker resentment of a modernizing economy. Industrialization required cultural as well as economic adjustments. Many people entered the factories with the pre-industrial work habits of farmers and artisans. Both native- and foreign-born "prefactory" peoples rarely shared the industrialists' notions of time and labor, and resisted adopting the work ethic so highly prized by cost-conscious managers. Accustomed to the irregular rhythms of agriculture, the farm folk often resented the rapid pace and rigid discipline of clock, steam, and electricity. The craftsmen watched in alarm as their status declined and their skills were rendered obsolete by machine production. Few welcomed the repetitive specialization of labor required by the factory system. Except for such examples as the Knights of St. Crispin, which struggled futilely to prevent the mechanization of boot and shoemaking in the 1870s and the scattered acts of machine-smashing during the 1877 railroad strike, however, organized expressions of worker hostility to modernization were rare. Yet the conflict between old ways and new expectations accounts for much of the popular malaise of the Gilded Age and is part of the social costs of economic progress.

THE FARMERS AND POPULISM

Farmers also suffered from the effects of modernity. Although their problems in the three decades after 1865 were varied and complicated, the most pressing were international in scope. Almost without realizing it, once largely self-sufficient American farmers had become commercialized growers, who raised specialized cash crops for a wildly fluctuating international market. They competed not just with other American farmers but with farmers in Canada, Argentina, Russia, India, Australia, and New Zealand. The origins of this process can be traced to the staple-exporting economy of the colonial period (see Chapter 9). The process speeded up with the emergence of a national market economy in the early Republic and matured in the post–Civil War age of steam and electricity. The farmers' world was transformed by the revolutions in communication and transportation, which came with the intercontinental steamships, transcontinental railroads, and transoceanic cables that shrank the globe and forged an integrated international market.

In such a market — where vast new crop lands had opened and productivity had increased with the application of machines and science — supply quickly outstripped demand, and the price of farm commodities fell. Saddled with the high fixed costs of land and machinery, farmers responded by growing ever larger crops, further aggravating their problems. They sold the products they raised in a free market, but had to buy the manufactured goods they needed from a tariff–protected market. The consequences for the farmers were chronic indebtedness and acute distress.

Although the uncertainties of modern agriculture were often international in origin, farmers generally blamed conditions closer to home. Agriculturalists believed that the money supply was inadequate and inflexible and that retiring greenbacks, decreasing the number of banknotes in circulation, and above all taking silver out of the currency had been mistakes. Also, they blamed exploitative intermediaries: the railroads and grain elevators with their high rates, the bankers with their usurious interest, and the tariff–protected farm implement combines with their monopoly prices.

These ills were compounded in two regions by local conditions. The overexpanded wheat farmers of the plains were hit by devastating droughts, and in 1887 an especially sharp price fall toppled their inflated credit structure. Southern farmers found that the sharecrop and crop-lien systems, which had evolved during the postwar shortage of capital, served neither the landlords nor their tenants well. The region suffered, moreover, from an oppressive racial climate that subordinated all issues to that of white supremacy. Occasionally and in only a few southern states did agrarian radicals, spokesmen for white dirt-farmers, make common cause with black farmers against railroads and landlords. Discontented poor whites were apt to blame their troubles on their black neighbors and to classify their enemies as "nigger lovers."

Though independent and, in many ways, conservative, farmers of all sections were not reluctant to organize or to ask the government to help relieve their distress. Their demands took two forms: inflation to bring their prices up, and regulation to bring their costs down. Toward these ends they turned, in succession, to the Patrons of Husbandry (the Grange), the Greenback-Labor party, the Farmers' Alliance Movement, and the Peoples' (or Populist) party. Of these, the two parties were avowedly political. The other two, the Grange movement and the Alliances, *officially* eschewed politics in favor of social and educational functions and such activities as cooperative grain elevators, marketing associations, and general stores. Both, however, were effective political pressure groups and influenced state legislatures. Reaching peak strength in 1874 with more than one million members, mostly in the South and Midwest, the Grange gave its name to state laws regulating railroads and grain elevators; many of these Granger laws were invalidated by the Supreme Court in the 1880s. The Alliances, really three distinct networks (the Northwestern, the Southern, and the Colored Alliances), flourished in the 1880s with a combined membership of four to five million. These organizations advocated reforms like free coinage of silver, a

federal income tax, direct election of senators, and regulation or nationalization of transportation and communication companies. In 1890, Alliance
candidates ran so well in the gubernatorial, legislative, and congressional
races of southern and plains states that the movement formed the Peoples'
party two years later.

The first Populist platform, drawn up at the party's initial national convention in Omaha in 1892, summarized, in angry and dramatic language,
most of the discontent of the period. It called for inflation by using legal
tender notes, silver, and other methods. Railroad land grants were to be
recovered, and aliens were to be forbidden land ownership. Railroads and
telephone and telegraph industries were to be nationalized. In an effort to
attract labor support, the platform called for the eight-hour day, immigration
restriction, and the abolition of Pinkerton industrial detectives. Miscella-
neous radical sentiment was cultivated by denunciation of land monopoly,
demand for the income tax, and a general statement that the powers of government should be extended as much as was necessary to secure the end of
injustice and poverty. Finally, expressing the deep confidence in increased
democracy of most American radicalism, the platform praised the *initiative*
(a petition by which voters propose a law) and the *referendum* (the submis-
sion of a law to popular vote) and called for direct election of senators. Running on this platform, General James B. Weaver, the first Populist candidate
for the presidency, received a million votes.

Stirred by this promising first effort, some hopeful radicals believed that
the Populist movement was going to sweep to power, uniting all the diverse
kinds of discontent, upsetting the two-party system as the Republicans had
in 1856–1860, and driving out the monopolists and "gold bugs" (advocates
of a single monetary standard: gold).

CLEVELAND'S LAST STAND

Despite the Populist showing, their goals had no currency with the winning
Democratic candidate, Grover Cleveland. The 1892 election brought to the
presidency a conservative representative of the eastern and hard-money
wing of the Democratic party. When the Panic of '93 swept banks and railroads into bankruptcy and depression set in and unemployment soared, he
doggedly opposed not only the high tariff but inflation. At every cost, he
believed, demagogues and meddlers must be restrained while the immutable law of supply and demand effected recovery.

Cleveland's immediate problem was an inadequate supply of gold to meet
current treasury obligations. The prohibitive rates of the McKinley Tariff
had cut federal income, while expenditures had been increased during the
previous administration by political appropriations for internal improvements, pensions, and especially payments for silver under the Sherman Silver Purchase Act. Cleveland succeeded in repealing the act. To cut federal
spending further, he vetoed pensions and other pork-barrel legislation; to
replenish gold reserves, his administration sold government bonds for gold

and borrowed from the Morgan banking syndicate. These actions met the crisis of a continuing gold drain, but they alienated many Democrats. As a result, Cleveland lost congressional support for effective tariff reform and later lost control of his party.

In the congressional elections of 1894, the Republican opposition swept Congress and the Populists increased their popular vote by 40 percent. That year the Pullman strike, the most serious of the period, began after the financially pinched company fired one-third of its workers and slashed wages by 30 to 40 percent. Pullman workers then flocked to join Eugene V. Debs's American Railway Union, and the strike spread west beyond Chicago. With turmoil threatening to tie up essential transportation, a federal judge (under authority of the Sherman Anti-Trust Act) ordered Debs to end it. That order failed, so Cleveland ill-advisedly sent in federal troops on the request of the union-busting railroad General Managers' Association. Debs went to jail; when he emerged, he was a socialist.

The Pullman strike aroused fears of widespread social disorder in a time of severe depression. Conservatives were alarmed again when an "army" of the unemployed marched on Washington under the leadership of ex-Green-backer Jacob Coxey and others. Neither large nor revolutionary, the object of these groups was to dramatize the plight of the jobless and to demand federal works programs. While trying to address a rally near the Capitol, Coxey was arrested for walking on the grass. His army, only about 500 men, women and children, peacefully melted away.

Although Cleveland remained confident that his laissez-faire policies would cure the nation's economic problems, a challenge to the status quo far more formidable than Coxey's would soon emerge from his own party.

THE BATTLE OF '96

Republican presidential candidate William McKinley was a former congressman and governor from Ohio. Nominated on a hard-money, protectionist platform, McKinley was best known for the high tariff that bore his name. Behind him stood Senator Marcus Alonzo Hanna, an Ohio industrialist and talented Republican party kingpin. To run opposite McKinley, the Democrats offered 36-year-old William Jennings Bryan. At their national convention, the former Nebraska congressman, a political spellbinder who backed the free coinage of silver, had swept Democrats off their feet by his "cross-of-gold" speech.

For the first time since 1860, the parties were clearly divided on a single issue. To the silver forces, Bryan was a knight in armor riding to do battle for the little man. His credentials as the "great commoner" were so impeccable that he ran as the presidential nominee of the Populists and the National Silver Republicans as well as the Democrats. To conservative gold-bugs, on the other hand, he was an anarchist, an atheist, and a wild-eyed "Demo-Pop." No radical, he was thoroughly traditional in religion and morality and reflected the aspirations of millions of Westerners and Southerners who felt alienated by an industrial order. When the votes were counted, however, McKinley had won handily.

Among the possible explanations for Bryan's defeat are the rise in farm prices and Republican pressure tactics reportedly used on factory workers. Another plausible reason is that in 1896 the forces of discontent were either not strong enough or not united enough to prevail against a skillful and well-financed opposition. Conservatives thought McKinley's victory ended the threat to the status quo and gave a green light for prosperity. This impression deepened when good times returned soon after the election. Discoveries in South Africa and Alaska increased the supply of gold and thus of dollars. European crop failures and rising industrial production helped to raise the farmer's prices. For the next several decades, many farmers would enjoy a golden age, and the disadvantaged seemed to have no taste for crusades.

In the South, similarly, normality of a sort returned. In North Carolina at the height of the Populist excitement, some blacks had achieved political office. Now the frustrated agrarian radicals nearly all returned to militant segregationism, a position many of them had never left. For another two generations, Southerners stood united in defense of white supremacy.

Critics of the status quo, however, had not lost all. In the fashion of American third parties, the Populists did not win the presidency, but most of their programs eventually won the favor of one or both major parties. Moreover, a small minority of determined radicals emerged from the Pullman strike and other defeats of the 1890s to provide articulate criticism of American society in the next generation. The Socialist party, formed in 1901, became something close to a coalition of American radicals under the leadership of Eugene V. Debs.

Few of the middle-class reformers who had been aroused by late-nineteenth-century problems returned to a belief in laissez faire. Though they did not agree on any overall social analysis or program, they continued to press for particular governmental actions to redress grievances. Thus the 1890s laid down the lines on which conservatives, liberals, and radicals would argue for the next half-century. In domestic controversy and, as we shall see, in foreign policy the second Cleveland administration marked both an end and a beginning.

CONFLICTING HISTORICAL VIEWPOINTS: NO. 8

Was Populism Constructive?

Until after World War II, historians were generally sympathetic to Populism. Openly critical of the values and excesses of a business civilization, such early scholars as Solon Buck (The Agrarian Crusade, 1920) and John D. Hicks (The Populist Revolt, 1931) saw much to admire in the Populist critique of industrializing America. In his enormously influential synthesis, Hicks portrayed the Populists as constructive liberal reformers in the tradition of Jefferson and Jackson. Although their programs failed and their movement disintegrated, Hicks concluded that they not only focused the nation's attention on many of its gravest problems but offered an agenda for twentieth-century reform.

Hicks's classic study remains the best point at which to begin a serious study of Populism; it has never been surpassed as a general account of agrarian discontent. But during the 1950s, numerous revisionists questioned its interpretation. Disturbed by wartime fascism abroad and postwar McCarthyism at home, these scholars probed the darker side of Populism. Unlike Hicks, they fastened on its antisocial and negative, rather than its constructive and positive, features. In Populism, they discovered the antecedents of much that was distasteful and evil in American society. In an essay in The Radical Right *(Daniel Bell, ed., 1963), Peter Vierick, for example, found in Populism "a mania of xenophobia, Jew-baiting, intellectual-baiting, and thought-controlling lynch-spirit"; Victor Ferkiss uncovered "Populist influences on American Fascism"* (Western Political Quarterly, *June 1957). The behavioral scientists were generally the most critical, but it was the historian Richard Hofstadter who offered the most persuasive revision of the Hicks thesis. In his Pulitzer Prize-winning* Age of Reform *(1955), this distinguished scholar acknowledged "much that is good and usable in our Populist past." Yet he noted much more that was retrograde and sinister. He faulted the benighted Populists for their chimerical remedies and romantic longings for a "lost agrarian Eden" as well as for their nativism, anti-Semitism, and paranoia — irrational obsessions that he believed foreshadowed twentieth-century authoritarianism.*

At its best, as in Hofstadter's work, revisionism presented a subtle and suggestive argument that enriched our knowledge of agrarian unrest. More often, however, Populism's critics were neither temperate nor convincing. Yet, while their conclusions said more about their fears for the present than about their understanding of the past, they did provoke a re-examination of the nature of Populism. In the 1960s, a decade of reawakened interest in radical causes, a body of widely varying studies emerged to rehabilitate the Populist image in scholarly literature. Among the first of these was C. Vann Woodward's "The Populist Heritage and the Intellectual" (American Scholar, *1959), a moderate and judicious essay that praised the southern Populists for their noble, but abortive experiment in racial accommodation. Similarly, Walter Nugent's* The Tolerant Populists *(1963) celebrated broadminded Kansas agrarian reformers, and Norman Pollack's* The Populist Response to Industrial America *(1962) portrayed humane and radical midwestern farmers who sought realistic solutions to the evils of industrialism. Robert F. Durden's* The Climax of Populism *(1965) denied that Populists were radical, but he absolved them of retrogressive and nativist tendencies; Michael Rogin's* The Intellectuals and McCarthy *(1967) used statistical methods to prove that Populism was not the ancestor of McCarthyism.*

The most recent celebration of Populist virtue is Lawrence Goodwyn's Democratic Promise: The Populist Moment in America *(1976). Although uncommonly passionate and tendentious, this important study has been widely hailed as the successor to Hick's* Populist Revolt, *a new standard history in its field. Praising the noble, unsuccessful effort of the Populists to build a "multisectional, black-white, urban-rural, farmer-labor coalition of democratic reform," Goodwyn viewed their movement as a valid alternative to both socialism and capitalism. Its legions were the architects of a "culture of generosity," the hopeful builders of a cooperative commonwealth, and the "last American reformers with authentic cultural credentials to solicit mass support for the idea of achieving the democratic organization of an industrialized society."*

FOR FURTHER READING

The most complete survey of the period's social thought is Sidney Fine's *Laissez-Faire and the General Welfare State* (1956), but Daniel Walker Howe's *Victorian America* (1976) is an important anthology. Daniel Aaron's *Men of Good Hope* (1951) is a series of essays on reformers. H. F. May in *Protestant Churches and Industrial America* (1949) discusses the development of Protestant social criticism, and Jacob Henry Dorn's *Washington Gladden* (1967) examines a leading social critic. Rex Burns in *Success in America* (1976) and I. G. Wyllie in *The Self-Made Man in America* (1954) examine the impact of change on social thought and myth. The starting place for city problems is *The Rise of the City* (1933) by A. M. Schlesinger, Sr. Leo Hershkowitz's *Tweed's New York* (1977) is a brilliant revisionist defense of a much-maligned boss. Oscar Handlin in *The Uprooted* (1951) and Philip Taylor in *The Distant Magnet* (1971) convey the immigrant's point of view, while Thomas Pitkin in *Keepers of the Gate* (1975) studies the reception of immigrants at Ellis Island. John Higham in *Strangers in the Land* (1955) analyzes native hostility to immigrants; John S. Haller, Jr., in *Outcasts from Evolution* (1971) surveys scientific racism during the period; and both Paul F. Boller, Jr., in *American Thought in Transition* (1969) and Richard Hofstadter in *Social Darwinism in American Thought* (1944) consider the impact of evolution on the Gilded Age. Harold C. Livesay's *Samuel Gompers and Organized Labor in America* (1978) is a good brief introduction to the early history of the AFL. For the perspective of a radical labor spokeswoman, see the memoir of anarchist Emma Goldman, *Living My Life* (1931). A crucial farm problem is examined by George H. Miller in *Railroads and the Granger Laws* (1971), while Ari and Olive Hoogenboom offer a *History of the ICC* (1976). The campaign of 1896 is examined in several of the works in the essay above, but see also Paul W. Glad's *McKinley, Bryan, and the People* (1964). Among the many fine autobiographies, see especially those of Jane Addams, Samuel Gompers, and William Allen White. The following are a sampling of innumerable biographies: C. A. Barker, *Henry George* (1955); Clifford H. Scott, *Lester Frank Ward* (1976); Paolo E. Coletta, *William Jennings Bryan* (3 vols., 1964–1971); C. Vann Woodward, *Tom Watson* (1938), on Southern Populism; and Ray Ginger, *The Bending Cross* (1949) on Eugene V. Debs. Robert H. Wiebe's *The Search for Order, 1877–1920* (1967) is a penetrating analysis, useful for this chapter and the three following.

MAP 7: AMERICAN OVERSEAS EXPANSION TO 1917

DOMINICAN REP.
VIRGIN IS. 1916
PUERTO RICO 1898
HAITI
CUBA
PANAMA
Canal Zone 1903
NICARAGUA

CANADA

UNITED STATES

MEXICO
Tampico 1914 ☆
Vera Cruz 1914 ☆
Pershing border
expedition, 1916 ☆

ALASKA
1867

ALEUTIAN IS.

PACIFIC OCEAN

HAWAIIAN IS.
1898

SAMOA IS.
Condominium 1889,
divided 1899

Territory acquired by U.S.
CUBA Protectorates
☆ Armed intervention

RUSSIA

JAPAN

GUAM
1898

PHILIPPINE IS.
1898

1,200 miles
600
0
0   600   1,200 kilometers

21

★ ★ ★ ★ ★ ★

Imperial America,
1898–1914

FROM THE PEACE of Ghent in 1814 until almost the end of the nineteenth century, the United States remained aloof from international power politics. It was able to do so because of a fortunate combination of circumstances: the European balance of power, British control of the high seas, and growing American *potential* for armed resistance. Very few nineteenth-century Americans realized the transitory nature of this combination. Most believed that American freedom from foreign danger was permanent and "natural." The United States, Americans believed, was the greatest nation on earth. Following the advice of the founders, the Republic chose to demonstrate this greatness only by peaceful growth.

Once colonial expansion was completed, public interest in foreign affairs, where it existed at all, concentrated on four traditional concerns. The first was a great sympathy for republican and constitutional institutions and a belief that the world was moving toward free government. Second, the public felt that the United States had a special interest in the Western Hemisphere since the Monroe Doctrine and should increasingly claim dominance in the Caribbean. Third, Americans had a special, and highly ambivalent, relationship with England. This led to frequent clashes over such issues as the boundaries of New World British possessions, American sympathy for Canadian rebellion, use of the Newfoundland fishing grounds, and British interest in Central America. These clashes often led to violent denunciation from both sides, but all were settled peaceably, usually by British concessions made partly in the interest of commerce. The fourth concern was the desire to expand foreign trade, especially in the Far East. Partly the unrealized dream of a commercial minority, this concern led to the establishment of relations with Japan, China, and Korea, the acquisition of a few tiny Pacific islands, and the development of a protectorate in Hawaii.

THE END OF ISOLATION

Historians have often seen the Spanish-American War of 1898 as a watershed, a clear departure from the past, the point of American emergence into world politics. Yet the extent of change can be exaggerated. All four traditional concerns mentioned above were involved in the crisis of the 1890s. There was no sudden increase of American might; since industrialization, the United States had been a potential great power. Nor did 1898 mark a sudden, permanent shift in popular interest. After a flurry of argument over imperialism, most Americans resumed, in the early twentieth century, their habitual concentration on home affairs. However, 1898 did mark something of a change in American commitments. From this point on, both the United States and the European powers assumed that America had some interest in world crises ranging from North Africa to the Far East.

Many reasons have been given for this change. The most obvious suggestion embodies the traditional economic interpretation of imperialism: the American economy had reached maturity and therefore America, like other advanced industrial countries, needed new raw materials and foreign markets. Some historians, arguing that the growing economy still absorbed most of the nation's productive energies, would deny substantial connection between American expansion abroad and internal American economic development. The connection, however, was frequently made by turn-of-the-century farmers and business people who, particularly after the depression of 1893, saw a relationship between domestic prosperity and foreign markets. Although most business leaders, like most citizens, were probably anticolonialists, there was nonetheless a highly articulate and influential group of business leaders who believed that industrial overproduction and recurrent panics required secure overseas markets and sources of natural supply. Similarly, western farmers, who were themselves business people and under pressure from mounting surpluses, frequently were among the expansionists who looked to outside markets for relief. Although American foreign policy was not driven by the single engine of materialism, economic considerations played a leading role in the tragicomedy of American expansion.

Other explanations for the departures in foreign policy include the revival and restatement of "manifest destiny" in the form of Anglo-Saxonism — the idea that the racially superior "Anglo-Teutonic" American nation had a civilizing mission beyond its New World continent. In an age when many native whites confidently claimed superiority over blacks and new immigrants, whites believed that the world's savage, heathen masses would benefit from the extension of white civilization. Often racism of this kind was linked to the pseudoscience of Social Darwinism; strong races, it was alleged, needed warlike competition to maintain their virility.

Divine obligation was another factor in foreign policy changes. Evangelical Protestants — particularly denominations with foreign missions — promoted an imperialism of righteousness in which Americans would lead, not merely by remote example but by their physical presence among the unredeemed races. The most influential exponent of this doctrine was the Reverend Josiah Strong, author of the best-selling *Our Country* (1885); he urged the United States, with its Anglo-Saxon "genius for colonizing," to spread the blessings of Protestantism and democracy "down upon Mexico . . . Central and South America, out upon the islands of the sea, over upon Africa and beyond." Strong reminded his readers of the practical implications of America's overseas presence: the civilizing process creates "more and higher wants," and "commerce follows the missionary."

For equally practical, though military reasons, Strong's grandiose vision was also shared by the nation's naval lobby and especially by Captain Alfred T. Mahan, president of the Naval War College and student of seapower's influence on history. A modern agricultural and industrial nation, Mahan reasoned, needed overseas markets for its surpluses, and exploitation of overseas markets required an efficient merchant marine and the protection of a strong navy, both of which, in turn, meant acquiring overseas harbors and coaling stations. Thus, a great nation must be expansionist.

Expansion in general and an enlarged navy in particular were strongly advocated by the nation's "foreign policy elite," a group of able and highly placed men, most of whom had upper-class eastern backgrounds. An early representative was William H. Seward, the secretary of state (1861–1869) who added Alaska and Midway Island to the national domain and who spoke as early as 1850 of "the empire of the seas" as the only true empire. At the turn of the century, the elite's brightest and most articulate members included: Senator Henry Cabot Lodge of Massachusetts, member of the Senate Foreign Relations Committee; Theodore Roosevelt, McKinley's assistant secretary of the navy; and Elihu Root, a future secretary of war. Roosevelt was perhaps the most aggressively imperialist and belligerent, but his attitudes were not unrepresentative of his time and class. A historian of American naval and Indian fighting as well as a politician, Roosevelt believed that war — any "righteous" war — would unite the country, divert it from "sordid" issues, and promote manly virtues in its youth.

American expansionism must also be viewed in the wider context of the balance of power and a second great era of European imperialism. Many of the major European nations, driven by much the same forces that were driving Americans to expand, were already vying for territory and influence in the world's underdeveloped regions. These examples whetted the American appetite for empire. Having carved up Africa, the European powers began looking toward two remaining areas: the Near East occupied by the weak Ottoman Empire, and the Far East occupied by the still weaker empire of China. Each empire was thought to be too rich a plum to fall to any single European power, however, so the western nations agreed to support the independence of both empires, while staking out their own spheres of economic influence and uneasily eyeing each other.

A final reason for change in U.S. foreign policy was the fact that established patterns of influence were in flux. Since the German victory over France in 1871, the continent had been dominated by a recently unified Germany and its allies, while the seas were controlled by Great Britain. In the 1890s, the situation grew more fluid. Germany, under its ambitious young ruler Wilhelm II, challenged Britain with a program of naval construction. Britain, sensitive to threats to her sprawling empire, began to cast about for allies. In the Far East, a new power, Japan, was challenging traditional Russian interests in Korea and Manchuria. Inevitably, the newfound interest of the United States in world affairs drew the attention of the other nations.

All these forces are reflected in the developments of 1898. First the United States became involved in an avoidable, if minor, conflict for a seemingly traditional reason: political liberty in the Western Hemisphere. Then the war shifted to the Far East, where the American dream of commerce with the Orient was reawakened. Backed by a rising chorus of imperialist arguments, the nation became involved in great power politics.

FORERUNNERS OF EXPANSION

Some political leaders and many influential opinion shapers showed an early interest first in the Caribbean and then in the Pacific area. Secretary of State Seward had acquired the first noncontiguous territories for the nation, but he had failed in his post–Civil War dream of annexing Caribbean bases. President Grant also had expansionist aspirations toward the Dominican Republic. In the 1880s, struggling against the high tide of popular isolationism, Secretary of State James G. Blaine (1881, 1889–1892) sought unsuccessfully again for Caribbean footholds and wrangled with Britain over rights to build a canal across the Isthmus of Panama. His successor, Frederick Freylinghuysen, negotiated a canal treaty with Nicaragua in 1884 that died in the Senate. Back as Secretary of State in 1889, Blaine broached the idea of Pan-Americanism: Western Hemispheric unity under U.S. leadership. The Pan American Conference of 1889 was ineffectual, however, and Pan-Americanism itself was damaged by Blaine's high-handed efforts to mediate South American disputes. Hemispheric unity was also impaired in 1891 when the United States seemed to threaten war with Chile over a waterfront riot involving American sailors.

The most important overseas ventures in this period took place in the Pacific. American interest in the distant and primitive Samoan archipelago was primarily naval, and a clash with Germany led, in 1889, to the establishment of a joint Anglo-German-American protectorate in Samoa. U.S. involvement in the Hawaiian Islands was more significant. Since the beginning of the 1800s the islands had been visited by American traders, whalers, and missionaries. Their descendants had become prosperous sugar planters who held the power in the islands' picturesque native monarchy. From 1842 on, the United States repeatedly asserted its claim to Hawaiian trade; in the 1880s Secretary Blaine warned potential rivals that the islands were "essentially part of the American system." Under an earlier treaty (1875), Hawaiian sugar entered the rich American market duty free, and in 1887 the United States was granted exclusive rights to Pearl Harbor. Political absorption came after 1893 when the white minority — its sugar economy jeopardized by new tariff arrangements and its influence threatened by the Hawaiian nationalism of a new native monarch — toppled popular Queen Liliuokalani. The revolution was encouraged by the American ambassador and was assisted by American troops. Although this planters' republic was immediately recognized by the United States, efforts to gain formal annexation were frustrated by anti-imperialists (some of whom feared to absorb a racially mixed territory) until 1898.

Although the delay in Hawaii's annexation may be largely attributed to the anti-colonialist sensibilities of President Cleveland, even he had no reluctance in asserting American hegemony in the Caribbean. For some time the British had tried to redraw a disputed boundary between British Guiana and Venezuela; in 1895, when Britain rejected American pressure to arbitrate, Secretary of State Richard Olney warned that the United States was "practically sovereign in this hemisphere." Anglophobes called for war, and for once the Cleveland administration was almost popular. Preoccupied with a colonial crisis in South Africa and concerned about its lack of allies, Britain submitted to arbitration. While the episode did not indicate that the United States was in fact sovereign in the whole hemisphere, it did suggest that American power in the Caribbean might soon equal its interest there.

The most pressing challenge to American control of the Caribbean was in Cuba. A remnant of Spain's once-great New World empire, Cuba was chronically rebellious, yet no Spanish government could afford to let it go. Following a bloody and failed insurrection ending in 1878, Cuba enjoyed comparative prosperity, sustained by the American sugar market and enhanced by the McKinley Tariff of 1890, which made sugar duty-free. Then in 1894, when the sugar duty was restored by the Wilson-Gorman Tariff, Cuba faced a depression, and another insurrection set in. The insecure Spanish talked of eventual concessions but embarked on brutal repression of the Cubans. Spanish atrocities and Cuban suffering, exaggerated but not unfounded, were deplored in the sensationalist American newspapers of Joseph Pulitzer and William Randolph Hearst. Patriotic groups, labor organizations, reformers, and members of Congress demanded American intervention. President Cleveland resisted pressure for war and urged Spain to grant Cuba autonomy.

"THE SPLENDID LITTLE WAR"

Inaugurated in 1897, President McKinley represented a more expansionist party and was himself an advocate for a strong navy. Nevertheless, he was devoted to peace on religious grounds. His government appeared to be progressing toward obtaining major Spanish concessions in Cuba when two accidents killed all chance for peace. First, the de Lome letter fell into the hands of the American press; this unflattering characterization of McKinley was written by the Spanish minister in Washington. Second and far more important was the loss of the *U.S.S. Maine* in February 1898. Sent to Cuba on a "courtesy visit," the American naval vessel was blown up at anchor in Havana Harbor, and 260 men were killed.

Although prominent political and business leaders urged calm, "yellow journalists" and other hawks called for war. McKinley temporized, hoping to preserve the peace, while jingoists in his own party likened his backbone to "a chocolate eclair." The Spanish to avoid war recalled de Lome, expressed sympathy for the dead, and denied (with truth, it seems almost certain) responsibility for the marine disaster. On American demand, Spain abandoned its concentration camps for Cuban civilians and with reluctance and delay agreed to request an armistice with the rebellious Cubans, but not to submit to American mediation.

But the pressure for war against Spain was too great in the United States. Alarmed by the swelling martial spirit, reluctant to divide the country, and afraid that Congress might declare war against his will, McKinley on April 11 requested authority to use arms to restore order in Cuba. A formal declaration of war came two weeks later. Although some thought it folly to fight for a territory that would not be annexed, anti-imperialists in Congress pushed through the "Teller Resolution" binding the United States not to take over the island.

War with Spain, it seemed, offered something to everyone. Many business people, although initially not eager for a war for Cuban independence, now agreed with farmers and agro-industrialists like meatpackers and flour millers that Spain had been an obstacle to developing a flourishing export market. Expansionists saw the war as an opportunity for new territory. Humanitarians and evangelicals hoped that the banishment of the Catholic oppressor would bring opportunities of another sort.

Most Americans, however much they saw opportunities in Cuba, knew little about Spain's larger colony in the Far East, the Philippine Islands, where another colonial rebellion was under way. Theodore Roosevelt, as assistant secretary of the navy, was aware of these Pacific islands and had directed Commodore George Dewey to assemble the United States Asiatic Squadron at Hong Kong and to prepare, in the event of war over Cuba, to attack the Spanish fleet in Manila Bay. Roosevelt's purpose — whether it was American rule of the Philippines or obtaining a new coaling station — is subject to debate. On May 1, however, Dewey issued his celebrated order: "You may fire when ready, Gridley." The Spanish fleet of 10 ships was destroyed, without any American lives lost. This victory delighted press and public, and one newspaper called it "the greatest naval engagement of modern times." Dewey had no force to occupy Manila; troops arrived months later, and with the support of the Filipino leader Emilio Aguinaldo, they took the city the day after the war ended. Native insurgents and Spaniards were left to dispute posession of the rest of the archipelago.

Meantime, in the Caribbean the war proceeded far less favorably at first. American coastal cities panicked at mythical reports of Spanish raids, and mobilization was inefficient. Confusion marred the encampment of American forces in Florida and their embarkation for Cuba. Fortunately for the United States, Spanish equipment, tactics, and morale were in worse shape.

With the Spanish fleet cornered in Santiago Bay, in mid-June the Americans landed an invasion force of 17,000 troops. Among them were four regiments of black soldiers whom awed Spaniards called "Smoked Yankees"; also present were two other units: "Teddy's Terrors," the horseless regiment of Ivy League polo players, cowboys, and western badmen who made up Roosevelt's fabled Rough Riders; and the soldiers led by "Fighting Joe" Wheeler, the aging, former Confederate officer who reportedly cried, "We've got the damn Yankees on the run!" A number of small but bloody engagements during the approach to Santiago gave Americans, including Colonel Roosevelt, a chance to prove their courage under fire. On July 3 the decrepit Spanish fleet sailed bravely out of the harbor to meet certain destruction by American naval gunfire, and on July 17 Santiago surrendered, leaving the United States in control of eastern Cuba. In early August, General Nelson A. Miles completed a nearly bloodless conquest of Spain's Puerto Rico, and the fighting ended.

Even so, the United States was not in an easy position. American forces occupied only one end of Cuba and one city in the Philippines. Dressed in blue winter uniforms, equipped with obsolete Springfield rifles, and fed on hardtack and repulsive canned meat (called by the press "embalmed beef"), American forces in Cuba were ridden with dysentery and malaria and threatened with yellow fever. Lieutenant Colonel Roosevelt, among others, was demanding their recall. At home in the Florida camps, because of disgraceful neglect of sanitation, disease was spreading. Many more lives were lost by disease than by enemy action; of the 5,462 American dead, only 379 died in combat.

Fortunately for the United States, Spain, without a navy and even more poorly prepared than the Americans, had no hope of continuing hostilities. On August 12, 1898, scarcely four months after war began, an armistice was signed. Secretary Hay pronounced it "a splendid little war." Colonel Roosevelt later allegedly declared, "It wasn't much of a war, but it was the best war we had."

PEACE AND EMPIRE

As armistice terms, the United States insisted that Spain withdraw from Cuba and cede to the United States Puerto Rico, an island in the Ladrones (Guam), and the city and harbor of Manila. The fate of the rest of the Philippines (more than 7,000 large and small islands with about eight million people) was decided during the peace conference. At first reluctant to annex much distant territory, McKinley feared another upsurge of public opinion like that which had swept the country into war. Eventually he convinced himself that it was the duty of the United States to "uplift and civilize" the entire Philippines. Reluctantly, Spain agreed to cede them in exchange for $20 million.

In the Senate, the treaty faced serious opposition from the anti-imperialists. This diverse coalition included most northern Democrats and the familiar minority of eastern, reform-minded Republicans. It brought together such contrasting individuals as Bryan, Cleveland, Andrew Carnegie, Samuel Gompers, and Mark Twain. Libertarians argued passionately that empire over subject peoples would violate the Declaration of Independence and the Monroe Doctrine. Others pointed out that the Constitution provided no way of governing territories never destined to become states. Racists insisted that Filipinos were unassimilable, and strategists argued, more persuasively, that a Far Eastern possession would endanger American security.

On the other side, the treaty's proponents argued that the flag, once planted overseas, should not be pulled down, that annexation represented the will of God, and that it was America's duty to Christianize the Philippines (which were actually one of the principal outposts of Christianity in the Far East). The strong interest of Japan and Germany in the spoils of the Spanish Empire furnished another argument for annexation. Germany eventually picked up the Caroline Islands and all the Ladrones (Marianas) except Guam. The business community, in its concern for the expansion and protection of foreign trade, favored retention of the Philippines. Annexationists also pointed to strategic considerations: both Hawaii and the Philippines would be useful to the United States in resisting European encroachment on China.

Reluctantly the conservative Senate leadership agreed to go along with the president. Yet the opposing sides remained fairly even. The treaty would not have passed had not Bryan, as head of the Democratic party, decided to support the treaty and fight the issue of annexation in the coming election.

In their 1900 convention, the Democrats declared that anti-imperialism was the "paramount issue"; the Republicans accepted the challenge. Theodore Roosevelt, one of the war's principal heroes, campaigned as McKinley's running mate. It cannot be proved that McKinley's solid victory constituted an endorsement of annexation, however. Many voted once more for the gold standard, the high tariff, and prosperity.

Perhaps the strongest real reason for retaining the Philippines was the lack of a clear alternative. It was obviously out of the question to suppress the revolt and return the islands to Spain, and nobody wanted to hand them to Germany or Japan. Disunited and in places uncivilized, the islands seemed unable to sustain independence without at least the protection of the United States. Yet many continued to feel that annexation was a mistake, both moral and strategic.

The imperialist tide carried with it not only the Philippines, Puerto Rico, and Guam, but also Hawaii and Samoa. Increased American concern with the Far East in general, together with a competing Japanese interest in the Hawaiian Islands and Hawaii's commercial and military usefulness, furnished decisive arguments for their annexation in 1898. In 1899, the Samoan protectorate was ended and the islands were divided between Germany and the United States.

Meanwhile in Cuba, which the United States had sworn not to annex,

American forces, performing a heroic job of cleaning up yellow fever, quarreled with their Cuban allies. In 1902, the Americans withdrew, but not before the Platt Amendment was incorporated into the Cuban-American treaty and the Cuban constitution, making Cuba a virtual American protectorate. This measure granted the United States both the right to intervene in Cuban affairs to insure continued Cuban independence and stability (and it did intervene in 1906 and several times thereafter), and an American naval station (Guantánamo) on the island. The much-resented Platt Amendment was abrogated during the 1930s, leaving Cuba politically, but not economically, independent of the United States.

America's imperial experience started tragically. Aguinaldo's Filipino insurgents, bitter at not receiving the national independence that they thought had been promised, proclaimed a Philippine Republic and turned their guerrilla tactics against the United States. In the ensuing war, which lasted until 1902 (and broke out occasionally until 1906), about 5,000 Americans, 20,000 guerrillas, and 200,000 Filipino civilians died in combat or from disease. Having promised to bring these Asians "the good-will, the protection, and the richest blessings of a liberating rather than a conquering nation," the United States grossly underestimated Filipino desires for independence and paid both moral and material costs of empire. Although both sides committed atrocities, humanitarians recognized that American counterinsurgents employed the same savage measures that Spain had used in Cuba. As if to complete the mockery of the nation's ideals, the Supreme Court in the so-called Insular Cases ruled that the Constitution did not follow the flag and that its safeguards (including protection against internal tariffs) need not be fully applied to "unincorporated territories."

Despite these ironies, the colonial record of the United States was relatively good, and its imperialism was more economic than political. Throughout its dependencies, American investments and exports mounted sharply, and despite the ruling of the Insular Cases, substantial free trade was established; good work in education, sanitation, and civil authority was undertaken. Movement toward popular government began with the establishment of a legislature in Puerto Rico in 1900, and the Puerto Ricans were given American citizenship in 1917. In 1901, civil goverment replaced military rule in the Philippines, which received an elective assembly in 1907. The Filipinos were slated for eventual independence (which came following World War II) and were, therefore, not granted citizenship.

POWER POLITICS

The American venture into empire fulfilled neither the worst fears of the anti-imperialists nor the grandest expectations of the imperialists. Yet its effects on foreign policy were profound. American hegemony in the Caribbean was underlined, and Britain, long the chief rival, acknowledged it. In the second Hay-Pauncefote Treaty of 1901, England acceded to American demands for exclusive control of the proposed Isthmian canal, abrogating her own treaty rights to equality in this venture. Conditioned in part by a developing German-British rivalry, Anglo-American accord flourished. British support during the Spanish-American War, British agreement on the common goals of stability and the status quo in the Caribbean and the Far East, and a common cultural and (some believed) racial heritage pleased many Americans. In the twentieth century, the great rapprochement was completed. As the great powers chose sides for the next war, it seemed logical that the United States would favor the Atlantic, rather than the Central European, powers.

The developing friendship between the United States and Britain proved useful in the Far East, where the American foothold was tenuous. Annexation of the Philippines greatly increased the United States' stake in world trade and global politics, a fact underscored by Asian developments at the close of the century. Since 1895, China, the "Sick Man of Asia," had been forced by Japan and the European colonial powers to surrender spheres of exclusive economic interest. Expressing concern for the "territorial integrity" of the disintegrating empire, Secretary of State John Hay dispatched the first of his Open Door notes. In identical messages to the six leading imperial rivals (Austria, England, France, Germany, Japan, and Russia), Hay asked for a guarantee of commercial equality for all nations within their spheres. The idea sat well with the British (its original authors), but the Russians refused and the others equivocated. Nonetheless, the audacious Hay announced that the powers had agreed to leave open the door to the China trade.

In 1900, Chinese resentment of foreign exploitation overflowed in the so-called Boxer Rebellion. In nationalistic rage against the "foreign devils," members of the secret Boxer society besieged the international legations in Beijing (Peking). The United States joined Japan and the European powers in suppressing this uprising. Hay, fearing that the disorders invited further dismemberment of the Celestial Kingdom, demanded "equal and impartial" trade arrangements for all nations throughout all of China.

The Open Door was more a reaffirmation of traditional American opposition to international trade barriers than it was a new policy. Although successive generations of Americans would interpret U.S. opposition to partition of China as a act of friendship, it was also aimed at protecting an Oriental market for American goods. Explicitly stating a long-standing principle, the Open Door notes became pillars of American diplomacy.

The new century brought a new president but no substantial change in foreign policy. Upon McKinley's assassination in 1901, Theodore Roosevelt became chief executive. Roosevelt was an expansionist who believed that peace and stability required the firm but benevolent supervision of the enlightened great powers. More knowledgeable and interested in foreign affairs than his immediate predecessors, he understood the relationship between power and policy. Yet in contradiction to his much-quoted adage, he often did not speak softly and his stick was sometimes not big enough.

A friend of John Hay and an apostle of what many called the "large policy," the Rough Rider dabbled in the troubled waters of the far Pacific with the enthusiasm that was his trademark. Suspicious of Russian designs on China and eager to maintain the balance of power in Asia, he supported "tiny Japan" in the Russo-Japanese War, fought over rival interests in Korea and Manchuria from 1904 to 1905. After a series of Japanese victories, he mediated the Peace of Portsmouth, which unfortunately satisfied neither belligerent. Try as he did thereafter, he found no effective way to cement Japanese-American relations nor to offset Japan's rising power. In the Taft-Katsura Agreement (1905), he won Japanese recognition of the American place in the Philippines by conceding Japanese suzerainty over Korea. When Japan protested the segregation of Oriental school children in San Francisco, he arranged an international compromise that ended the segregation (but not other forms of discrimination) and restricted Japanese immigration under a "gentlemen's agreement" (1907). So that this conciliatory gesture would not be seen as weakness, he dispatched the navy's Great White Fleet on a "practice cruise" around the world. Although the long-range effect of this ploy was probably an East-West naval arms race, it may also have produced the Root-Takahira Agreement (1908), in which the United States and Japan agreed to respect the "integrity of China" and the status quo in the Pacific. This agreement acknowledged Japan's dominance in Manchuria, and seemed to guarantee the safety of the Philippines. It had little effect, however, on the continuing slide of United States–Japanese relations.

BAD NEIGHBOR POLICY

In the Western Hemisphere, Roosevelt wielded policy with greater confidence. He viewed Latin America as a semi-barbaric American dependency in need of Anglo-Saxon guidance. Under his leadership, U.S. dominance of the Central American and Caribbean areas was all but completed. His most important initiative was getting an isthmian canal constructed. The Senate chose the Panamanian route over the Nicaraguan partly to appease powerful investors in the French Panama Canal Company. Panama was a Colombian province, however, and the Republic of Colombia refused the American terms. Never one to permit the "interest of collective civilization" to be blocked by "Dagoes," Roosevelt considered seizure, but decided on subtler tactics. With tacit American support, agents of the French company prompted restive Panamanians to declare their independence and to negotiate a canal-zone treaty favorable to the United States. The revolution succeeded only through Roosevelt's connivance and the timely intercession of the American navy; the affair represented a dark chapter in bad neighbor politics, and gave credibility to Latin cries of "Yankee imperialism." Later Colombia was compensated, and in 1914, the Panama Canal was opened on equal terms to all nations.

On two earlier occasions, the president had intervened when Venezuela and the Dominican Republic were threatened by foreign creditors for their bad debts. These experiences convinced him, however, that if the United

States wished to prevent European intrusions in the Western Hemisphere, it must police the "wretched republics" itself. This Roosevelt Corollary claimed for the United States, a "civilized nation," the right of intervention to prevent "chronic wrongdoing." The policy distorted the spirit of the Monroe Doctrine, and offered fresh evidence of an old determination to make the Caribbean an American lake. Although under the later administrations of Herbert Hoover and Franklin Roosevelt the United States did modify its policies and eventually repudiate the right of unilateral intervention, it intervened in the internal affairs of at least six hemispheric countries from 1900 to 1920.

Under William Howard Taft, Roosevelt's successor, American interventionism took a decidedly economic turn, while later under Woodrow Wilson, it assumed the form of a "missionary imperialism" in which the president asserted the American right to enlighten and uplift, by force if necessary. To the nation's southern neighbors, both variants seemed familiar. Far more than his predecessor, Taft believed in using American foreign investment as an instrument of policy. Skeptics called this "dollar diplomacy," but the Republican chief executive argued that furthering private ventures led to peace and prosperity for the recipient nations. But in the Caribbean, dollar diplomacy involved the United States in unpopular military ventures, while in the Far East, it led to a startling departure from realism. Roosevelt had recognized the limits of American power in Asia; Taft and his Secretary of State Philander Knox, on the other hand, tried to force American participation in Chinese railway development and to pry open the door to the Japanese sphere in Manchuria. Neither effort succeeded.

The liberal, idealistic Wilson administration repudiated the diplomacy of both Roosevelt's big stick and Taft's dollars. President Wilson promised a new diplomacy based not on American self-interest but on the highest humanitarian ideals. Some have found in his high moral purpose the standard for American international policy; others saw in it a naive misunderstanding of the nature of humanity and nations. Harbingers of the promised Wilsonian departure included: the appointment of William Jennings Bryan as secretary of state, perhaps the first pacifist to serve as foreign minister to a great power; the negotiation of a Senate-aborted treaty of compensation and apology for Colombia; the negotiation of some 30 unilateral "cooling-off treaties" designed to render war obsolete; and the appointment of a governor-general to prepare the Philippines for self-government.

Wilson, for all his sincere anticolonialism, was capable of expediency. He believed that capitalism marched hand in hand with democracy and that the spread of both was in the interest of all. He also agreed with Theodore Roosevelt that the autonomy of Latin American nations was conditional on the needs of American national security (particularly the Panama Canal) and on the orderly processes of just government. When the occasion required (as it seemed to occur more often under Wilson than under Roosevelt or Taft), he promoted stability and American ideals in Latin America with the U.S. Marines. He intervened in Cuba, established American protectorates in Haiti and the Dominican Republic, and supported a dictatorship in Nicaragua.

The most egregious conflict between principle and practice came during the Mexican Revolution, when he carried the United States to the brink of war in order to teach troubled Mexico "to elect good men."

Wilson's Mexican policies were apparently shaped more by his idealism and support for the liberal, democratic revolution initially led by Francisco Madero, than by the $2 billion in American investments in Mexico. Yet, though Wilson resisted the all-out war demanded by Rooseveltian nationalists and the business interests, he eventually emerged as the enemy of the revolution he had hoped to assist. The affair began in 1913 when, contrary to long-standing American precedent, Wilson withheld U.S. recognition from the government of General Victoriano Huerta, Madero's assassin, on the grounds that it had come to power undemocratically. Persuading the British to withdraw recognition, Wilson supplied arms to Huerta's major rival, Venustiano Carranza, and found a pretext to block a German munitions shipment to Huerta by seizing the Mexican port of Vera Cruz. Huerta abdicated in favor of Carranza.

Wilson then found the new provisional regime too radical and ill-disposed to American guidance, so he shifted his support from Carranza to Francisco "Pancho" Villa. Wilson thought that the picturesque border bandit was a broadly popular social reformer. Upon realizing his mistake, Wilson moved toward friendlier relations with Carranza, so Villa, desperate to provoke American intervention, raided a New Mexican town. Wilson sent a punitive expedition of 11,000 troops some 300 miles into Mexico. The elusive Villa escaped and the American troops were withdrawn, but not before they had clashed with Carranza forces. In the end, increasingly preoccupied with the war in Europe, Wilson formally recognized Carranza in March 1917.

That Carranza fulfilled many of the ideals of Mexico's revolution cannot be credited to Wilson. Despite promising a moral diplomacy, Wilson had intervened more high-handedly in the affairs of Latin America than either Roosevelt or Taft. However well intentioned, his spiritual imperialism left a heritage of inter-American mistrust.

CONFLICTING HISTORICAL VIEWPOINTS: NO. 9

Why Imperialism in 1898?

In 1968, at the very summit of the national debate over American interests in Southeast Asia, the historian Walter LaFeber wrote (Texas Quarterly, Winter 1968): "The line from the conquest of the Philippines in 1898 to the attempted pacification of Vietnam . . . is not straight, but it is quite traceable." This interpretation of the events of 1898 was timely, but it was not new. Well before LaFeber's birth, Charles Beard had also concluded that America's turn-of-the-century imperialism was no accident but the result of "the present economic system."

While others, notably Samuel Bemis (Diplomatic History of the United States, 1936), viewed the Asian adventure of the 1890s as "The Great Ab-

beration," *unplanned and unrepeated, Beard* (Rise of American Civilization, 1927; Idea of National Interest, *1934) dismissed any "fortuitous aspects" in the events ending with the annexation of the Philippines. The road to empire, he believed, was paved with economic interest, and the Americans who followed it to Manila were unbashed commercial expansionists. To the dean of the "Old Left" historians, then, American imperialism, the natural culmination of "over a century of commercial development," owed little "to fate, the accidents of history, the current of events, destiny, and the gifts of the gods." In this judgment, LaFeber, perhaps the most gifted of the New Left scholars, agreed. His* New Empire: American Expansion, 1860–1898 *(1963) emphasized "the economic forces which resulted in commercial and landed expansion," and his 1968 essay concluded that "the Spanish-American conflict can no longer be viewed as only a 'splendid little war.' It was a war to preserve the American system."*

The economic interpretation, although the oldest and most durable, has many critics. The most influential of these, Julius Pratt, author of The Expansionists of 1898 *(1936), after painstaking examination of the commercial press, asserted that "an overwhelming preponderance of the vocal business interests of the country strongly desired peace." Conceding that the business community wanted an expanded overseas trade, he contended nonetheless that most of them became imperialists only after the Spanish-American War began. To Pratt and many others, the Spanish-American War, although spurred by a yellow press and a martial temper, was a war to liberate Cuba. To be sure it brought imperial opportunities that were welcomed by the business community — but these were windfalls.*

The question, of course, remains: Why imperialism? By reading these works and those listed below, the student can perhaps formulate his or her own answer.

FOR FURTHER READING

An informative, reliable history of recent American foreign policy is Richard W. Leopold's *The Growth of American Foreign Policy* (1962). Charles S. Campbell's *Transformation of American Foreign Relations* (1976) is admirable synthesis of scholarly work in the period from 1865 to 1900. An excellent account of the emergence of the United States into power politics is Ernest R. May's *Imperial Democracy* (1961). But see also Walter LaFeber's studies mentioned above; William A. Williams's revisionist classic, *The Tragedy of American Diplomacy*, rev. ed. (1962); and David Healy's *U.S. Expansionism* (1970). R. L. Beisner in *Twelve Against Empire* (1968) and E. B. Tompkins in *Anti-Imperialism in the United States* (1970) focus on the opponents of expansion. A lively and sometimes penetrating history of the McKinley administration is Margaret Leech's *In the Days of McKinley* (1959). It should be compared to Howard Wayne Morgan's provocative, but not influential biography, *William McKinley and His America* (1963). Tyler Dennett in *John Hay* (1933), Kenton J. Clymer in *John Hay*, and Charles S.

Campbell in *Special Business Interests and the Open Door Policy* (1951) illuminate an important chapter in American foreign policy. Both Walter Millis's *The Martial Spirit* (1931) and Graham A. Comas's *An Army for Empire* (1971) are useful studies of the Spanish-American War; H. G. Rickover in *How the Battleship Maine was Destroyed* (1976) traces the disaster to an internal and accidental explosion; Frank Freidel's *The Splendid Little War* (1958) is a highly entertaining pictorial history; and Willard Gatewood's *"Smoked Yankees" and the Struggle for Empire* (1971) tells the black soldiers' story. Roosevelt's foreign policy is examined by Howard K. Beale in *Theodore Roosevelt and the Rise of America to World Power* (1956). The history of the interoceanic waterway is told by David McCullough in *Path Between the Seas* (1977) and by Walter LaFeber in *The Panama Canal* (1978). W. V. and Marie V. Scholes examine *The Foreign Policies of the Taft Administration* (1970); Dana Munro's subject is *Intervention and Dollar Diplomacy in the Caribbean* (1964). Gordon Levin offers a study of *Woodrow Wilson and World Politics* (1968), and Wilson's career, diplomatic and political, is meticulously detailed in the multivolume work of Arthur Link, *Woodrow Wilson* (1947–1965).

TABLE 12. THE PROGRESSIVE ERA, 1898–1916

Year	President	Domestic events	Foreign policy: Europe, Asia	Foreign policy: Latin America
1898			Spanish-American War. Open Door Policy.	
1900	McKinley R (September 6, 1901, assassinated)	Gold Standard Act.	Boxer Rebellion.	
1901				Platt Amendment.
1902		Newlands Reclamation Act.		Venezuela Incident.
1903		Elkins Act. Coal strike settled. Panic of 1903.		Panama Affair.
1904	Roosevelt R	Northern Securities case.		
1905			Russo-Japanese War and Peace of Portsmouth.	"Roosevelt Corollary."
1906		Hepburn Act. Pure Food and Drug Act.	Algeciras Conference on Morocco.	
1907		Panic.	"Gentlemen's Agreement" on Japanese immigration.	

Year	President	Domestic events	Foreign policy: Europe, Asia	Foreign policy: Latin America
1908	Taft *R*	Conservation conference.	Root-Takahira Agreement.	
1909		Payne-Aldrich Tariff.		Mexican Revolution.
1910		Mann-Elkins Act.		
1911		"Rule of Reason" decisions.	Chinese Railway Consortium.	
1912	Wilson *D*			
1913		Underwood Tariff. Federal Reserve Act.		"Watchful Waiting" in Mexico.
1914		Federal Trade Commission Act. Clayton Anti-Trust Act.	**August** War in Europe.	Tampico and Vera Cruz incidents.
1915			**May** *Lusitania* sunk. **May** United States threat and German concession on submarine warfare.	
1916	Wilson *D*	Federal Farm Loan Act. Adamson Act.		Mexican border warfare.

22

★ ★ ★ ★ ★ ★

THE PROGRESSIVE ERA, 1901–1917

THE NEW sense of power abroad that marked the turn of the century was accompanied by a new nationalism and a quest for order at home. No one embraced these related matters — imperialism and progressivism — more readily than the irrepressible Theodore Roosevelt.

Young and dynamic, Vice President Roosevelt became president when William McKinley was killed by an assassin in September 1901. Although this tragic incident is often taken as the beginning of a new period of adjustment and reform, the Progressive era was not born of one violent act. Its sources lay deep in the economic, social, and moral history of the country.

A series of reform initiatives rather than a single reform movement, progressivism was animated by varied, confusing, and sometimes contradictory impulses: efficiency and social justice, scientific management and fair play, and professional reorganization and moral regeneration. Complex, diffuse, pluralistic, the meaning of the movement and the characteristics of its adherents defy easy analysis and historical consensus. For all its ambiguities, the aggregate of causes known as progressivism can be understood as an essentially urban, middle-class response to social and economic change and a search for order and equity in a rapidly changing age. As Thomas Alva Edison confided to Henry Ford, there was reason to believe that sweeping demographic and technological changes had thrown the nation "out of gear." Not content, in the inventor's words, "to run a new civilization in old ways," the progressives set out to "make the world over."

THE MATURE ECONOMY

By 1900 the American economy was relatively mature. It was no longer necessary to concentrate all resources and efforts on the expansion of productive capacity. Production continued to increase fairly rapidly in the new century, but not at the fantastic rate of the previous period.

Progressivism owed some of its nature, if not its existence, to the fact that the period 1901–1914 was one of relatively stable prosperity. There was no prolonged depression like those of the 1870s and 1890s, and there were only two brief financial panics (1903 and 1907). The farmer, that perennial step-child of the American economy, entered a rare period of relative content-ment. Of course, many farmers were continually having a hard struggle, and some farm evils like tenancy were still increasing. But average farm income, for a change, was moving upward. This was partly due to the demand by city populations at home and abroad, which were increasing faster than farm produce. By 1900 only 35 percent of Americans lived on farms.

For some of the new urban population, crowded into slums and immigrant ghettos, things were less than cheerful. Real wages for industrial labor rose more slowly than in earlier decades. Never were social contrasts more ex-treme, from the multimillionaire with a Fifth Avenue palace and a 50-room Newport cottage, to the tubercular child working in a cotton mill or the garment worker in the tenement sweatshop. America led the world in the number of industrial accidents. Thus it is only with careful qualification that the Progressive era can be called a time of contentment. It was more a pe-riod of hope, especially for the politically articulate middle class.

Business consolidation reached a peak at about the turn of the century. During the Progressive era, the largest firms retained but did not increase their share of the nation's industry. However, this was enough to make big business the main target of progressive criticism. Its defenders argued that not all consequences of bigness were bad; for instance, there was more money for such advances as electrification and research laboratories. Public relations and advertising received much attention from progressives and so did the new scientific management of Frederick W. Taylor. Taylor, originally an engineer, urged that each movement of each worker be made as efficient as possible through close study, minute division of function, and rigorous supervision. Working toward similar objectives with less theory, Henry Ford began production of his Model T in 1909; by 1914 he was producing a quarter of a million cars a year, all black.

One aspect of business consolidation that received a great deal of pro-gressive attention was the tendency toward banker control. Only a dozen great investment houses, led by J. P. Morgan's, could float the securities necessary for the period's gigantic mergers, like that of U.S. Steel in 1901. These private bankers, controlling insurance and trust companies as well as industries and railroads, could draw on a large part of the national savings as well as on their foreign connections. Proponents of stability, he and his allies tried to end what they called cutthroat competition, to prevent risky investment, and to rescue sick industries before their financial collapse. In return, they exacted not only high fees but control. Through seats on the governing boards of railroads, steel companies, and many other corpora-tions, they could enforce their own ideas of sound operation on American business. Sometimes the bankers were unimaginative and unenterprising (they were very reluctant, for instance, to back automobile manufacturers). They did not worry much about working conditions in the industries they controlled. And as the period's two panics testify, they did not always achieve the stability at which they aimed.

THE PROGRESSIVE MIND

The main complaint of the progressives was directed against what they regarded as immoral and irresponsible power, personified by Morgan and the mighty, invisible "Money Trust." Antimonopoly feelings were as old as the Republic. Most of the remaining progressive ideology continued the previous period's ambiguous social concerns, concerns that reflected both an acceptance of the need to organize and modernize and at the same time a yearning to return to the less complex world of farms, small towns, and moral individualism. Settlement workers were still coping with urban poverty; social gospel ministers continued to reinterpret Christianity in terms of temporal human needs, and social scientists were still challenging the basis of nineteenth-century individualism. But the discontent of the early twentieth century had a new tone, set by an optimistic, though not complacent, middle class. Leaders of progressivism were fairly prosperous professionals or members of the business community, usually in their early forties, often Anglo-Saxon and Protestant; they were motivated by moral indignation and personal ambition.

Although historians generally agree that progressives were moderates who sought political and socio-economic amelioration, not revolutionary change, the age had its radicals. In the century's first decade, one congressman and many local officials representing the Socialist party were elected. In 1912, Socialist presidential candidate Eugene V. Debs garnered 6 percent of the popular vote. Radical intellectuals, including writers Randolph Bourne, Upton Sinclair, and Jack London, confidently looked forward to the nation's socialist future. On the far left were the syndicalist Industrial Workers of the World (IWW), organized in 1905 and led by William D. (Big Bill) Haywood and the legendary Mother Jones. The IWW offered a mix of interracialism, industrial unionism, and Marxian class conflict to workers unserved by, or dissatisfied with the conservative trade unionism of the AFL.

For most progressives, however, the pressing questions were not humanitarian but moral and political. Their primary aim was not the eradication of poverty or class disparities, but the creation of a rational, stable, and efficient political and social order. First, progressives wanted to end corruption, to throw out the crooks and to return power to "good citizens" like themselves. Their urban reforms were more notable for their efficiency and centralization than for their responsiveness to constituent pressures. Second, progressives wanted to control big business, not in the interest of socialism or of social leveling, but in the interest of a more humane and rational free enterprise system. Some of them, including the followers of jurist Louis Brandeis, wanted to break up large corporations and return to a more competitive age. Others, Theodore Roosevelt among them, concluded that trusts were not inherently evil and, properly regulated in a partnership between government and business, might provide socially useful economies of scale.

Because they found American life fundamentally good, progressives wanted to preserve its promise for the future. Rejecting nineteenth-century determinism, they believed that science, government, and the public morality were all changing, and changing for the better. Although most subscribed to moral absolutes, they generally saw no other immutable laws. Following philosopher William James, they were usually pragmatists; they rendered judgments on the basis of concrete experiences or consequences, rather than according to general metaphysical principles. In educational theory, John Dewey and his fellow instrumentalists insisted that children should be taught to solve problems arising in their environment, rather than to learn the wisdom of the past. The law and the Constitution were reinterpreted as guides to action, rather than as changeless codes of universal and literal application. At the height of the Progressive era, people talked not only of the New Freedom of Woodrow Wilson and the New Nationalism of Theodore Roosevelt, but also of the new literature, the new psychology, the new woman, and less frequently the "new negro."

Optimism gave these middle-class reformers much of their confidence and courage; it also blinded them to some intractable contemporary problems concerning minorities. A few reformers — among them Oswald Villard, Lillian Wald, Jane Addams, and Clarence Darrow — agitated for Afro-American rights and joined the black militant W. E. B. Du Bois in organizing the National Association for the Advancement of Colored People (NAACP) in 1909. But progressivism was largely for whites only, and most adherents shared the nearly universal belief that blacks were inherently inferior and socially unassimilable. The movement's moral blind spot is shown in the career of Governor (and later Senator) James K. Vardaman of Mississippi. A fire-eating white supremacist who rose to power by agitating the racial fears of his poor white constituents, Vardaman was nevertheless a champion of the red-neck and the first Mississippi governor to qualify as a democratic reformer. His racism, of course, was cruder and more blatant than that of most other reform governors of his age. But his racial values differed from those of his more genteel counterparts more often in degree than in kind.

A similar attitude of indifference verging on hostility was applied to the new immigrants who crowded the cities after 1880. Although appalled by urban slum conditions, otherwise humane and tolerant reformers rarely challenged nativism. Indeed, some of them led campaigns aimed at restricting southern and eastern European immigration.

THE PROGRESSIVE ACCOMPLISHMENT

Exposure of corruption fueled the reform movement. A vogue for sensational accounts of corruption and monopoly began with books like Henry Demarest Lloyd's attack on Standard Oil (*Wealth against Commonwealth*, 1894).

The new fashion was taken up by sensational newspapers like those of Hearst and by a new crop of popular, cheap, ably edited magazines led by *Mc-Clure's*. Muckrakers, as Roosevelt called the new journalists, attacked big business, the unions, the churches, the press itself, state and city government, and finally the U.S. Senate. While many people read the muckrakers for sheer excitement, some were stirred to action.

Some of the most important progressive crusades started outside politics in such fields as charity organization, education reform, or juvenile courts (concern for the young was characteristic). Sooner or later, however, most concrete accomplishments had to be registered in political action.

The first progressive political offensive was directed against the most obvious target: America's swollen cities, where grafting utilities and protected vice were all too obvious. City reform got under way in the 1890s, and in the first decade of the century many cities moved from boss rule to reform. Some moved back soon enough, but often the cycle left a heritage of public waterworks, public or highly regulated street railways, tenement laws, and playgrounds.

Still more was accomplished in the states, perhaps the most important laboratories of reform. In 1900, Robert M. La Follette, one of the most militant and uncompromising progressive leaders, became governor of Wisconsin. Working closely with experts from the state university, he made Wisconsin a "laboratory of democracy." Reformers won control of one state after another in the Middle West and then in the far West, East, and South. Typical state reforms featured devices intended to keep the bosses and the railroads out of power and the people — or at least the respectable middle class — in control. The direct primary, preferential popular election of U.S. senators (still officially chosen by legislatures), and woman's suffrage fostered this aim.

FEMINISM AND REFORM

Women, too, benefitted from the reform impulses of the age. Although many progressive leaders, Presidents Roosevelt and Wilson among them, were reluctant and belated supporters of woman suffrage, the political aspirations of American women could no longer be denied. By 1896 the four western states of Wyoming, Utah, Colorado, and Idaho had granted women the vote. But no further gains were made until suffragists in Washington and California won referendums in 1910 and 1911. Despairing of success through state-by-state action, the "woman movement" (as it was then often called) swung its considerable energies behind the "Anthony Amendment" to enfranchise all adult women at a single stroke. The movement's modern origins dated from 1848, but not until the National American Woman Suffrage Association (NAWSA) was formed from two rival organizations in 1890 was there significant unity of action. Led first by Elizabeth Cady Stanton and Susan B. Anthony and after 1900 by Carrie Chapman Catt and Anna Howard Shaw, NAWSA focused on federal legislation. Essentially middle-class and moderate, the association sometimes cooperated and sometimes clashed with such radical feminists as Alice Paul and Lucy Burns of the Congressional Union (later called the Woman's party). In 1914, the cause won the official support of the conservative and influential General Federation of Women's Clubs. In the end, suffragists of all persuasions won. The Nineteenth Amendment cleared Congress during 1919 and was ratified and became law in August 1920 in time for the presidential election of that year.

Having won the battle for suffrage, many women believed that the war for women's rights was over. In fact, it was scarcely begun. The concerns of working-class women, for example, centered more often on the conditions of life and labor than on the ballot. Suffrage meant less to these denizens of the textile and garment sweatshops than to the middle-class women who dominated the women's movement. Moreover, the most advanced women's rights advocates, the social feminists, recognized that the franchise brought few real social changes and that the list of women's grievances remained painfully long. Women were still hemmed in by male notions of "true womanhood"; the woman's "sphere," not unlike the black's "place" remained one of subordination. Like Charlotte Perkins Gilman (*Women and Economics*, 1898), social feminists advocated the emancipation of women from smothering gentility and enforced domesticity. Like her they favored a comprehensive redefinition of women's status in society and the elimination of gender-related impediments to economic opportunity. Progress in these areas, however, came very slowly and major breakthroughs would come only in the 1960s and 1970s.

By 1910 one-fifth of the American work force was female and one fifth of all adult women (7.8 million) worked outside the home. The great majority worked as domestic servants or as unskilled factory labor, particularly in textile and garment sweatshops. Black women were nearly always confined to such menial work as agricultural day laborers, laundresses, cooks, and servants. A growing number of white women did find work as stenographers, typists, and bookkeepers, but these clerical positions — like those of school teaching and nursing — were already defined as "woman's work" and pay was accordingly very low. Only a few entered the professions of law, medicine, or higher education. By 1920 a "lady lawyer" was a great rarity and only 5 percent of the nation's medical school graduates were women. In sum, the domestic stereotype still prevailed; even educated women were generally expected to forgo careers for the "natural" female duties of housewifery and child rearing.

Nonetheless, there were modest advances. By 1900 the great majority of high school graduates were female. Traditional sexual barriers to higher education continued to erode and by 1920 most colleges and universities in the United States were coeducational. Divorce became increasingly common, particularly in urban areas. The double standard of sexual and social behavior, though still very much in force, was slowly giving way. The "revolution in morals and manners" commonly identified with the 1920s was rooted in the social ferment of the Progressive era.

Most important, many middle-class women assumed leadership roles in progressive crusades for social justice. In the field of social work and urban reform, Jane Addams and Florence Kelley, both of Chicago's Hull House, and Lillian Wald of New York City's Henry Street Settlement House, were preeminent. Ida Tarbell, among the most notable investigative journalists of her time, exposed the monopolistic practices of Standard Oil. Mary White Ovington championed civil rights for blacks. And both Emma Goldman and Margaret Sanger defied public convention and the medical profession to pioneer in the field of birth-control education. These and countless other women agitated not only for the Nineteenth Amendment but for such progressive causes as industrial safety standards, consumer protection, judicial and penal reform, child and female labor laws, kindergartens, and temperance. Indeed much of the behind-the-scenes research and lobbying that sustained local, state, and federal reform legislation was performed by women.

THE PROGRESSIVE HERO

Theodore Roosevelt's inauguration brought to the presidency, for the first time since Jackson, a popular hero, and Roosevelt was the first president since Lincoln to stretch the powers of his office. On the surface he was ever the irrepressible Teddy — noisy, impulsive, even violent, given to dramatic self-promotion and a boyish affinity for the strenuous life. Most of his impulsiveness, however, came either early or late in his career or was confined to minor issues. His major domestic decisions as president were usually shrewd compromises that served his administration and his nation well. An aristocrat by birth, a public servant by inclination, he brought to the office political experience, a keen mind, and broad learning. Even without McKinley's untimely demise, he would likely have become president.

Roosevelt was a master of timing. When McKinley died, Republican leader Mark Hanna cried, "That wild man . . . that damned cowboy is President." But Roosevelt quickly reassured conservative business and financial interests, which dominated his party, that he would continue McKinley's policies and cabinet. At the same time, he put out a trial balloon by denouncing the trusts and moved further in that direction when public response was favorable. In 1904, he easily defeated a conservative Democrat, Judge Alton B. Parker, for re-election. President in his own right and conscious of the progressive tide throughout the country, he moved further toward reform objectives. Then in 1907, when the financial panic seemed to demand caution, he followed the suggestions of J. P. Morgan. Finally, in 1908–1909, about to leave office, he called for a host of drastic reform measures. This accomplished nothing immediately but left a program that his successors could not ignore.

The domestic accomplishments of his administration are important, but his dramatization of domestic reform issues and his demonstration of the possibilities of the presidency had greater effect. Roosevelt assumed office as "His Accidency" and as heir to a tradition of congressional ascendancy dating from Andrew Johnson's impeachment; thus, he was inaugurated president of a republic that expected little from its chief executives. With the exception of Cleveland, his predecessors since Lincoln were mediocre, colorless men, and political power had rested with congressional leaders like Hanna and state party bosses like Thomas Platt of New York. Alternatingly bold and cautious, he reveled in the exercise of political power. Under his leadership and that of Wilson, the initiative returned to the White House and the president assumed primary responsibility for shaping public opinion and the congressional will.

During his first years in office, Roosevelt won recognition as a proponent of labor and an opponent of trusts. In both cases his reputation was unduly inflated. During the bitter anthracite coal strike of 1902–1903, he broke precedent and refused to send troops to the coal fields to restore order. Angered by the intransigence of the operators and impressed by the legitimacy of the miners' demands, he persuaded both sides to submit to arbitration. Improved hours and wages (but no union recognition) resulted — a milestone in labor history. But he never again intervened on labor's behalf. His fame as trustbuster can be traced to his first message to Congress, in which he urged creation of a Department of Commerce and Labor, including a bureau of corporations, to keep tabs on interstate commercial and industrial abuses. His administration successfully challenged the legality of Northern Securities, a massive railroad holding company, and went on to begin similar proceedings against the so-called Beef Trust, Standard Oil, American Tobacco, and several dozen other corporate behemoths. But Taft busted more trusts than Roosevelt, who believed that, properly regulated, these inevitable aggregations of power and wealth could serve the public interest.

His role in the development of the federal regulatory state was modest. In 1903 he signed the Elkins Act, supported by the railroads themselves, and in 1906 the Hepburn Act. These measures outlawed the rebate and gave the feeble Interstate Commerce Commission additional supervisory authority over railroads, including the power to set aside existing schedules and determine reasonable rates pending court review; they represented compromises between the demands of reformers and those of stand-pat conservatives. Additional consumer protection came in 1906 with the federal Pure Food and Drug Act and the Meat Inspection Act. Roosevelt initiated neither measure, but supported them once convinced of their need. His most systematic regulatory contribution came in the areas of conservation and wilderness preservation. A celebrated outdoorsman and champion of the national interest, Roosevelt won public acceptance for comprehensive land-use planning and scientific conservation. Over opposition of ranchers, miners, timber companies, and other interests accustomed to private use of public resources, he set aside millions of acres of public land as permanent wildlife refuges, mineral and water-power reserves, and national forests and parks.

Having promised not to seek re-election in 1908, Roosevelt arranged the nomination of his friend, Secretary of War William Howard Taft, who handily defeated two-time loser William Jennings Bryan. Roosevelt, who went on an African safari, left undone two of the nation's most pressing tasks: tariff reform and banking regulation.

TAFT AND THE INSURGENTS

A former judge, governor of the Philippines, presidential troubleshooter, and cabinet officer, Taft was an intelligent administrator, well qualified for the office. Yet his presidency was marked by failure and the disruption of his party. Critics caricatured him as a fat and lazy reactionary; his problems lay not in his weight (nearly 350 pounds) but in his inexperience in elected office and in his limited conception of the presidency. His devotion to Roosevelt's policies was genuine and he worked hard for programs in which he believed. But his cramped view of presidential prerogatives and preference for the ordered gentility of conservatives over the "yelping and snorting" of reformers poorly served the progressive cause.

Perhaps no Republican coming to power in 1909 could have succeeded. Since the Panic of 1907, times had been less prosperous and increasingly impatient progressives demanded attention to unsolved problems: trusts, taxes, and tariffs. Roosevelt had adroitly sidestepped these issues. But even his magic could only have deferred the developing conflict between Republican reformers (called insurgents) and the Republican old guard. Stand-pat conservatives still controlled party machinery, but aggressive, ambitious Republican progressives, mostly from the Midwest, were increasing their congressional power with each election.

Blaming the rising cost of living on the high Dingley Tariff (1897), reformers easily pushed a modest downward tariff revision through the House of Representatives. In the Senate, however, the protectionists won out, and the resulting compromise bill was anything but a triumph for reform. To the dismay of progressives in both parties, Taft signed the Payne-Aldrich Tariff and called it the best ever passed by Congress. The insurgents also felt betrayed by other Taft actions. Although he favored the reform effort to end Speaker Joseph G. Cannon's absolute control of the all-important House Rules Committee, he sided publicly with the reactionary "Uncle Joe," lest the old guard frustrate his administration's programs. Taft again alienated the reformers when he exonerated Richard A. Ballinger, his controversial development-minded Secretary of the Interior, of charges that he not only had opened to private sale previously closed public lands and waterpower sites, but also had fraudulently assigned federal coal reserves to commercial interests. Taft also fired Ballinger's implacable accuser, Chief Forester Gifford Pinchot, Roosevelt's friend and fellow champion of the national interest. At this point (although Ballinger was later replaced with an arch-conservationist) the breach was irreparable between the president and the insurgents who saw him as a reactionary and a traitor to the Roosevelt heritage.

Appearance is not necessarily reality, however. Despite his political ineptitude, Taft was a committed conservationist, and his record of progressive accomplishment compared favorably to Roosevelt's. He actively supported the Sixteenth Amendment (income tax), and he worked for other important measures: the Mann-Elkins Act (1910) strengthening the Interstate Commerce Commission, the Postal Savings and Parcel Post acts, and the establishment of a federal Bureau of Mines and a Children's Bureau. Taft was a more literal interpreter of the Sherman Act than Roosevelt and instigated twice as many antitrust proceedings as the trustbuster.

REPUBLICANS AND PROGRESSIVES, 1910–1912

Divisions within the Republican party widened further during the off-year elections of 1910, when the administration threw its powers, including patronage, against its own party's progressive wing. The insurgents, in turn, denounced dollar diplomacy, tariff betrayal, and conservation setbacks, and sometimes supported progressive Democrats. The Republicans suffered an electoral drubbing and the old guard was repudiated. In the congressional races, the Democrats won control of the House, and a coalition of Democrats and insurgent Republicans seized the Senate. Taft's problems, of course, grew worse; his renomination seemed in doubt.

Roosevelt's role in the coming Republican debacle of 1912 was conditioned by his personal ambition, his appetite for controversy, and his personal sympathies for the insurgent cause. While abroad, he had been kept apprised of the developing confrontation by both sides. Following his famous "New Nationalism" speech in Osawatomie, Kansas (August 1910), the long-rumored rift between Roosevelt and his old friend Taft broke into the open. Subsequent Roosevelt addresses were watered down for the consumption of eastern conservatives, but in Kansas progressives had been electrified and the old guard alarmed by his call for an extension of government regulatory authority and the subordination of private interests to the public welfare. Taft lashed out unmistakably at "political emotionalists" and "neurotics," and Roosevelt soon characterized Taft as a reactionary "fat head." In 1912, Roosevelt, urged on by seven progressive Republican governors, announced that his hat was in the presidential ring. Meanwhile, a second challenge to Taft came from the Progressive Republican League, established by the insurgents in 1911; initially La Follette was its favorite, but when the Wisconsin senator faltered, the insurgents enthusiastically switched their support to Roosevelt.

Waging a vigorous campaign for the Republican nomination, Roosevelt defeated Taft in those states that had adopted the new direct primary system. But Taft controlled party and convention machinery and enough delegates to ensure his own renomination. The Roosevelt following withdrew from the GOP, formed its own organization, and promptly nominated its hero by acclamation. The Bull Moose party's platform contained a long list of reforms: legislation prohibiting child labor and establishing minimum wages for women and social insurance; the initiative, referendum, and recall; direct election of senators; preferential presidential primaries; and woman suffrage. Its foreign policy planks, though favoring international peace, were distinctly Rooseveltian and nationalistic.

More than a group of Roosevelt worshippers, the Progressive party of 1912 was an attempt to adapt traditional American individualism to new conditions and to combine old and new ideas. Its uneasy mix of practicality and moral uplift was to find echoes in the New Deal.

Roosevelt's venture turned out badly for his supporters and himself. It deepened the Republican split, for a time handing over the party to the old guard and thus paving the way for the conservative new era of the 1920s. The defeat destroyed Roosevelt's important role in American politics, and it retarded the job of adapting traditional liberalism to twentieth-century realities. The split assured a Democratic victory.

WILSON AND THE PRESIDENCY

Woodrow Wilson had a varied and largely academic career before he became the Democratic presidential candidate in 1912. The son of a Presbyterian minister and a Virginian, Wilson was trained both as a lawyer and a political scientist. A scholar and university lecturer, he became president of Princeton University; in 1910 after a quarrel with university regents, he left and was nominated for the governorship of New Jersey at the age of 53. A Jeffersonian devoted to individual liberty and state rights, he had opposed the Populists, organized labor, and the social service state. Influential Democrats had identified him as a possible savior of the party from "Bryanism."

To the dismay of corrupt New Jersey party leaders, Wilson would not be a figurehead, and gradually emerged as a progressive. He pushed a comprehensive program of reform through the state legislature, including a direct primary law, utilities' regulation, a corrupt practices act, and a workmen's compensation law. A presidential hopeful by this time, he conciliated Bryan and other progressives, while retaining the support of some conservative elements in the party. To many Democrats, delighted by Republican discord, he appeared to be a unity candidate, likely to heal the long-standing rift between Democratic factions: Bryan's rural, southern and western, reform-minded group and Cleveland's urban, Eastern, business-minded contingent.

During the ensuing campaign, one of the liveliest in American history, Socialist Eugene V. Debs and Taft were quickly overshadowed by the contest between the New Freedom of Woodrow Wilson and the New Nationalism of Theodore Roosevelt. Wilson's campaign speeches were as progressive as Roosevelt's but strikingly different in style and content. Though both were bookish, strong-willed, and moralistic, the barrel-chested and toothy Roosevelt was warm, gregarious, and enthusiastic, while the lean and eloquent Wilson tended to be cool, aloof, and detached. The public made Roosevelt the most popular living American and fondly called him Teddy and TR. Wilson, on the other hand, inspired respect, not popular affection; he exuded dedication, high-mindedness, and at times self-righteousness. Where Roosevelt called for a federal regulatory state powerful enough to control inevitable, and in many ways beneficial business corporations, Wilson argued the need for destroying monopolies and returning to a decentralized, competitive economy. Neither was a proponent of laissez faire, but

Wilson was the most suspicious of the power of big government. While Roosevelt advocated a broad program of social justice and political reform, Wilson insisted that the restoration of business competition would minimize the need for government paternalism. No candidate commanded a majority of the popular vote, but Wilson placed first with 42 percent. Roosevelt garnered more votes than any third-party candidate in history, running well ahead of Taft, but he was buried by Wilson's electoral-college landslide.

Many doubted that a former college professor with little practical political experience could hold together the coalition of immigrants, white Southerners, Bryanites, and eastern commercial interests that made up the Democratic party. Nor did Wilson's personality always inspire confidence. Often inflexible, rarely torn by self-doubt, he sometimes viewed complex issues in terms of dogmatic absolutes. Yet he brought superb gifts to the presidency. Wilson proved to be a principled statesman, a sensitive interpreter of the public will, and a skillful, tough-minded, and forceful politician who brought progressivism to full flower.

As president, Wilson's first concerns were the tariff and banking. With the help of progressives of both parties, the Democratic president guided through Congress the Underwood Tariff, reducing the rates to about pre–Civil War levels; the tariff bill also included a moderate income tax to offset the loss of revenue. His banking reform was the most sweeping in U.S. history.

The Federal Reserve Act of 1913 steered a middle course between the advocates and the enemies of a central bank and between the proponents of either public or private control. The Federal Reserve System divided the country into 12 districts, each with a Federal Reserve Bank owned by member banks and governed by a mixed public-private board. Acting as agents of member banks, Reserve Banks were empowered to pool resources in times of financial crisis and to issue a new and elastic currency, the Federal Reserve note (the paper money used to the present day). The entire system was supervised by a presidentially appointed board, which could regulate the money supply and interest rates as the economy seemed to require. Although the act was generally hailed by progressives and condemned by bankers, it was a shrewd compromise between the public and the private interest — regionally decentralized, privately owned, and publicly controlled.

The third major accomplishment of Wilson's first years was new trust legislation. The Federal Trade Commission Act established a presidentially appointed board with power to investigate corporate practice and issue cease-and-desist orders (subject to judicial review) against unfair methods of competition. The next law, the Clayton Anti-Trust Act, prohibited specific practices, including discriminatory prices leading to monopoly, and interlocking directorates; it also exempted labor organizations from its anti-trust provisions. For a time at least, business leaders consulted the government before attempting further consolidation.

With these major enactments, Wilson announced that his reform program was completed. Following the business panic of 1914, he seemed unduly conciliatory of conservative opinion; he appointed bankers to the Federal Reserve Board, refused support for either women's suffrage or child labor legislation, opposed federal loans for farmers, and sanctioned racially segregated facilities in federal departments. To go beyond the limited reforms of the New Freedom, he told unsatisfied reformers, would violate state rights, and undermine individualism.

In 1916, however, he moved left. Finding his own initial program too limited and also recognizing the need to win progressive votes, he supported and signed in an election year the measures he had earlier opposed: an act providing long-term rural credits, a child-labor law (later held unconstitutional), an interstate highway construction program, a federal aid to vocational education law, and an act establishing an eight-hour day for railroad workers — thus embracing much of Roosevelt's New Nationalism. In the national election, however, he faced a unified Republican party with Roosevelt back in the GOP fold. Although he defeated Republican reform governor and later Chief Supreme Court Justice Charles Evans Hughes, he was again denied a popular majority, with 49.4 percent of the vote.

THE MEANING OF PROGRESSIVISM

The Progressive era left a mixed record of failure and achievement. It had not produced, or tried to produce, a new social system. It had made only the barest beginning toward the redistribution of wealth or the control of private accumulations of power. While ultraconservatives lamented the end of free enterprise, the million or so Americans who wanted to move toward socialism were impatient with progressive caution. Despite the efforts of southern white progressives, the South still lagged far behind the rest of the country in health and wealth. The deepest rooted American form of inequality was almost untouched, North or South. In the face of massive discrimination, many blacks accepted the program of Booker T. Washington, who counseled the temporary acceptance of social discrimination and the adoption of modest economic goals. A few black intellectuals, led by W. E. B. Du Bois, joined a few progressive whites to form the NAACP. But the crusade for racial justice attracted little support, and civil rights for blacks would not become a tenet of American liberalism until World War II.

Some progressive accomplishments proved impermanent. It was plain to close observers, even before 1917, that the reform fervor was declining and the opposition gathering strength. Soon, in wartime, much of the progressive program was to take on a different meaning, and in the postwar decade many progressive enactments were emasculated or abandoned. During the 1920s, a period of conservative Republican ascendancy, the regulatory agencies fell into the hands of the interests they were meant to control. Conservative state and federal courts qualified and in many cases struck down progressive legislation designed to protect workers and consumers. Some measures, including those designed to reform city politics and initiative and referendum, failed to achieve the desired results of greater citizen participation and more responsible government.

But all progressive effort was not in vain. Big business, neither destroyed nor much weakened, was never again as defiant of public opinion as it had been. Immensely valuable national resources had been saved for the future. New paths for possible later government action were made possible by the income tax and other measures. Outside the arena of politics, dedicated reformers left countless playgrounds, schools, clinics, and parks. In architecture, poetry, social science, and psychology, innovation had characterized the Progressive era.

More important than any concrete accomplishment of the progressive movement was its general reassertion of the will to adapt. Like other countries, America had been confronted by the huge problems of industrial civilization. Faced with this challenge, the country had not failed to find resources of courage and vitality. More than anyone realized, these resources were to prove indispensable in the coming decades.

CONFLICTING HISTORICAL VIEWPOINTS: NO. 10

Who Were the Progressives?

Few phenomena of American history are more controversial than the Progressive movement. For more than six decades, scholars have offered conflicting answers to such questions as: Why did the movement begin and end when it did? What were its major objectives? Was its impact on the national experience salutary or otherwise? What was its relationship to other reform movements before and since? On these topics there is so little agreement among historians that Peter Filene has written "An Obituary for the 'Progressive Movement'" (American Quarterly, Spring 1970), arguing that the very concept should be abandoned as a figment of the scholarly imagination.

The nature of this continuing historiographical debate is perhaps best suggested by conflicting assessments of the social origins of the reformers. In his analysis of The Progressive Movement *(1915), Parke De Witt, the first scholar to study progressivism, accepted the interpretation offered by the reformers themselves. Like them, he viewed their movement as an uncompromising onslaught against big business. The period, he concluded, was one of conflict between "the people" and "the interests." Essentially the same idea pervaded the two most famous historical studies written during the 1920s. Vernon L. Parrington's* Main Currents in American Thought *(3 vols., 1927–30) and Charles and Mary Beard's* The Rise of American Civilization *(1927) viewed progressivism as the lineal descendant of a reform tradition that stretched back in American history to the age of Jefferson and Jackson. Pitting the masses against business moguls and crooked politicians, the movement was the twentieth-century phase of the age-old struggle between democracy and aristocracy, equality and privilege. The Progressives, then, were the people themselves, rank-and-file, democrats with a small* d, *who waged the battle for reform in defense of their national birthright.*

Writing from within the progressive frame of reference, such scholars as De Witt, Parrington, and Beard were, in effect, involved participants whose sympathetic and simplistic analysis of progressivism was not shared by historians of subsequent generations. The events of the 1920s and 1930s offered new historical vantage points from which to view the movement. To those who lived through the political reaction of "normalcy" and the economic crisis of the Great Depression, progressivism generally seemed less idealistic and much less effective than earlier scholars assumed. As early as 1932, John Chamberlain, a young Marxist, studied the era closely and then bade Farewell to Reform. *The progressives, he concluded, were nostalgic conservatives seeking to restore a simpler past, not liberal reformers responding to the challenges of industrialism and urbanism. Although Harold U. Faulkner could still celebrate progressivism as* The Quest for Social Justice *(1931), most scholars from Chamberlain's time forward shared his doubts about the nature of the movement.*

Thus both George Mowry's The California Progressives *(1951) and Richard Hofstadter's* The Age of Reform *(1955) portrayed the era as one in which the urban middle class sought to restore its position of leadership. The progressives were not selfless crusaders for popular democracy, these scholars affirmed, but bourgeois victims of status anxiety. Drawn from the old and established professional elite (lawyers, educators, ministers, editors), whose standards of morality and order had been offended by political bosses and a flood of new immigrants and whose influence had been eclipsed by a new class of industrial and financial plutocrats, the progressives struggled to restore traditional standards of probity and to regain their lost power and deference.*

In a vein somewhat different from Mowry and Hofstadter, Samuel P. Hays in The Response to Industrialism, 1885–1914 *(1957) and Robert Wiebe in* Businessmen and Reform *(1962) cast additional doubts on the traditional view that progressivism was basically a people's crusade against big business. In fact, both argued that special interests often favored meaningful reforms that the people opposed. In their view, the progressives were neither disinterested do-gooders nor disquieted bourgeois but realistic conservatives, a new class of bureaucratic-minded professionals who sought to bring order and efficiency to a chaotic and wasteful society.* The Search for Order, 1877–1920 *(1967), Wiebe's second book and the most systematic expression of this interpretation, suggested that in their quest for stability and system, the new middle-class progressives often found ready allies in big corporate managers.*

Not all recent scholars trace the social origins of reform to the middle class. J. Joseph Huthmacher (Mississippi Valley Historical Review, *1962) and Michael Paul Rogin and John L. Shover* (Political Change in California, *1970) emphasize working-class (particularly Catholic and immigrant) support for progressive programs. David P. Thelen in* The New Citizenship *(1972) went further to argue the futility of attributing social movements to particular social groups. Noting that Wisconsin Progressives, not unlike their conservative critics, drew their ranks from farmers, workers, professionals, and business people, he emphasized issues more than classes, and concluded that "no particular manner of man became a progressive."*

Since World War II, then, historians have redefined the sources of progressivism and its relationship to the business community. Although delineating the conservative tendencies inherent in the progressive mind, most scholars still accept the traditional equation of progressivism with reform. New Left historians, however, have denied even that. Gabriel Kolko, for example, has described the movement as The Triumph of Conservatism *(1963). In his view, the progressives were not reformers at all, and the chief characteristic of the era was not orderly change in the public interest but complete control by business interests. Clearly, Kolko's is a minority view, but his total inversion of the traditional interpretation serves as a reminder that history is art not science.*

FOR FURTHER READING

Overviews of the period include the books by Samuel P. Hays, Richard Hofstadter, and Robert Wiebe mentioned in the essay above, but also see William O'Neill's popular *The Progressive Years* (1975). Among several studies of the Rough Rider are George Mowry's *The Era of Theodore Roosevelt* (1958), H. F. Pringle's *Theodore Roosevelt* (1931), J. M. Blum's *The Republican Roosevelt* (1954), and W. H. Harbaugh's *Power and Responsibility* (1961). H. F. Pringle's *William Howard Taft* (2 vols., 1939) and Paolo Coletta's *The Presidency of William Howard Taft* (1973) are both sympathetic portraits. Of the immense literature on Wilson, the most valuable biography is Arthur Link's multivolume study; Link summarizes Wilson's first administration in *Woodrow Wilson and the Progressive Era* (1954). John Garraty's *Woodrow Wilson* (1965) is a brief biography, and John M. Blum's *Woodrow Wilson and the Politics of Morality* (1956) is a suggestive interpretation. Blum's *The Progressive Presidents* (1980) examines a tradition of strong executive leadership from Theodore Roosevelt to Lyndon B. Johnson. There are good accounts of important figures of the age; see, for example, Daniel Levine's *Jane Addams and the Liberal Tradition* (1971), Allen Davis's *American Heroine: The Life and Legacy of Jane Addams* (1973), David Kennedy's *Birth Control in America: The Career of Margaret Sanger* (1970), William Holmes's *The White Chief: James K. Vardaman* (1970), and David Thelen's brief *Robert M. La Follette and the Insurgent Spirit* (1976). Among the many valuable autobiographies, see especially William Allen White's (1946). Books on the urban scene include Mevin Holli's *Reform in Detroit* (1969), Zane Miller's *Boss Cox's Cincinnati* (1968), and Bradley Rice's *Progressive Cities* (1977). Statewide studies include George Mowry's *The California Progressives* (1951) and Sheldon Hackney's *Populism to Progressivism in Alabama* (1969). There are uncounted histories of particular reform topics. Among these see Sheila Rothman, *Woman's Proper Place* (1978); Aileen Kraditor,

The Ideas of the Woman Suffrage Movement (1965), and William O'Neill, *Everyone Was Brave* (1969), on feminism; Harold Wilson, *McClure's Magazine and the Muckrakers* (1970), and David Chalmers, *The Social and Political Ideas of the Muckrakers* (1964), on the new journalism; and Temple Kirby, *Darkness at the Dawning* (1972), and August Meier, *Negro Thought in America* (1963), on blacks. Socialism's story is told, in part, by David Shannon's *The Socialist Party of America* (1955) and Melvin Dubofsky's *We Shall Be All* (1969). Intellectual histories of the period include H. S. Commager's *The American Mind* (1952), Morton White's *Social Thought in America* (1949), and David Noble's *The Progressive Mind* (1980).

23

★ ★ ★ ★ ★ ★

The Era of the First
Overseas War, 1914–1920

THE WAR that began in August 1914 brought to an end a century of relative peace, apparent democratic progress, and European domination of the world. It helped bring about the first Communist revolution. For the United States it ushered in a period of economic world power and political isolation. It brought far greater steps toward governmental direction of the economy than most progressives had dreamed of. All this drastic innovation produced intense emotional confusion: Americans moved in a rapid zigzag from neutrality to crusading excitement to disillusion and revulsion. President Wilson's progressive idealism and moralism seemed to connect the nation at peace to the nation at war.

THE WAR AND AMERICA

In 1914, most Americans found it hard to understand why all Europe went to war over the murder by a Serb of the heir to the throne of Austria-Hungary. Actually, the European great powers, all heavily armed, had long been engaged in a struggle for empire and prestige. They were organized in two huge, approximately equal alliances, each fearful of the other. One consisted of the two Central European empires of Germany and Austria-Hungary (with the doubtful adherence of Italy); the other consisted of Britain, France, and Russia. When Austria-Hungary, afraid of the disintegration of its multinational empire, demanded severe punishment of Serbia, Germany backed its ally's demands. Russia felt it necessary to assist Serbia, and France was linked to Russia. When Germany invaded France through Belgium (whose neutrality had been internationally guaranteed), England came somewhat reluctantly into the war. Later the Central Powers were joined by Turkey and Bulgaria; the Western Allies by Italy, Japan, Greece, Rumania, and other countries.

TABLE 13. THE WAR AND THE TWENTIES, 1914–1929

Year	President	Political events	Economic conditions	Foreign policy	Miscellaneous
1914			1914 Depression.		
1915			1915–1916 Recovery: war orders.		1915 Movie, "Birth of a Nation."
1916	**Wilson D**				
1917		1917–1918 War prosperity.	**April** War declared.		
1918		Republicans win Senate.		**January** Fourteen Points. **November** Armistice.	
1919		**September** Wilson's collapse. Volstead Act.	1919 Inflationary boom strikes.	**June** Versailles Treaty signed.	Red Scare. First regular radio station. Sinclair Lewis, *Main Street*.
1920	**Harding R**	Prohibition and women's suffrage in effect. Palmer's raids.	Deflation and recession.	**March** Treaty finally defeated in Senate.	19th Amendment.
1921		Immigration quotas established.	1921 Depression.	1921–1922 Washington Conference.	
1922		Fordney-McCumber Tariff. Progressive gains in Congress.	Recovery.		Sacco and Vanzetti trial.
1923	**August** Death of Harding. **Coolidge** becomes president.	1923–1924 Exposure of "Harding Scandals."	Prosperity $\longrightarrow$		

Year	President	Political events	Economic conditions	Foreign policy	Miscellaneous
1924	Coolidge *R*	La Follette Third Party Movement. National Origins Act — immigration quotas.		Dawes Plan for Germany.	
1925					Scopes Trial. Klan membership peaks. Theodore Dreiser, *American Tragedy;* F. Scott Fitzgerald, *Great Gatsby.*
1926					
1927		Coolidge vetoes McNary-Haugen farm bill.	1927 Decline in construction and auto industries.	U.S.–Mexican differences compromised.	Lindbergh flight. Marcus Garvey deported.
1928	Hoover *R*			United States renounces right of intervention in Latin America under "Roosevelt Corollary."	
1929			**September–October** Wall Street crash.	Young Plan for Germany.	Ernest Hemingway, *Farewell to Arms;* William Faulkner, *The Sound and the Fury.*

When war broke out, most Americans, believing themselves secure and immune, thought that their country could and should stay out of it. Many quoted, or misquoted, the country's founders on the subject of foreign entanglements. Progressives often associated war with reaction, and socialists thought of it as a product of dying capitalism. To ensure American neutrality, Jane Addams, Lillian Wald, and other social reformers joined the American Union Against Militarism, and feminist Carrie Chapman Catt organized the Women's Peace party. Both Andrew Carnegie and Henry Ford subsidized the peace movement; Ford sent a "peace ship" to Europe in 1915 to promote an early armistice. Some intellectuals and many idealists on both sides of the Atlantic, having convinced themselves that humankind had outgrown its need for the cruder forms of international violence, expressed shock that civilized, twentieth-century nations would resort to war.

President Wilson advocated a scrupulous neutrality, partly because he saw no compelling American interests at stake and partly because he recognized that the ethnically diverse American nation was not united on whether to intervene. Most of the eastern, Anglo-Saxon elite, including many editors and journalists, rated British law and literature highly and identified their own values with those of Western European civilization. Large groups remembered the Marquis de Lafayette, holding a traditional sympathy for France, and felt outrage over the invasion of neutral Belgium. Some influential individuals argued, on less lofty grounds, that American safety depended on British control of the seas. For two decades the United States had moved toward rapprochement with Britain; a British defeat, these Anglophiles believed, would threaten Wilsonian designs for an open world of free commerce and national self-determination.

Though Allied war propaganda fell on many friendly ears, a sizable portion of Americans favored the Central Powers. Most Irish-Americans and many Midwesterners continued to associate Britain with empire, aristocracy, and oligarchy. Some progressives identified Great Britain as the center of the hated international Money Trust, and reformers often thought of Germany as the birthplace of government-sponsored social meliorism. To the well-organized and articulate German-American minority, the Fatherland was an innocent victim of Allied encirclement.

More obvious than in Jefferson's day, neutrality was made difficult by economic and strategic considerations. In 1914 the country was entering a depression, and war orders promised economic recovery. From the beginning, America took the traditional position that all belligerents were free to buy war materiel wherever they chose. Because of British naval power, only the Allies could buy desperately needed American goods. Originally inclined to insist on cash sales, Wilson and his first Secretary of State Bryan early withdrew their opposition to loans and bank credits. By 1915, American industry was booming, and American prosperity was bound up in Allied success. A German victory, an embargo on munitions, a prohibition of loans, or a sudden peace would have meant financial crisis.

Undoubtedly this economic involvement influenced some American opinion. Yet business, and particularly big business, was by no means dominant in the formation of American foreign policy. Some progressives were against whatever business leaders supported. And the president, who bore the responsibility for foreign-policy decisions, had demonstrated in the Mexican crisis a deep hostility to "selfish interests." While Wilson loved British culture and disliked German militarism, he was determined to maintain peace. He was also determined, as always, to defend America's national honor and its power. Both were essential to the overriding goal: the promotion of worldwide democratic progress. The president's most influential advisers, including his close friend Colonel Edward House, were strongly and openly pro-British. Like the president, they believed that the two Atlantic nations were "bound together by common principle and purpose."

Thus the forces affecting American policy were fairly evenly balanced. Most Americans wanted to stay out, and most hoped for Allied victory. Neither economic interest nor Allied sympathy was strong enough to counter the traditional dislike of becoming involved in Europe's troubles. Perplexed by conflicting emotions, many Americans responded most to surging nationalism. Only a direct challenge to American rights and feelings could tip the balance toward war. This challenge arose out of a familiar problem: neutral rights at sea.

Once again, as in the time of Napoleon, a great land power and a great sea power were fighting an all-out war. Each preferred to remain on good terms with America, the world's most powerful neutral. Neither, in the long run, could afford to give up any weapon necessary to victory. The British, as expected, used their navy to blockade Germany and to deny it essential supplies. The Germans countered, attempting to cut off British trade with a new weapon, the submarine or U-boat.

Enormously effective, the submarine was also vulnerable and ethically, and (in terms of international law) perhaps legally questionable. Under the conventions of war, a warship was required to warn an enemy merchant vessel and to remove passengers and crew before sinking her. If, however, a U-boat did surface to warn its victim, it could be destroyed by an armed merchant ship. In at least one famous case, a German submarine that had surfaced for this purpose was sunk by a British decoy ship, disguised as an American merchant vessel. Thus the Germans, throughout the war, faced a difficult choice. They could not use their only effective sea weapon in the only effective manner without killing civilians. Yet killing civilians, in 1914, was regarded by the West as illegal and brutal. Submarine warfare, which might bring Germany victory, could at the same time add to Germany's enemies and thereby bring defeat.

In dealing with blockade and counterblockade, the Wilson administration had three possible choices, each with its advocates. The first was strict neutrality, favored by Secretary Bryan, many congressional Democrats, and much midwestern opinion. Of the many methods proposed to implement such a policy, the most plausible was to prohibit American citizens from traveling on armed ships and thus to prevent the most dangerous kind of incidents. Under this plan, protests against both German and British blockade excesses would be filed for postwar negotiation. This policy, or any policy of abandoning or diminishing American neutral rights, was rejected by Wilson on grounds of national honor.

The opposite extreme would have been to intervene early on the Allied side. This would not only have ended the dilemma about neutral rights, it would have shortened the war and given America a more decisive voice in the peace. This action was advocated by Theodore Roosevelt, which hardly recommended it to Wilson. Such a choice was completely contrary to tradition and would have divided the country disastrously.

The third choice, and one that attracted Wilson from time to time, was American mediation, either to moderate the war or to end it. With Europe immersed in the carnage of total war, the president accepted personal and national moral responsibility to try to restore peace. Mediation efforts took two forms. The first was an effort to induce Britain to modify her blockade or cease from arming merchant vessels in return for German abandonment or modification of submarine warfare. The second was the attempt to persuade both belligerents to state negotiable war aims.

Both kinds of effort at mediation, sporadically pursued and probably illusory, had clearly failed by 1916. Neither side was willing to abandon weapons it considered essential, and neither would abandon the prospect of victory. As the bloodshed mounted, so did fear and hatred, until compromise became impossible.

To force peace, America would have had to threaten both sides with losing the war. To cut off munitions to Britain might result in German victory. To intervene on the Allies' side would require a heavily armed America with a united public opinion. Thus, effective mediation was made impossible by the whole nature of the American political system. Thus the policy adopted was, and perhaps had to be, a constantly shifting compromise among the three alternatives: neutrality, intervention, and mediation.

FROM NEUTRALITY TO WAR
IN FOUR ACTS

The first stage of American policy, from the outbreak of war to February 1915, was characterized by benevolent neutrality toward England. After the shocking invasion of Belgium, the Germans gave little direct offense to America, while the British blockade became increasingly rigid. In it, most commodities were gradually considered to be war contraband, neutral ships were stopped at sea and taken to port for search, and trade with other neutrals who might transship to Germany was severely rationed. Yet American protests were moderate in tone, British concessions were considerable, and, most important, no American was killed. The United States even accepted without much ill feeling the British proclamation of a mined war zone in the North Sea, where few American ships went.

The second stage, running from February 1915 until May 1916, was dominated by German submarine warfare. In February, Germany proclaimed a submarine war zone around the British Isles, cutting the main Atlantic sea lanes. From this point on, the U.S. administration refused to accept the legality of submarine warfare and announced that Germany would be held to "strict accountability" for American losses.

On May 7, 1915, the oceanliner *Lusitania,* unarmed but carrying some war cargo, was sunk off the Irish coast. Of the 1,198 passengers drowned, 128 were Americans. In a series of very strong notes, Wilson demanded that Germany accept responsibility for these losses and abandon its methods of submarine war. After repeated warnings, partial or temporary German concessions, and further sinkings, Wilson in March 1916 made it clear that a continuation of unrestricted submarine warfare would mean a break in German-American relations. Although Roosevelt had objected in the past to Wilson's "weasel words," the implication of war was unmistakable. Germany somewhat grudgingly promised that henceforth her raiders would warn before sinking. This seemed a major American victory. The nation was, however, practically committed to go to war if and when Germany changed her mind. To give some meaning to his implied threats of force, Wilson gave his backing in late 1915 to a preparedness program, including increased army and navy appropriations and heavy new taxes.

The third stage, from May 1916 to February 1917, brought somewhat less tense relations with Germany, increased irritation against England, and the peak of Wilson's efforts for a negotiated peace. In this period Britain, hard pressed in war and confident of American tolerance, stepped up her enforcement of the blockade. American mail was searched, and American firms believed to have dealt with Germany were blacklisted and barred from British trade. Wilson found these actions almost intolerable, and Congress made gestures of retaliation.

In November, Wilson narrowly won re-election, following a campaign in which he was attacked by isolationists who thought him a war monger and by internationalists who agreed with Roosevelt that he was "yellow." Wilson partisans pointed to his success in keeping America out of war, as well as to his increased domestic progressivism. Once elected, the president made his most ambitious mediation effort, a public request to both sides for a statement of war aims. When this effort failed and it became clear that neither side was interested in compromise, Wilson became increasingly disillusioned with the Allied cause. On January 22, 1917, in an eloquent speech, he declared that the world's only hope lay in a "Peace without Victory" for either side.

The fourth and final phase started a week later when Germany, in a desperate bid for victory, announced the resumption of unrestricted submarine warfare. Wilson had no alternative but to break relations, yet he still refused to ask for war. On March 1, the administration released to the press an intercepted German note, the so-called Zimmerman telegram, which proposed, in the event of war with the United States, an alliance with Mexico to recover lost territories. Meanwhile Wilson, despite a filibuster by Robert La Follette and other antiwar progressives, started arming American ships. Only at the beginning of April, after a series of new sinkings, did Wilson seek a congressional declaration of war. Among the few dissenting votes was that of Representative Jeannette Rankin of Montana, the first woman to serve in Congress. Averring that "peace is a woman's job," she voted no, and in 1941 repeated the act by opposing U.S. intervention in World War II.

AMERICA AT WAR: PATRIOTISM AND DISCONTENT

Though many Americans had expected limited, almost painless participation in the war, Allied exhaustion made limitation impossible. On the brink of starvation, Germany was still sinking British ships faster than they could be built; England, virtually drained of its young manhood, was beset with civilian and military labor shortages; the French army was demoralized and mutinous; and Russia, having suffered staggering casualties, was convulsed by revolution.

The first Russian Revolution in March 1917 had caused America to welcome Russia as a constitutional state and possible ally in the war against Prussian autocracy. In November, however, Lenin and the Bolsheviks overthrew the moderate Kerensky government. In March 1918 the Bolsheviks signed a treaty with Germany, surrendering large territories and releasing German troops for the Western Front. Germany began a series of major offensives that penetrated deeply into Allied-held territory and threatened to defeat the war-weary Allies before the Americans could arrive on the scene.

Faced with this crisis, the United States built a massive conscript army; by November 1918, 2,000,000 Yanks had safely been convoyed to France. American naval forces greatly reduced the German submarine menace. The American Expeditionary Force, initially distributed among Allied armies and later united under General John J. Pershing, played a decisive part in the bloody operations from mid-April to November 1918. In the first major American engagement, doughboys of the Second Division stopped a German advance at Château-Thierry, and then in June 1918 drove the enemy out of Belleau Woods. During July in the Second Battle of the Marne, one of the war's turning points, American troops helped halt another German drive against Paris. In the great Allied counteroffensive, the Meuse-Argonne engagement in September and October, General Pershing's forces cut German supply lines and drove the enemy back toward its frontier. By November, the war was over.

To support American military operations, the administration experimented with a planned economy in which the production, distribution, and consumption of American goods was regimented as never before. Money for huge loans to the Allies, as well as for America's war effort, was raised by a fairly democratic system of war finance. About one-third of the total was raised by taxes, compared to about one-fifth in the Civil War. For this purpose, incomes and corporate profits were taxed at unheard-of rates. In 1918, incomes of over $1 million were assessed a total tax of 77 percent. (In 1913, a top rate of 7 percent had seemed high.) Federal war bonds were sold to

65 million customers in four great drives. Even so, the war was financed partly by inflation and mostly through expansion of bank credit by action of the new Federal Reserve System.

After fumbling with various regulatory devices in the first war winter, Congress in the spring of 1918 gave the president almost dictatorial powers over the war economy. Under his control, 500 war agencies policed the productive effort. The War Industries Board allocated raw materials, determined priorities, and standardized products. The War Trade Board supervised foreign commerce. The War Labor Board opposed strikes and lockouts, but also promoted union recognition, the eight-hour day, and uniform wages. The Food Administration under Herbert Hoover guaranteed the purchase of, and set the prices for major farm commodities, thereby using powers granted by Congress (Lever Act) to increase food production. The Fuel Board and the Shipping Administration similarly increased production in their spheres. Railroads, telegraph, and telephones were taken over and efficiently managed by the Railway Administration.

Despite blunders and confusion, the United States achieved a fairly efficient, regulated economy — a form of state capitalism — that reached full-capacity production just as the war ended. Some advanced progressives prophesied that these gains for centralization would never be lost; most citizens, however, accepted the new system as the wartime expedient that it was, and supported it largely for patriotic reasons. Business flourished, as it always does in times of war. Corporate profits, buoyed by cost-plus federal contracts, increased at least threefold between 1914 and 1919. Yet business people objected to wartime taxes, resented labor's modest gains, and in general carped about governmental regimentation. Farmers, though faring well, resented the fixing of price ceilings and noted that price floors had never been set in a depression.

The labor shortage, exacerbated by male military enlistments and declining immigration, created unprecedented opportunities for minorities and women. Blacks, welcome only in the most menial industrial jobs up to this time, found their labor in high demand. Between 1916 and 1918, nearly 500,000 Afro-Americans left the South for wartime jobs in northern cities. Thousands of Mexican-Americans left the Southwest and moved in the same direction, but many more Hispanics, their numbers increased by relaxed immigration laws, found employment as agricultural workers in California and neighboring states. Although woman's place was still thought to be in the home, perhaps a million women out of a female workforce of eight million held jobs in war industries, and many others performed useful war-related volunteer work.

Thus, despite minor discontentments, governmental direction of the war economy marked a momentous step in a generally continuing direction. There was no return to laissez faire. After the war, the government was to act as a partner to business, and later, under Franklin Roosevelt's New Deal, wartime precedents were invoked to meet a national depression.

Like the president's war powers, radical steps were taken to manage public opinion, with frightening consequences. Despite evident popular enthusiasm, the government was concerned about national unity. The Committee on Public Information, administered by the progressive journalist George Creel, blanketed the country with some 75 million pamphlets and un-counted speeches about "Why We Are Fighting" and "The Meaning of America." The Post Office barred antiwar publications from the mails. The Espionage (1917) and Sedition (1918) acts cracked down on "spies" and "trai-tors" by forbidding abusive words and contemptuous deeds about, or against the U.S. flag, government, Constitution, uniform, or military. About 1,500 persons, including Eugene Debs, Emma Goldman, and most other leading socialists, were imprisoned for sedition, often on dubious charges, and a number of presumably undesirable aliens were deported. States and private vigilance organizations, such as the Boy Spies of America and the American Anti-Anarchy Association, committed even greater excesses. Self-appointed patriots declared open season on disloyalty, nonconformity, and "heresy" or radicalism. The German language, German-American actors, and German music were banished from schools, the stage, and concerts, respectively. Religious pacifists and other "slackers" were humiliated, physically abused, and in some cases lynched. Rigid censorship and political repression were imposed on educational institutions, the press, and the movie industry. Some mobilization of opinion may have been necessary, but official abuses of civil liberties during the Wilson administration were extreme in a democ-racy, and substantially worse than during either the Civil War or World War II. As the postwar Red Scare of 1919 would demonstrate, patriotism was more easily aroused than controlled (see Chapter 24).

Yet, for all the repression and hysteria, the American people knew little of the horrors of war. Few civilians knew or understood the remote and hideous world of the Western Front, a world of barbed wire and rat-infested trenches, of appalling butchery and rotting corpses, crowded field hospitals, poison gas, shrapnel, and shell shock. At war's end, Americans proudly noted that their arms and troops had tipped the balance in the Allies' favor. But the price paid in American lives was relatively small; in an intense six months of fighting, the United States sustained about 100,000 combat-re-lated deaths, about half in battle and half due to disease. By contrast, in four years the Russian combat dead numbered 1,700,000; the Germans, 1,600,000; the French, 1,400,000; and the British, 900,000 — 20,000 of them in a single day. All told, about 10 million people died in the bloodiest and most costly war in history.

THE FAILURE OF A WILSONIAN PEACE

Wilson became the worldwide prophet of a democratic peace, a singular spokesman for moral ideas in a world at war. In substantial measure, he had advocated intervention to give the Americans a decisive role in shaping a just and lasting postwar agreement between the warring countries. On Jan-uary 8, 1918, ten months before the armistice, Wilson outlined to Congress his famous Fourteen Points, the terms for peace.

The first five points were general liberal formulae: open treaty making, freedom of the seas, removal of trade barriers, arms reduction, and impartial adjustment of colonial claims in the interest of the natives. Most of the remaining points were concerned with the readjustment of boundaries in the interest of the Wilsonian principle of national self-determination even for small nations. The final point, the most important to Wilson, provided for an association of nations to maintain the peace. A number of the Fourteen Points were contrary to provisions in the secret treaties already negotiated among the Allies. Wilson knew of these treaties but ignored them, doubtless believing that he could force the Allies to abandon them.

Its military situation hopeless, Germany asked Wilson on October 6 for an armistice based on his announced program. Despite Allied objections, the Fourteen Points were accepted as the basis for peace, but not without several specific reservations. On November 11, military authorities finished negotiating a truce that disarmed Germany and made further resistance impossible.

In January 1919 at Paris, the victorious Allies started negotiating among themselves the peace terms to be imposed on Germany. Accompanied by an undistinguished peace delegation and a large corps of experts, Wilson left for Paris. Frantic ovations throughout Europe apparently convinced him that it was his mission alone to force a generous peace on the world. His bargaining power was limited by several factors, however. First, despite his misguided and narrowly partisan appeal for a Democratic Congress, the voters elected Republican majorities to both the Senate and the House in 1918. Thus, even as he attempted to check Allied ambitions, his leadership was apparently repudiated at home. Then, having negotiated a preliminary peace document with the provision for a League of Nations, he came back to Washington to find more than a third of the Senate opposed to the League convenant as then drafted. Returning to Paris, he had to face the Allied leaders with his authority further weakened. Another limiting factor was the fact that Allied leaders, bound by the secret treaties between them, were determined to secure their nations from further attack and to make Germany pay for the long struggle.

Despite a courageous fight, Wilson had to make many concessions from his original plan. To Italy he had to concede sizable German-speaking border areas. Japan secured not only Germany's island colonies (which were to play a crucial part in World War II), but also, against Chinese opposition, German interests in the Shantung Peninsula. To France, who desired the dismemberment of Germany, Wilson had to concede very severe terms regarding the defeated nation. Germany was stripped of colonies and merchant marine, disarmed, and forced to surrender border areas. Perhaps more important, Germany was required to admit its guilt for the war as a basis for reparations, whose sum would be fixed later by the Allies. With hindsight it is easy to see the inadequacies of the Versailles settlement. Too harsh to effect a reconciliation between conquered and conquering nations, it also failed to restore an Anglo-French world hegemony. Japan was thwarted, China chaotic, the colonial world restive, and all nonwhites irritated by the failure of a clause affirming racial equality.

In addition, Bolshevik Russia was proclaiming world revolution, and communist revolutions seemed to threaten both Asia and Central Europe. Hoping to smash Bolshevism before it could spread, Allied forces with American participation invaded Russian territory during her years of upheaval and civil war. Wilson also joined an Allied economic blockade and withheld American diplomatic recognition from the new Soviet state. These and other Allied anti-communist gestures figured importantly in Soviet alienation from the West and contributed to tensions leading 25 years later to the Cold War.

To Wilson, exhausted and implacable, all the faults of the Versailles settlement were compensated for by the gains for self-determination and above all by the establishment of the League of Nations. It would, he hoped, supervise the administration of former German colonies by their new masters under the mandate system. It would secure the reduction of armaments, preserve the independence and integrity of all nations, mediate disputes, and even use force against those resorting to war. For this great ideal, Wilson came home to fight an uncompromising moral battle for the covenant of the League.

At first, the treaty's chances looked good. Wilson's prestige was still great, and the idea of a League of Nations had long attracted American support. But the treaty aroused many kinds of opposition. Among its enemies were the disappointed minorities of German, Italian, and Irish descent, isolationists who feared that the League would involve America in European affairs, liberals who objected to the compromises of democratic principle, and a less easily identifiable, but large group of Americans reacting against wartime enthusiasm and sacrifice.

The Senate, where the treaty's struggle centered, was divided into three groups: loyal Wilsonian Democrats in favor of the treaty and the League; a group of about a dozen senators, including La Follette, Borah, and Johnson of California, who were "Irreconcilables," all-out foes of both issues; and "Reservationists," who were inclined to accept the treaty with certain changes defining and restricting the authority of the League.

In the long struggle, opposition to the treaty was marshaled by Henry Cabot Lodge, an enemy of Wilson and a master tactician. In order to attract the crucial Reservationists, Lodge proposed not rejection but alteration of the treaty. The changes were carefully calculated to sound plausible but to be unacceptable to Wilson. Lodge knew his opponent. Wilson forbade Democrats to accept the reservations, thus making impossible the two-thirds majority necessary for passage of the treaty. Without reservations, the treaty was opposed by Irreconcilables and Reservationists; with reservations, it was opposed by Irreconcilables and loyal Democrats.

Refusing to accept defeat, Wilson embarked on a nationwide speaking tour. The people, he said, must not allow the Senate to "break the heart of the world" by rejecting the treaty. Prematurely aged and emotionally exhausted, Wilson broke down in the midst of his tour and had to be taken back to Washington. There he suffered a severe stroke and was partly incapacitated for the rest of his presidency. Sick, isolated, but grimly determined, he continued to forbid his followers to compromise. Wilson's loyal followers rejected the reservations, and the treaty failed to get ratification.

Once more Wilson appealed to the final authority, the American people, announcing in the spring of 1920 that the coming presidential election would constitute a "solemn referendum" on the treaty. In the campaign, the Democratic candidate, Governor James M. Cox of Ohio, supported the treaty and the League. The Republican candidate, Senator Warren G. Harding of the same state, opposed it only ambiguously, and some of his supporters favored it equally vaguely.

Harding won by the most sweeping majority since Monroe. It is impossible to prove that the election constituted a real referendum on foreign policy. It was certainly affected by many domestic issues, including the breakdown of Wilson and, to a considerable extent, of his administration. In another sense, however, the election of 1920 was a major decision; the campaign, the press, and the results indicated that the American people wanted a president as little like Woodrow Wilson as possible, and this is what they got.

CONFLICTING HISTORICAL VIEWPOINTS: NO. 11

Why Did America Enter World War I?

Contemporary accounts of U.S. intervention in World War I were generally favorable to Wilsonian policies. The war was a noble and necessary war, many first-hand observers agreed, and Americans could take pride and satisfaction in their role in it. Reinforcing this initial view were two semi-autobiographical publications: Burton Hendrick, ed., The Life and Letters of Walter H. Page *(3 vols., 1922–26), and Charles Seymour,* The Intimate Papers of Colonel House *(4 vols., 1926–28). Both House and Page had helped shape American policy and neither questioned the wisdom of U.S. intervention.*

*A revisionist interpretation, however, was not long in developing. Disillusioned by the failures of Wilson's peace and threatened by the gathering clouds of war in Europe and Asia, many Americans in the 1920s and 1930s traced the nation's involvement not to idealism or self-interest, but to folly, sentimentalism, and greed. Scholarly advocates of this view included Harry E. Barnes (*Genesis of the World War, *1926), C. Hartley Grattan (*Why We Fought, *1929), and C. C. Tansill (*America Goes to War, *1938), all of whom argued that Wilson's policies were neither wise, necessary, nor beneficial to the United States. In their accounts, U.S. intervention was attributed to the pernicious influences of misguided Wilsonian Anglophiles, skillful British propagandists, and grasping American munitions makers and international bankers.*

Although the revisionist view was in many ways an accurate reflection of popular, or at least congressional, sentiment during the postwar and

Depression years, it has not been widely accepted by historians. A more satisfactory argument was offered by Charles Seymour, whose American Diplomacy during World War I *(1934) has been called "the first historian's history of intervention." Treating American involvement as a historical problem rather than as a moral issue, this Yale professor asserted that Wilson, although pro-Allies, struggled valiantly to remain neutral. Anticipating such relatively recent interpretations as Arthur Link's* Wilson the Diplomatist *(1957) and Ernest May's* The World War and American Isolation *(1959), Seymour concluded that Wilson had little choice but to lead the nation into war. In the final analysis, he believed, the German submarine was the cause of American intervention. In close agreement, Link and May have stressed the tragedy of Wilson's dilemma and the limited range of his alternatives. While they, too, endeavored to avoid judgment, their studies stress the essential correctness of presidential policy.*

*Also critical of revisionism were such "realist" historians as George Kennan (*American Diplomacy, *1950) and Robert Osgood (*Idealism and Self-Interest in America's Foreign Policy, *1953) who argued that in 1917 the United States entered the right war for the wrong reasons. Having experienced World War II, realists doubted that the United States could have avoided World War I. Their primary complaint, then, was not that Wilson carried the nation into war, but that he did so in the name of morality and legality, not national security and self-interest.*

Radical historians, on the other hand, denied that American intervention could be attributed to altruism and idealism. In their view, the war was waged not to make the world safe for democracy, but to make the world's markets safe for American economic expansion. Although perhaps best argued in William A. Williams's The Tragedy of American Foreign Policy *(1962), a subtle and challenging variation on this theme is presented in N. Gordon Levine's* Woodrow Wilson and World Politics *(1968). According to this scholar, it was Wilson's aim to build "a new rational international-capitalist order, safe from war and revolution and open to [American] commercial and moral expansion."*

FOR FURTHER READING

In addition to the studies mentioned above, students interested in the diplomacy of American interventionism should consult Thomas A. Bailey and Paul B. Ryan's *The Lusitania Disaster* (1975) and Patrick Devlin's *Too Proud to Fight* (1974). Also of interest to the conduct of the war are Gerd Hardach's *The First World War* (1977) and Ellis Hawley's *The Great War and the Search for a Modern Order* (1979). Different phases of the social and economic history of the home front are described in P. W. Slosson's *The Great Crusade and After* (1937); R. D. Cuff's *The War Industries Board* (1973); Charles Gilbert's *American Financing of World War I* (1970); Maurine Greenwald's *Women, War, and Work* (1980); and Florette Henri's *Black Migration* (1975). The wartime state of civil liberties is described by Zachariah

Chafee in *Free Speech in the United States* (1941); by Paul Murphy in *World War I and the Origin of Civil Liberties* (1979); and by William Preston in *Aliens and Dissenters* (1966); and Emma Goldman's *Living My Life* (1931). The misuse of history by wartime historians is the subject of Carol S. Gruber's *Mars and Minerva* (1975) and G. T. Blakey's *Historians on the Home Front* (1971). The rejection of the treaty is analyzed by T. A. Bailey in *Wilson and the Peacemakers* (1947), and Ralph Stone has written an able account of *The Irreconcilables* (1971). The beginnings of Soviet-American relations are described in W. A. Williams's *American-Russian Relations* (1952) and in George Kennan's *The Decision to Intervene* (1958).

24

★ ★ ★ ★ ★ ★ ★

The Twenties: Prosperity and Social Change

AMERICANS today view the postwar decade in at least three ways. It was the Jazz Age, the Roaring Twenties, and the romantic heyday of flappers and flivvers. It was also the period of Coolidge prosperity, conservative retrenchment, and isolation. Finally, it was the period of the "lost generation," of Ernest Hemingway, F. Scott Fitzgerald, and T. S. Eliot — an era marked by literary rebellion and experimentation.

Even at the time, different kinds of people saw America from differing angles. Entrepreneurs and farmers, Freudians and fundamentalists, all were reacting at varying rates and ways to a changing social and economic order. Some changes, like industrialization and urbanization, had been going on for a long time and were accelerating. Others, like the importation of challenging new ideas (among them psychoanalysis and relativity), had begun before the war. Still other changes directly resulted from the war, which was itself a traumatic break with national tradition.

Some Americans accepted change passively, if not willingly; others clung tenaciously to tradition and fought every departure from old ways. Other Americans, among them notably Henry Ford, accepted innovation in areas like technology and transportation, but fought it in areas like manners and morals. Even for the most conservative, however, tradition seemed hard to define, let alone restore.

This period of flux was cushioned by relatively good times. For many Americans, though clearly not all, the Twenties were years of peace and prosperity — the last to occur for a long time.

POSTWAR ADJUSTMENTS, 1918–1920

Ironically, high-minded Woodrow Wilson, not vacuous Warren G. Harding, ushered in the spiritually cramped postwar reaction and disillusionment. Wilson more than any evangel of the resurgent Old Guard set the tone of the "New Era."

316

The immediate aftermath of the war was anything but placid. The fight over the treaty was only the first round of a frustrating struggle to liquidate the war and, less consciously, the idealism that led to America's involvement in it. In 1919, advanced progressives and labor leaders were talking about planned and masterful nationwide reconstruction and some were predicting the nationalization of basic industries. Actually, nothing was further from popular demand or administration intent. From the armistice on, government contracts were canceled, employees dismissed, and regulatory powers abandoned. Soldiers were rapidly discharged with only minimum provisions for re-employment.

Congress abandoned regulation and reform less rapidly than the administration. Immediately after the war, two progressive causes reached nationwide victory. The Eighteenth (prohibition) Amendment, pushed hard by the Methodist Church and the Anti-Saloon League, was passed through a combination of moral zeal, desire to conserve resources, and dislike of German-American brewers. In October 1919, the Volstead Act was passed over Wilson's veto and ended forever (most of its friends and enemies thought) the manufacture, sale, transportation, and possession of intoxicating beverages. In the same year, the Nineteenth Amendment made women's suffrage a nationwide reality.

In dismantling controls, the postwar Congress had a mixed record. The railroads, returned to private hands by the administration, were placed under stringent regulation by the Esch-Cummins Act of 1920. This law's purpose, however, was partly to promote, rather than to prevent, consolidation into fewer systems. From then on, the railroad industry, threatened with truck and bus competition and overbuilt in places, was treated more like an invalid than like a tyrannical giant. The government-built merchant marine was returned to private interests, and here too subsidy was needed more than control. In the vital area of water power, Congress established in 1920 a new regulatory agency, the Federal Power Commission, to license development and operation.

For the most part, however, the wartime-directed economy was dismantled without planning and without disaster. In the spring of 1919, after a very brief postwar slump, business began to pick up. At the time, the upturn was credited to unsatisfied consumer demand, but economists today credit government spending, temporarily continued in the form of loans to the Allies and European relief operations. Rapidly, recovery turned into speculative boom, as wholesale prices rose by about 30 percent.

Instead of Imperial Germany, the main public enemy in 1919 seemed to be the high cost of living. Salaried people on fixed incomes were badly pinched by runaway inflation. Labor was restive, fearful that its wartime gains might be lost and threatened by increasingly anti-union employers. Four million workers, more than ever before, went on strike for higher wages, shorter hours, and better conditions. Though these were traditional union objectives, conservatives in most cases portrayed work stoppages as revolutionary acts inspired by Bolsheviks. This portrayal was successful particularly in the Seattle general strike, the United Mine Workers' strike, the bitter and bloody steel strike, and the Boston police strike. Public opinion, local and state governments, and the Wilson administration sided strongly with management, and the unions generally lost these battles.

Along the nation's troubled racial front, there was also violence and disorder. Beginning with the savage East St. Louis riot of 1917 and climaxing with a violent eruption in Chicago during the Red Summer of 1919 (so called because of the bloodshed), American cities began a painfully uneasy adjustment to the growing presence of new waves of black migrants. Pushed out of the South by discrimination and violence and drawn to northern industrial centers by wartime employment and the promise of a better life, blacks by the thousands came to occupy the blighted slums of Buffalo, Chicago, Cleveland, Detroit, New York, and other cities. In time, these black newcomers found somewhat better economic, political, and educational opportunities. But during the war and its aftermath, their presence was bitterly resented by whites who feared social equality and job competition. There were at least 26 urban race conflicts during the Red Summer, and in Chicago alone a chain of white violence, black counterviolence, and official repression left 23 blacks dead and thousands more homeless. Outraged by these bloody encounters — and the 83 lynchings of 1919 — the NAACP and allied organizations launched a campaign that resulted in 1921 in the first antilynching bill ever passed by the House of Representatives. In the Senate, however, a southern filibuster prevented its enactment. During the postwar decade, lynch mobs killed at least 330 Americans, nearly all of them southern blacks.

Many white citizens blamed racial unrest, strikes, the high cost of living, and foreign crises on one simple cause: radical conspiracy. The Third International, calling from Moscow for world revolution, was echoed by the two new American communist organizations: the Communist Labor party (cofounded by John Reed) and the Communist party (composed largely of aliens). Although the parties could legitimately claim no more than 50,000–70,000 members, their very presence alarmed many Americans. Public opinion was also aroused by a few unexplained bombings believed to be of anarchist origin. Many conservative citizens feared — and a few ardent radicals hoped — that revolution was at hand.

In January 1920, politically ambitious Attorney General A. Mitchell Palmer ordered a series of raids on alleged foreign radical organizations. Using intelligence dossiers compiled by J. Edgar Hoover, director of the new Bureau of Investigation, Palmer's agents summarily arrested more than 4,000 people in 33 cities; some 250 alien radicals, including Emma Goldman, were deported to the USSR aboard the "Soviet Ark." Little evidence of dangerous revolutionary activity was uncovered, but many zealous individuals, organizations, and governmental units turned their hostility from Germans to radicals. Eager to win congressional support for a peacetime sedition act, Palmer even warned that revolutionaries planned to overthrow the United States government on May Day of 1920. The New York legislature expelled five duly-elected Socialist representatives; some communities required school teachers to take loyalty oaths; several states made it illegal to fly the red flag of Bolshevism. In 1921, two philosophical anarchists, the hapless Nicola Sacco and Bartolomeo Vanzetti, were arrested for a robbery and murder on evidence that seemed to rest on public hostility toward alien radicals. Despite impassioned agitation for their release, they were finally executed in 1927. Half a century later, they were posthumously pardoned.

Well before this execution, in fact before the end of 1920, the Red Scare began to ebb. Though Palmer's excesses were widely ridiculed, the public's fear of the alien, the dissenter, and the nonconformist continued to manifest itself in race riots and lynchings, in anti-Semitic whisperings, in crusades against alarming ideas, and in suspicion of foreigners. All these tendencies play a part in the growth of the Ku Klux Klan, a secret organization founded in 1915 in imitation of its Reconstruction namesake. Stronger in the West and Midwest than the South — and with surprising strength in some larger cities and in New England — the Klan was militantly anti-Catholic, anti-Semitic, antiforeign, antiliberal, and antimodern. At its peak in the early 1920s, thousands participated in "One Hundred Percent Americanism" parades, perhaps 5 million enrolled in the Klan (and bought hoods and bedsheet robes), and at least two states came under its political control. Only in the mid-1920s, when most kinds of hysteria gave way to complacency, did the Klan lose strength.

In 1919–1920, many Americans came to associate Wilsonian idealism with frustrated hopes and divisive emotions, with the unsolved problems of Europe, with war propaganda and foreign entanglements, and with the high cost of living and the Red Menace. Even the most devoted Wilsonians had to admit a shattering contrast between the vigorous leader of 1913 or the inspired prophet of 1917 and the sick, stubborn, old man of 1919, presiding over an administration zealous in hounding radicals but helpless in dealing with social or economic problems. Unsurprisingly, the country turned with relief toward a completely opposite type of leadership.

INDEPENDENT INTERNATIONALISM

Warren G. Harding was a small-town editor, a regular McKinley and Taft Republican, and a handsome, genial man with a modest intellectual endowment and undemanding moral standards. Conceivably, he was a more forceful and able president than the bumbling misfit that several generations of historians have portrayed him to be. But even his most sympathetic biographer concedes that his term of office was scarred by gross mismanagement. To his credit, he announced a plan to staff his administration with his party's "best minds." A few of these were secured, including Charles Evans Hughes as the new secretary of state, Henry C. Wallace as secretary of agriculture, and Herbert Hoover as secretary of commerce. In too many cases, however, the administration was staffed with presidential cronies. A major center of power was the notorious "little house on K Street," where members of the "Ohio Gang" exchanged male jokes, played poker, and drank prohibited whiskey. Harding's heterogeneous group of the talented and the tawdry made decisions of great importance, most of them highly popular in their time. Indeed, a nation that had seemed reluctant to embrace such exceptionally able chief executives as Lincoln and Wilson gave its heart to the good-natured and second-rate Harding.

In his campaign, Harding, whose oratory rarely rose above platitudes, avoided defining his foreign policy. Much of the Republican party was bitterly isolationist, but an important faction including ex-President Taft insisted that a new administration work out a less offensive substitute for the League of Nations. Whatever the election really meant (and clearly it was no "solemn referendum" on the League), Harding drew from it the conclusion that American entry into the League was a dead issue. U.S. membership in the World Court, which Harding and his Republican successors favored, was blocked by conservatives in the press and Senate.

Despite strong isolationist sentiment, total disengagement from world affairs proved impossible. The United States pursued what has been called an independent internationalism. As the world's greatest manufacturing, exporting, and creditor nation, it could hardly return to its traditional isolationism, and American policies during the 1920s vigorously promoted the nation's overseas trading advantages. American exports more than doubled during the decade; American investors, encouraged by both the State Department and favorable tax laws, penetrated foreign markets as never before. Private American capital sustained the new German Republic, propped up congenial governments throughout Latin America, and helped the relatively moderate banking and industrial regime in Japan. Americans vied with the British and French for Near Eastern oil areas, and developed copper interests in Chile. Because all these ventures were done in the name of profit rather than politics and, above all, because military force was invoked only in minor instances in the Caribbean, the Republican administrations of this decade could appease isolationists with pious references to the founders' anti-entanglement doctrines.

In the Far East, the original home of the Open Door Policy and the traditional center of Republican foreign interest, Secretary Hughes and other key Harding international advisers endeavored to stabilize the balance of power. During the war, Japan had taken steps to dominate China and to gain military hegemony in East Asia. Traditional American commitments to the trading and territorial integrity of China still ran well beyond America's military power. Attempting to limit naval armaments and to promote Far Eastern stability, the Harding administration sponsored the multinational Washington Conference of 1921. Participating nations included Great Britain, France, Italy, the Netherlands, Portugal, Belgium, China, and Japan. Here the United States entered into a series of interlocking multilateral treaties that limited the construction of capital ships, partially rolled back Japanese territorial expansion, terminated the embarrassing Anglo-Japanese Alliance, recognized the Pacific status quo, and reaffirmed the Open Door. In return for these concessions (many from the Japanese), the United States surrendered the possibility of naval superiority and agreed not to fortify its possessions in the western Pacific. Renewed Japanese expansion in the next decade prompted Americans to denounce these agreements. At the time, however, the United States was in no mood for a costly arms race or for rivalry of Japan's control of the western Pacific. The Washington settlement seemed reasonable, and Japanese-American tensions relaxed temporarily.

Isolation from European affairs was also impossible. During and immediately after the war, the United States made huge loans to Allied nations. Although these war debts were generally viewed by Europeans as American contributions to the common struggle, most Americans thought of them as conventional business obligations. With great European resentment, "Uncle Shylock" negotiated a series of funding agreements that extended repayment to the United States over 25 years, and scaled interest rates according to ability to pay.

Obstacles to repayment seemed insurmountable, despite scaled interest rates. The European gold supply was dwindling; a second avenue of repayment, heavy American imports of European goods, was virtually closed by short-sighted American protectionism. Having flirted with freer trading policies during the Progressive era, the United States returned to high tariffs during the postwar Republican ascendancy. Congress passed the Emergency Tariff in 1921 and the steeply protective Fordney-McCumber Tariff in 1922. Then in 1930, over the protest of 34 nations, Congress enacted the prohibitive Smoot–Hawley Tariff, the highest in U.S. history.

Closely related to the issue of war debt was that of reparations. Unable to sell their goods in volume in the American market, the former Allies argued that they could meet their American obligations only through German reparation payments to them. But in 1923, the Germans defaulted, as the country was racked by inflation and resentful of the sole war guilt principle on which reparations were based. France promptly occupied the industrial Ruhr area of Germany and was challenged by passive resistance from the German population. This situation, clearly threatening prosperity and peace, was a major test for the new foreign policy, and the test was passed. An international commission of experts, headed by an American banker, negotiated the Dawes Plan in 1923, and six years later a like group worked out the similar Young Plan. The basis of these plans was: (1) successively scaled-down German payments; (2) stabilization of the German currency; and (3) an international loan to Germany to make these steps possible.

INTERNAL READJUSTMENT

Although isolation from foreign affairs was impossible, Americans could at least control immigration. Well before the war, fear and dislike of the new immigrants from southern and eastern Europe had become widespread. Pseudo-scientific racists pointed to the "criminal tendencies" and other alleged genetic deficiencies of the unwanted newcomers. Labor unions had long opposed the admission of cheap labor, and technological advances brought less demand for unskilled workers. During the war and the postwar

Red Scare, nativism and xenophobia peaked. Congress responded during 1921–1924 with a series of measures designed to decrease the number of immigrants sharply and to set quotas to bring in a majority of northern and western European immigrants. The 1924 National Origins Act established a quota system limiting immigration from each country to 2 percent of its proportion of resident aliens according to the census of 1890. To the anger of the Japanese, a special provision totally excluded Orientals as "aliens ineligible to citizenship." This decision, which reduced immigration from a flood to a trickle, broke decisively with a major American tradition and wounded the feelings of important minorities. In the long run, however, its results were far different from those intended by some of its supporters. The end of free immigration, like the disappearance of the frontier, lessened the wide-open, competitive, mobile tendencies of American life. It also speeded assimilation. Without the familiar flood of desperate, exploitable new arrivals, the foreign-born and their children were to insist with increasing force on a full place in American life and politics.

The economic policies of the Harding administration were developed in a time of instability. Late in 1920, the postwar boom turned into depression as government supports of basic commodity prices ended and European demand temporarily fell off. In the face of plummeting prices and mounting unemployment, government policy was simple: to do everything possible to encourage business leadership and prosperity. Secretary of the Treasury Andrew Mellon, the Pittsburgh aluminum king and one of the nation's richest people, called for strict economy in government expenditures and proposed sharp cuts in taxes on corporate profits and high incomes. Initially frustrated by progressives, Mellon's efforts to shift most of the tax burden from the wealthy to lower income groups were successful by 1926. The Republicans also completed Wilson's postwar policy of withdrawal from all forms of government economic enterprise and cooperated more fully in industry's anti-union endeavors. Hoover's Department of Commerce strove to further foreign investment and encourage the formation of trade associations to prevent "unfair" competition. Pro-business appointments to the courts and to such agencies as the Interstate Commerce, the Federal Trade, and the Tariff and Power commissions effectively repealed progressive regulatory legislation.

These economic policies won business's approval, and the economy soon recovered from its postwar slump. The nation seemed to bask in "Republican prosperity," except for areas like agriculture. Early in the 1920s, the farmers' wartime boom ended. Increased world competition, improved technology, and bumper crops pushed production beyond demand, and farm prices fell disastrously. Caught in an all-too familiar cost-price squeeze, farmers turned for relief to organizations that ranged from the semisocialist Non-Partisan League of North Dakota to the more conservative Farm Bureau Federation. In Congress the powerful Farm Bloc secured considerable relief legislation of familiar kinds, such as encouragement of cooperatives, facilitation of credit, and regulation of packers and speculators.

Farmers were not the only people to show their discontent with the Harding policies. Prewar progressivism, with its underdog sympathies and anti–big-business sentiments, lived on in the hearts of millions of teachers, preachers, social workers, unionists, and others. In the new postwar circumstances, however, both high morale and unity seemed hard for progressives to attain.

In 1922, the most promising of a series of progressive coalitions took shape in the form of the Conference for Progressive Political Action (CPPA), a federation of farm organizations, discontented labor groups, moderate Socialists, and assorted Bull Moosers and other progressives. In the congressional elections of 1922, the CPPA scored some startling successes. Harding Republicans lost many seats to both the Democrats and the progressive Republicans.

In the Sixty-Eighth Congress, Senate investigations disclosed a series of scandals equaled only in the Grant administration. Harding cronies in the Veterans Bureau, the Departments of Justice and Interior, and other agencies had dispensed favors for financial inducements. The worst revelation was that government oil lands (held for naval needs) at Teapot Dome, Wyoming, and Elk Hills, California, had been secretly transferred to private speculators. Betrayed by his appointees, Harding complained that the presidency was "a hell of a job." "I have no trouble with my enemies," he confided to a journalist. "But my friends, my God damned friends."

Harding fell ill while returning from an Alaskan junket; on August 2, 1923, he died of a stroke in San Francisco. His office was assumed by Vice President Calvin Coolidge, the "High Priest of Stability" and the perfect incarnation of conventional Republican morality. In all fairness, this taciturn Vermonter (the most cruelly caricatured of presidents) was not entirely the political cipher of the "Silent Cal" joke. He was, in fact, conventional and uninspiring. His most memorable expression seems almost self-mocking: "The business of America is business." Much in his public career was virtuous, and he brought to the presidency more knowledge of domestic and foreign affairs than he has been credited with.

During 1922–1924, many people thought that the Harding scandals and the progressive gains foreshadowed a political upheaval. The CPPA backed the redoubtable "Fighting Bob" La Follette as a "Progressive" presidential candidate. The La Follette platform had an oddly dissonant reform ring for 1924: antimonopoly, public ownership of railroads, conservation, farm relief, and curbing of the Supreme Court. The Wisconsin Senator, whose antiwar record was now an asset in his own region, looked formidable enough to unnerve conservatives. The Republicans, renominating Coolidge on a status quo and laissez-faire platform, denounced La Follette and his "radical" following. Meanwhile the Democrats, deeply divided on such issues as the Klan and Prohibition, finally settled on an unpromising conservative candidate, John W. Davis. In the election, La Follette carried nearly 17 percent of the popular vote and ran ahead of Davis in many western states, but Coolidge won in a landslide. A business-oriented public voted for more of the same.

THE NEW ERA

For the rest of the decade, American prosperity took center stage. The basis for the good times was an increase in productivity based on advances in technology, mass production, and scientific management. Industrial output and foreign investments soared; worker productivity in manufacturing rose by one-half. New industries abounded, including automobiles, commercial aviation, and chemicals. The most spectacular advances came in the production of electric power and light and such durable consumer goods as refrigerators, vacuum sweepers, and washing machines, and in the construction of suburban houses and urban skyscrapers. By 1925, Ford's "Tin Lizzy" cost $260, well within the reach of many families; by 1929, one American in five had an automobile. Radios, household appliances, and prepared foods became standard fixtures of the "good" American life.

Changing patterns of consumption, stimulated by the new mass-advertising industry and assisted by credit and installment-plan purchasing, seemed to render obsolete the Puritan virtues of hard work, self-denial, and saving. As a workweek of five and one-half days became increasingly common for industrial workers, leisure and the pursuit of amusement became possible for great numbers of people. With extra time on its hands and money in its pockets, the public turned its attention to a new pantheon: movie stars, athletes, and heroes like Charles Lindbergh, the Lone Eagle, whose solo flight across the Atlantic in 1927 made him the most popular American. Close in popularity were the sports heroes: baseball's Herman "Babe" Ruth, boxing's Jack (the "Manassa Mauler") Dempsey, and collegiate football's Harold "Red" Grange, (the "Galloping Ghost"). In an increasingly collectivized, motorized, and standardized mass society, the triumphs of these individuals — including that of Gertrude Ederle, the first woman and the first American to swim the English Channel — captured newspaper headlines and the popular imagination. The nation's appetite for fantasy was fed by the cinematic exploits of dashing Rudolph Valentino, sultry Clara Bow (the "it" girl), and Theda Bara (the "vamp").

The screen and the sports arena were not the sole amusements for postwar Americans. Some turned to jazz, the unique, black musical idiom. Perfected by such Afro-American band leaders and instrumentalists as Joe "King" Oliver and Louis Armstrong, jazz was popularized by such white band leaders as Ted Lewis and Paul Whiteman. Other middle-class pastimes included golf, tennis, and the frivolities that gave the "Era of Wonderful Nonsense" its name — six-day bicycle races, marathon dancing, the Charleston, mah-jongg, and flagpole-sitting. Collegians, it was said, not only strutted the latest dances in bellbottoms and sleeveless dresses, but swallowed goldfish! A "revolution" in sexual morality, apparently more widely discussed than exercised, seemed to herald the death of Victorian prudery. Some historians, as the Viewpoint essay argues, have made too much of these popular diversions to the neglect of an emerging machine and business civilization, but this decade of evanescent prosperity was notably an age in which urban Americans in growing numbers learned to play.

The postwar boom brought with it a new ideology as well as fads. American business, according to its enthusiasts, had accomplished the dreams of past radicals without coercion or class struggle. Poverty and war were both overcome, and cutthroat competition had been replaced by economic co-operation and social service. The new business leaders, it was said, were committed to high wages and deeply interested in employee welfare. Some firms introduced paid vacations, recreation halls, group insurance, and old-age pensions. Thus, in a new era of enlightened "welfare capitalism" and uncritical popular support for business, there was no further use for labor unions or radicalism.

THE CRITICS OF THE 1920s

The benefits of the new affluence were not universally shared, nor was there a universally sanguine view of the benefits of cultural change. The farmers' depression began at the beginning of the decade, and business failures were widespread. Real wages for industrial workers rose, but not in proportion either to productivity or profits. Economic statistics for the period are un-reliable, but some economists place the unemployment rate at 10–13 per-cent; 50 percent of the people, by one estimate, lived below the poverty line. In 1929 the average factory worker made less than $1,500 annually; the combined income of the richest 0.1 percent equalled that of the poorest 42 percent. Although the middle and upper classes were thriving, large num-bers of Americans — coal and textile workers, southern dirt farmers, sea-sonal laborers, unorganized workers, the elderly, single women, most blacks and Hispanics — were experiencing hard times.

Later developments would demonstrate that the prosperity of the New Era was as unsound as it was uneven. Business consolidation, after a brief pause in the trust-busting years, flourished again and often led to dangerous practices. Prices were more often administered than competitive. Insider groups sometimes built crazy pyramids of holding companies. In the late 1920s, too much money went to outright speculation in land or stocks, and not enough into genuinely productive investments. Chain stores crowded out local retailers of food, merchandise, and pharmaceuticals. Most serious was the distribution of income that put little purchasing power in the pay-checks of average consumers.

Important minorities also refused to join in the chorus of complacency. Surviving congressional progressives, led by Senator George Norris of Ne-braska, prevented the administration from turning over to private interests the government-built nitrate plants on the Tennessee River. (In turn, Coo-lidge and his successor were able to block Norris's own plan for a govern-ment-run Tennessee dam and power system.) Prodded by the Farm Bloc, Congress passed ambitious farm relief laws. Of these, the most discussed was the McNary-Haugen bill, vetoed in 1927. This was a complex scheme providing for government purchase and sale abroad of surplus farm commodities.

Other important dissenters expressed themselves outside the political arena. Many people, often those living in isolated and provincial areas, resented modern ways, machines, and large cities. Uneasy in an increasingly complex and uncertain world, these Americans clung to the conventions of a simpler past, their identity and moral values rooted in family, church, and community. The Klan, the Red Scare, the immigration restriction movement, Prohibition, and even the evangelism of Sister Aimee Semple McPherson and Billy Sunday reflected the discontent of those who recoiled from the apparent secularism, materialism, and hedonism of an urban age. The most dramatic expression of this clash of cultures was the Fundamentalist crusade that seemed to pit the Bible against Darwinian science. Sixty years after the publication of Charles Darwin's *On the Origin of Species*, a number of southern Bible-belt states proscribed the teaching of evolutionary theory in the public schools. In 1925, when the American Civil Liberties Union challenged the first of these laws in the famous Scopes trial in Tennessee, no less a figure than William Jennings Bryan appeared to champion the "Old Time Religion."

Equally hostile to the dominant tendencies of the age were the literary insurgents and other intellectual critics of the culture of materialism. Although the Lost Generation had its roots in an exuberant prewar rebellion against moral and esthetic conventions, its members became more deeply alienated in the Twenties. Repelled by postwar intolerance and by what they thought to be the vulgar materialism and spiritual emptiness, many American intellectuals expressed their worries about its culture in lectures and in print. Some fled to more congenial environs — to the sophistication of Paris, the primitivism of Mexico, or New York's Greenwich Village. Whether in exile or at home, the nation's literary avant-garde experimented with new expressive forms and assailed the "organized stupidity" of the American "boobosie."

The most perceptive of the discontented recognized that more was at stake than any set of national mores. Old questions, put in new forms, were raising doubts about human nature itself. Americans were confronting problems common to all people but particularly distressing to those who inherited a tradition of individual freedom. To some popular behaviorist psychologists, the human person was a bundle of predictable and controllable responses to physical stimuli. To Freudians, human beings were ruled by emotional drives far below the level of consciousness. Neither view seemed to offer much hope to those who cared most for individual freedom. Squarely confronting these and other intellectual challenges, some Americans produced excellent and profoundly serious novels or poems. Others laid the foundation for a deeper and richer criticism of contemporary civilization than had yet been possible.

Afro-Americans, perhaps more than any other group, indulged in this spirit of national self-criticism and personal re-evaluation, and explored the failures of American society. The black literati of the Harlem Renaissance shared the discontented white intellectuals' distaste for bourgeois values and joined their insurrection against traditional literary forms. But the alienation of the black artists seemed more firmly rooted in the day-to-day realities of American life. In a rich outpouring of poems and novels, they celebrated the emergence of a "New Negro" — race-proud and militant, impatient with white injustice, determined to fight for basic human dignity. Joined by a confident new generation of black musicians, dancers, painters, and actors, they struggled to work out a new attitude toward blackness and the cultural heritage of their African past. In a parallel development, the inarticulate black denizens of the nation's industrial slums found a symbol of race pride in the exotic figure of Marcus Garvey and his Universal Negro Improvement Association. Unlike either Booker T. Washington or W. E. B. Du Bois, Garvey stirred the imagination of the impoverished black masses. His back-to-Africa movement, like his dream of an African empire, died in embryo. But his immense popularity (estimates of his following range from one to four million) exposed the depths of Afro-American despair.

The discontent of some intellectuals and the dissatisfaction of much of its black minority were not widely shared by other segments of the population. Indeed, traditional Lost Generation accounts have doubtless exaggerated the degree and the depth of alienation and dissaffection among even the most discerning and sensitive elements of society. Everybody was not happy or rich in the mid-1920s, but prosperity was still a substantial fact, and those who were the most satisfied were also the most influential. More people than ever before moved to the suburbs, drove to the beach, or dreamed of a summer in Europe. Prosperity could be measured not only in baseball gate receipts but in such substantial terms as houses, schools, and hospitals. What civilization, complacent citizens could legitimately ask, had ever done so much for so many?

Ignoring his critics, President Coolidge continued to issue his laconic and reassuring statements, take his afternoon naps, continue his predecessor's probusiness policies, and remain generally popular. The federal government persisted in trimming its costs, and Secretary Mellon assured the continued support of business.

In foreign affairs, success seemed equally conclusive. In Europe, the mid-1920s were an era of apparent economic stabilization, of Franco-German rapprochement, and of increased prestige for the League of Nations. Despite congressional suspicion, the administration was able to develop a habit of unofficial cooperation with the League for many purposes. In Mexico, where conflict between the forces of social revolution and American business interests dragged on, the Coolidge administration managed to compromise serious differences over subsoil oil rights. Americans also believed that they could attain lasting international peace. Barred by Congress from toying with collective security, the Coolidge administration made further but generally unsuccessful efforts to negotiate disarmament in 1927, an effort carried on by Hoover with somewhat more success in 1930. In August 1928, largely through American efforts, 15 nations signed the Kellogg-Briand Pact renouncing war as an instrument of national policy.

HOOVER AND SMITH

In 1928 the two major presidential candidates presented a colorful contrast, though in retrospect their platforms did not. Both were essentially pro-business moderates, and except for Prohibition, their views were similar. Alfred E. Smith, the Democrat, did have a more progressive record in civil liberties and labor. The candidates, however, seemed to embody the post-war cultural conflicts that divided rural and urban, native and alien, provincial and cosmopolitan, traditional and modern. Hoover, his roots in a small Iowa town, came from old-immigrant stock and was a Protestant (Quaker) and a "dry." Smith was a New Yorker, an Irish-Catholic, and a "wet"; he had Jewish advisers and ties to Tammany Hall. Without question the campaign was sullied by intolerance and bigotry, particularly anti-Catholicism. But the Republicans had prosperity on their side, and in the end the election turned on economic issues, not on Smith's religion. Herbert Hoover, architect of the New Era, promised four more years of the good life, and that was enough for many voters.

The larger significance of the election is open to question. Some historians have attributed future Democratic triumphs to Al Smith's success with urban voters. Others, however, argue that Franklin D. Roosevelt's election and the new Democratic coalition are explained by the Depression, not by Smith's impressive showing in the cities.

Whatever the election's meaning for the future, the new Hoover administration seemed to promise increased efficiency and broader humanitarianism within the framework of the Harding-Coolidge policies. Yet Hoover, the ablest of the three postwar presidents, encountered disaster at home and menace abroad. Whether one looked at the peaceful and prosperous 1920s with nostalgia or distaste, the era would soon seem a strange interlude in the tragic and turbulent history of the twentieth century.

CONFLICTING HISTORICAL VIEWPOINTS: NO. 12

Were the Twenties Roaring and Reactionary?

Few decades in American history have suffered more superficial analysis than the 1920s. In popular thought and in all too many serious works of history, the years between the armistice and the crash have been described — after a contemporary newspaper advertisement for a motion picture — as years of "beautiful jazz babies, champagne baths, midnight revels, [and] petting parties in the purple dawn." Most studies of the postwar decade, like the talkies, are animated by stock characters typecast as "flaming youth," "discontented intellectuals," or "self-complacent Babbits."

This conception of the 1920s as the Jazz Age of a Lost Generation was the work of many hands. But its chief architect was the self-styled "retrospective journalist" Frederick Lewis Allen, whose Only Yesterday *(1931) is probably the most readable and most read account of the decade. In Allen's view, it was a unique segment of American life with an atmosphere and style of its own. Isolated somehow from its past and curiously unconnected to its future, the decade was a frivolous interlude in which a nation, on the rebound from Wilsonian idealism, plunged into "a revolution of manners and morals."*

Allen's portrait, however impressionistic and superficial, profoundly influenced a generation of historians who viewed the period as an unfortunate interregnum between progressivism and the New Deal. The two best overviews of the period, William E. Leuchtenburg's lively social history (The Perils of Prosperity, 1958) and John D. Hicks's political, economic, and diplomatic survey (Republican Ascendancy, 1960), emphasize the decade's more frivolous and retrograde impulses.

In the late 1950s, however, more subtle and complex images of the 1920s began to emerge. Growing numbers of scholars became skeptical about conventional emphasis on the spectacular, the bizarre, and the unique. Upon close examination, many found continuity as well as change in the postwar decade. Parting the curtain of speakeasies, marathon dances, and raccoon coats, they perceived what Arthur Link has called "the exciting new frontier of American historical writing." A good example of this new view is Roderick Nash's Nervous Generation (1970), which did much to mute the roar in the Roaring Twenties. A survey of formal thought and popular culture, this study pointedly de-emphasized the degenerate bohemian and the flagpole sitter and argued that the period was notable for neither disillusioned cynicism nor happy revelry.

Similarly, recent political and diplomatic histories no longer teem with one-dimensional political Philistines and resolute isolationists. Arthur Link (American Historical Review, July 1959) and Clark Chambers (Seedtime of Reform, 1963), for example, revealed powerful reform currents at work in a decade once presumed to be conservative. Robert K. Murray (The Harding Era, 1969), Donald McCoy (Calvin Coolidge, 1967), and David Burner (Herbert Hoover, 1978), among others, have offered provocative new studies of these Republican presidents that help dispel familiar, oversimple notions and that differ sharply in important particulars from earlier and markedly less sympathetic biographies. And foreign relations specialists, notably William A. Williams, have challenged "The Legend of Isolationism in the 1920s" (Science and Society, Winter 1954).

Thus, in the past decade or so, historical perceptions of the 1920s have been altered. Although many areas of disagreement remain, there is broad scholarly discontent with Jazz Age stereotypes. However enjoyable and enchanting, the traditional, breezy survey à la Allen lacked the depth and complexity historians now bring to their analyses of the 1919–1929 decennium.

FOR FURTHER READING

The works mentioned above by Allen, Leuchtenburg, and Hicks, however flawed in emphasis, are still useful introductions to the period. Francis Russell's *Shadow of Blooming Grove* (1968) and William Allen White's *Puritan in Babylon* (1938) are biographies of Harding and Coolidge.

Economic history is excellently summarized by George Soule in *Prosperity Decade* (1947). Irving Bernstein's *The Lean Years* (1960) is a revealing history of labor from 1921 to 1933. Foreign policy is illuminated by Selig Adler in *The Isolationist Impulse* (1957), and Joan Hoff Wilson in *American Business and Foreign Policy* (1971). Robert Murray examines the *Red Scare* (1955); Kenneth Jackson surveys *The Ku Klux Klan in the City* (1967); and Ray Ginger's *Six Days or Forever* (1958) analyzes the Scopes trial. Garvey's career is the subject of E. David Cronon's *Black Moses* (1955), and Nathan Huggins has surveyed the *Harlem Renaissance* (1971). An influential contemporary sample of American society is R. S. and H. M. Lynd's *Middletown* (1929). President Hoover's Research Committee on Social Trends summarizes a great mass of interesting material in *Recent Social Trends* (2 vols., 1933). Andrew Sinclair's *Prohibition* (1962) and Norman H. Clark's *Deliver Us from Evil* (1976) are both provocative interpretations of the "noble experiment." James J. Fink in *The Car Culture* (1975) examines the rise of American "automobility"; and Marshall Smelser's *The Life that Ruth Built* (1975) is a biography of a popular legend. For literary history, the best source is contemporary writing, and the best introductions are Alfred Kazin's *On Native Grounds* (1942) and Malcom Cowley's *Exile's Return* (1951). Darwin Payne's biography of Frederick Lewis Allen, *The Man of Only Yesterday* (1975), offers a portrait of one arbiter of the decade's taste.

The Great Depression and the New Deal

The Great Depression in 1929 began with the stock market crash in October 1929. This photograph of Wall Street in New York City shows the milling crowds outside the stock exchange in that fateful month. *(Brown Brothers)*

Full recovery from the Depression did not come until mobilization for World War II created jobs. Many banks that closed their doors in the early Depression years did not reopen; this one in Haverhill, Iowa, photographed in 1939, is an example. *(Library of Congress)*

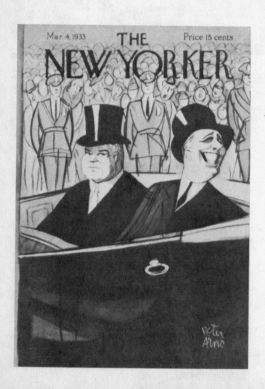

The election of the optimistic Franklin D. Roosevelt ended over a decade of Republican political ascendancy. This cover of the *New Yorker,* with its portrayal of a gloomy Hoover and a victorious Roosevelt on their way to the inaugural in 1933, was never published. Apparently it was considered inappropriate after there was an attempt to assassinate Roosevelt. (*Franklin D. Roosevelt Library*)

Jobless Americans haunted the cities, looking for work and seeking food doled out by private and public agencies. Photographed during the early 1930s, the long bread line near the Brooklyn Bridge in New York City shows graphically the impact of the Depression. (*Library of Congress*)

Union strength grew during the Depression, and New Deal legislation fostered workers' rights. CIO strikers are shown picketing a New York City radio station in December 1937. (*Library of Congress*)

The Depression extended through the 1930s, despite government intervention. Millions of workers were still unemployed, and many Americans lived in extreme poverty. This family in the sawmill town of Gibbs City, Michigan, was photographed in 1937. *(Library of Congress)*

The New Deal and its proliferation of government agencies received mixed reviews. Cartoonist Clifford Berryman in 1934 drew a skeptical view of these alphabetical remedies. *(Library of Congress)*

The effects of the Depression hit not only industrial workers and farmers but also white-collar workers. Many middle-class men found employment as manual laborers in federal projects. WPA workers here are shown excavating a trench in a New York City Park. (*Brown Brothers*)

Threshing Wheat
shows a midwestern
farm in the 1930s
painted by Thomas
Hart Benton. Shown
also on the cover of
*Volume II: Since the
Civil War* of this text,
the painting
dramatizes the farm
environment. *(1939,
tempera on panel,
26 × 42 in.,
unframed.
Permanent
Collection, The
Sheldon Swope Art
Gallery, Terre Haute,
Indiana)*

25

★ ★ ★ ★ ★ ★

Depression and New Deal, 1929–1938

IN THE SUMMER of 1929, while stock prices rose beyond all relation to earnings or dividends, most industrial and financial experts predicted nothing but permanent prosperity. Signs of trouble, including a general decline in consumer spending and particularly sharp reductions in the production and sale of housing and automobiles, went unnoticed. In September the market hesitated nervously, and then in late October a devastating series of crashes canceled 40 percent of the paper values of common stocks.

Despite the continuing optimism of government and business leaders, the crash of 1929 was not a mere correction of inflated values. Like the panics of 1873 and 1893, it turned into a severe and prolonged depression. In the years from 1929 to 1933, as stock prices fell ever lower and confidence evaporated, manufacturing production was halved and building nearly stopped. Banks and businesses failed; farm income, already low, was cut in half; worst of all, unemployment grew steadily. By 1932, at least one in every four Americans were jobless. Prosperity, and with it the spirit of the New Era, had disappeared.

The impact of the Great Depression on those who lived through it is hard to exaggerate. At the lowest economic level, the unemployed faced the threat of starvation when charities, cities, and states ran out of relief funds. Apple selling and bread lines became common sights; shanty towns sprang up on the edge of cities; men and women were sometimes seen pawing through restaurant garbage. At the opposite end of the scale, some respected financiers were caught misusing investors' funds; only a few killed themselves or fled to Europe. Both bankers and big businessmen rapidly lost public prestige. In the large, previously contented middle class, people unused to disaster lost savings, houses, jobs, and hope. Even those who suffered no personal privation found it hard to dispel fear. Anyone might be the next victim of a disaster that nobody understood.

Why did catastrophe paralyze the richest and most productive country in the world? At the time, many blamed the more obvious weak spots in the economy: the loose and ill-coordinated banking structure and the irresponsible financial manipulation that had piled one holding company on another. Later, New Dealers insisted that Republican policies had crippled foreign trade, encouraged inequality and concentration, fostered the boom, and then clung doggedly to financial conservatism after the crash. On the other hand, President Hoover was always to believe that the Depression was almost beaten when the election of a Democrat destroyed business confidence. In the long run, many historians have concluded that the causes were the unsoundness and inadequacy of the previous decade's prosperity. In the 1920s, prosperity depended as never before on mass consumption, but inequality in the distribution of profits and a too rigid price structure limited consumption. By 1929, demand for automobiles and some other products was apparently about filled. Attractive outlets seemed to be lacking for large-scale investment. In other words, the prosperity of part of one country in a poor world could not continue. The New Era picture of liberal and enlightened American capitalism, while not totally false, was not true enough.

HOOVER AND THE DEPRESSION

On entering office in 1929, President Hoover found himself confronted by two familiar problems of the Twenties: farm relief and the tariff. Each of these grew more difficult with the Depression. Like Coolidge, Hoover fought off farm bloc proposals that seemed to involve subsidy and price fixing. In their place, Hoover secured the passage of a complex measure establishing a Federal Farm Board empowered to promote such time-honored remedies as cooperative marketing. By 1930 the Stabilization Corporations also created by this law were buying and storing surplus wheat and cotton. Already the government was up to its neck in nondisposable surpluses, and prices were still going down.

As part of his farm program, Hoover proposed another old panacea — tariffs — on agricultural products. This led Congress to further demands for industrial protection and the enactment of the Smoot-Hawley Tariff, signed by Hoover despite the protest of more than 1,000 economists. The high rates of this measure ended all prospects of reviving foreign trade.

In his anti-Depression measures, President Hoover, the elected representative of New Era know-how, broke sharply with the past. When Secretary Mellon recommended that the government allow prices and wages to fall until recovery set in according to traditional laissez-faire formulae, Hoover decided that such a drastic purge might kill the delicate patient. His first action, following New Era doctrine rather than nineteenth-century economic theory, was to call conferences of business leaders in which employers were urged to maintain wages and production. When this proved ineffective, Hoover used available government machinery to cut taxes, liberalize credit, and prop farm prices.

By 1930 the administration turned to more drastic remedies. In that year, however, the long-brewing revolt against the Republicans was brought to a boil by the Depression, and Hoover lost the support of Congress. Many administration measures failed, but the president managed to secure large public works appropriations and measures to refinance home mortgages and further stimulate credit. A new agency, the Reconstruction Finance Corporation, lent large sums to banks, railroads, and businesses and also eventually to states, cities, and agricultural credit corporations. To stem international financial disaster, Hoover called successfully in 1931 for a one-year moratorium on German reparations and Allied debt payments.

Thus, in a major break with the past, the Hoover administration assumed governmental responsibility for fighting an economic crisis. Yet the Hoover measures, sweeping and large-scale as some seemed by the standards of the 1920s, were not adequate to the dimensions of the crisis. Moreover, the president flatly refused to meet two widespread demands. First, he opposed currency inflation. Second, he fought all direct, federal unemployment-relief measures. Either of these actions, he sincerely believed, would have grave effects on American tradition and character.

As the plight of the unemployed became desperate, Hoover was wrongly perceived as heartless by the public. By 1932, dejection, apathy, and bad luck seemed to have destroyed the administration's earlier vigor. In that year, a "Bonus Army" of unemployed servicemen assembled in Washington to demand immediate cash payoff of 20-year insurance policies provided for World War veterans by legislation in 1924. Panicking at a minor threat to order, the administration directed the U.S. Army to destroy the veterans' camp with tanks and tear gas. This episode helped to make Hoover, a sensitive man, the worst-hated president since Cleveland. Although not without personal warmth and humor in his private life, the public Hoover too often appeared to be a dour and dogmatic technocrat, aloof, uncompassionate, more troubled by falling corporate profits than by soaring unemployment.

Having forecast during the campaign "the day when poverty would be banished from the nation," his name quickly became the byword of personal misfortune and mass suffering. In a matter of months, his reputation collapsed, and the "great humanitarian" of 1928 became the scapegoat of the nation's worst economic disaster. His re-election was obviously unlikely.

Whether through political inexperience or through personality limitations, the hapless president lost the confidence of the nation and never managed to project the jaunty, crowd-winning confidence or the style of easy leadership that endeared his Democratic successor to a generation of Depression-weary voters. Democratic Governor Franklin D. Roosevelt of New York was little known to most of the public. A Hudson River aristocrat from the Democratic branch of his family, he had been influenced by his cousin Theodore as well as by Wilson, whom he had served as assistant secretary of the navy. After a losing campaign for the vice presidency in 1920, Roosevelt had been crippled by poliomyelitis. Though he never again walked unassisted, he recovered his physical strength and resumed his political career. In 1924 and 1928 he supported the presidential campaigns of

Al Smith, and kept his own name before the party's leaders. In 1928, bucking a Republican trend, he was elected governor of New York, where he tackled depression problems with great energy. Although sometimes dismissed during the presidential campaign as an unknown quantity with no particular ideas of his own, Roosevelt's years in Albany had nevertheless been uncommonly fruitful. As governor of the nation's most populous state, he was a champion of social welfare and reform legislation, which included the first state relief agency, social security and labor measures, public works programs, and regional planning. His gubernatorial years had also demonstrated that he was a master of radio, a skilled manipulator of public opinion with a resonant voice and a winning manner.

The trait that the public immediately saw in the Democratic Roosevelt was a gay, unflappable confidence — a welcome opposite to Hoover's dogged gloom. To Roosevelt's critics, his cheerful nonchalance, his willingness to experiment, his tolerance of contradictions, and his impatience with theory meant superficiality and arrogance. To his admirers, however, his flexibility seemed to reflect a bedrock of courage and a genuine humanitarian and religious concern for the underdog. Either way, FDR's energy, his zest for life and leadership, and most of all his infectious optimism were welcomed by a dispirited people.

Nominated by adroit maneuvers in a close Democratic convention, FDR pledged "bold, persistent experimentation" and "a new deal for the American people." Beyond these pledges, his campaign stances were vague and sometimes contradictory. He called for public power development and other progressive reforms, but the Democratic platform promised a 25 percent cut in spending and a balanced budget. Hoover, meanwhile, asked the people to sustain his own battle with the Depression and grimly predicted disaster if his opponent won. The result was hardly in doubt; the Roosevelt landslide approximately equaled the Hoover victory of 1928.

During the interregnum before the new administration could take over in March 1933, Hoover tried hard to persuade the president-elect to commit himself to a balanced budget, maintenance of the gold standard, and other central Republican policies. Roosevelt committed himself to nothing and was blamed by Republicans for a further economic downturn. In February, the Governor of Michigan announced a bank holiday to prevent financial collapse, and other states followed suit. By inauguration day, all banks were shut, and some cities turned to issuing temporary currency. In the Midwest, farmers resorted to old methods of semiviolent protest against a hopeless situation; milk trucks were overturned and mortgage sales forcibly halted. Unemployed vagrants, many of them boys, were roaming the country. As never before, the stage was set for masterful presidential action.

THE FIRST NEW DEAL

In his arresting inaugural, Roosevelt promised that he would, if necessary, ask for powers to fight the Depression equal to those given presidents in wartime. America's resources were adequate for the task ahead; the only thing it had to fear was "fear itself." Resounding with confidence and vigor, the speech committed the administration to no single course. For a while, nearly all Americans, from bankers to tenant farmers and unemployed, counted on Roosevelt to give them their demands. The New Deal, taking various forms through the next years, is best understood as a continuing experimental response to these demands. Behind each measure demanded by the president lay group pressures, party needs, presidential advisers, and congressional blocs. To understand the New Deal fully, one would have to understand two profound mysteries: American society and Franklin D. Roosevelt.

In the spring of 1933, Congress passed a series of administration measures with unheard-of speed. Roosevelt later summarized his objectives as "Relief, Recovery, and Reform," and this First New Deal can be described in terms of these Three Rs.

Relief for the country's most urgent needs started with legislation to open and sustain the sounder banks, leaving the weaker ones shut. Direct federal help for the unemployed began with the Civilian Conservation Corps (the CCC), which set young men to work on reforestation and other conservation projects. Larger unemployment relief programs included federal grants to states and plans for vast public works. Relief for home and farm owners was the main purpose of further legislation to refinance mortgages.

Recovery of the economy called forth the most spectacular measures of the First New Deal, measures that demonstrated its lack of consistent economic theory. Approaches to recovery included the Economy Act, which reflected the traditional belief that government spending somehow caused economic decline; the Trade Agreements Act, which gave the president power to negotiate low-tariff agreements in order to revive foreign trade; and even the Beer and Wine Revenue Act, which legalized one promising industry. (By year's end the Twenty-first Amendment swept away Prohibition completely.) The most important recovery programs of the First New Deal, however, relied on two main methods: first, raising prices by restricting output and controlling competition; and second, inflating the dollar, now irresistibly demanded by western Democrats.

During the campaign, Roosevelt and some of his advisers had declared that the expansion of the American economy, like that of the frontier, was finished. In the future, better distribution and planned production would replace violent competition. This theory owed something to Herbert Croly and the Bull Moose movement and something to Herbert Hoover and the trade associations of the 1920s. The ambitious National Industrial Recovery Act (NIRA) gave industry the legal right to agree on binding codes of common practice. These codes would, it was hoped, end sharp practices, unfair treatment of labor, and unjust, below-cost cuts in prices. How much they would permit prices to *rise* was never clearly settled. To make such agreements possible, the antitrust laws were suspended. To compensate for this favor to industry, workers were promised in the famous Section 7A of the NIRA the right "to organize and bargain collectively through representatives of their own choosing . . . free from the interference, restraint, or coercion of employers. . . ."

Reflecting a somewhat similar purpose, the Agricultural Adjustment Act (AAA) of 1933 sought primarily to raise farm prices by many complex methods. Its most striking feature was a system of subsidies to be given farmers who agreed to decrease production. Such payments were to be financed by taxes on the industries that processed agricultural products.

Inflation, the other principal recovery device, was provided for in an amendment to the AAA, sponsored by Senator Elmer Thomas of Oklahoma, who remembered Bryan's crusade against gold. The Thomas Amendment gave the president power to inflate the currency in many ways. Moving reluctantly at first, Roosevelt took the dollar off gold, sanctioned special measures to support the price of silver, and eventually stabilized the currency at about 60 percent of its former value.

Reform — that is, deliberate effort to render the social system more just or humane and preclude future depressions — could be seen in the new programs to regulate stock exchanges and investment banking, in the labor clause of the NIRA, and, most clearly of all, in the Tennessee Valley Authority (TVA). This daring project, bringing to fruition the long frustrated dreams of Senator Norris and other progressives, was designed to remodel a whole river system by building a series of dams. Among its objectives were cheap power and fertilizer, flood control, soil and forest conservation, the improvement of inland waterways, and new recreational areas. Reform and recovery were both objectives of the National Housing Act of 1934, which provided insurance of loans to promote repair and modernization of homes, farms, and small plants.

NEW DEMANDS AND A SECOND NEW DEAL, 1934–1936

Through these and other laws, the First New Deal seemed to have scored a qualified success. Its first actions brought a sharp rise in production and prices. Then the rate of recovery slowed, and people realized that the Depression had not disappeared. The elections of 1934, increasing the already large Democratic majorities, showed clearly that a majority approved the administration's efforts. But more was needed; the First New Deal had brought to light a whole series of new demands.

Farmers had benefited from price rises but were still distressed. Some of them had been disturbed by the destruction of crops and animals undertaken as an emergency measure in time of surplus. Then in 1934, the worst drought in the nation's history threatened to change surplus to shortage. Thousands of tenants and sharecroppers were driven from the land and left destitute. In part caused by the drought, this hardship also seemed in part to be caused by the AAA, which encouraged landlords to mechanize and cut acreage. So far, it seemed to many angry small farmers, the New Deal farm program had most helped the richest.

The unemployed demanded faster relief than was provided by the cautious handling of public works. Organized labor, which had reached a low point in 1933, took new courage from Section 7A with its guarantees of freedom to organize. But as new millions rushed into the ill-prepared unions, problems arose. Employers, many of them still hostile to "outside" organizations, thought that Section 7A had authorized them to form more or less docile company unions. Workers insisted that only national organizations could be effective. The National Labor Board, formed by the president to arbitrate multiplying controversies, lacked both authority and consistent policy.

Business and industry, at first eager for New Deal help and willing to promise drastic reform, had become restless with partial recovery. Despite gains made through NIRA codes, many business leaders resented excessive government interference in the details of their operations. Some hoped to exclude the government altogether and to make the program into one of simple business self-regulation on the Hoover pattern. On the other hand, progressives were charging that big business already dominated the codes and gouged consumers. Worried liberals, looking both at NIRA and AAA, doubted whether raising prices and cutting production were the best answers to widespread scarcity.

Thus the administration, which had tried to please everybody, found itself attacked from right and left. Conservatives looked back with nostalgia at the probusiness policies of the Republican years or lamented the end of laissez-faire and traditional individualism. Just below the surface of some fervent complaints ran an undercurrent of fear that the balance of power in the country was shifting away from those who ought to be in charge, in the direction of the shiftless, the irresponsible, and the foreign born. Not a few outraged citizens concluded, with no foundation in fact, that the whole New Deal was a socialist conspiracy against free enterprise, sound money, and American tradition.

At the other extreme, the tiny Communist party of the United States had made some progress. It was aided in 1935 by a sharp change in the international communist line. Instead of denouncing all non-communist efforts at reform as insipid and useless, communists were now to call for a "United Front" and to make every effort to work with "progressives" and "anti-Fascists." During the period from 1935 to 1939, while this line endured, the communist movement achieved some influence among American intellectuals and among some elements of labor. More important than actual communist gains, which remained numerically small, was the conviction, or half-conviction, fairly widespread among intellectuals, that capitalism could not recover.

Still more important in practical politics was the rapid spread of economic panaceas. Most of these appealed, as in the past, to disgruntled rural and small town people, and most involved a combination of currency tinkering and old-fashioned anti–big-business rhetoric. Among them were the Townsend Plan for liberal old-age pensions; the inflationary suggestions of Father Coughlin, the radio priest who denounced international bankers in speeches having anti-Semitic overtones; the sweeping production-for-use plan of Upton Sinclair in California; and the glittering, enticing "Every Man a King" proposal of Huey P. Long, a talented, ruthless spokesman of the dispossessed, who became governor and near-dictator of Louisiana. All these plans, however illusory, gained their strength from two undeniable truths. First, the richest country in the world had too many poor people. Second, the New Deal had not yet produced a convincing remedy.

Disappointed by the bitter response of the wealthy (his own class) and concerned by these threats from the left, the president backed a new set of measures. This Second New Deal, often seen as more liberal than the first, was not aimed at systematic alteration of the economic or social system. Indeed, one important group of the new young advisers who prepared it were under the influence of Louis D. Brandeis, who had helped to prepare Woodrow Wilson's "New Freedom" program and had imbued his followers with a dislike of bigness and a fervent belief in competition and diversity. The Second New Deal contained no measures aimed at economic planning or direct regulation of business on the NIRA scale, and none whose objectives were as sweeping as those of the TVA. Its main object, like that of its predecessor, was to get the economy going and to correct in the process some obvious injustices. Some measures had the further, highly traditional purpose of breaking up concentrations of power.

The new measures were sometimes proclaimed in combative tones. Often they were carried through with hard-boiled political efficiency. Obviously, some of them reflected the demands of newly articulate groups. It is not surprising that members of the business community, remembering the placid 1920s, were both resentful and alarmed. To many young people and to believers in social experiment, on the other hand, the Second New Deal brought a time of excitement, when almost any goal seemed possible and almost any method worth a try.

In the sphere of unemployment relief, the administration committed itself to the conservative principle of providing work rather than welfare. A special agency, the National Youth Administration, provided jobs for unemployed youths and assisted students to stay in college. The Second New Deal's principal relief agency was the gigantic Works Progress Administration (WPA) led by former social worker Harry Hopkins, a devoted, self-sacrificing, and sometimes imperious New Dealer. The army of WPA workers built roads, schools, parks, and countless other projects. In addition to construction work, the WPA offered different kinds of employment for actors, painters, musicians, and writers. Astounded conservatives and delighted liberals found the government sponsoring symphony concerts, excellent guidebooks, colossal murals of varying quality, and theatrical productions — some of the last were experimental, and others left-wing.

Existing farm programs were supplemented by efforts to help the poorest, most neglected farmers. The Resettlement Administration tried to move families from submarginal land, and the Rural Electrification Administration brought power lines to areas not served by private utilities.

In the Social Security Act, the United States, entering the field much later than other leading industrial countries, laid the foundations for a system of old-age, unemployment, and disability insurance financed largely by employer and employee contributions. The Revenue Act of 1935, though whittled down in Congress, sharply increased taxes on high incomes, corporations, and estates. The Banking Act of 1935 increased the power of the Federal Reserve Board to buy and sell government securities in the open market for stabilization purposes, and the Public Utility Holding Company Act restricted the practice of piling one company on another in the fashion popular in the late 1920s.

Finally, as the new labor problems became more and more pressing, the president, in 1935, gave his backing to a bill long advocated by Senator Robert F. Wagner of New York. The Wagner Act outlawed employer coercion and support of company unions. Henceforth an employer was required to bargain with the union chosen by a majority of his employees in government-supervised, secret-ballot elections.

Sweeping changes in the size and shape of organized labor were partly a cause and partly an effect of new government policies. Since NIRA days, organizers had turned their attention to the long-unorganized millions in such great industries as steel, automobiles, rubber, and textiles. Inevitably, swelling numbers and this change of direction strained the traditional craft organization of the American Federation of Labor (AFL). Led by John L. Lewis, the colorful and domineering head of the United Mine Workers, a group of rebels formed within the AFL a Committee for Industrial Organization. This group, expelled in November 1935, became in 1938 the independent Congress of Industrial Organizations (CIO).

In a series of hard-fought, sometimes bloody, strikes, the CIO attacked the long-defended bastions of American heavy industry. This time the outcome of labor warfare was a sweeping union victory. Beginning with the surrender of U.S. Steel and General Motors in 1937, America's most powerful corporations were to make agreements with CIO unions. By that year, organized labor had already grown from a Depression low of under 3 million members to more than 7 million, and it was still growing fast.

Not only the size but the nature of the American labor movement was changed. Most of it, unlike the labor movements of other industrial countries, continued to accept the capitalist system of production. (An important faction of the CIO, later to be expelled, was under communist influence.) But American labor by the mid-1930s was far more deeply committed to political action to further its social objectives than it had been before.

In 1936 the Republicans, sharply denouncing the New Deal, nominated Alfred M. Landon, the moderately liberal governor of Kansas, to oppose Roosevelt. In a victory that surpassed all but Harding's, Roosevelt got more than 60 percent of the popular vote and carried all states but Maine and Vermont. In this election, the Democrats were supported for the first time by an emerging, powerful, but unstable coalition consisting of labor, most farmers, recent immigrants, blacks, and the South; the Republicans had the support of most people in business. Though this pattern was to vary from election to election with changing circumstances, it would affect American politics for several decades.

DEADLOCK AND A THIRD NEW DEAL,
1937–1938

Despite the resounding election victory in 1936, the New Deal in 1937 and 1938 ran into a series of partial defeats. The first was in its conflict with the Supreme Court; seven of the court's nine members were Republican appointees, four of these unyielding conservatives. In its sessions of 1935 and 1936, the court threatened to dismantle the New Deal, overturning such measures as the NIRA and the AAA. According to a majority of the justices, Congress had unconstitutionally delegated detailed legislative power to administrative agencies and had gravely misinterpreted the taxing power, the interstate commerce clause, and other intentions of the Constitution's framers.

To the president and many advisers, the majority opinions appeared not only unduly narrow but menacing to the whole structure of New Deal reforms. Both the Wagner Labor Relations and the Social Security acts seemed doomed. Determined to make the court more responsive to the popular will, but fearing that a constitutional amendment would take too long, Roosevelt proposed, in February 1937, judiciary reorganization legislation. Under its authority, the court's conservative composition could be altered by the appointment of up to six additional judges, one for each justice over the age of 70. Some people — including Democrats in Congress — were shocked by Roosevelt's "court-packing plan," and many resented his disingenuous plea for greater judicial "efficiency." While argument raged, the court itself shifted unexpectedly to a pro–New Deal tack. A number of important statutes, though similar to those nullified earlier, were suddenly sustained by the court, and one laissez-faire justice retired. As one wag said, this "switch in time saves nine," for it made court reform less pressing. Roosevelt's bill was defeated, but he later claimed, with some justification, that though he had lost the battle, he had won the war. He did eventually appoint eight Supreme Court Justices (including Hugo Black, William Douglas, and Felix Frankfurter), and the Roosevelt court built a distinguished, liberal record in the areas of civil liberties, civil rights, and labor law. The bill, however, was probably FDR's greatest political mistake, for it damaged Democratic unity and impaired his leverage in Congress.

Presidential prestige was further injured by the onset of a new economic recession. In the summer of 1936, production, profits, and wages (though not employment) edged toward the levels of 1929. Apparently this was partly because of large government spending for New Deal purposes and for payment of the veterans' bonus (finally provided by Congress over Roosevelt's veto in 1936). The president, worried about deficits and mounting debt, acted to tighten credit and cut the budget, particularly WPA funds. In the fall, a sudden collapse seemed to bring back conditions of 1932. Farm prices headed down again, unemployment grew, and some critics concluded that the administration had failed to find a solution for the Depression.

Whether this was true or not, the New Deal proved in 1937–1938 that it had not lost its energy. Expenditures were sharply increased for relief, public works, and, under the Wagner-Steagall bill, for public housing. Whereas earlier governmental expenditures had usually been defended only as humanitarian necessities, now spending was advocated partly as a means of inducing recovery. This reflected the increasing influence among economists, in and out of the administration, of the theories of the English economist J. M. Keynes. Keynes argued impressively that in time of depression, deficit spending by government was necessary in order to induce recovery and "prime the pump" of private investment.

Partly to further recovery by breaking up price fixing (a direct reversal of the First New Deal's objective), antitrust prosecutions were vigorously increased. A new Farm Security Administration tried hard to help the tenant farmers and migratory workers, who were still America's most poverty-stricken people. A new AAA sought to raise all farm income by many devices, including new measures for crop restriction and government loans on stored surplus crops. Finally, the Fair Labor Standards Act of June 1938, made possible by the Supreme Court's new attitude, established modest minimum wages and maximum hours for most employees and killed that old and tough enemy of American progressives, child labor. Some innovations of this last New Deal, including compensatory spending and wage regulation, proved to be among the most permanent and substantial changes brought about in the whole period.

THE MEANING OF THE NEW DEAL

The 1938 congressional elections ended the New Deal period. Not only did conservative Republicans gain sharply in the West, but conservative Democrats in the South beat off Roosevelt's daring attempt to defeat them and thereby turn the Democratic party into a clear-cut New Deal organization. Though Roosevelt remained popular and existing New Deal measures remained in effect, further concerted or rapid reform action was impossible. For the next quarter-century, the same conservative coalition was normally to control Congress.

Why did the New Deal lose momentum in 1938? The most obvious reason is that foreign crisis began to draw the country's attention away from domestic reform. But many have blamed the slowdown partly on the program's own shortcomings — particularly its shifting approach to economic problems, its effort to combine incompatible groups of supporters, and its dependence on Roosevelt's personal leadership. Conservatives and radicals heatedly disagree as to whether the New Deal attempted too much or too little. Whatever the reasons for the New Deal's decline, this much is certain: there were still 10 million unemployed persons in 1938. Not until the United

TABLE 14. THE NEW DEAL, 1932–1938

	Labor	Agriculture	Business and industrial recovery	Relief	Reform	Miscellaneous
1932			Reconstruction Finance Corporation established.	Relief and Construction Act. Federal Home Loan Bank Act.		Bonus March. Election of **Roosevelt**.
1933	Section 7A of NIRA. 13 million unemployed.	Agricultural Adjustment Act. Farm Credit Act.	Thomas Amendment to AAA (inflation). Emergency Banking Act. Economy Act. Beer and Wine Revenue Act. Banking Act of 1933 (guaranteed deposits). National Industrial Recovery Act.	Civilian Conservation Corps. Federal Emergency Relief Act. Home Owners Loan Act. Public Works Administration. Civil Works Administration.	Tennessee Valley Authority. Federal Securities Act.	Twenty-First Amendment (Repeal of Prohibition).
1934		Cotton Control Act. Federal Farm Bankruptcy Act.	Gold Reserve Act. Silver Purchase Act. Trade Agreement Act (reciprocal trade treaties).	Civil Works Emergency Relief Act.	Securities Exchange Act. National Housing Act.	Johnson Act.

	Labor	Agriculture	Business and industrial recovery	Relief	Reform	Miscellaneous
1935	National Labor Relations (Wagner) Act.	Resettlement Administration. Relief Electrification Administration.		Works Progress Administration and National Youth Administration.	Banking Act of 1935. Social Security Act. Public Utility Holding Company Act. Revenue Act (wealth tax).	First Neutrality Act.
1936		Soil Conservation and Domestic Allotment Act.				Neutrality Act extended. Soldier's Bonus. **Roosevelt** re-elected.
1937		Farm Security Administration. 7.5 million unemployed.		Business recession begins.	Court Reorganization Bill (not passed). Wagner-Steagall Housing Act.	Neutrality Act revised. Depression (fall).
1938	Fair Labor Standards Act.	Agriculture Adjustment Act of 1938. 10.4 million unemployed.				Billion dollar naval expansion. Republican gains in Congress.

States mobilized for World War II would it emerge from the Depression. Though the Roosevelt administration did not fully solve the problems of modern industrial society, it was not alone. No other nation completely succeeded, and several, including Germany and Italy, abandoned their liberties in the process of trying.

In retrospect, though Republicans and conservative Democrats still decry Roosevelt's "radical innovations," the New Deal seems notable for its essential conservatism. The administration clearly had no quarrel with the wage system, wealth and profits, or private property. Roosevelt addressed the worst American crisis since the Civil War, as he said, from the perspective merely of "a Christian and a democrat." Under the New Deal dispensation, the harsher edges of the nation's political and economic system were softened. If democratic capitalism was not precisely saved, it was surely revitalized. While much of the world was turning to collectivism either of the extreme right or extreme left, Roosevelt steered a middle course. Without upheaval, without even major constitutional change, the government under his leadership ameliorated the effects of the Depression and assumed major responsibilities not just for the welfare of business but for the general public's welfare. The significance of the New Deal years is to be found not in the success or failure of particular policies or programs, but in a revival of creativity, confidence, and hope — qualities sorely needed in the decades ahead.

CONFLICTING HISTORICAL VIEWPOINTS: NO. 13

How New Was the New Deal?

To many conservative observers, the New Deal was a destructive experiment in socialism. Al Smith angrily denounced the "Brain-Trusters" as Marxists in Jeffersonian clothing, and Herbert Hoover shuddered when he contemplated the horrors of "New Deal collectivism." Yet, with the exception of Edgar Robinson — whose deprecatory The Roosevelt Leadership *(1955) is read largely for its novelty — this contemporary judgment has found no support among historians. Whatever else it was, scholars generally agreed, the New Deal was not socialism. Richard Hofstadter* (Age of Reform, *1955) called it the "New Departure" and Carl Degler* (Out of Our Past, *1959) termed it the "Third American Revolution." They both agreed that the New Deal departed in fundamental ways from the American reform tradition, but neither viewed it as particularly radical or dangerous. The New Deal was something of a break with the past, these liberal scholars argued, but it was also an essentially constructive and healthy response to the challenge of the Great Depression.*

The argument for benign discontinuity was widely, although not universally, accepted. Many distinguished historians, including Arthur Link, Henry Steele Commager, and Eric Goldman, believed that Roosevelt's programs evolved naturally from traditional American reform impulses. In

Rendezvous with Destiny *(1952), Goldman discovered the New Deal's antecedents in the ideas and policies of Theodore Roosevelt, Woodrow Wilson, and even Herbert Hoover. The roots of the New Deal, he concluded, were firmly fixed in the soil of traditional American values.*

Although once heatedly debated, the revolution-evolution controversy is no longer an issue dividing the scholarly community. In recent years, historians have worried less about the origins of the New Deal and more about its effectiveness. Liberal sympathizers, most notably Arthur M. Schlesinger, Jr., have cast the Roosevelt administration in a most favorable light. Sharply contrasting New Deal dynamism with the static "Old Order," Schlesinger's brilliant Age of Roosevelt *(3 vols., 1957–60) portrayed FDR as a commonsense democrat who spurned "dogmatic absolutes" and sought a middle way between the extremes of "chaos and tyranny," laissez faire and collectivism. Other liberal scholars, including James MacGregor Burns* (Roosevelt: The Lion and the Fox, *1956) and William E. Leuchtenburg* (Franklin D. Roosevelt and the New Deal, *1963), however, were less laudatory. Although generally favorable, Leuchtenburg focused on the limited effects of New Deal recovery and reform measures; Burns, though not without sympathy for Roosevelt, faulted the Democratic president for failing to embrace Keynesian economics and to recast his party as the party of reform.*

More recently, radical scholars offered vastly more damning analyses. Such New Left scholars as Howard Zinn (ed., New Deal Thought, *1966) and Barton J. Bernstein (ed.,* Towards a New Past, *1967) attempted to expose the poverty of the New Deal imagination and the essential conservatism of its leadership. In their view, Roosevelt was the creature of corporate capitalism; he failed to solve the problems of the Depression, and he made no effort to create an equitable society.*

The radical interpretation has won much support among younger historians who find little that was bold or innovative in the New Deal record. Many older scholars, however, have attacked the New Left for measuring the past with the yardstick of the present.

FOR FURTHER READING

President Hoover's revealing *Memoirs* (3 vols., 1951–1952) describe his own administration well and comment without admiration on the policies of his successor. Arthur M. Schlesinger, Jr., in *The Crisis of the Old Order* (1957) provides an unflattering portrait of Republican leadership from a liberal Democratic point of view. The more sympathetic studies of Harris Gaylord Warren (*Herbert Hoover*, 1967), Joan Hoff Wilson (*Herbert Hoover*, 1975), and David Burner (*Herbert Hoover*, 1978), reflect an emerging revisionist consensus on the first Depression president. The 1929 debacle and the onset of depression are illuminated by John Kenneth Galbraith in *The Great Crash* (1954) and by Peter Temin in *Did Monetary Forces Cause the Great Depression?* (1976). *The Bonus March* (1971) is analyzed by Roger Daniels;

Hoover's long lame-duck period is the subject of Jordan A. Schwarz in *The Interregnum of Despair* (1970).

The Roosevelt literature is exceptionally full. Frank Freidel's *Launching of the New Deal* (1973), the fourth and latest volume in his multivolume *Franklin D. Roosevelt* (1952–) is indispensable for the early years of FDR's leadership. It should be supplemented with the more comprehensive studies by Burns, Leuchtenburg, and Schlesinger. Some of the most interesting and contradictory works are those by FDR's contemporaries. Compare, for example, Frances Perkins's *The Roosevelt I Knew* (1948) and Raymond Moley's *After Seven Years* (1939). Lyle W. Dorsett in *Franklin D. Roosevelt and the City Bosses* (1977) considers the impact of New Deal welfare programs upon urban machine politics. Dixon Wecter's *The Age of the Great Depression* (1948) is an introduction to the period's fascinating social history. Studs Terkel's *Hard Times* (1970) contains many personal accounts. Of an enormous literature on American Marxism in the 1930s, one of the most readable and understanding accounts is Murray Kempton's *Part of Our Time* (1955). In *Turbulent Years* (1970), Irving Bernstein writes brilliantly of the labor movement; in *American Welfare Capitalism, 1880–1940* (1976), Stuart D. Brandes briefly considers an important facet of corporate union-busting; and in *Cry from the Cotton* (1971), Donald Grubbs focuses sympathetically on southern tenant farmers. Harvard Sitkoff describes *A New Deal for Blacks* (1978); Abraham Hoffman analyzes the world of the *Unwanted Mexican-Americans in the Great Depression* (1974); and the impact of the depression on women is assessed by William H. Chafe in *The American Woman* (1972) and by Winifred Wandersee in *Women's Work and Family Values* (1981). Aspects of the era's intellectual history are detailed by C. C. Alexander in *Nationalism in American Thought, 1930–1945* (1969), and by Arthur A. Ekirch, Jr., in *Ideologies and Utopias* (1969). Otis L. Graham, Jr.'s *An Encore for Reform* (1967) is a sensitive examination of the relation between the New Deal and the Progressive Era.

26

★ ★ ★ ★ ★ ★

The Reversal of Foreign Policy, 1931–1941

DURING MOST of the 1930s, American attention was centered on domestic problems. Yet foreign events, occurring in the same period, were to affect the United States even more profoundly than the New Deal. The fragile international order established at Versailles and propped by prosperity broke down. Aggressive military states threatened to dominate Europe and Asia. To meet this challenge, America moved from relative disarmament to colossal military power, and American opinion swung from an extreme of isolationism to unprecedented acceptance of worldwide commitment. This commitment was to prove permanent, and under its stress American tradition and society were to be profoundly altered.

THE BREAKDOWN OF ORDER, 1931–1933

When Hoover took office, he intended to carry on, with only slight revision, the foreign policies of the New Era. More internationalist in outlook than Coolidge, he carried much further the policy begun under Coolidge of substituting conciliation for intervention in Latin America. Cautiously, the Hoover administration moved closer to cooperation with the League of Nations. In any efforts to preserve world peace, however, he was determined to stick to noncoercive political or economic methods. At the London Conference of 1930, the administration worked hard, with some success, to reduce further naval armament according to the pattern set by the Washington Conference of 1921. This was the last victory for disarmament. The effort to limit land armies at Geneva in 1932–1933 resulted in complete failure. By that time, the very idea of arms limitation was rejected by several powerful states.

The Versailles order in Europe had always been unstable. With American power withdrawn, France and England confronted fascist Italy, the Soviet

347

Union, and defeated, unstable Germany. If these discontented powers were to be united and armed, their strength could outweigh that of the defenders of the status quo.

In the late 1920s, the Central European order was upheld to some extent by American investment. In 1931, partly because of the withdrawal of American funds, a major Austrian bank failed, and panic threatened to spread to Germany. To prevent further collapse, Hoover suggested a one-year suspension of payments of both German war reparations and Allied debts to the United States. After a damaging delay caused by French suspicions, this "Hoover moratorium" was accepted. Frightened by the growing power of the aggressive Hitler movement in Germany, the Western Allies finally, in 1932, agreed to cancel almost all reparations — but they were too late to save the German Republic. The United States refused to cancel war debts in a parallel manner. While most countries paid the first installments due after the end of the moratorium, these were, in most cases, the last payments made.

In 1931, Britain, the home of laissez-faire economics, found it necessary to abandon the gold standard for a managed currency, and many other countries promptly followed suit. Hoping to restore currency stability, the United States helped plan a World Economic Conference that would give first priority to stabilizing the international monetary exchange rate.

The most dramatic collapse of international order occurred in the Far East. Since the Washington Conference, Japan had been ruled by conservative cabinets, and American-Japanese relations had been relatively good. The Japanese military leaders, however, were becoming increasingly angry at arms limitation and civilian control. Since Theodore Roosevelt's Treaty of Portsmouth, Japan had possessed railroad and port rights in Manchuria, where many Japanese saw an opportunity to acquire raw materials and living space. In 1931, taking advantage of incidents in Manchuria produced by rising Chinese nationalism, the Japanese army embarked on a program of conquest in this vast, nominally Chinese region. This action, carried out apparently against the will of the civilian government in Tokyo, violated not only the League Covenant but also the Republican party's security structure, consisting of the Washington Nine-Power Treaty and the Kellogg Peace Pact. The Open Door and Chinese integrity, moreover, were part of Republican tradition.

Thus Hoover had to act, but once more American commitments in the Far East outran American power. Furthermore, the deepest beliefs of the Quaker president ruled out either military reprisal or cooperation with the League in economic sanctions. In addition, England, whose collaboration would have been necessary for effective action, had no wish to provoke Japanese threats to its own huge Asian holdings. Resorting to purely moral force, Secretary of State Henry L. Stimson announced that the United States would not recognize any situation brought about by force in violation of the Open Door or Chinese integrity. After much hesitation, the League took a somewhat similar stand, advising its members not to recognize the Japanese puppet state of Manchukuo. Neither the so-called Stimson Non-

Recognition Doctrine nor world disapproval deterred Japan in Manchuria, although Japan did withdraw from a brief military occupation of Shanghai undertaken in 1932 in retaliation for a Chinese boycott. At the same time, despite Hoover's abhorrence of coercive international action, the United States had become further involved in the defense of the crumbling international order.

THE NEW DEAL AND THE WORLD,
1933–1937

In the first years of the New Deal, American isolationism reached its peak. To the disillusion of the 1920s was added the new disillusion of the Depression. A host of plays, movies, and novels depicted the horrors of war, and in 1935 a Senate investigation seemed to show that munition makers caused most wars for the sake of sordid profits. Many Americans believed that European propagandists had made a sucker of the United States in 1917 and were trying to do it again. At the same time, former American allies were defaulting on their obligations and finding it difficult to sustain their own League of Nations. (Throughout the decade, European appeasement and American isolationism were called on to justify each other.)

Traditional suspicion of Europe was only one of a number of components, all powerful and some mutually contradictory, of the isolationist frame of mind. Many young people were deeply affected by pacifism, and some liberals wanted to concentrate on building a good society at home. On the other hand, conservatives were suspicious of foreign threats to American tradition. Many Midwesterners and most Irish-Americans maintained their historic suspicion of British imperialism.

As Japanese expansion slowed down to assimilate its gains, American-Japanese relations seemed to improve. And though nearly all Americans disliked the brutal Hitler regime that took power in Germany in 1933, few proposed to do anything about it.

In the early years of the New Deal, Roosevelt failed to challenge the dominant isolationist creed, though as a follower of his cousin Theodore and Wilson, he could hardly accept it. He was primarily concerned with getting his program of national economic reform through Congress and into action, and he badly needed the support of midwestern isolationist progressives. Therefore, he refrained from opposing such measures as the Johnson Act of 1934, which forbade loans to nations in default.

In cooperation with some isolationists or continentalists, Roosevelt supported a modest program of naval building and continued the program of improving relations with Latin America. The nonintervention policy was restated and backed in practice by abandonment of the direct right of intervention in Panama and Cuba. But when the nationalist and moderately radical government of Ramon Grau San Martin came to power in Cuba in 1933, Washington, thinking that government "too radical," withheld recognition and encouraged its overthrow by an army sergeant, Fulgencio Batista, in

1934. Batista remained the strong man of Cuba until overthrown in 1959 by Fidel Castro. In 1938 the expropriation of all foreign-owned petroleum company properties by Mexico was accepted, after much bitter opposition by the oil magnates, and compensation agreed upon. At the Inter-American Conference in 1936, intervention by one state in the affairs of another was condemned, and mutual consultation provided for in case of threats to the peace of the hemisphere. This Good Neighbor Policy, though it by no means ended all Latin American suspicion of the United States, was to produce good results in wartime when most Latin American countries were to be first friendly neutrals and then allies.

In economic matters, the main drive of the early New Deal was nationalistic. In order to save his own program of raising prices through currency inflation, Roosevelt abruptly reversed his early approval of exchange stabilization and, in so doing, broke up the World Economic Conference in London. On the other hand, Cordell Hull, the new secretary of state, had a deep southern-Democratic belief in lower tariffs, and Roosevelt succeeded in getting congressional backing for the Hull program. From 1934 on, the administration negotiated mutual tariff reductions through reciprocal trade treaties. Hope for a revival of international trade was also involved in Roosevelt's decision in 1933 to recognize Soviet Russia. This action, long prevented by ideological hostility, was supported by political realists and business leaders who prophesied (mistakenly) a major expansion of Russian-American trade.

American isolationist policies were little changed by the new challenges to world order that occurred in the mid-1930s. In 1935, Mussolini's Italy invaded Ethiopia, and in the same year Adolf Hitler felt strong enough to remilitarize Germany in defiance of the Versailles Treaty. In the next year, German troops marched into the Rhineland where the same treaty prohibited their presence. In July 1936, Francisco Franco opened a Fascist rebellion against the republican government of Spain, and in 1936–1937 the Berlin-Rome-Tokyo Axis united the major dissatisfied, essentially aggressive states. All these actions were dealt with ineffectually by the Western European powers. In the Ethiopian affair, the League invoked only half-hearted sanctions, England condoned German rearmament in a naval treaty, and western countries, through a policy of nonintervention, denied munitions to the Spanish government. Turning increasingly to the left, that government got some aid from Russia, while the Spanish rebels were more effectively supported by Germany and Italy.

American policy toward these crises was dominated by a determination to keep out of war rather than to keep war from occurring. The neutrality legislation of 1935–1937 was designed to prevent the particular kinds of mistakes that were believed to have drawn America into World War I. The first neutrality law, passed in 1935, forbade arms shipments to all belligerents, rejecting an administration wish to discriminate between aggressor and victim. In the Ethiopian crisis, this was supplemented by a "moral embargo" on oil, the commodity most needed by Mussolini. American refusal to take stronger action gave an excuse for the League to refuse an outright oil embargo. The second neutrality law (1936) forbade loans to belligerents. In 1937 a congressional resolution, requested by the president, extended the application of the neutrality system from international war to the Civil War in Spain; thus, American arms were shut off from the Loyalist government, which helped to ensure Franco's success. Finally, the neutrality law of 1937 made the existing prohibitions permanent and, in addition, forbade American travel on belligerent ships. It also gave the president power, for two years, to list commodities other than munitions that belligerents would be required to pay for and transport in their own ships (the cash-and-carry provision). Thus the United States had reversed the policies of Woodrow Wilson. Neutral rights were waived in order to stay out of war. It seemed clear to the aggressive nations that they had little to fear from American counteraction, as long as America itself was not attacked.

DEEPENING CRISIS AND CAUTIOUS CHANGE IN POLICY, 1937–1939

Once more, a shift in American policy was brought on by events in Asia, not Europe. Japan, which had continued to press from Manchuria into North China until 1933, made a truce in that year. In 1937, fighting broke out again near the Beijing-Tientsin railway for which Japan had certain treaty privileges. Since the ensuing war, though full-scale, was undeclared, the American neutrality legislation was not automatically applied. Partly in order not to cut off arms to China, and partly to keep some anti-Japanese action in reserve, Roosevelt refrained from invoking the neutrality laws, and America shipped some war materials to each belligerent. However, in October 1937, Roosevelt expressed his feelings about Japanese action with new vigor. Referring to a "spreading epidemic of world lawlessness," he suggested that aggressors be "quarantined."

Alarmed isolationist reaction made it plain to the president that he had moved beyond public opinion. The United States joined in the League of Nations' condemnation of Japanese action but opposed sanctions. In December, when Japanese planes sank the American gunboat *Panay* on the Chiang Jiang Zangbo (Yangtze River) in China, apologies were accepted without much excitement. Once more, world disapproval without action failed to deter Japan, and its forces proceeded to bomb and occupy the principal Chinese cities. By 1938, it had set up a puppet government in China and committed itself fatefully to the establishment of a New Order in East Asia.

Lacking a clear European policy, the United States played only a minor role in the major European events of this period, periodically and fruitlessly appealing for moderation and conciliation. In 1938, Hitler absorbed Austria and began threatening Czechoslovakia. This led to the Munich Agreement among Britain, France, Italy, and Germany, which forced Czechoslovakia to surrender certain strategic frontier districts inhabited by German-speaking people. This settlement was brutally nullified in March 1939 when Hitler took over the rest of Czechoslovakia. During the same spring, Italy invaded

Albania, while Hitler seized the Lithuanian town of Memel and unmistakably began threatening Poland. This time, however, Britain and France promised to aid the prospective victim, and it became evident that major war was imminent.

Roosevelt, who shared this opinion, believed also that Britain and France could win with American material help. He therefore called for a cautious and moderate program of rearmament, mainly on the basis of continental naval and air defense. He also asked Congress to repeal the arms embargo to make it possible for belligerents to buy American munitions on a cash-and-carry basis. Though most press opinion favored this action, it was defeated by isolationists in Congress. This was to be their last major victory.

In the summer of 1939, while Britain and France were making a half-hearted effort to make a defensive alliance with Russia, Stalin instead suddenly concluded pacts of trade and nonaggression with Hitler. This apparently left Germany free to attack Poland without becoming involved in a major two-front war, and on September 1, Hitler's troops crossed the Polish frontier. France and England, this time, declared war as they had promised. Poland, destined to be the most tragic victim of World War II, was quickly overrun. As German troops advanced through western Poland, Russian troops occupied the eastern part of the country.

With war a reality, Roosevelt was able (in November 1939) to prevail on Congress to repeal the arms embargo and place shipments of both munitions and other commodities on a cash-and-carry basis. Once more, as in 1914, the Western Allies were free to come and get American arms, provided that they could pay cash and provide shipping. This seemed enough to assure western victory without further American commitment. Most observers predicted that the major belligerents would settle into a long stalemate, confronting each other across "impregnable" French Maginot and German Siegfried lines.

CATASTROPHE AND THE END OF NEUTRALITY, 1940–1941

In the spring of 1940, the stalemate war came to a sudden end as the Germans conquered first Denmark and Norway and then the Low Countries. In a lightning assault from Belgium, mobile German units poured into France and in a month had crushed and demoralized the French army, supposed by many to be the world's strongest. It seemed impossible to resist the new German combination of parachutists, dive-bombers, and tanks. On June 22, France surrendered. The Germans occupied half the country, leaving the collaborationist government at Vichy in charge of the rest.

Thinking he had won his war, Hitler hoped that England would make a compromise peace. Instead, though isolated and almost without land armament, the British replaced ineffective Neville Chamberlain with Winston Churchill as prime minister. He announced his determination not only to resist but ultimately to destroy the Nazi regime. In the air battle of Britain, though British cities were heavily bombed, the Royal Air Force defeated the German effort to clear the way for invasion. It began to seem possible once more that American support might sustain England, and many Americans wanted to do this at all costs. Others, however, insisted that the most important objective still was to keep America out of war.

In the ensuing foreign policy argument, one of the most important in American history, both sides were made up of diverse elements. On the anti-interventionist side with the traditional midwestern isolationists were: Anglophobes, including many Irish-Americans; people who thought Britain's cause hopeless; pacifists; young people who had heard with horror about the intolerance and hate generated by World War I; middle-aged people who had shared the postwar disillusionment; progressive reformers reluctant to give up domestic objectives; and some, but not by any means all, of those who disliked Roosevelt because of his domestic policies. This diverse coalition was supported by the small group influenced by the Communist party, which had supported collective security until 1939 and was to support war after 1941, but which was isolationist during the two years of the German-Soviet alliance. Those who favored drastic action in support of Britain included, as in 1914, many influential Americans conscious of deep ties to British culture. These were joined by those who were outraged by atrocity stories, this time true, about Nazi barbarism. Most important, perhaps, were the increasing numbers who felt that American security would be seriously threatened by Nazi control of the Atlantic.

Most Americans, probably, were neither isolationists nor outright interventionists. Most wanted to help Britain and also to stay out of the war. The decisive question was which of these last objectives was the more important. Before the fall of France, opinion polls seemed to show that most Americans wanted first of all to keep out of war. After it, the majority gradually shifted; most concluded that British survival came first. This decision, however, was neither universal nor clear-cut, and the administration did not help to clarify the choice.

Insofar as one can understand Roosevelt's policy, he appeared by no means neutral in his sympathies and clearly wanted to contribute as much material aid as possible to Britain. This policy, he said, would keep America out of war. At first, he doubtless believed that this *would* be so, and until very late he hoped that it *might* be the case. Always conscious of the dangers of hostile public reaction, and once more desperately anxious to put over his program, he continued to say that America would stay out of war when he must have known that this was no longer certain. Whether a franker policy would have had better results, either at the time or in the long run, will long be debated.

The steps taken by the administration and approved by a majority of Congress and public opinion, were drastic enough. In May, Roosevelt called for increased defense appropriations and for airplane production of 50,000 a year. At Charlottesville, Virginia, on June 10, he promised continued material help to "opponents of force." In September, by executive agreements, he traded 50 over-age destroyers, desperately needed by Britain, for defense bases in British Western Hemisphere possessions. In the same month, Congress adopted the first peacetime conscription law in American history.

In the fall of 1940, foreign policy argument was channeled into an election campaign. Because of the national emergency, the Democrats broke the anti–third-term tradition to renominate Roosevelt. His opponent Wendell Willkie, though a utility company president who had fought TVA, was a representative of the liberal wing of the Republican party. Accepting much of the New Deal, Willkie attacked mismanagement and bureaucracy. Since Willkie accepted the necessity of aiding Britain and since both candidates promised that America would stay out of actual foreign war, there was little difference on foreign policy. In the closest victory of his presidential career, Roosevelt got 55 percent of the popular vote.

Once more in office, Roosevelt asked for and got a still more binding commitment to British victory. In March, Congress passed the lend-lease bill, giving the president authority to transfer equipment, rather than money, directly to nations whose defense was vital to that of the United States. In response to urgent appeals from the beleaguered British, munitions were furnished in enormous quantity. In the spring of 1941, British and American staff officers discussed common strategy in the event of American belligerency. In August, Roosevelt and Churchill, meeting at sea, committed themselves to the liberal principles of the Atlantic Charter, promising a free and warless world "after the final destruction of the Nazi tyranny."

Committed to Hitler's defeat, America could not allow its shipments of munitions to be destroyed by the increasingly powerful German submarine offensive. In the summer of 1941, the United States entered into undeclared naval warfare with Germany. American ships reported submarine sightings to the British. American troops occupied Greenland and Iceland, and American ships began convoying British and American shipping to Iceland, half-way across the Atlantic. Sinkings occurred, and in September, Roosevelt denounced German "piracy" and ordered American naval vessels to "shoot on sight."

Meanwhile, the war in Europe had profoundly changed. Unable to knock Britain out of the war before American deliveries became effective, Hitler decided to secure his continental flank. Germany already controlled Hungary, Rumania, and Bulgaria, and in April 1941, its armies conquered Yugoslavia and Greece. Germany's moves toward the East intensified Hitler's growing difficulties with his quasi-ally, Stalin. In June 1941 the Germans invaded the Soviet Union, penetrating so deeply that it looked for some months as if they would win another major victory. Promptly both Churchill and Roosevelt announced that any enemy of Hitler was a friend of theirs, and lend-lease aid to Russia began. While Russian participation stimulated anti-interventionism in some quarters, it reduced it in others. For the first time, it seemed, a coalition existed that could actually destroy the Nazis, and the United States was a member of it in all but actual land fighting.

For some time, Roosevelt had concluded that official American participation in war would be desirable, and a majority of the public had decided, according to the polls, that war would be preferable to British defeat. Hitler, however, was by no means eager to provoke further American intervention and add another great power to his already formidable list of opponents. Once more, the crucial development came from the other side of the world.

WAR WITH JAPAN

In the Far East also, the Hitler breakthrough of 1940 precipitated great changes. To Japan, it seemed to offer a last chance to consolidate her new East Asian order and thereby to end the costly and indecisive "China incident." By moving southward toward the colonies of occupied France and Holland and hard-pressed Britain, Japan could secure needed supplies of oil, rubber, and tin.

So far, Roosevelt, concentrating on the European danger and not eager for involvement on another front, had continued the rather ambiguous U.S. policy toward Japan with one important change. In July 1939 the United States threatened future economic measures by giving a six-months' notice of the abrogation of her 1911 commercial treaty with Japan. In July 1940, sensing that a Japanese forward movement was at hand, the president prohibited the export of some kinds of oil and scrap metal. Later measures tightened this embargo and increased the pressure on Japan to find alternate sources.

In September 1940 the Japanese, with Hitler's diplomatic assistance, forced the Vichy government to concede ports and bases in the northern part of French Indochina. In that same month, Germany, Italy, and Japan signed the Tripartite Pact, forming the Axis alliance and obliging each to help the other in case of attack by any power not now at war. Since a special article excluded Russia, this could mean only the United States.

There were still, however, powerful Japanese who hoped to achieve Japan's goals without war with America. Through much of 1941, the attitudes of both countries were set forth in a series of negotiations. Japan was willing, at most, to refrain from armed aggression in Southeast Asia and even to "interpret" in America's favor the promises of the Tripartite Pact. But to pay for peace in the Far East, even in the event of war with Germany, the United States would have had to restore Japanese-American trade, help Japan to obtain oil supplies from the Netherlands East Indies, and recognize (or at least cease to obstruct) her new order in China. The United States was unwilling to accept these terms and offered instead to restore trade and help Japan gain some of its economic goals provided it gave up its military objectives both in Southeast Asia and China. Once more, the American commitment to the Open Door and Chinese integrity assumed enormous importance.

In July 1941, following Germany's invasion of the USSR, Japanese forces moved into southern Indochina and headed for Malaya and the Dutch East Indies. Roosevelt promptly responded by freezing all Japanese funds in the United States. In August, still hopeful of keeping the United States neutral, Prince Konoye, the Japanese premier, requested a "Pacific Conference" with Roosevelt. Though Konoye suggested the possibility of further important concessions, Roosevelt refused to meet unless there was some preliminary agreement on basic issues. In October, the Konoye government fell, and the new Tojo government prepared for war.

Well before the complex Washington discussions of November 1941, the positions of each side had been made clear, and the two positions had proved incompatible. The American government considered trying to gain time by presenting proposals for a temporary Pacific truce, but decided against this. Knowing that an attack was at hand, the Americans restated for the record their earlier position. On December 7, 1941, Japanese planes attacked and severely crippled the American fleet at Pearl Harbor, in the Hawaiian Islands. The next day, Congress declared war, and three days later Germany and Italy declared war on the United States.

Later, Roosevelt was much criticized, first for not pursuing further the effort for peace with Japan and second for not preventing the Pearl Harbor disaster. It was even argued (though never convincingly) that his real objective was to force Japan to attack the United States and thereby to get America into war with Hitler. A compromise with Japanese ambition, short of surrendering old American commitments and betraying American allies, would probably have been difficult to achieve. It is arguable, however, that a Roosevelt-Konoye meeting might have gained time and, less plausibly, that it might have strengthened the opponents of Japanese militarism. As for the second charge, it seems that by late November 1941 the American government had decided that war was inevitable and that further stalling would be of no use. Roosevelt knew before December 7 that a Japanese movement was actually under way, and warnings were sent to American Pacific bases to that effect. Apparently because an attack was expected farther west, the warnings to Pearl Harbor were insufficiently frequent and emphatic, and defensive action was neglected. Thus a small cloud remained over the official version of the Pearl Harbor incident. At the time, however, the Japanese "sneak attack" united the American people for war as nothing else could have.

FOR FURTHER READING

An able study of *American Diplomacy in the Great Depression* (1957) is offered by Robert H. Ferrell. Lloyd Gardner examines *Economic Aspects of New Deal Diplomacy* (1964). The most formidable attacks on the Roosevelt foreign policy are Charles A. Beard's *President Roosevelt and the Coming of the War* (1948) and C. C. Tansill's *Back Door to War* (1952). Wayne S. Cole, in *Charles A. Lindbergh* (1974) and Thomas C. Kennedy in *Charles A. Beard and American Foreign Policy* (1975) examine the work of two prestigious opponents of American interventionism. Roosevelt is defended by Basil Rauch in *Roosevelt: From Munich to Pearl Harbor* (1950). W. L. Langer and S. E. Gleason's *The Challenge to Isolation, 1937–1940* (1952), and *The Undeclared War, 1940–1941* (1953) are well-documented and informative studies, generally favorable to U.S. policy. Other notable accounts include: Donald Drummond's *The Passing of American Neutrality* (1955); Robert Divine's *The Illusion of Neutrality* (1962); Arnold Offner's *American Appeasement: United States Foreign Policy and Germany* (1969); and Roberta Wohlstetter's *Pearl Harbor: Warning and Decision* (1962). American relations with Japan are assessed by Herbert Feis in *The Road to Pearl Harbor* (1950) and by Paul Schroeder in *The Axis Alliance and Japanese-American Relations, 1941* (1958). Richard Triana examines *American Diplomacy and the Spanish Civil War* (1968); and in *Prelude to Downfall* (1967), Saul Friedlander surveys American relations with Nazi Germany on the eve of war.

27

★ ★ ★ ★ ★ ★

War for the World, 1941–1945

FROM DEFEAT TO VICTORY, 1941–1944

Through the winter and spring of 1941–1942, the United States confronted its most serious challenge since 1861. One headline after another reported successful Japanese invasions: Malaya, Guam, Wake, Hong Kong, Singapore, the Dutch East Indies, Burma, and the Western Aleutians. On May 6, 1942, the last organized American forces in the Philippines surrendered at Corregidor. The New Order in Greater East Asia was almost a fact. Any counteroffensive against Japan, it seemed, would have to conquer concentric rings of islands scattered over vast ocean areas.

Hitler, meanwhile, held firmly the productive power of Western Europe. His first invasion of the Soviet Union was turned back in the winter of 1941–1942 after reaching the outskirts of Moscow. His second, beginning in June 1942, reached deep into the Caucasus Mountains and entered Stalingrad on the Volga River. Britain was threatened with the collapse of her Atlantic supply line. Sinkings mounted after American entry, many of them occurring within sight of American coastal cities. The worst fears of western leaders were that the Soviet Union would collapse and Britain starve long before American power became really effective.

Already Anglo-American staff conferences had decided that the main Allied offensive must be directed against Germany, the more formidable enemy, while a holding action was carried on in the Pacific. But any offensive seemed a long way away, and even a holding action was not immediately apparent.

By summer and fall of 1942, more hopeful news began to appear. Japanese naval power, checked at the Coral Sea in May, was ended as an offensive threat at Midway in June. In August, American troops began a grim and

TABLE 15. WORLD WAR II, 1939–1945

	Diplomatic	Pacific theater	European theater	Home front
1939 — Outbreak	March 14 Germany annexes Czechoslovakia. March 31 Anglo-French pledge to Poland. August 23 German-Russian Pact.		September 1 Germany invades Poland. October 14 Soviet Union invades Finland.	November 4 Neutrality Act of 1939 (cash and carry).
1940 — Disaster	September 3 United States–British "Destroyer Deal." September 27 Japan-Germany-Italy Tripartite Pact.	September 22 Japan gets bases in French Indochina.	April 9 Germany invades Norway, Denmark. May 10 Germany invades Benelux. June 22 German-French armistice. August–September Battle of Britain.	September 16 Selective Service. November 5 Roosevelt defeats Willkie.
1941 — Intervention	July 26 United States freezes Japanese funds. August 14 "Atlantic Charter" statement by Roosevelt and Churchill. November United States–Japanese Washington negotiations.	July 24 Japan occupies French Indochina. December 7 Pearl Harbor.	April Germany invades Greece, Yugoslavia. April–May United States extends protective action in Atlantic. June 22 Germany invades Soviet Union.	March 11 Lend-Lease Act. June Fair Employment Practices Committee. November 17 Neutrality Acts repealed. December 8 Declaration of War.

(Continued on page 360)

TABLE 15. WORLD WAR II continued

	Diplomatic	Pacific theater	European theater	Home front
1942 — Low point	May Molotov in Washington. June Churchill in Washington. August Moscow Conference (Stalin, Churchill, Harriman).	February 15 Singapore surrenders. May 6 Corregidor surrenders. May 7–8 Coral Sea. June 3–6 Midway. August–February Guadalcanal.	January–June German offensive in North Africa. Summer German offensive in Soviet Union. September–February Stalingrad. November 4 El Alamein. November 8 U.S. landings in North Africa.	1942–1945 6 million women enter labor force. January 30 Office of Price Administration established. February–March Japanese-American "relocation." November Republican gains in Congress. December 2 First self-sustaining nuclear reaction (Chicago).
1943 — Allied unity	January 14–24 Casablanca Conference (Roosevelt, Churchill). August 11–24 Quebec Conference (Roosevelt, Churchill). November 22–26 Cairo Conference (Roosevelt, Churchill, Jiang [Chiang]). November 28–December 1 Teheran Conference (Roosevelt, Churchill, Stalin).	Throughout year Allied gains in South Pacific (Solomons, New Guinea). November 21 United States invades Gilberts (Tarawa) (start of central Pacific offensive).	January–May Allied victory in North Africa. July–December Russian offensive. July 10 Sicily invaded. September 9 Italy invaded (Salerno).	November 5 Senate resolution for international organization. Summer Urban race riots.

1944 — Victory in sight	**July 1–22** UN Monetary and Financial Conference (Bretton Woods). **August 21–October 7** Dumbarton Oaks Conference (plans UN). **October 9–18** Second Quebec Conference.	**January 31** Marshalls invaded. **June 18** Marianas invaded. **October 23–25** Philippine Sea. **November 24** Beginning of air attack on Toyko.	**June 6** Normandy invaded. **July 25** St. Lô breakthrough. **September 12** United States enters Germany. **December** "Battle of the Bulge" (German counteroffensive).	United States reaches twice Axis war production G.I. Bill of Rights. **November 7** Roosevelt defeats Dewey.
1945 — The Atomic Age	**Februrary 4–11** Yalta Conference. **April 23–June 26** San Francisco UN Conference. **July 17–August 2** Potsdam Conference (July 26, ultimatum to Japan). **September 2** Japan surrenders.	**February** Manila recaptured. **February–March** Iwo Jima. **April–June** Okinawa. **August 6** Hiroshima. **August 9** Nagasaki. **August 14** V-J Day.	**March 7** Rhine crossed. **April 25** United States and Soviet forces meet on Elbe. **May 8** V-E Day.	**April 12** Roosevelt dies; Truman takes office. **July 16** First atomic bomb exploded, Alamogordo, New Mexico.

bloody offensive in the Solomon Islands. In October, the British stopped the German drive toward Suez at El Alamein; the next month, American forces landed in North Africa and began fighting German troops. In the gigantic battle of Stalingrad, in many ways the turning point of the Second World War, the Russians, while sustaining incredible losses, captured a German army and began the reconquest of the vast territories they had lost.

In 1943, the Allies passed decisively to the offensive. After hard fighting, German forces were cleared from Africa, and in the summer and fall Anglo-American forces invaded Sicily and Italy. Though Mussolini fell from power and Italy surrendered, the Italian dictator escaped, and bitter German resistance formed in central Italy. In the Pacific War, the island-hopping strategy provided the means of American victory. Sea and air power made it possible to isolate and bypass Japanese garrisons; it would not be necessary to reconquer the vast Japanese holdings one by one. Bitter fighting brought control of the Solomons, and in November the battle of Tarawa began the Central Pacific campaign.

By this time, the technique of amphibious warfare was so highly developed that it became possible to land on any hostile shore with sufficient preparation, provided one was willing to accept immense casualties. The crucial difficulty was maintaining a beachhead after landing. This was borne out in June 1944 in the long-awaited landing in Normandy. This attack on the heavily defended French coast, the greatest amphibious operation in history, was seriously endangered by bad weather and stubborn resistance. By the end of July, however, a breakthrough at St. Lô ended the Normandy campaign and opened the campaign of France. American tank units were able to sweep around the defenders as German forces had in 1940. By November most of France and Belgium had been liberated by Anglo-American forces, but in December a fierce counterattack surprised Americans in the Ardennes Forest.

On the eastern front in 1944, the Russians entered Poland, Yugoslavia, Hungary, and even East Prussia. In the Pacific the island-hopping campaign continued through the Marshalls, Marianas, and Carolines. In November, bombers from the Marianas began devastating raids on the Japanese home islands. In the Philippines, American re-entry brought on the greatest naval battle in history at Leyte Gulf, where the remaining power of the Japanese navy was broken. By the end of the year, though much fighting remained in Europe and on the Pacific, victory and the problems of victory were in sight.

THE HOME FRONT

Perhaps the greatest single factor in this victory was American production of ships, tanks, planes, and the infinitely varied tools of modern war. In 1941, only a halting buildup of war production had begun, and shipments to Britain had depleted American supplies. Once more, organizing a democratic capitalist nation for war purposes proved difficult. Despite bureaucratic battles, bottlenecks, and waste, however, the task was handled with imagination and astonishing scale. By 1943, the vast American industrial complex was oriented to the war effort, and by 1944 America was producing twice the total war output of the Axis powers.

This achievement came, moreover, without the extreme measures of coercion urged by experts. There was no single production czar and no draft of labor. Incentives worked better than compulsion. Industrialists received very high rewards in depreciation allowances and government war-plant construction, though corporation profits and high individual incomes were heavily taxed. Business, and especially big business, played a major part in planning; it accepted a partnership with the government as it had in World War I and had not in the New Deal period. Labor, too, cooperated in the war effort. Strikes, much deplored in the press, were few. Labor kept the gains of the New Deal, including a 40-hour week with time and half for overtime. Wages rose rapidly, and unions expanded from 10 million to nearly 15 million members.

War brought prosperity and with it fundamental social change. The mechanism of economic growth, true to Keynesian theory, was government spending on an unprecedented scale. In 1936, the biggest New Deal spending year, a comparatively modest federal outlay of $8 billion had caused much alarm. In 1945, when federal expenditures reached $98 billion, unemployment practically vanished, and the country seemed to reach new levels of production and prosperity. As war industry redistributed the population, the Pacific Coast gained wealth and power. High wages and farm prices, together with war taxes, produced a greater measure of economic equality than ever before.

In a full employment economy, blacks were accepted in jobs previously closed to them. Pressed by A. Phillip Randolph and the March on Washington Movement, Roosevelt created the Fair Employment Practices Commission in a partially successful effort to ensure equal employment opportunities. The military, however, remained rigidly segregated. The one million black men and women in uniform were generally assigned to menial tasks, and (with such signal exceptions as Brigadier General Benjamin O. Davis) Afro-Americans were rarely accepted as officers. Racial ill-will was manifested in riots on military bases, and in bloody riots in 1943 in Harlem, Los Angeles, Mobile, Newark, and other cities. The war brought both black militance and black gains; black leaders promoted the "Double V," victory at home as well as abroad. Many historians now regard these years as the seed-time of the postwar civil rights revolution.

Women, too, entered the war economy in unprecedented numbers, many as clerical workers and many more, in the fashion of Rosie the Riveter, as factory hands. Black women left domestic service for higher paying industrial jobs. Married women with children left home and nursery to join the war effort. Although wartime labor shortages temporarily undercut traditional notions of "woman's place," women war workers were paid less than men, and most were expected to retire "when the boys come home."

Many changes accelerated or begun during the war proved to be permanent. Neither wages, prices, employment, government expenditures, nor taxes were to return to prewar levels. Control of inflation, as well as prevention of depression, became federal responsibilities. In addition to the economy, government became deeply involved in race relations, public information, and the promotion of scientific endeavor. Minorities and women would never again be content with prewar patterns of exclusion and discrimination. Perhaps most fateful of all, the size, political influence, and economic importance of the armed forces in the United States had been enormously and permanently expanded, although few Americans suspected this and that demilitarization would not come with peace.

In politics, the war brought a superficial unity. Since the United States had been attacked, overt opposition to the war was negligible. Startling worldwide commitments seemed to be accepted; and it appeared that isolationism had died at Pearl Harbor. The government under Roosevelt and Attorney General Francis Biddle engaged in few of the Wilson administration's excesses during World War I. Allied to the Soviets, Americans felt less threatened by radicals. German-Americans, Italian-Americans, and even fascist sympathizers generally enjoyed the protection of the Constitution. One national group, however, presents a staggering exception to such tolerance: 117,000 Americans of Japanese ancestry, two-thirds of them citizens of the United States, were interned at the start of hostilities. Responding to white racism and military pressure, the administration moved Japanese-Americans from their West Coast homes — first to temporary, barbed-wire concentration camps and then to isolated "relocation centers" in the interior. Most Japanese-Americans were resettled in the East or Midwest before war's end and some eventually received financial recompense, but an ugly precedent had been set.

If there was less overt opposition and less hysteria than in World War I, there was also less idealistic enthusiasm. The Four Freedoms (freedom from hunger, fear, injustice, and oppression), Henry A. Wallace's glowing picture of a "Century of the Common Man," Wendell Willkie's commitment to "One World" were highly effective in liberal circles. None of these, however, came as close to producing a nationwide response as Wilson's appeal to "make the world safe for democracy." For many Americans, this was less a crusade than (as Roosevelt called it) a "War for Survival."

American opinion, deeply divided in 1941 over both the New Deal and Roosevelt's interventionist foreign policy, was not magically reunited in wartime. But division had to manifest itself in indirect ways — in hostility to the Europe-first policy, resentment of price control, exaggeration of strikes, and (despite much countereffort) criticism of the Allies. Some liberals attacked the government for its tactical compromises with Vichy or alleged tenderness toward the British Empire. A larger group remained deeply suspicious of collaboration with the Soviet Union, and a still larger faction was determined to prevent the postwar survival of the New Deal.

In 1942 the Republicans sharply increased their strength in Congress. In 1944, Roosevelt, like Lincoln, won a wartime election, this time against the rather ineffective opposition of Thomas E. Dewey. In the same year, many arch isolationists lost their seats in Congress. Thus Franklin Roosevelt, again like Lincoln, retained the decision-making power of a wartime president. But for this he paid a price. It was necessary — or so he decided — to postpone discussion not only of important unsettled domestic controversies, but also of some of the thorniest unresolved international problems. The only goal on which all could agree was military victory.

THE GREAT ALLIANCE

In international relations, America did not follow precedents set during World War I. Then the United States had been gingerly cobelligerent; now it was a full-fledged ally, bound to refuse a separate peace. America led in efforts to form a second international organization, and this time public opinion and even the Senate seemed heartily to back the proposal for a new United Nations.

President Roosevelt placed his hopes both for victory and postwar stability on the "Four Policemen": Britain, China, the Soviet Union, and the United States. But only with Britain was full cooperation possible. Similar national traditions, plus the mutual admiration of Roosevelt and Churchill, helped make the Anglo-American war effort the most successful international operation in history. But, despite this closeness, major differences appeared.

The Americans were used to thinking of war in terms of an all-out drive for victory followed by a return to peace and normality. The British had some experience of victory's delusions and costs. Many American leaders were suspicious of British efforts to cling to empire. Above all, Roosevelt and Churchill differed in the later stages of the war over Soviet relations.

In 1942, American political and military leaders demanded an immediate cross-channel invasion of Europe, partly to prevent collapse of the eastern front in the Soviet Union. Churchill accepted the necessity of such an operation in the future, but thought it impossible without further buildup and fought hard for diversionary operations in southern Europe. After 1943, his reasons were partly political: western penetration of the Balkans and Central Europe would prevent Russian domination of these areas. This argument was settled by compromise. To Stalin's chagrin, the Normandy invasion was put off until 1944, while the North African and Italian campaigns represented a partial concession to Churchill's views. A Balkan front was never opened.

Roosevelt's program for making China a great power was a failure because it was based on an illusion. He backed Jiang Jieshi's (Chiang Kai-shek's) Nationalist government, which shared control of the huge country with a well-entrenched Communist movement led by Mao Zedong (Mao Tse-tung). Each side fought the other as well as Japan. Exhausted by the long war, the oppressive Nationalist regime was further weakened by corruption. Neither General Joseph Stilwell nor anybody else could bring about a major Chinese contribution to victory. Yet at Cairo in November 1943, Roosevelt, Churchill, and Jiang agreed that after the war China would get back Manchuria as well as Formosa and the Pescadores. The first of these pledges was largely nullified by the Yalta Agreement, and the second became the source of long-term trouble. No amount of Anglo-American wishing could make a divided China a stable ally.

By far the most difficult relationship was, of course, with the Soviet Union. America began this wartime association with a recent past of deep hostility toward that nation. During the period of the Russo-German Pact, American opinion had been outraged by Soviet moves into eastern Poland and Rumania; by the absorption of the three small Baltic states — Latvia, Lithuania, and Estonia; and, above all, by the Winter War with Finland, which had refused to surrender certain border districts considered by the USSR necessary to its defense. With the German-Soviet break, however, both Roosevelt and Churchill immediately recognized the crucial importance of Russian contributions to the war. To help keep Germany occupied in the east, America sent the Soviet Union lend-lease aid amounting to $11 billion. Temperamentally optimistic and used to thinking in terms of only one opponent at a time, many Americans managed to convince themselves that the USSR had fundamentally changed. Many presumed that the two countries would remain friendly after the war, and that this accord would be the mainstay of world peace. This opinion, many historians once believed, was shared by Roosevelt and his principal advisers, liberal and conservative, civilian and military. Recent research, however, suggests that the administration was less than optimistic about postwar Soviet-American relations.

Through 1943, some success was achieved in shaping common military objectives. Good feeling reached its height in late November 1943, when Roosevelt, Stalin, and Churchill met at Teheran, Iran. There the coming offensive against Hitler was roughly coordinated. It was agreed that German military power must be permanently eliminated, perhaps by division of the country. In Yugoslavia, Allied aid was to go only to Tito, the communist leader of one branch of the underground. Both the eastern and western frontiers of Poland were to be shifted radically to the west. From here on, as Soviet armies penetrated Eastern and Central Europe, postwar control of this area became the principal subject of inter-Allied argument. While fully aware that the USSR's losses entitled it to some security and realistic about its unquestioned power in the area, Churchill wanted to bargain sharply with Stalin. He was willing, for instance, to concede Soviet predominance in Rumania and Bulgaria in return for British predominance in Greece and equality in Yugoslavia and Hungary. Poland presented a harder problem. Russian forces had set up a government in Poland independent of the exile government in London; the latter had contributed large fighting forces to the Allied side, and on its behalf Britain had gone to war. Churchill was willing to put pressure on the London Poles to accept the realities of Soviet power, but he was not willing to recognize the unqualified sovereignty of the Soviet-supported Polish government. He wanted to use Allied bargaining power, including troop dispositions, to secure as favorable a Polish settlement as possible.

Roosevelt was unwilling to concur completely in Churchill's policy of firmness. He too was concerned about Polish freedom and could not ignore the

MAP 8:   THE EUROPEAN WAR

Hitler's Greater Germany
Allied with Germany
Occupied by Germany and its allies
Advances by Allied forces
Major battle

SOVIET UNION
Russian front, Dec. 1941
Stalingrad
Volga R.
CASPIAN SEA
Moscow
L. Ladoga
Leningrad
FINLAND
Helsinki
NORWAY
SWEDEN
Stockholm
BALTIC SEA
DENMARK
Copenhagen
NORTH SEA
GREAT BRITAIN
Battle of Britain (Fall 1940)
London
Dunkirk
English Channel
NORTHERN IRELAND
IRELAND
Invasion of Normandy (June 6, 1944)
NORMANDY
ATLANTIC OCEAN
NETHERLANDS
Amsterdam
Rotterdam
BELGIUM
Bastogne Battle of the Bulge (Dec. 1944)
Sedan
Western front Feb. 1945
FRANCE
Paris
Vichy France (Occupied Nov. 1942)
Vichy
RHÔNE R.
SWITZERLAND
GERMANY
Berlin
POLAND
Warsaw
Posen
Lodz
Russian front Feb. 1943
Kiev
UKRAINE
Riga
CZECHOSLOVAKIA
AUSTRIA
Vienna
HUNGARY
Budapest
ROMANIA
Bucharest
BULGARIA
YUGOSLAVIA
Belgrade
ITALY
Rome
Monte Cassino (May 1944)
Anzio
Salerno (Sept. 1943)
Italian front Feb. 1945
Bologna
SICILY (July 1943)
ALBANIA
GREECE
Athens
CRETE
BLACK SEA
Yalta
TURKEY
Ankara
SYRIA
CYPRUS
LEBANON
PALESTINE (Br. Mandate)
TRANS-JORDAN (Br. Mandate)
Suez Canal
Cairo
Nile R.
EGYPT
Alexandria
El Alamein (Summer 1942)
MEDITERRANEAN SEA
MALTA (Gt. Br.)
Tunis
TUNISIA
Rommel defeated in Tunisia (May 1943)
ALGERIA (Vichy France)
Algiers
LIBYA
SPAIN
Madrid
PORTUGAL
Lisbon
Gibraltar (Gt. Br.)
SP. MOROCCO
FRENCH MOROCCO
Casablanca (Nov. 1942)

strong feelings of Polish-Americans, but he was aware also of America's historic dislike of power politics. Confident of his own diplomatic skills, he was eager to mediate Russian-British differences and willing to defer inter-Allied disagreements about sovereignty until after the war. While not naive about Soviet ambitions, he believed that the survival of the Grand Alliance was the best hope of a peaceful world.

At the February 1945 Allied conference in Yalta in the Russian Crimea, the approach of victory made postwar planning unavoidable. Germany's ultimate fate was left undecided, but the Allies agreed temporarily to divide it into four zones of military occupation by the Big Three (the United States, Britain, and the USSR) and France. Germany was to be assessed heavy reparations, but a decision on the amount was postponed. Poland's boundaries were settled: Russia gained rights to large territories in Eastern Poland for which Poland was compensated with German territories to its west. Stalin also reluctantly agreed to a more representative interim Polish government and to free Polish elections. Elsewhere in liberated Eastern Europe, the Soviets accepted the principle of "broadly representative governments." In the Far East, Churchill and Roosevelt recognized the Soviet puppet state of Outer Mongolia (nominally Chinese), and ceded to Russia the Asian territories lost to the Japanese in 1904–1905. In return, Stalin not only pledged to enter the war against Japan, but to sign a treaty of friendship with Jiang's regime rather than with Mao's.

At Yalta, the Big Three also agreed to meet in the United States to form a United Nations Organization. Some of its structure had already been determined at a conference in Dumbarton Oaks in Washington. Of the world organization's two most important organs, the Assembly and the Security Council, the latter was to act by unanimity. Its effectiveness, all understood, would require close collaboration, for neither the United States nor the USSR would surrender the power of veto.

Later, during the Cold War, the Yalta Agreement was bitterly attacked by American conservatives as a betrayal of China and a sellout to Stalinism in Eastern Europe. Some alleged treason; many came to believe that Roosevelt was too sick to be competent. In fact, though not well, the president was able to bargain realistically. The agreement represented a series of tradeoffs, more or less mutually unsatisfactory, and it was probably as favorable as time and circumstance permitted. Because they were uncertain of the effectiveness of the untested atomic bomb and expected fanatical resistance to invasion of the Japanese home islands, Roosevelt and his military advisers were more than eager to have Soviet forces participate in the final stage of the Pacific war, for which enormous numbers of casualties had been projected. Moreover Russian troops were already occupying much of Eastern Europe, including Poland, and the treaty represented not so much a concession to Stalin as a recognition of postwar realities. Given the context, even the vague agreement on free elections seems reasonable, if not wholly realistic. Roosevelt recognized that the American people were not prepared to impose their will in areas occupied by Soviet arms. Most important, the president had won Soviet approval for a United Nations, an American conception that would be organized and headquartered on American soil. The great powers emerged from Yalta with their alliance intact. In retrospect, FDR's judgment seems valid. The agreement was, he said, "the best I can do."

When Roosevelt returned from his long journey, exhausted but optimistic, most Americans gratefully accepted his statements that a future of democracy and peace had been assured. In the months ahead, Soviet actions in some parts of Eastern Europe made it clear that free elections and broad representation meant different things to the Soviets than they did to Western Allies. Having been attacked so often from the west, the USSR was not likely to allow governments hostile to it to exist in states along its western border. In some of these countries, notably Poland and Rumania, it was equally doubtful that governments that would be democratically chosen could be friendly to the Soviets. When American commanders discussed with German agents in Switzerland possible surrender terms for German forces in Italy, Stalin suspected the United States of plotting to deny the USSR a role in the peace negotiations. Depressed by increasing friction, Roosevelt came to doubt the future he had planned. Before these doubts could lead to action, however, he died of a cerebral hemorrhage on April 12, 1945. America mourned his passing, and people on both sides of the Atlantic recognized that the world had lost one of its most gifted statesmen.

FROM YALTA TO HIROSHIMA

The victory of 1945 was clouded by Allied dissent and darkened by cruelty and destruction. In the spring of that year, however, this was not apparent to the American people, and even the president's death failed to spoil the news of success on every front. In Europe, the German counteroffensive had been stopped at Bastogne, Belgium, before the end of 1944. By March 1945, American forces had crossed the Rhine. In early April, when American troops reached the Elbe River, General Dwight D. Eisenhower decided on military grounds not to push forward toward Berlin, but first to make sure of the Southern Alpine redoubt where it was believed that the Nazis might make a last stand. This decision, communicated to Stalin, was protested by Churchill. It was, however, upheld by Harry S Truman, the new president, on the basis of prior agreements among the Allies on zones of occupation. A little later, Eisenhower refused to press toward Prague, Czechoslovakia, and the Russians occupied both Central European capitals. On May 1, while Soviet troops were entering Berlin, Hitler killed himself, and three days later Germany surrendered to England, the Soviet Union, and the United States.

As American forces drew closer to the Japanese home islands, they continued to meet fierce resistance. No Pacific battles were harder fought than Iwo Jima in February or Okinawa in May. Off the latter island, as in the Philippines, Japan made use of a strange and effective weapon, the suicide plane. Hundreds of kamikaze pilots dove deliberately at American ships.

This and other fanatical behavior convinced most Americans that they were in for a desperate fight in Japan itself.

Actually, Japan's resistance was almost at an end. American submarines had cut off necessary supplies, and since November, American bombers had inflicted terrible destruction. In June, the Japanese war cabinet fell, and a new government began unsuccessfully to seek Soviet mediation.

President Truman and Winston Churchill, meeting at Postdam, demanded on July 26 that Japan surrender. If Japan did, they promised, the Japanese would neither be destroyed nor enslaved; if it did not, it would meet "utter destruction." Since Truman had received word of the first explosion of an atomic bomb, he was in a position to carry out this threat. It had long been decided that the new weapon would be used against the enemy for maximum effect, rather than being dropped first on uninhabited territory as a warning. Some of the president's advisers believed that use of the new weapon would greatly increase the power of the United States in the postwar settlement, particularly in relations with the Soviet Union. On August 6, an atomic bomb was dropped on the city of Hiroshima. On August 8, the USSR hurriedly entered the war in advance of the agreed time. The next day, another atomic bomb hit Nagasaki, and on August 14, Japan agreed to the Postdam terms. A formal surrender was signed aboard the *Missouri* in Tokyo Bay on September 2, 1945.

Even in the euphoria of victory celebrations, some Americans could not avoid asking themselves how it happened that their country, with its deeply humanitarian traditions, had been the first to use history's most terrible weapon. The Hiroshima bomb killed 80,000 people and injured many more, some of whom died horribly in the ensuing weeks and months. Yet in 1915, the United States had been genuinely outraged by the death of 1,198 civilians on the *Lusitania*. Throughout the 1930s, and as recently as 1939, Americans had denounced aerial bombing of civilian populations.

The advent of the atomic bomb typified several tendencies, good and bad, that ran through the history of the war. The bomb was, in the first place, a typical result of the American civilian war effort. It depended on a bold decision based on immensely complex science and engineering and was conceived by scientists from many countries, some of them refugees. Thus, the atomic bomb was a product of a liberal society associated with some of the best American traditions.

At the same time, the bomb's use in war was the climax of a period of mounting inhumanity for which all major nations bore some responsibility. The worst atrocity of the period was the systematic German annihilation of 6 million Jews. In places, Russian treatment of political and national minorities was almost as bad. Bombing of cities was carried out by Axis nations from Shanghai in 1932 to Rotterdam in 1940. Destruction of German cities was carried to new lengths by Britain and America in 1943–1944, when 300,000 civilians were killed. The American fire bombings of Japan — including the incendiary bombing of Tokyo in March 1945, the most destructive air raid in history — killed about 330,000. Thus the atomic bomb could be viewed as just another weapon and the annihilation of Hiroshima and

MAP 9: THE PACIFIC WAR

Japanese-held areas
Limit of Japanese conquest
United States advance
Atomic bomb explosions

ALASKA

ALEUTIAN IS.

ATTU

KISKA 1943

1942

MIDWAY IS.

HAWAIIAN IS.

OAHU

Pearl Harbor

PACIFIC OCEAN

WAKE

MARSHALL IS.

GILBERT IS.

1943

1942

NEW HEBRIDES

MARCUS I.

MARIANAS IS.

TINIAN I.

1944

GUAM

CAROLINE IS.

SOLOMON IS.

GUADALCANAL

CORAL SEA

IWO JIMA

1945

JAPAN

Tokyo

Hiroshima

Nagasaki

OKINAWA

1945

1945

1944

1944-45

PHILIPPINE ISLANDS

LEYTE

NEW GUINEA

1943

1942

AUSTRALIA

FORMOSA

Hong Kong

LUZON

Manila

1944

FR. INDOCHINA

NETHERLANDS EAST INDIES

Singapore

U.S.S.R. 1945

MANCHURIA

Beijing (Peking)

CHINA

OUTER MONGOLIA

UNION OF SOVIET SOCIALIST REPUBLICS

Chongqing (Chungking)

Ledo

Stilwell Rd.

Lashio

Burma Rd.

BURMA

THAILAND

Nagasaki could be taken for granted by callous people. More sensitive individuals could still defend the action as a means of shortening the war and thus reducing both Japanese and American losses in the long run.

Postwar examination by American experts seemed to indicate that Japanese resistance had been almost over before Hiroshima. (Somewhat similarly, precision bombing of industries and transport turned out to have been far more decisive than city destruction in Germany.) But whatever the military or other judgments on the use of the atomic bomb in 1945, its existence became henceforth a major and incalculably frightening fact.

Thus the United States came to the end of a period of great and revolutionary achievement. From a policy of isolation, it had emerged to a stance of worldwide involvement. It had helped to build a great alliance, and through this and its productive and military achievements, the United States had helped destroy in Nazi Germany one of the worst regimes in history. All this had been accomplished without the destruction of either economic or political liberty at home.

The price for these great achievements started with a million American casualties, but that was only a beginning. Millions of people in Europe and Asia were starving in their ruins. Hate and fear were rampant as never before in modern history. Another totalitarian state, the Soviet Union, had been brought to immense worldwide power. The peaceful, democratic world promised by Roosevelt, and by Wilson before him, was soon to seem nowhere in sight.

CONFLICTING HISTORICAL VIEWPOINTS: NO. 14

Why Was the Atom Bomb Used on Japan?

Soon after the destruction of Hiroshima and Nagasaki, President Truman's mother commented: "I'm glad Harry decided to end the war. He's no slow person. He gets where he's going in short order." But where was he going? More particularly, was the decision to level the Japanese cities purely a military one, or did it have political and diplomatic dimensions as well? Was the use of the "ultimate weapon" designed to defeat Tokyo or to intimidate Moscow? In short, did the Cold War with the Soviet Union begin before the hot one with Japan ended?

For a decade and more, these questions have stirred scholarly debate. In Truman's own Memoirs (Vol. 1, 1955) and the writings of his Secretary of War, Henry L. Stimson (Harper's Magazine, February 1947), the decision to bomb the island nation was described purely in humanitarian and military terms. In Stimson's words, the nuclear devices were used "in order to end the war in the shortest possible time and to avoid the enormous losses of human life which otherwise confronted us. . . ." Some scholars, however, questioned the candor of the president and his secretary. Among the earliest to do so was P. M. S. Blackett, a British physicist whose Fear, War, and the Bomb (1948) asserted that "the dropping of the atomic bomb was not so

much the last military act of the second world war as the first major oper-
ation of the cold diplomatic war with Russia."

Blackett's conclusion won support from Gar Alperovitz, a Harvard
scholar and one time State Department employee who sharply criticized the
Truman administration's Atomic Diplomacy (1965). Drawing heavily upon
Stimson's own diaries, he addressed the question of "the influence of the
bomb on certain questions of diplomacy." Admittedly, the reverse question
— "the influence of diplomacy upon the decision to use the bomb" — could
not be answered from available sources. Yet he found evidence that "strongly
suggests" — and he so implied in much of his book — that the weapon was
used chiefly to demonstrate American power and, thereby, to make the
USSR more manageable in Central and Eastern Europe.

The critics of Truman's "atomic diplomacy" have critics of their own. Michael Amrine, author of The Great Decision (1959) and other studies of
American atomic policy, condemned Alperovitz as a "cold-blooded cousin of
. . . Dr. Strangelove," and charged that his thesis was based on unsubstan-
tiated and highly convoluted conjecture. The distinguished diplomatic historian Herbert Feis agreed with Amrine. In his own study, The Atomic
Bomb and the End of World War II (1966), a revision of an earlier work
entitled Japan Subdued (1961), Feis concluded that Secretaries Stimson and
Byrnes were aware that the A-bomb might not only "subdue the Japanese"
but also "monitor Russian behavior." He warned, however, that this awareness should not be "distorted" into accusations of "atomic blackmail," saying
"the impelling reason for the decision to use [the bomb] was military."

The most recent and balanced addition to the controversy is Martin Sherwin's A World Destroyed (1975), a thoughtful analysis of the complex inter-
actions of science, policy, and diplomacy. Although placing himself closer to
Alperovitz than to Feis, Sherwin disputed the revisionist thesis that the
bomb was used primarily, if not exclusively, to impress the Soviets. The
American nuclear arsenal was created solely to win the war, he argued, and
Truman used it to that end. But Sherwin also believed that both Roosevelt
and Truman intended to wage atomic diplomacy against the Soviets. Discov-
ering an unsuspected degree of continuity in American wartime and postwar
policies, he contended that Roosevelt, perhaps not less than Truman, shared
Churchill's deep suspicions of Stalin's intentions. Together, the wartime president and prime minister secretly plotted to retain exclusive control of atomic
energy as insurance against postwar Soviet ambitions. The Anglo-American
partnership died with Roosevelt, but his successor continued short-sighted
wartime nuclear policies that, in Sherwin's view, contributed to the origins
of the Cold War. Thus, whether through cause or effect, the end of one war
and the beginning of another were one.

FOR FURTHER READING

For military and diplomatic history, probably the single most valuable work
is Churchill's monumental though not infallible *The Second World War* (6

vols., 1948–1953). American involvement is traced in detail by A. R. Buchanan in *The United States and World War II* (2 vols., 1964). Walter Millis's *Arms and Men* (1956) is a humane and enlightened study of American military policy from the beginning and is especially valuable for this period. Robert A. Divine's *Roosevelt and World War II* (1969) is brief and sympathetic; while James MacGregor Burns's *Roosevelt: The Soldier of Freedom* (1970) is more detailed and critical. The tangle of Washington bureaus is to some extent unraveled by Eliot Janeway in *The Struggle for Survival* (1951). Richard Polenberg in *War and Society* (1972) and John Morton Blum in *V Was for Victory* (1976) contribute to an understanding of the homefront. The tragic tale of Japanese-American internment is told by Roger Daniels in *Concentration Camps USA* (1971), and by Michi Weglyn in *Years of Infamy* (1976). Lawrence S. Wittner examines the peace movement during and after the war in *Rebels Against War* (1969). One of the most thorough accounts of inter-Allied negotiations is Herbert Feis's *Churchill, Roosevelt, Stalin* (1957). Robert Sherwood's *Roosevelt and Hopkins* (2 vols., 1948) gives a highly favorable picture of the American effort to achieve good relations with the USSR. Chester Wilmot in *The Struggle for Europe* (1952) provides a stimulating and intelligent English criticism of American strategy and diplomacy. Diane Shave Clemens in *Yalta* (1970) offers a revisionist view. Developing East-West tensions are explored in John Gaddis's *The United States and the Origins of the Cold War* (1972), and in Daniel Yergin's *Shattered Peace* (1977). Among important memoirs are those of Secretaries of State Cordell Hull, Edward R. Stettinius, and James F. Byrnes; of Admiral William D. Leahy; and of Generals Dwight D. Eisenhower and Omar Bradley.

28

★ ★ ★ ★ ★ ★

The Perils of Peace, 1946–1961

ALTHOUGH the origins of the East-West tension known as the Cold War date back to the time of the Bolshevik Revolution, Russo-American antipathy took an ominous turn in the aftermath of World War II. At best, the Grand Alliance of the United States, Britain, and the USSR had been a marriage of convenience. Faced by a common enemy, the Big Three worked in relative harmony for the war's duration. As victory approached, however, it became clear that Allied unity was fragile.

In July 1945, following the German surrender, Truman, Stalin, and Churchill (soon to be replaced by Clement Attlee as Britain's prime minister) met in Potsdam, Germany. They issued an ultimatum to Japan and they agreed on demilitarizing Germany, along with prosecuting Nazi war criminals. But they could agree on little else. Unable to reach accord on the future of Germany and Eastern Europe, they reaffirmed the Yalta agreements and postponed decisions for future conferences of their foreign ministers. The American president left the conference, his first meeting with Stalin, convinced that the Soviets "were planning world conquest." He was cheered by news of the successful atomic bomb tests because the bomb would hasten the defeat of Japan and because "I'll have a hammer on those boys [the Soviets]." Even as the Axis collapsed, the wartime partners were becoming postwar antagonists.

NEITHER PEACE NOR WAR

When Roosevelt died, Truman told reporters, "The moon, the stars and all the planets fell on me." Indeed, the world in which he was unexpectedly asked to play a leading role was turbulent and perilous. The only nation to

MAP 10:   THE COLD WAR UP TO 1960

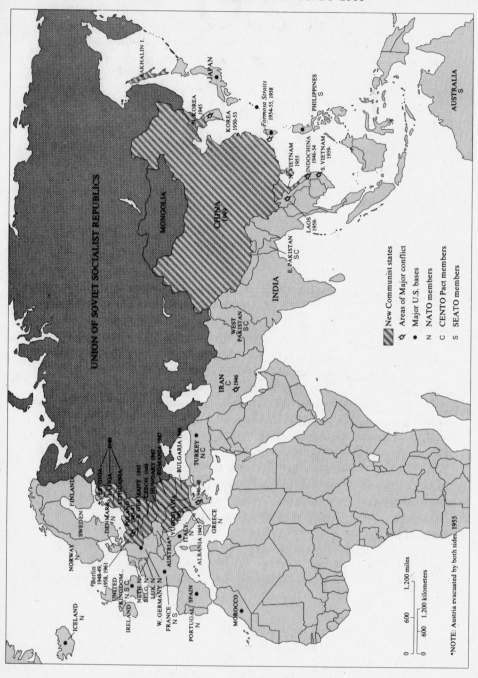

AUSTRALIA
S

UNION OF SOVIET SOCIALIST REPUBLICS

MONGOLIA

CHINA
1949

SAKHALIN I.

JAPAN

KOREA
1945

KOREA
1945

KOREA
1950-53

Formosa Straits
1954-55, 1958

PHILIPPINES
S

VIETNAM
1955

INDOCHINA
1946-54

S. VIETNAM
1959

LAOS
1959

E. PAKISTAN
SC

INDIA

WEST
PAKISTAN
SC

IRAN
C
1946

FINLAND

SWEDEN

NORWAY

DENMARK

ESTONIA

LATVIA

LITHUANIA

POLAND
1945

E. GERMANY 1945

Czech. 1948

HUNGARY 1947

ROMANIA 1947

BULGARIA 1946

YUGOSLAVIA

AUSTRIA*

ITALY
N

GREECE
N

ALBANIA 1945

1946-48

TURKEY
NC

Berlin
1948-49,
1958, 1961

UNITED
KINGDOM
N S C

NETH. N

BELG. N

LUX. N

W. GERMANY N

FRANCE
N S

IRELAND

ICELAND
N

PORTUGAL
N

SPAIN

MOROCCO

New Communist states

Areas of Major conflict

Major U.S. bases

N   NATO members

C   CENTO Pact members

S   SEATO members

0   600   1,200 miles

0   600   1,200 kilometers

*NOTE: Austria evacuated by both sides. 1955

emerge from the war with its military and economic strength enhanced, the United States was the sole remaining global power. Western Europe, once a center of world power, was physically shattered; its economies were prostrate. England's might and wealth, like its once great empire, were greatly diminished. France, an occupied country during the war, groped haltingly toward national reunification. Germany was literally torn asunder, a divided and disputed battleground between East and West. In the Far East, both the old colonial order and Japan's New Order were on the brink of destruction. Restive colonial peoples in the Orient, the Middle East, and Africa were astir with nationalist strivings. All the world seemed in flux.

Although ill-prepared, Truman mastered his job quickly and proved to be an uncommonly knowledgeable, hardworking, and resolute chief executive. Faced from the outset with awesome and dangerous decisions, he made all of them with courage and some with intelligence. From first to last, he was primarily concerned with the developing Russo-American power struggle. As international tension mounted over time, the rivalry assumed global dimensions.

For the moment, East-West rivalry centered on Eastern and Central Europe, where American hopes for a democratic and capitalist world order collided with Soviet security needs. The advantage in that region, of course, lay with the Soviets. Because of the war offensives, Russian troops already occupied these areas and could impose Soviet-oriented governments on the states liberated from Nazi control.

Given the clash of ideologies and national interests, given the dangerous vacuum created by the collapse of the Axis nations, conflict between the two surviving world powers was perhaps unavoidable. Both were operating in an unstable climate of fear and suspicion, and were entrapped by their own inflexible perceptions and simplistic rhetoric. But neither side understood the sources of the other's anxieties. All too quickly, the United States and the USSR abandoned diplomacy for bombast and confrontation.

Conscious to the point of paranoia that its European approaches were vulnerable and determined never again to be invaded from the west, the USSR would settle for nothing less than a buffer of Soviet-directed nations on its borders. Unwilling to brook serious opposition within its newly claimed sphere of influence, the Soviet Union imposed its harshest policies on Poland and Rumania, where its interests were most crucial and anti-Russian sympathies nearly universal. Somewhat more subtly, coalition governments in Hungary, Bulgaria, and Albania were also subverted; in 1948, democratic Czechoslovakia fell to a Soviet-inspired *coup d'état*. Except for neutral Finland (which ceded territory and paid reparations to the Soviets) and Marshal Josep Broz Tito's independent Marxist state, Yugoslavia, all of Eastern Europe was under direct Soviet control. In the Middle East, the Soviets only honored a wartime agreement to withdraw from Iran on the oil-rich Persian Gulf due to western prodding. Stalin also pressed hapless Turkey for a toehold on the strategic Black Sea straits.

Although the reasons for the tightening Soviet grip on Baltic, Central and Eastern European, and Balkan states have been interpreted in various ways,

TABLE 16. THE TRUMAN YEARS, 1945–1952

Year	Domestic	The atom	Europe	Asia
1945	April 12 Death of F.D.R. Truman becomes president. November Coal strike.		July 17–August 2 Potsdam Conference. August 21 End of lend-lease. November 20–October 1 Nuremburg trial.	August 14 Sino-Soviet Treaty. December Beginning of Marshall mission to China.
1946	June–November End of price controls. November 5 Republicans capture both Houses.	Baruch Plan rejected. McMahon Act (AEC).	November 4–December 12 Foreign ministers complete treaties with German allies (ratified 1947).	January–April Iran incident.
1947	March 22 Truman loyalty program. June 23 Taft-Hartley Act. July 26 National Security Act.		March 12 Truman Doctrine (aid to Greece and Turkey). June 5 Marshall Plan announced. November–December London Conference (Britain, Russia, United States) breaks up over German question.	January End of Marshall mission to China.
1948	June Selective Service revised. November 2 Truman defeats Dewey.		February Communist coup, Czechoslovakia. June Yugoslav-Russian break. June 24 Berlin blockade begins.	May 15 Israel independent, recognized by United States.

Year	Domestic	The atom	Europe	Asia
1949	October 14 Smith Act convictions.	First Russian atomic explosion.	April 4 North Atlantic Treaty. May Russians agree to end Berlin blockade.	January 20 "Point Four" announced. Chinese Nationalists defeated. December 8 Jiang to Formosa.
1950	January 21 Hiss convicted. February 9 McCarthy attacks State Department. September 23 McCarran Act. November 7 Republican election gains. December Hoover attacks Truman foreign policy.	United States starts work on hydrogen bomb.		January Acheson "defense perimeter" speech. June 25 North Korean attack. November 26 Chinese attack in Korea.
1951	1951–1952 Corruption disclosures, foreign policy and communism argument.		April Eisenhower Headquarters in Paris opens.	April 11 MacArthur recalled. July 10 Korean Peace talks open. September 8 Japanese Peace Treaty.
1952	April 8 Truman seizes steel mills. June 30 McCarran-Walter (Immigration) Act. November 4 Eisenhower defeats Stevenson.	British atomic explosion. United States hydrogen explosion.	August 2 West German peace Contract (occupation ends).	

many scholars believe that Stalin's policies were defensive in character, though provocative and brutal. Mindful of Allied military intervention in Russia following World War I and fearful of a resurgent Germany and continued "capitalist encirclement," Stalin violated his Yalta agreements. But his postwar aims were limited and conditioned not by Marxist doctrines but by traditional Russian national security considerations. His ambition was not world conquest but the establishment of a Soviet sphere of influence, one to offset the admittedly more benign American spheres in Western Europe and Latin America.

Timely Western concessions to Stalin's minimum-security demands, some now argue, could have moderated Soviet behavior and eased East-West tensions. This view of Soviet motives for expansion and possible alternative Western responses differs sharply from the traditional historical interpretation. This traditional or "orthodox" argument posits (see Viewpoint No. 15) that America reluctantly but valiantly responded to the challenge of Soviet expansion. Clearly the revisionist view runs counter to what President Truman and his closest advisers thought to be the lesson of the Munich agreement with Hitler. The Western democracies, they noted, had attempted and failed to appease the aggressive designs of one dictator in 1938. They would not now try to appease another; they would not, as Truman said, continue to "baby" Stalin. The administration feared that having "sovietized" Eastern Europe and ruthlessly consolidated his personal power within the USSR, the insatiable Soviet dictator now sought westward extension of communist control. Still reeling from the war, Western European economies were faltering, and Communist parties were active and strong in France and Italy. By 1947 the administration had concluded that only a "get tough" American policy could stem the rising "Red tide."

CONTAINMENT

To counter this perceived danger from the East, America had only limited options. Churchill's proposal for a frank division of Europe into spheres of influence had been rejected out of hand by Roosevelt. In Truman's cabinet, only Secretary of Commerce Henry Wallace favored a relatively "free hand" for the Soviets in Eastern Europe, and he was soon fired by a president who was out of patience with "parlor pinks" and "crackpots." Liberal hopes for resolving international disagreements through the United Nations were frustrated at every turn by Great Power suspicions and by the veto provision that severely limited the international body's coercive authority. Stalin's refusal in 1946 to cooperate in the Baruch Plan — which provided for the abandonment of the American nuclear monopoly *after* the world's atomic energy was brought under international control — was particularly disappointing. (Stalin proposed that American stockpiles be destroyed *first*.) "Hardliners," on the other hand, hoped to use American power to challenge Soviet gains and to push toward the traditional American goals of democracy and the Open Door everywhere. Toward this end, economic leverage was clumsily applied in 1945 when the United States abruptly terminated Soviet lend-lease (including shipments already at sea) and conveniently misplaced a Soviet loan request. If these gestures were intended to make the USSR more tractable, they backfired. Some wanted to use the U.S. atomic advantage to roll back the communist threat. But the Soviets could not be easily intimidated, and a "preventive" war was not only morally repugnant to Americans, but was politically impossible in an open, democratic society. In the end, the logical and perhaps only practical response was containment.

Although this policy was in formation since 1945, it was not formally articulated until the publication of George F. Kennan's "Mr. X Paper" in 1947. In this unsigned article, Kennan wrote: "The main element of any U.S. policy toward the Soviet Union must be that of a long-term, patient but firm and vigilant containment of Russian expansive tendencies." The unspoken concession was American acceptance of Soviet control in Eastern Europe as an accomplished fact. But there the line was drawn. There should be no bluster, no threats, Kennan believed, but only "the adroit and vigilant application of counter-force" wherever further Soviet extensions threatened.

The first major application of counterforce came with the Truman Doctrine, announced in March 1947. Responding to Soviet pressures on Turkey for joint control of the key Bosporus waterway and to communist guerrilla attacks on the conservative British protectorate of Greece, Truman persuaded Congress to approve a $400 million program of military and economic assistance for those two beleaguered nations. The intention, the president explained, was to "support free peoples who are resisting attempted subjugation by armed minorities or by outside pressures." The withdrawal of Yugoslav assistance to the Greek leftists, together with American military aid, allowed the Greek government to defeat the insurgency and to end the civil war. Having committed itself to counterrevolutionary policies, the United States found itself, as it would repeatedly in the years ahead, supporting an undemocratic and unpopular regime merely because it was anticommunist.

In June 1947 the Truman administration proposed a more general program of European economic recovery. In a speech at Harvard, General George Marshall, then secretary of state, offered to assist the recovery of *all* European nations. The USSR denied its satellites this opportunity, and few Americans believed that the United States would in fact provide aid for communist nations. But Western European countries promptly presented a united recovery plan. After considerable debate, and some conservative opposition, Congress established the European Cooperation Administration; by 1952, when the aid program ended, nearly $13 billion had been appropriated for its purposes. This "Marshall Plan" or, as it was officially called, European Recovery Plan (ERP), was the greatest success of American postwar policy. It laid the basis for the startling European recovery and unprecedented European unity of the 1950s. It also served American strategic and economic interests by strengthening Western European capitalism and enlarging the American export market. Because ERP provided credits rather than cash — and thus assured that aid dollars would be spent in the United

States — it promoted one of the greatest peacetime economic booms in U.S. history. Similarly, in 1949, the administration proposed Point Four, a technical aid program designed to undermine the appeal of communism by extending the benefits of American scientific and industrial progress to underdeveloped nations, and particularly to Latin America. Again, American economic self-interest was linked to the crusade against communism.

Stalin responded to these initiatives by tightening his grip on Eastern Europe. Midway through the congressional debate on the Marshall Plan, a communist coup d'état brought Czechoslovakia into the Soviet orbit. Denouncing the European economic recovery program as American imperialism, Soviet leaders organized the Warsaw Alliance of satellite nations and the Cominform (Communist Information Bureau) to ensure orthodoxy throughout their sphere. The most threatening Soviet countermove, however, came in Germany, a vital East-West pressure point. Reacting to American efforts to promote the economic stability and political unification of Trizonia, the three western zones, Stalin boycotted the Four Power Control Commission and closed all surface access to Berlin (located 100 miles inside the Soviet sector).

The most severe test of American resolve so far, the Berlin blockade threatened with starvation the city's western garrisons and West Berlin's 2 million pro-Western inhabitants. The object of the blockade was to force the Western Allies out of Berlin and/or to frustrate Western plans for a united West Germany. No doubt the Soviets feared a resurgent, anti-communist Germany. The Berlin blockade, many Truman advisers believed, left the United States with but two unattractive alternatives: capitulation or force. In the spirit of the containment policy, however, Truman chose instead an around-the-clock airlift of American supplies into the beleaguered city. After 324 days and nearly 300,000 flights of cargo totalling 2.5 million tons, the Soviets lifted the blockade. Armed confrontation had been avoided, but the division of Germany was complete. In September 1949 the (West) German Federal Republic was proclaimed at Bonn, and in the following month the (East) German Democratic Republic was created, having as its capital East Berlin.

Alarmed by the fall of Czechoslovakia and the Berlin blockade and encouraged by economic recovery, Western Europe moved toward unity and asked for American defense commitments. In April 1949 the United States broke with its historic distaste for binding alliances and joined the North Atlantic Treaty Organization (NATO), a 20-year pact proposed by Truman to link the United States, Canada, Great Britain, France, and eight other Atlantic nations (and later Greece, Turkey, and West Germany) in mutual defense. Under the NATO agreement, an attack on one would be interpreted as an attack on all. The Soviet Union protested this "violation" of the United Nations' spirit and, not without justification, again cried "encirclement."

The creation of NATO in 1949 represented a militarizing of containment, a process that only gradually developed in the early Cold War years. Under popular and congressional pressures for rapid demobilization following World War II, the administration reduced both the army (from 8.3 million troops in 1945 to 593,000 in 1950) and the navy (from 3.4 million to 382,000). Truman maintained low defense budgets through 1949, resisting the military's request for drastic defense increases following the Berlin blockade. The president also denied a defense establishment request for military control of the atomic weapons' stockpile. The stockpile itself remained small — 11 bombs, all of the "fat-man" type used on Hiroshima — until tests in 1948 allowed for the production of more advanced bombs. Although the National Security Act (1947) was designed to unify the military establishment (as well as to create the National Security Council and the Central Intelligence Agency), genuine unification did not occur, and the president remained skeptical of the conflicting demands of the armed services for budget increases.

Only in the crisis year of 1949, with the "fall" of China and the detonation of a Soviet atomic device in August, did Truman move quickly. First he increased the atomic weapons' stockpile, and second and more important, he authorized the development of a hydrogen bomb. This decision to build a bomb one thousand times more powerful than the "fat-man" was opposed on moral grounds by some of the nation's top scientists, and George Kennan and Albert Einstein warned that "general annihilation beckons." But Truman, pressured by the Joint Chiefs of Staff and convinced that the Soviets were developing their own H-bomb, made the decision without public discussion or congressional authorization. As the nuclear arms race rapidly developed, a joint committee of the Departments of State and Defense prepared NSC-68, a policy statement that would militarize and globalize containment. NSC-68 proposed that the defense budget be tripled and that the United States should no longer distinguish between national security and global security. Truman approved the plan in the fall of 1950 as the Cold War turned hot in Korea.

RED SHADOW OVER ASIA

The singular American postwar success story in Asia was Japan's occupation by the U.S. armed forces and its reconstruction. American power was not seriously contested by the USSR. General Douglas MacArthur issued his orders through Emperor Hirohito and received a surprising measure of cooperation from the Japanese. Japanese industry and U.S. funds helped MacArthur carry through a political and economic program that helped remake the Pacific nation along more democratic and nonmilitaristic lines.

Elsewhere, Asian problems defied American solutions. At war's end, two groups vied for control of China: the Nationalists of Jiang Jieshi (Chiang Kai-shek) and the Communists of Mao Zedong (Mao Tse-tung). The Nationalists enjoyed the recognition of most nations, including the Soviet Union. Not eager for a strong and united China, and no doubt finding Mao too independent, the Russians in this case honored their Yalta agreements. The United States briefly encouraged a coalition government; when that collapsed in the face of renewed civil war, Truman resumed American support (totalling $3 billion) for Jiang. In the end, Jiang lost the struggle through lack of popular support and ineptness; in 1949, the Nationalist Chinese remnant followed him in flight to the island of Formosa (Taiwan), and Mao was victorious. The red flag now flew over the whole Eurasian mainland, from the Baltic to the Yellow Sea.

The political fallout from Mao's victory in China severely damaged both Truman's leadership and congressional foreign policy bipartisanship. Although time would demonstrate that the Sino-Soviet powers were uneasy ideological bedfellows — that communism was not the international monolith many Westerners thought it to be — most Americans were alarmed by the prospect of a mainland Communist China. Neo-isolationists and Asia-firsters — like archconservative Republican Senator William Knowland of California, but also Democrats like Representative John F. Kennedy — blamed the Truman administration for the "betrayal" of Jiang and the "fall" of China. Senator Joseph R. McCarthy spoke darkly of the treason of "egg-sucking liberals." Some saw partisan advantage in the administration's apparent failures. Other observers recognized that in 1948 and 1949 the United States had neither the troops nor the will for the massive intervention that would be required to save the Nationalists. In retrospect, it is arguable that by rebuffing Mao's several early diplomatic overtures and then by not recognizing his mainland government, the United States lost (as it did in North Vietnam's Ho Chi Minh) a chance to nurture an "Asian Tito" — a popular nationalist leader, a communist, but one who was independent of Moscow. In 1950, Mao signed an accord with Stalin.

The next Asian crisis came in Korea, where postwar zones of Russian and American military occupation had solidified into hostile northern and southern political entities. Following Japan's defeat, the United States supported Korean reunification under UN supervision; the Soviets blocked the attempt. Both sides withdrew their occupying forces by 1948. Although Korea (and Formosa) was excluded when Secretary of State Dean Acheson defined American strategic interests in the Pacific in January 1950, Syngman Rhee's Republic of (South) Korea received both military and economic aid from the United States. Little noticed at the time, Acheson's omission stood out boldly on June 25 when Kim Il-sung's North Korean troops suddenly invaded South Korea.

The origins of the Korean War remain obscure. Many historians now argue that North Korea acted on its own without either the encouragement or the knowledge of the Soviets. American leaders at the time thought otherwise. Assuming that Moscow was behind the invasion, Truman ordered supplies to South Korea and the U.S. Seventh Fleet into the straits between China and Formosa. Because the USSR happened to be boycotting the United Nations and was not there to exercise its veto, President Truman obtained from the UN Security Council a demand for North Korean withdrawal and an appeal for member nations to aid in South Korea's resistance. With no other authorization, he became the first (but not the last) American commander-in-chief to wage a foreign war without congressional consent. Within a week of the invasion he unilaterally sent in U.S. air, sea, and ground forces. Although the counterattack was waged as a UN international police action and 15 other nations sent in small contingents, General Douglas MacArthur was in supreme command, and 90 percent of his forces were either American or South Korean.

At the outset, MacArthur boasted that given a free hand by Washington, he could end the war with "one arm tied behind my back." Later he promised to have the troops home first by Thanksgiving and then by Christmas. Instead, UN forces were initially hurled back by the invaders. But MacArthur, who acted under a mandate from the UN General Assembly for a "unified and democratic Korea," recouped skillfully and drove the North Koreans across the 38th parallel and pushed northward toward the Chinese boundary at the Yalu River. Begun as a limited intervention to repel the invaders, the Korean War became a crusade to destroy the communist regime in the North. Chairman Mao, President Nehru of India, and others warned that an expanded war to unify Korea risked Chinese intervention. General MacArthur assured the president that even in that unlikely eventuality, American might could prevail. In October, the North Korean capital at Pyongyang was captured. In November, as American aircraft bombed bridges on the Korean-Chinese border, MacArthur's troops were poised for final victory, only to be surprised by the direct entry of China into the war and a massive Chinese counteroffensive; they were flung southward once again. By December, 1950, the communists again controlled the North.

Chagrined by these reverses and convinced that the primary communist threat now lay in Asia, MacArthur demanded permission to carry the war into China. Truman himself thought briefly of using the atomic bomb. But fear of a protracted land war in China and possible Soviet intervention prevailed. MacArthur's request was denied. The general, defying tradition and the Constitution, announced that there was "no substitute for victory" and repeatedly appealed the commander-in-chief's decision to the press and people. He was removed from his post in April 1951 for insubordination.

Scholars generally agree that the president acted wisely, both in limiting the war to Korea and in relieving his gifted but headstrong general of command. Such military advisers as General George Marshall, then secretary of defense, and General Omar Bradley, chairman of the Joint Chiefs of Staff, suggested that the recall of MacArthur was overdue. It was nevertheless a politically costly decision that precipitated an angry public and congressional debate. Never popular, the president was burned in effigy, and his popularity ratings slumped further. Republican leaders talked of impeachment. Senator Joseph McCarthy and Representative Richard M. Nixon raised the specters of appeasement and possible treason. Trial "MacArthur-for-President" balloons were sent up, but the controversy slowly died and the general faded from public view.

The Korean stalemate, however, dragged on and the administration successfully pressed its case for rearmament under NSC-68. In 1950–1951, only partly for Korean purposes, the military budget was quadrupled, and the number of armed forces was increased to 3,500,000. In Europe, where recovery was well advanced, American aid shifted from an economic to a military emphasis. NATO built a combined force with General Dwight D. Eisenhower in command. Seemingly on every front the administration continued to search for anti-communist military advantages. First, the Allies formed a European Defense Community, but France refused (for the moment) to permit independent West German rearmament. Also, treaties were signed with Japan that permitted American forces to remain in Japan and that lifted economic and rearmament restrictions on that nation (which, remarkably, refused to rearm). Finally, the United States entered mutual defense pacts with the Philippines, Australia, and New Zealand.

The hot war in Korea and especially the Truman-MacArthur controversy revealed an American dissatisfaction with containment as a foreign policy strategy. Preferring tidier solutions to international problems, the American people longed for decisive victory, a quick and total resolution of postwar tensions. The North Korean invasion had been repulsed without provoking World War III. But 25,000 American soldiers had died in the first year of fighting, and an end to the war was not in sight. Nor had the larger struggle against a perceived communist menace produced satisfactory results. What began as a regional problem in Eastern Europe had become a crisis of global proportions. Instead of guarding a limited defense perimeter, the United States seemed committed to resisting communist encroachments in the most remote and difficult theaters. China was "lost," Europe was apparently divided permanently, and the German problem continued to defy solution. Postwar rearmament brought its accompaniment of conscription, inflation (comparatively moderate by more recent standards), and high taxes. Spy exposés in the United States, Canada, and Great Britain suggested that Soviet agents had penetrated the highest levels of the Allies' governments. Both the USSR and the United States were developing bombs vastly more powerful than those dropped on Hiroshima and Nagasaki. Unsurprisingly, national confidence was shaken, and many Americans were profoundly disquieted.

FOREIGN POLICY DEBATE AND RED SCARE II

Popular unrest first took the form of a public debate over foreign policy — similar in some ways to the debates of 1898–1900, 1914–1917, and 1939–1941, but less reasoned than any of them. Extremists, usually of the opposition party, suspected conspiracy in such Roosevelt-Truman domestic and foreign policies as the New Deal, Pearl Harbor, the alliance with the USSR, the Yalta "sell-out," the "theft" of atomic secrets, the "betrayal" of China, the no-win stalemate in Korea, and the deposing of MacArthur. Less hysterical critics argued, as former President Hoover did in 1950, that it was a mistake for America to make any commitments on the continents of Europe or Asia. Republican Senator Robert Taft promoted greater reliance on air power, less on ground troops. Many urged that timid or uncooperative allies be disregarded and that the United States impose its own peace on a troubled world. Demoralized liberals, on the other hand, faulted the administration for propping up reactionary regimes and relying too much on military, rather than economic, anti-communist measures. A number of Americans, then, found truth in the Republican campaign slogan: "To err is Truman."

The president's critics offered more vitriol than they did feasible alternatives. Increasingly the argument centered on one issue: communists in government. Although this great postwar fear and the witch hunt it engendered became known as McCarthyism, the junior senator from Wisconsin did not create it; he merely proved to be the most successful exploiter of pervasive public anxieties. Dread of domestic subversion, although subsiding after the post–World War I Red Scare, had sporadically troubled the American political scene since 1917. Anti-Roosevelt conservatives gravitated easily to the issue of subversion. From its formation in 1938 the House Un-American Activities Committee (HUAC) had devoted most of its energies to imaginative exposures of "communist influence" on New Deal agencies and programs. The Smith Act of 1940 was passed to limit free speech and assembly of radicals and other "subversives." Following the sensational exposure of apparent Soviet wartime spying within the Canadian government, Truman instituted a "loyalty program" (1947) and, somewhat later, evoked the Smith Act to prosecute American communists for conspiracy. His intention, in large part, was to deprive Republicans of the communists-in-government issue; perhaps he also sought public support for his anti-Soviet foreign policies by overdramatizing the menace within. By 1951, some 2,500 alleged security risks (including suspected alcoholics and homosexuals) were dismissed from federal employment without due process. Despite attempted safeguards, the probe led to widespread abuse and uneasiness. In time, it also seemed to legitimize a wider and infinitely more destructive anti-communist crusade.

Though deplored by civil libertarians, these measures neither departisanized the internal security question nor allayed popular alarm. In 1947, HUAC began searching for communists among Hollywood screen writers and directors. The next year, self-confessed former Soviet agent Whittaker Chambers identified Alger Hiss, once a middling State Department employee who had accompanied Roosevelt to Yalta, as a communist and Russian spy. Hiss denied the allegation, and liberals generally rallied to his defense. Truman referred to HUAC proceedings against the former New Dealer as a "red herring" designed to divert public attention from Republican failings. But Chambers's charges (relentlessly pursued by Representative Richard Nixon, who took personal charge of the investigation) proved hard to refute. Recent research seems to implicate Hiss in at least low-level espionage activities. In January 1950, he was tried and convicted of perjury in his denial of Chambers's charges (the statute of limitations on espionage having run out). The next month, Truman ordered the production of the hydrogen bomb, and the British revealed that nuclear scientist Klaus Fuchs had spied for the Russians at the U.S. Los Alamos atomic-bomb project. Fuchs's confession led investigators to Julius and Ethel Rosenberg; these two Americans were arrested some months later (and convicted and electrocuted in 1953) as his accomplices. These espionage cases set the stage for Senator Joe McCarthy.

McCarthy began his crusade in February 1950 with the claim that he had a list of 205 communists known to Secretary Acheson who were employed by the State Department. The administration vehemently denied the charge, and a Senate Foreign Relations subcommittee found it to be "a fraud and a hoax." Amid rising public furor, McCarthy twice changed the number of State Department "reds" (to 57 and 81) and never produced his list. But he brashly (and without foundation) named other communist "agents," "dupes," and "traitors," including General Marshall and Secretary Acheson. The entire Democratic party, he averred, was stained with "historic betrayal." Having played midwife at the birth of a second Red scare, Truman now found his party and administration to be the object of its attack.

Some responsible conservatives in both parties initially objected to this mudslinging. But McCarthyism was good politics, and the Senator quickly won financial support from the extreme anti-communists of the radical right. At first offended by McCarthy's "recklessness," Senator Robert A. Taft, "Mr. Republican" himself, began to encourage attacks on liberals and Democrats. "If one case doesn't work," he advised his Wisconsin colleague, "then bring up another." During the congressional elections of 1950, several McCarthy critics were defeated. Other politicians employed his tactics, notably California Congressman Nixon in his Senate race against the allegedly "pink lady," liberal Democrat Helen Gahagan Douglas.

As in the anti-German hysteria of World War I, states, cities, and private organizations took up the crusade. Self-appointed patriots purged libraries and in some cases burned books. Teachers and government employees were required to sign loyalty oaths. The broadcasting and motion picture industries black listed allegedly subversive writers and actors. Adrift in a sea of character assassination and guilt by association, the nation seemed prepared to sacrifice individual freedom, decency, and common sense for internal security. A two-thirds majority in the House and Senate overrode Truman's veto and enacted the McCarran Internal Security Act (1950), which among other drastic measures provided that *suspected* subversives could be interned, without trial, by presidential order in time of "international security emergency." Although Truman denounced the McCarran Act as "a long step toward totalitarianism," his administration, as the law required, selected sites for the construction of what even the most strident congressional Red-baiters called "concentration camps." Congress did not fund camp construction, and the bill was repealed some two decades later.

During McCarthy's reign of slur and innuendo, few people or institutions of power openly opposed him. Although opinion polls suggest that his mass support has been overestimated, he was widely thought to be the most powerful figure in Washington and politically invincible. Conservatives and even such Republican moderates as Eisenhower (elected president in 1952), who loathed his methods, found the senator too useful to repudiate. Liberals and Democrats, stung by conservative charges of "fellow traveling" and eager to protect their own anti-communist credentials, generally remained silent. Except for major metropolitan newspapers, the nation's press was broadly sympathetic. The Senate, true to its tradition of noninterference, ignored McCarthy's excesses as long as possible. Only when the senator overreached himself, and began to smear "communist sympathizers" in the Protestant clergy, army, Eisenhower administration, and Senate was he finally called to task. In 1954, during the Army-McCarthy television hearings, the senator's swaggering manners and unethical methods shocked the nation. Soon thereafter, the Senate condemned him for conduct unbecoming a senator. Ignored by his colleagues and by the press, he quickly lapsed into obscurity and died in 1957.

Having run its course, the second Red scare faded with McCarthy. Later in the decade, the Supreme Court, presided over by Earl Warren, a liberal Republican, delivered a number of decisions that restricted the scope of congressional committees and in other ways reaffirmed the importance of traditional individual freedoms. At the polls, the congressional elections of 1954 demonstrated that the Red issue had lost its potency, and in 1956 it was hardly used. In the prosperity and complacency of the middle Eisenhower years, hysteria died down more quickly than it might have under more vigorous counterattack. Yet the costs of tolerating McCarthyism were high. An ugly image had been presented to the world, sections of the government service had been demoralized, and some important issues of foreign policy seemed to have been placed beyond the range of effective discussion. As McCarthyism waned, a shrill minority on the Far Right added Eisenhower and Warren to their list of worldwide conspirators.

MASSIVE RETALIATION AND THE NEW LOOK

In the election of 1952, both presidential candidates (Democrat Adlai E. Stevenson and Republican Dwight David Eisenhower) were political moderates who shared Truman's perceptions of the origins and nature of the Cold War. Of the two, "Ike," the grandfatherly war hero, was the popular favorite. The articulate and witty Stevenson, on the other hand, was often dismissed as an intellectual. His major handicap, however, was voter discontent with Truman. The political opposition portrayed Truman as an incompetent president, surrounded by traitors and crooks, committed to a hopeless war. The election of Stevenson, the Republicans alleged, would bring more of the same: "Korea, Communism, and Corruption." Republican vice presidential candidate Nixon called Stevenson "Adlai the appeaser," and McCarthy impuned his patriotism with sly references to "Alger Stevenson." Eisenhower, for the most part, stayed above the unseemly fray, while his running mate led the assault on the Democrats. In October, General Eisenhower promised that if elected he would fly to Korea to end the war. That and his attractively bland and reassuring manner helped to produce a Republican landslide.

TABLE 17. THE EISENHOWER ADMINISTRATION, 1952–1960

Year	Domestic	Space and the atom	Europe	Asia, Latin America, and Africa
1952	November Eisenhower elected.	November 1 Eniwetok hydrogen explosion (United States).		December Eisenhower visits Korea.
1953	1953–1954 McCarthyism. Recession.	August 20 Russian H-bomb.	March 5 Stalin's death. June Riots in East Berlin.	July 27 Korean armistice.
1954	April–June Army-McCarthy hearings. May 17 Supreme Court outlaws school segregation. November Democrats capture Congress.	March 1 Bikini H-bomb (United States).	August 30 France rejects EDC.	May–June Guatemala Crisis. July 21 Geneva Agreement. September 8 SEATO Pact.
1955	July 11 Dixon-Yates contract cancelled.		May 15 Austrian Peace Treaty. July 18–23 Geneva meeting (Eisenhower, Bulganin).	

Year	Domestic	Space and the atom	Europe	Asia, Latin America, and Africa
1956	**November** Eisenhower elected with Democratic Congress.	Stevenson proposes H-bomb ban.	**February** Khrushchev denounces Stalin crimes. **October–November** Hungarian insurrection.	**October** Suez Crisis.
1957	Recession. **September 24** Troops to Little Rock. Civil Rights Act.	**May 15** British H-bomb. **October 4** Sputnik.	**March 28** European Common Market.	**January 5** "Eisenhower Doctrine" in Middle East.
1958	**November** Democratic gains in Congress.	**January 31** United States satellite. **March 31** Russia suspends tests (United States follows).		**May** Lebanon Crisis.
1959	**July** Steel strike.	**September 13** Soviet "Lunik" hits moon.	**September** Khrushchev visits United States.	**February 16** Castro premier of Cuba.
1960	Recession. **November** Kennedy elected.	**February 11** French atomic explosion. **July 20** Polaris sub launches missile.	**May** U2 incident. **November** West Berlin threatened.	**June** Tokyo riots. **June 30** Congo independent; civil war. **August** Laos Crisis.

During most of Eisenhower's presidency, his principal foreign policy adviser was Secretary of State John Foster Dulles, a man of formidable experience, energy, and consistency. A committed cold warrior, Dulles seemed to view American-Soviet rivalry in starkly simple terms of good and evil. Though possessed of a shrewd and sometimes subtle mind, his inflexible anti-communism and his bellicose rhetoric were not well suited for diplomacy. During the presidential campaign, he called for the "liberation" of Soviet satellite countries and promised to "unleash Jiang" and to "roll back" the Iron Curtain; as secretary of state, he alarmed many Americans and their allies by boasting that the administration had gone to the brink of war three times in pursuit of peace. Yet Dulles enjoyed the president's confidence. He may have played the role of pugnacious international stalking horse for a president who generally shared his world view, but not his confrontational style of leadership.

Having promised peace, economy, and a "dynamic" alternative to the "negative, futile, and immoral policy of 'containment,'" Eisenhower and Dulles proclaimed a bold new solution to international problems. Instead of reacting to every communist challenge with expensive but limited and indecisive counterpressure, Dulles said, the United States would assume the initiative and resort to "massive retaliation" at times and places of its own choosing. Expenditures and conventional forces would be cut back, and nuclear weapons would be further developed and air-strike capabilities expanded. The development of a powerful nuclear deterrent force — and a well advertised willingness to use it — would make further communist challenge, even Soviet aggression by proxy, unthinkable. Corollaries of this "new look" in defense were more emphasis on anti-Soviet defense pacts and the development of additional air bases from Spain to Iran. NATO armies in Europe would also be equipped with tactical atomic weapons.

The Eisenhower strategy drew heavy criticism abroad and at home. Some thought it inappropriate in light of a new Soviet emphasis on peaceful coexistence following the death of Stalin in March 1953 and the subsequent rise of the more conciliatory Nikita Khrushchev. Critics noted that however ideologically satisfying, the proposed Republican alternative to containment was absurd and technologically obsolete — a transparent bluff that would only tie American hands in the face of Soviet adventurism. Would the United States, they asked, risk a nuclear exchange over a single, limited aggressive act? Under Khrushchev the Soviets shifted from Stalin's steamroller techniques to subtler forms of East-West competition in underdeveloped countries. Would the United States counter Soviet attempts to exploit revolutionary nationalism in the former colonies of the Third World with possible international holocaust? A new balance of terror, moreover, suggested that the United States lacked the nuclear supremacy on which massive retaliation was premised.

In 1953, the Soviet Union tested its first hydrogen bomb only months after the Americans had exploded theirs. Further evidence of advanced Soviet weapons technology came in 1957 with the launching of Sputnik, the world's first space satellite.

CONTAINMENT REPUBLICAN STYLE

In reality, the Republican administration departed from the foreign policy of its Democratic predecessor only in its rhetoric. Faced with complex and perilous international situations and eager to mollify the conservatives who had harried the "no win" strategy of Truman and Acheson, the administration talked change and practiced continuity. Anti-Soviet, nationalist uprisings in East Berlin (1953) and Hungary (1956), for example, were encouraged by American promises of support. But when these challenges to Soviet hegemony were brutally crushed, the administration protested through the United Nations, but prudently attempted neither "liberation," "roll back," nor "massive retaliation." Similarly, Eisenhower permitted Dulles briefly to "unleash" Jiang in 1953 and ordered the Seventh Fleet (then patrolling the Straits of Formosa) to refrain from preventing a Nationalist attack on the People's Republic. Nationalist commando raids subsequently harrassed the mainland, and the Communists responded (in 1955 and 1958) with artillery bombardments of Jiang's garrisons on the off-shore islands of Quemoy and Matsu. Jiang could not invade in force without American support, and Eisenhower, after consulting allies, would not risk a second major Asian war.

Even before his inauguration, Eisenhower went to Korea; Dulles later threatened to end the war with atomic weapons. That threat and pressure from Khrushchev may have moved the North Koreans to resume negotiations. The armistice of July 1953 brought a troubled peace on essentially the same terms as Truman had sought. After the expenditure of more than 33,000 American lives and some $50 billion dollars, American policy makers had no realistic choice but to redivide the Korean peninsula at roughly the old boundary, with the United States committed to assist and defend South Korea.

Elsewhere in the Far East (see Chapter 30), the administration addressed a crisis in Indochina with much the same mixture of bellicosity and restraint and again decided to contain, rather than roll back, a perceived communist menace. After the 1954 defeat of French colonialism by communist-led Vietminh (Indochinese nationalists), the administration took part in the partition of Indochina and the division of Vietnam, and committed the United States to supporting an anti-communist but undemocratic regime in the South. The United States also organized an "Asian NATO," the Southeast Asia Treaty Organization (SEATO), which pledged signatory nations (Great Britain, France, Australia, New Zealand, Pakistan, the Philippines, Thailand, and the United States) to construe an attack on one as an attack on all. A special protocol extended the treaty to cover the Indochinese nations of Laos, Cambodia, and South Vietnam. In the Far East, as in Europe, the "new look" looked much like the old.

In the Middle East, Eisenhower's policies were influenced by sometimes contradictory concerns. One was the region's immensely important oil resources, long defended by Britain and coveted by the USSR. To protect growing American economic interests in the region and to offset Soviet influence, the administration looked to the Arabs, who as Moslems seemed to be logical foes of communism. That objective, however, was enormously complicated by another American objective, the survival of Israel. Most of Israel's neighbors, particularly the displaced Palestinians, resented the Israelis as interlopers and denied the right of the Jewish state to exist.

The magnitude of the problem is suggested by the administration's relationship with Gamal Abdel Nasser, an independent Arab nationalist. Frustrated by the Egyptian leader's profession of neutrality in the Cold War, Eisenhower and Dulles first attempted to win his support with the promise of aid for the construction of the Aswan High Dam, and then withdrew the offer when he turned to the Soviet bloc for arms. Nasser promptly seized the Anglo-French Suez Canal, allegedly to finance the dam. When the French, British, and Israelis invaded Egypt, the Soviet Union threatened to send "volunteers"; Eisenhower persuaded the invaders to withdraw. The incident strained U.S. relations with its allies and greatly damaged Western prestige in the Middle East. Nasser moved closer to the Soviets, who financed his dam. Alarmed by this turn of events, the administration augmented the anti-Soviet Baghdad Pact or Central Treaty Organization (CENTO) of 1954 with the Eisenhower Doctrine, which pledged American aid to Middle Eastern nations threatened by communist aggression. Under it, the United States intervened in Jordan and Lebanon in 1957 and 1958 to counter Nasser's influence.

In the Western Hemisphere and elsewhere among developing nations, the Republicans fared little better. During Truman's administration, there had been such promising developments as the Rio Pact in 1947 (a collective security treaty signed by all American nations) and the formation of the Organization of American States (OAS) in 1948, (the most encouraging symbol of inter-American unity). Latin America remained, however, a place of social misery, political instability, and anti-Yankee sentiment when the Republican administration took office. Clearly secondary to Europe in U.S. concerns, the region was not included in the Marshall Plan. Not unlike most of the Third World, its people worried more about encroaching want than communist advances.

The Eisenhower administration's meddling in Guatemala served only to underscore U.S. preference for compliant, reactionary regimes, rather than for social progress under revolutionary movements. Prodded by the American-owned United Fruit Company, Dulles terminated U.S. aid to that nation's leftist but constitutional government. The hard-pressed Guatemalans turned to the Soviet Union for financial support. Its darkest suspicions apparently confirmed, the administration used Central Intelligence Agency (CIA) agents to promote a right-wing coup in 1954 and immediately recognized the repressive new military government. Widely applauded in the United States but condemned by NATO allies, this ill-advised intervention seemed all too familiar to Third World countries, where American talk of democracy and morality often met with skepticism. In 1953, the CIA had also subverted a popularly elected but uncompliant government in Iran. American support (sometimes administered through the CIA) propped up numerous right-wing dictatorships, notably in Cuba, the Dominican Republic, Nicaragua, and Portugal. In 1958, Americans were shocked to discover the intensity of anti-Yankee sentiment in Latin America when Vice President Nixon's good will tour was cut short by violent demonstrations in Venezuela.

COEXISTENCE

Amid these uncertainties and setbacks there was one bright spot: the on-again, off-again thaw in the Cold War. Encouraged by Khrushchev's softer line at home and abroad, his support for a negotiated settlement in Korea, and his willingness to accept a reunified, independent Austria (1955), Eisenhower (over Dulles's opposition) met the Soviet leader in Geneva. No substantive agreements were reached, on either the unification of Germany or the arms race. But the fragile "Spirit of Geneva" seemed briefly promising, and the two sides exchanged delegations of ballerinas, farmers, and other goodwill ambassadors. In 1958, following unsuccessful efforts to negotiate a nuclear test-ban treaty, the two powers (under immense international pressure) temporarily suspended atmospheric testing. The following year (after Dulles's death), Eisenhower invited Khrushchev to tour America and discuss Soviet plans to terminate further Western access to Berlin. Again nothing was settled, but Khrushchev delayed on Berlin and the strained cordiality known as the "Spirit of Camp David" offered cause for hope. Then another summit conference and a presidential tour of the Soviet Union were aborted in 1960 when an American spy plane was downed deep inside Soviet territory.

At best, Eisenhower left a mixed legacy. For reasons largely beyond American control, the nation's relative power in the world had declined. The Soviets had achieved nuclear parity; developing nations chafed under Great Power dominance; and Europeans, particularly the French, grew less dependent on the United States and more critical of NATO. Administration support for repressive governments in Latin America and U.S. opposition to revolutionary nationalist movements everywhere undermined the nation's prestige and cast doubt on its claim to leadership of the "free world." Despite a temporary thaw in East-West relations, the administration did not fully exploit the opportunities for long-term accord with the USSR in the post-Stalinist era. Yet the administration's deeds were generally more restrained than its rhetoric. Under Eisenhower the nation enjoyed eight years without direct involvement in war. Ike should also be remembered for his interest in arms reduction and his somber admonition about the dangers posed by the military-industrial complex.

CONFLICTING HISTORICAL VIEWPOINTS: NO. 15

Who Started the Cold War?

The governments of the Soviet Union and the United States have offered remarkably similar explanations for the origins of the Cold War. Each side

*has characterized the conflict as a morality play in which the other is cast
as the villain. Both have presumed to act in the name of the world's "peace-
loving" peoples, and each portrayed the other as an imperialist power bent
on global conquest.*

*Articulated initially by top officials in the Truman administration, includ-
ing George F. Kennan* (Foreign Affairs Quarterly, *July 1947*), *head of the
State Department Policy Planning Staff, the official American interpretation
of Cold War origins was not seriously questioned by most historians in the
United States until the 1960s. Although scholarly accounts were often less
hysterical than those by journalists and other popular writers, historians
generally agreed that the Soviet Union's aggressive designs threatened the
stability of the postwar world. Indeed, one of the most methodical and au-
thoritative apologists for American diplomacy was Herbert Feis, a State Department adviser-turned-historian. In a series of books* (Roosevelt-Chur-
chill-Stalin, *1953;* Between War and Peace, *1960;* The Atomic Bomb and the
End of World War II, *1966; and* From Trust to Terror, *1970*), *Feis argued
that in its Cold War policies the United States was merely responding to a
Soviet challenge. Fomenting revolution and seeking conquest, the Soviet
state, he believed, shattered the Grand Alliance, violated its Yalta agreements, and forced a reluctant and war-weary United States to assume the
leadership of a threatened free world.*

*Although the orthodox view dominated popular and scholarly writing
throughout the 1950s, there were from the beginning of the Cold War a few
precocious dissenters who raised disturbing questions about American policy. Years before popular disenchantment with the war in Vietnam found
reflection in a multitude of revisionist attacks on American postwar policy,
the philosopher-journalist Walter Lippmann* (The Cold War, *1947*) *questioned the rationale for containment. And such "realist" historians as Hans
Morgenthau* (In Defense of the National Interest, *1951*) *and William McNeill*
(America, Britain, and Russia, *1953*) *offered early challenges to prevailing
assumptions of exclusive Russian guilt. But the first systematic revision of
the traditional interpretation was probably William A. Williams's* American-
Russian Relations, 1871–1947 *(1952). In this volume and in such later works
as* The Tragedy of American Diplomacy *(1959) and* The Contours of American History *(1961), Williams attributed the onset of the Cold War to the
dollar diplomacy of the United States. Linking American foreign policy to
the "needs" of American capitalism, he viewed containment as the latest
manifestation of a traditional American diplomacy of economic expansionism
dating at least from the days of the Open Door. American counterrevolutionary activities, then, were designed not to contain communist aggression
but to promote commercial penetration of Eastern Europe.*

*In recent years, Williams's thesis has been documented and extended by a
number of New Left scholars. In* The Politics of War *(1968) and* The Roots
of American Foreign Policy *(1969), Gabriel Kolko, for example, has offered
the least temperate indictment of American policy yet available. Although
typical of much New Left scholarship on the period, Kolko's work is more
extreme than studies by such thoughtful radicals as Walter LaFeber and*

Lloyd Gardner. *In his balanced* America, Russia, and the Cold War *(1967), LaFeber surveyed the entire era and concluded that both powers must share the blame for the war of nerves. In* Architects of Illusion *(1970), Gardner was also highly critical of American policy shapers, but he too conceded that "neither side could fully control events, or even freely respond to them in many instances."*

The critics of revisionism are numerous, and many historians reject the economic determinism of the New Left. But recent scholars have shown little willingness to defend the simple pieties of the orthodox interpretation. Thus, in The United States and the Origin of the Cold War *(1972) and* Strategies of Containment *(1982), among the most persuasive postrevisionist studies, John Gaddis concluded that "leaders of both super-powers sought peace" and that "neither side can bear sole responsibility for the onset of the Cold War." In much the same nonaccusatory vein, Daniel Yergin has argued in* Shattered Peace *(1977) that in the confusion of postwar events, well-intentioned American policy makers misread clumsy, even brutal, but defensive Soviet behavior.*

Though the question of Cold War origins remains open, there is clearly widespread scholarly belief that the orthodox answer is no longer satisfactory.

FOR FURTHER READING

In addition to the studies above, students should compare the conflicting judgments of John Spanier's *American Foreign Policy Since World War II* (1960), Louis Halle's *The Cold War as History* (1967), and Thomas Paterson's *Soviet-American Confrontation* (1973). Brief overviews of the period include John Lukacs's *A History of the Cold War* (1961), Norman Graebner's *Cold War Diplomacy* (1962), and Thomas Paterson's *On Every Front* (1979). Robert J. Maddox's *The New Left and the Origins of the Cold War* (1973) harshly criticizes revisionist scholarship. The memoirs of both Truman and Eisenhower are useful, and those by Kennan and Acheson are indispensable. Students interested in exploring the Soviet point of view should read *History of the USA Since World War I* (1976) by N. Sirachyou and E. Yazkov, which is a tendentious challenge to "bourgeois" history. Robert Griffith in *The Politics of Fear* (1970) and Richard Fried in *Men Against McCarthy* (1976) consider aspects of the McCarthy phenomenon. William F. Buckley and L. Brent Bozell's *McCarthy and His Enemies* (1951) is a spirited defense. Allen Weintein in *Perjury* (1978) and John Cabot Smith in *Alger Hiss* (1976) offer opposing answers to the celebrated Hiss question.

29

★ ★ ★ ★ ★ ★

People of Plenty,
1946–1961

THE RETURN of full employment during World War II did not cure the "depression psychosis" of a people grown accustomed to hard times. Remembering the soup kitchens and breadlines, and the idle farms and darkened factories of the 1930s, Americans entered the postwar period with mixed emotions. They welcomed an end to the blood letting, but feared that wartime boom would become peacetime want. In 1939, the last prewar year, there were still 9.5 million persons unemployed; in 1945, Americans doubted that a demobilized economy could absorb 10 million war workers plus the 12 million men and women who had been in the armed forces.

This fear of unemployment proved groundless. The high employment war years were followed by the longest sustained period of peacetime prosperity in history. The gross national product (GNP, the sum value of all goods and services produced), which had reached $100 billion in 1929 and fallen to $70 billion during the Depression, soared by 1948 to $174 billion (using the same dollar value), and was still climbing. Farm income fell after 1947, but industrial wages rose and so did labor's share of total national income. Although the cult of motherhood and domesticity was intensified by the postwar baby boom, women — and particularly married women — continued the wartime employment trend, taking jobs in the expanding postwar economy in substantial numbers. By 1950, one in four American wives worked outside the home; by 1960, 31.6 million women (40 percent of the total) were gainfully employed, up from 16.8 million in 1946. Businesses, big and small, flourished. Veterans, under the "G.I. Bill of Rights," flocked to colleges in unprecedented numbers. In the warm glow of economic expansion, the doubts and anxieties of the Depression generation gradually evaporated.

RESURGENT PROSPERITY

Inflation, not depression, proved to be the most pressing economic problem. Their earnings fattened by high wages, their savings accounts bulging by a half-decade of full employment, consumers weary of wartime privations gave into their pent-up desire for things. Supplies, however, were limited in the early reconversion period; shortages quickly developed in nearly everything: houses, automobiles, clothes, shoes, sugar, butter, refrigerators, beefsteak, and small appliances. As wartime price controls were relaxed, the overall cost of living rose 70 percent between 1946 and 1950. Though vexing, the problem was short-lived. During the next twenty years, few Americans worried much about inflation. The economic picture was generally so excellent that even the minor recessions of 1949, 1952, 1957, and 1961 caused little anxiety. Swept along by enormous government expenditures in the Cold War arms race, by swollen military spending during the Korean and Vietnam conflicts, and by the unflagging consumption of a burgeoning population, the American economy slackened only when it was overtaken early in the 1970s by a crisis of "stagflation" that brought ominously high levels of both inflation and unemployment.

During the period from World War II through the Vietnam War, the GNP quadrupled. Although expanding more slowly than that of some industrializing nations, the American GNP, in absolute terms, outperformed all others. Some older industries, including coal and textiles, declined, but others, notably steel, grew steadily. Still others — housing, automobiles, and aircraft — expanded spectacularly, and the new "glamour industries" — chemicals (including plastic and synthetic goods), electrical appliances, and electronics (radios, tape recorders, phonographs, and television) — grew at rates that astonished even optimistic investors. Perhaps most gratifying of all, disposable per-capita income more than doubled, and the average wage earner benefited more fully from the industrial system than at any other time in the national experience.

The new prosperity was not universal. Agriculture, which claimed an increasingly smaller share of the labor force (8.5 percent in 1960), continued to be a problem sector. Technological and scientific innovations contributed to the overproduction of staple crops, which forced prices down and small growers out. The trend from family farms to agribusiness seemed irreversible. Elsewhere in the economy, disparities in income and wealth remained about as great as in the 1920s. By the late 1950s, the richest 5 percent received more income than the poorest 40 percent. In any given year, depending on economic fluctuations, one-fourth to one-third of the population lived below the government's poverty line. More than half of the elderly, nearly 20 percent of the whites, and more than half of the nonwhites were officially classified as poor. Ill-fed and ill-housed, generally born into deprivation, the poor were tucked out of view in urban slums and *barrios* or in migrant camps and rural hovels. Although carefully documented in the 1960s, this "culture of poverty" was easily overlooked amid the otherwise impressive prosperity of the complacent fifties.

In their celebration of a triumphant capitalism, Americans also overlooked a new wave of business concentration that surpassed the consolidation movements of the McKinley and Coolidge eras. Despite federal anti-trust legislation dating to the 1890s, large-scale enterprise dominated nearly every area of the economy. By 1960, some 600 businesses (0.5 percent of the total) controlled more than half of all corporate income in the United States. The most conspicuous example was the once-competitive automobile industry; smaller manufacturers went out of business during the 1950s, leaving the domestic market to General Motors, Ford, Chrysler, and the much smaller American Motors. The postwar merger movement, moreover, took new forms, such as the conglomerate and the multinational, in which business ownership transcended not only related enterprises but national boundaries.

BABY BOOM AND SUBURBIA

A primary symbol of postwar affluence was population growth. Depression couples, with their shrunken expectations, married late and normally limited family size to two children. The birth rate fell to 6.5 per thousand in 1933, and averaged only 18 per thousand for the entire decade of the thirties. Beginning with a crop of "furlough babies" during World War II and increasing during the "nesting" phase of the postwar period, the rise in birth rate mounted to 25.8 per thousand in 1947, and remained at 25 or above every year from 1951 to 1957.

The baby boom was both a cause and an effect of the economic boom. A cyclical phenomenon, population growth brought increased demands for goods and services, which created more jobs, which heightened prosperity, which stimulated population growth. Viewing this self-sustaining process, demographers and other experts (perhaps some who had earlier projected a long-term population decline) worried that the nation would soon have standing room only. In the 1960s, however, domestic environmental and economic concerns and a global population explosion fostered an appreciable reduction in American population growth. In the prosperous fifties, however, an increasing birth rate combined with a declining death rate to give the United States a rate of increase roughly equal to India's.

Among the first concerns of the growing American family was a better place to live. During the 1930s the national housing standard deteriorated badly. New construction all but stopped, as hard-pressed families pooled their resources in single dwellings. A dozen occupants in a one-bedroom apartment were not unusual in many cities. The return of good times brought increased demand for shelter; the federal government and private developers tried to meet this demand by the construction of large-scale urban, suburban, and all too few public housing developments. During the 1950s, new housing expanded faster than new households, at a rate of more than one million dwellings a year. By 1960, at least half of all existing dwellings had been built since World War II. The federal role in this suburban growth was particularly great. Through the grace of the Federal Housing

Administration (FHA), the Veterans' Housing Administration (VHA), and income tax deductions on mortgage interest payments, a majority of Americans for the first time in the twentieth century owned their own homes. Federal highway programs, chiefly for the construction of an interstate system, also accelerated the movement from city to suburb.

Often the postwar homemakers found themselves in standardized tracts, with row upon row of nearly identical "ticky-tacky" houses on small, treeless lots. Frequently, these were mushroom communities built almost overnight by fast-buck speculators, without planning or government oversight. They appeared on the outskirts of cities and along the new freeways. Occasionally, as with the Levittowns on Long Island and in Pennsylvania, the builders and merchandisers of low-cost, mass-produced developments created not merely "bedroom towns" but self-contained settlements complete with churches, recreational facilities, and shopping centers.

Although often physically and socially more differentiated than their detractors alleged, these postwar projects were widely described as indistinguishable "warrens for the middle class." They were said to be homogenous centers of stultifying "togetherness," of harried commuting fathers and child-centered, mother-dominated homes, of credit-poor consumers anxiously accumulating gadgets and conveniences to "keep up with the Joneses." In time, much of suburbia was to be swallowed by the almost uninterrupted metropolitan sprawl that linked Boston to Washington (Boswash) or San Francisco to San Jose (San-San). However much they yearned for the bucolic life of small town and country, these Metro-Americans were destined to live in megalopolis, amid eight-lane highways, parking lots, rapid transit systems, and town-house complexes.

But if life beyond the city limits was not universally appealing, it nevertheless had its attractions. Encouraged by relatively low-cost housing and improved transportation — but also by city congestion and social disorganization — roughly as many people moved from the urban core to the suburbs in the 1950s as came from Europe in the peak years of immigration. By 1970, suburbia claimed more people than either the central cities or rural areas and small towns. Those left behind were generally poor, elderly, and nonwhite. As the white middle-class pursued its dreams in suburbia, the central cities increasingly became the preserve of minorities: blacks, Hispanics, and American Indians.

CONSUMERISM, "THE AMERICAN WAY OF LIFE"

The expanding population and housing market were matched by unparalled growth in the market for consumer goods. All but insatiable in its appetite for things, the postwar consumer society was sustained by constantly rising wages, easy flowing credit, and intensive advertising. Confident that higher future earnings would make repayment possible, if not painless, Americans borrowed as never before. Between 1945 and 1952, consumer credit increased by 800 percent. The nation's advertising budget soared, from $3 billion in 1945 to $12 billion in 1960. Bombarded by increasingly sophisticated sales campaigns in the print and broadcast media, Americans turned desire into need and indulged themselves in a welter of objects.

The stuff of nearly everyone's dreams was the automobile, the great American status symbol, the means of social as well as spatial mobility. During the 1950s, an average of nearly seven million new cars and trucks were sold every year. Although doomed to short life through planned obsolesence, the automobile was a luxury liner of gaudy convenience, comfort, and conspicuous consumption. Sporting "futuristic" styling and tail fins in the fifties and somewhat sleeker, though even larger, lines in the sixties, it often came equipped with an endless array of frills: stereo radios, tinted glass, air conditioning, and electrically powered windows, brakes, and steering. The ripple effect of the industry sustained a vast number of consumer services and enterprises, from motels and drive-in restaurants to filling stations and highway construction.

The television set was, if anything, more ubiquitous. Developed in the late twenties but still a rarity in 1945, television rapidly became the dominant medium of mass entertainment and advertising in the United States. By 1952, two-thirds of all families owned one; a decade later, at the close of television's "golden age," hardly any did not. In the 1970s, color TV, once the ultimate symbol of working-class success, became so commonplace that families without one felt deprived.

The social and cultural consequences of the national obsession with the tube remain little explored. Radio and film lost their central place in the entertainment field, but both responded creatively and survived in altered forms. Mass-circulation magazines, including *Look, Collier's,* and *Life,* eventually folded. Social dancing to the "big band" sound never recovered. Consumer response to the TV dinner suggested that family table talk was similarly doomed; social commentators worried that the art of conversation would be lost to the artfulness of Milton Berle and "Gun Smoke." By the mid-1950s, educators noticed that the baby-boom children, the first generation to grow up with television, were more preoccupied with the vapid fare of video than with the printed word. Optimists spoke of the salutary "homogenizing tendencies" of a medium that permitted all Americans, regardless of race, class, or region, to share the same visual and aural experiences; one scholar concluded that "the television set has democratized experience." Others feared that "high culture" would be swept away in the tidal wave of enthusiasm for home entertainment tailored for a mass audience.

Patterns of consumption varied to meet the lifestyles of the consumers, but the array and volume of goods met all tastes. In the fifties, home freezers and high-fidelity stereophonographs were accorded the status of "necessities." By the end of that decade, the houses and garages of suburbia were littered with sporting goods, power tools, tape recorders, automatic dishwashers, barbecues, boats, electric toothbrushes, can-openers, hair-dryers, and nail-groomers. Special markets were developed for particular consumer groups: anglers, amateur photographers, pet lovers, scuba divers, and backpackers. The teen-age market, once nonexistent, rapidly became a multi-billion-dollar business, specializing in records, cosmetics, surfboards, junk food, soft drinks, clothes, 3-D movies, and motorcycles.

New institutions catered to the demands of the consumer culture: supermarkets, shopping malls, and credit cards, to name a few. In the 1950s, the large retail food store became the envy of the world: a spacious, glistening shrine to American abundance where shoppers pushed overladen, stainless steel carts among rows of well-displayed and hygienically packaged cartons, cans, and frozen foods. The great shopping malls that spread in the 1960s contained even more goods. In these sprawling indoor emporia of shops, stalls, and stores, consumers could dine in a cafeteria or a pizza stand, buy a mink stole or a hula-hoop, play pinball, purchase a paperback book or a bayberry-scented candle — and in some cases ride an elephant or go skating. If the piped Muzak annoyed some, there was comfort in the air-conditioned and plant-laden atmosphere and in the knowledge that the credit card was rapidly making cash obsolete.

A PACKAGED SOCIETY

To most Americans the consumer culture was the supreme achievement of the world's most vigorous economy. Vice President Nixon, in his famous "kitchen debate" (1959) with Khrushchev, could think of no more effective rebuttal to the claim of communist superiority than the dazzling array of household appliances available in the United States. More skeptical observers, on the other hand, decried the ethic of accumulation and lamented the development of an "abundance psychology."

Books of social criticism, freed from the Depression-era preoccupation with hard times, analyzed *The Crack in the Picture Window* (1956) and *The Split Level Trap* (1960). The postwar American male was described as *The Organization Man* (1956) or *The Man in the Gray Flannel Suit* (1956) who was lost in the *Lonely Crowd* (1950) where "belongingness," the "organization ethic," and "other-directedness" were more highly prized than traditional values of thrift, individualism, and self-reliance. Members of the new white-collar class, it was said, were the victims of "status anxiety," and were manipulated and dehumanized by corporate greed. Suburban schools produced a standardized product, better trained in "life adjustment" and "peer orientation" than in the three *R*s. According to its critics, this was a "packaged society," an "air-conditioned nightmare," in which art, sex, politics, religion, and even the sentiment of Mother's Day were merchandised in a mass market.

In the 1960s, the social commentary grew shriller as the children of the middle class became disenchanted with the war in Vietnam and the supermarket society. Drawing in part on the experience of the nonconformist "beat generation" of the fifties — and the poetry and novels of Lawrence Ferlinghetti, Allen Ginsberg, and Jack Kerouac — the "counter culture" rejected the values, if not always the benefits, of the consumer culture. More recently, double-digit inflation, a slower growth rate, depleting energy supplies, and despoiled natural resources have cast other shadows across our affluent society and have forced Americans for the first time since the Great Depression to face diminishing expectations.

During the fifties, however, the detracters of American society were not listened to. For the moment, though turmoil, confusion, and national self-doubt lay just ahead, the People of Plenty took their material well-being for granted. Repeatedly assured that never in any nation had so many so much, they assured themselves that the good life lay within the grasp of every American who deserved it. It seems unsurprising, then, that the politics of the period was not notably committed to social causes.

THE POLITICS OF ABUNDANCE:
HARRY AND IKE

Harry S Truman, the first postwar president, like his successors, lived in the shadow of FDR. Chosen to his own astonishment as Roosevelt's running mate in 1944, he became chief executive by happenstance — Roosevelt's death. Lacking the New Dealer's elegant manner and patrician good looks, Truman was friendly, earthy, unmistakably middle-class. He had only a high school diploma; his brief career as a Kansas City clothier ended in bankruptcy. Except for his wartime role as chairman of a Senate investigating committee, his two terms in that body were distinguished only by his loyalty to the New Deal. But he was much more than the embodiment of the common man. Though never popular during his years in office, many historians now describe him as the most underrated chief executive, and some rank him as a "near-great" president.

In domestic affairs, Truman was committed to social justice and shared abundance. Beginning in September 1945, he proposed the long list of reforms later called the "Fair Deal": a full employment program; increased minimum wages and broader Social Security; public housing and slum clearance; additional TVA-like regional development projects; federal aid to education and health protection; federal control of atomic energy; and an end to racial discrimination in voting and employment.

Except for early action on the employment and atomic energy bills, the Seventy-Ninth Congress was uncooperative. The conservative coalition of southern Democrats and northern Republicans, who gave his foreign policy initiatives bipartisan support, blocked his domestic programs at nearly every turn. In 1946 — amid the chaos of reconversion and mounting public dissatisfaction with rising prices and strikes — the Republicans gained control of both House and Senate. The new Eightieth Congress, the first Republican Congress since the Hoover administration, quickly cut government spending and taxes. The controversial Taft-Hartley Act, passed over Truman's veto, indicated a conservative swing in labor policy, but it proved not to be the union-busting measure that management wanted. It authorized anti-strike injunctions, outlawed the *closed shop* (which forbade the hiring of nonunion workers), and permitted so-called right-to-work laws prohibiting the *union shop* (which required new workers to join the union).

As the election of 1948 approached, Truman's prospects seemed bleak. Conservatives of both parties opposed his domestic programs. Liberals faulted his handling of the 1946 railroad and coal-mining strikes and longed for the magic of FDR. The New Deal coalition and the Democratic party itself seemed to be falling apart. The left wing threatened to follow Henry A. Wallace, who favored more progress at home and more conciliation abroad. A strong civil rights plank in the platform brought the secession of many conservative Southerners, who supported the "Dixiecrat" movement of Governor J. Strom Thurmond of South Carolina. The confident Republicans, once more fighting their right wing, renominated Governor Thomas E. Dewey of New York.

The situation was actually more favorable to Truman than it seemed. The people were not yet deeply divided about foreign policy, and some had resented Republican efforts to frustrate reform and curb labor. The two Democratic secessions proved advantageous. Wallace's well-intentioned protest movement, compromised and thus doomed to insignificance by its Communist supporters, drew antiradical fire away from Truman. Thurmond carried only four Deep South states, and his candidacy helped keep northern blacks in the Democratic camp. The old New Deal coalition held, giving Truman an upset victory. The Democrats regained control of Congress.

Jubilantly, a newly confident president called once more for the enactment of the Fair Deal, to which he added a new farm program, additional civil rights measures, and repeal of the Taft-Hartley Act. Again, though Democrats nominally controlled the Congress, the conservative coalition held fast. Congress cooperated by extending some existing programs. Social Security was expanded, the minimum wage was increased, and new public housing units were funded. But there were no new departures — no new TVAs; no new farm program, no prepaid national medical plan, nor federal aid to education; no revision of labor legislation; and no break-throughs in civil rights law. Under his own authority as commander-in-chief, the president ordered the armed forces to begin desegregating; he also appointed blacks to important offices, intervened in federal court cases on behalf of black litigants, and strengthened the Civil Rights Section of the Department of Justice.

Beyond these achievements, however, Truman's domestic record is unimpressive. Called to lead in a period of economic abundance and international crisis, his first priority was always foreign policy. Inheriting the political stalemate of Roosevelt's last peacetime years, but not the sense of national emergency that gave the New Deal its broad support, Truman's domestic legislative struggles were waged against uneven odds. But he kept the reform tradition intact and before the national conscience. Future generations and future Congresses would be kinder to the man and more receptive to his programs than were his contemporaries.

In the presidential campaign of 1952, the Republicans made much of the "mess in Washington" (an allusion to minor scandals involving Truman's subordinates) and of "creeping socialism" (a reference to New Deal programs, particularly TVA). The party chose the moderate General Dwight David Eisenhower, not the conservative idol Robert A. Taft. Eisenhower called himself a "modern Republican" and a "dynamic conservative," by which he meant that he was "conservative when it comes to money and liberal when it comes to human beings." That ambiguous distinction, like much of the new president's syntax, baffled many observers. But it was a fair description of the character and style of an affable general-in-politics who preferred consensus to conflict and who was more frequently opposed by his party's right wing than by the Democrats.

More comfortable at presiding than leading, ill at ease with governmental solutions to national problems, he left his successors a back-log of unresolved social problems. If Ike mounted no new crusades, he also sounded no retreat from the reform tradition. He was immensely popular and well suited to the conservative national mood. Some historians argue that his executive talents have been underestimated, and many believe that, despite his failure to build a Republican majority, the general was not the political innocent he appeared to be. He was, as Vice President Nixon observed, "far more complex and devious . . . than most people realized."

Initially, the Republican administration offered a businessman's government. The president, whose reverence for business leaders bordered on awe, conceded that Senator Taft was "twice as liberal" as he on social welfare issues. The cabinet was dominated by wealthy corporate executives — "eight millionaires and a plumber" — who hastily dismantled Korean wartime controls and paid lip-service to the gospel of small government, balanced budgets, and free enterprise. Administration efforts to win business confidence included tax concessions, increased "partnership" of government and private enterprise in public power and atomic energy development, and support for state, rather than federal, control of tideland oil resources.

Midway through the first term, however, Eisenhower's economic and social policies shifted from right to center. The Treasury Department modified its conservative, anti-inflation measures to fight a recession in 1954, and recovery came swiftly. The Republican Congress, moreover, proved somewhat receptive to familiar kinds of reform. There were modest extensions of Social Security and public housing, and a Department of Health, Education, and Welfare (HEW), initially a Truman proposal, was created. The return to Democratic control of Congress after the 1954 elections brought little change to this moderate course. Such controversial programs as health insurance or federal support of education were regularly defeated or heavily amended. Secretary of Agriculture Ezra Taft Benson's efforts to revise Democratic farm policies resulted in lower price supports. But declining farm income and heavy pressure from farm organizations prompted the administration to support many New Dealish measures, including a "Soil Bank" scheme to reduce agricultural acreage.

Government spending, so long denounced as the road to socialism, was cut back only moderately after the Korean War. It remained higher than the 1950 post–World War II low of $45 billion and, by 1957, was to reach a new peacetime high of $82 billion — more than half directed to defense expenditures. Government decisions continued to affect every part of the economy. Eisenhower successfully blocked federal construction of a dam and hydroelectric plant in Hell's Canyon, Idaho. But his efforts to curb federal power production in the Memphis area by favoring a private utility group over TVA were frustrated by revelations of excess profits and conflict of interest. Also, Eisenhower's effort to remove federal controls on natural gas production ended in failure. When HEW Secretary Oveta Culp Hobby opposed the free distribution of polio vaccine as "back door" socialism, public indignation forced her resignation. Neither budgetary considerations nor fear of "statism" deterred presidential support for such massive federal works projects as the St. Lawrence Seaway (jointly undertaken with Canada) and the Interstate Highway System (the largest road-building program in history).

The most important social advance of the period, that made by Afro-Americans, was a product of judicial activism and black initiative, not administration action. At mid-century, blacks were still generally subject to enforced segregation in the South, and throughout the nation they were far behind whites in jobs, income, housing, education, and health. In 1954 — in *Brown* vs. *Board of Education*, a case brought by the NAACP — the Supreme Court reversed its 1896 "separate but [nominally] equal" doctrine, and ordered the desegregation of public schools. In 1955–1956, blacks in Montgomery, Alabama, led by young Martin Luther King, Jr., launched a successful boycott to end segregation in that city's buses. Similar nonviolent, direct-action campaigns by black and white civil rights activists eventually brought additional progress in voting, public accommodations, and housing. But change came slowly. The *Brown* decision (which was soon extended to all public institutions) and the emerging civil rights movement provoked fierce opposition in the South, particularly in the lower tier of states, where massive resistance campaigns were led by white supremacist Citizens' Councils.

Although he cautiously acknowledged the desegregation order as the law of the land, Eisenhower refused otherwise to lend his considerable moral authority to the crusade against racism. But in 1957, when Arkansas Governor Orval Faubus attempted to obstruct the court-ordered desegregation of a Little Rock high school, the president used federal troops to enforce the decree. He also signed the first Civil Rights Acts (1957 and 1960) passed by Congress since Reconstruction. In civil rights, as in other areas of human welfare, Eisenhower provided little executive support.

The diffidence of Eisenhower's leadership led some to dismiss him as "the bland leading the bland." But Eisenhower was the most effective Republican campaigner since Warren G. Harding; despite a heart attack in 1955, he was re-elected in 1956 by a landslide. Whatever his deficiencies, Eisenhower gave the great majority of Americans the kind of presidency they wanted. Eight years of "modern Republicanism" did not solve the nation's critical domestic and foreign problems; however, peace was preserved, general abundance (despite brief recessions) was maintained, and a once-corrosive political atmosphere was tempered.

In the presidential campaign of 1960, Eisenhower gave his nominal blessings to Vice President Nixon, and then stood by unenthusiastically while the new Republican standard bearer ran on the administration's record. The Democratic challenger, John F. Kennedy, a Roman Catholic, was then only 42 years old; he exuded confidence and vigor and promised to "get America moving again." Kennedy's victory was by the narrowest of margins, and its meaning was not readily apparent. Popular suspicions about Kennedy's great wealth and religion were offset by his personal charm and political skill. But Nixon's strong showing suggested that the nation was not ready for bold new directions. The Democrats retained control of Congress, but Republicans and conservatives of both parties registered gains. Although the presidential guard had changed, there was no mandate for the bold new programs Kennedy's campaign had promised. In time, of course, the election of 1960 would emerge as a point of transition from the politics of tranquility to the politics of reform. At the moment, however, one thing was certain: the people still liked Ike.

FOR FURTHER READING

Among the more thoughtful overviews are Carl Degler's *Affluence and Anxiety* (1968); William Leuchtenburg's *A Troubled Feast* (1979); and Eric Goldman's *The Crucial Decade and After* (1961). The social and intellectual impact of American affluence is treated in David Potter's *People of Plenty* (1954), but the books mentioned in the text should also be consulted. Douglas Miller and Marian Novak have described *The Fifties: The Way We Really Were* (1977), and Scott Donaldson analyzes *The Suburban Myth* (1969). Aspects of the period's economic history are delineated in Herman Miller's *Rich Man, Poor Man* (1964); J. K. Galbraith's *The Affluent Society* (1958); and Michael Harrington's *The Other America* (1962). Richard Kluger's *Simple Justice* (1975) is a history of the *Brown* decisions. Numan Bartley in *The Rise of Massive Resistance* (1969) and Neil McMillen in *The Citizens' Council* (1971) chronicle southern reactions to desegregation. Of the many books on the Truman administration, see especially Alonzo Hamby's *Beyond the New Deal* (1973); Robert Ferrell's *Harry S Truman and the Modern American Presidency* (1982); Robert Donovan's *Conflict and Crisis* (1977) and *Tumultuous Years* (1982); and Barton Bernstein, ed., *Politics and Policies of the Truman Administration* (1970). Useful studies of Eisenhower's presidency include Charles Alexander's *Holding the Line* (1975); Herbert Parmet's *Eisenhower and the American Crusades* (1972); and Fred Greenstein's *The Hidden Hand Presidency* (1982). Gary Richard's *The Reaffirmation of Republicanism* (1979) examines the 83rd Congress; and John Bartlow Martin's *Adlai Stevenson and the World* (1977) portrays one of the nation's more notable also-rans.

30

★ ★ ★ ★ ★ ★

Promise and Frustration, the 1960s

THE EARLY 1960s were notably optimistic years. Riding a wave of unprecedented affluence, the people looked confidently toward the fulfillment of the American dream. A new president, young and vigorous John F. Kennedy, was the self-proclaimed tribune of "a new generation," who had pledged to lead the nation out of drift and conformity. Bold federal initiatives against poverty and discrimination promised ready solutions to the most nagging American social ills. Abroad, the power and prestige of the United States remained immense. New divisions within the communist bloc carried assurances of diminished Soviet influence and the relaxation of East-West tensions.

By 1968, however, Americans were plagued by multiple domestic and international crises. The twin goals of social and economic justice seemed as illusive as ever. Politically and culturally polarized, deeply mired in an unpopular war it could not win, the nation was awash with discontent. Some observers worried that America had lost its social cohesion and was coming apart.

IN SEARCH OF THE NEW FRONTIER

John Fitzgerald Kennedy inspired public adoration more common to entertainers than to politicians. He was blessed with keen intelligence, an urbane and elegant style, and a self-deprecating sense of humor. Virtually alone among post–World War II presidents, his popularity seemed to increase with each month that passed. His public esteem, however, won him little congressional support. At the time of his assassination, less than one third of his legislative program had been enacted. Inevitably, his brief, tragic presidency raised expectations that could not be realized.

TABLE 18. THE KENNEDY-JOHNSON YEARS, 1961–1968

Year	Black revolution	Other domestic events	Vietnam War	Other foreign events
1961	Freedom Riders.	**January** Kennedy inaugurated.	**December** Kennedy pledges help to South Vietnam.	**April** Bay of Pigs. **August** Berlin wall.
1962	**October** Troops to Oxford, Mississippi.	**April** Steel price dispute. **November** Election; slight Republican gains.		**October** Cuban missile crisis.
1963	**April–May** Birmingham incidents. **August** March on Washington.	*Feminine Mystique* published. **September** Tax cut passed. **November 22** Kennedy assassinated.	**November** Fall of Diem.	**August** Above-ground test-ban treaty signed.
1964	**January** Poll tax amendment. **June 3** Civil rights workers murdered in Mississippi. **July** Civil Rights Act.	**August** Economic Opportunity Act. **November** Johnson wins election.	**August** Tonkin Gulf incident.	**October** Chinese atomic bomb.
1965	**August** Voting Rights Act. Watts riots.	**July** Medicare enacted.	**February** "Operation Rolling Thunder" begins. **June** U.S. troops in combat.	**April** U.S. troops to Dominican Republic.
1966	**January** Robert C. Weaver, first black cabinet member. Black Power movement. National Organization for Women formed.	**November** Election; Republican gains.	**June** Bombing of Hanoi, Haiphong.	**July** France withdraws from NATO command organization.
1967	**June** Thurgood Marshall appointed to Supreme Court. **July** Riots in Newark, Detroit.		**January** U.S. offensive. **September** Elections in South Vietnam.	**June** Israeli-Arab War.
1968	**April 4** Martin Luther King assassinated. **April 10** Civil Rights Bill passed.	**June 5** Robert Kennedy shot. **November** Nixon elected president.	**February** Tet offensive. **May** Paris peace talks. **November 1** Bombing of North Vietnam ended.	**August** Soviet invasion of Czechoslovakia.

The first challenge to the Kennedy promise — "to get the country moving again" — was a sluggish economy. Having inherited a lagging growth rate, 6 percent unemployment, and a staggering balance-of-trade deficit, the new administration encouraged economic expansion through increased civilian and military spending. To hold down inflation, the president issued wage-price guidelines and "jawboned" steel companies into rescinding a price hike.

Although Congress responded favorably to the administration's defense and space research-and-development programs, it turned down most social welfare proposals. Kennedy's stop-gap bills for investment tax-credits, employee retraining, public housing, and increased minimum wage and Social Security benefits were enacted. Congress also passed the landmark Trade Expansion Act (1962), which stimulated foreign trade through reciprocal tariff agreements. But the president's Area Redevelopment Act (1961), designed to aid chronically depressed areas, was so amended that most of the funding went for highway construction — more beneficial to business interests than to the poor. Conservatives blocked Kennedy's requests for nearly everything else: programs to assist unemployed youth and migrant workers, a new Department of Urban Affairs, expanded unemployment insurance benefits, Medicare for the aged, federal aid to education, and a tax cut designed to increase consumer spending.

Despite these setbacks to New Frontier reforms, the economy improved dramatically. Between 1960 and 1964, both the GNP and total federal expenditures (much of the latter for defense) increased by nearly 25 percent. The annual inflation rate (1 to 2 percent) was minimal, but the unemployment rate never fell below 5 percent.

In confronting the country's worst social problem, the unequal status of blacks, Kennedy was again sharply limited by the dominant congressional coalition of Southern Democrats and generally conservative Republicans. Defeated in several legislative battles and afraid of tying up all domestic and foreign action in a filibuster, the administration relied mainly on executive action. Blacks were increasingly appointed to office, pressure against discrimination was applied through government purchasing policies, and after some hesitation a presidential order forbade discrimination in federally financed housing. Robert F. Kennedy, the president's brother, was appointed Attorney General by the president, and vigorously attacked the problem of black voting rights in the South.

As in the 1950s, the most important advances for blacks were made through the increasingly militant, though nonviolent civil rights movement. Strongly supported by college students, clergy, and other white sympathizers from the North, the movement was opposed in the South by threats and mounting violence. By the end of 1962, the efforts of "freedom riders," supported by the Attorney General in the face of violent white resistance, achieved the end of segregation in transportation. In October 1962, federal troops were sent to Oxford, Mississippi, when mob violence and the resistance of the governor threatened to bar a black, James Meredith, from the state university. The threat of similar action prevailed the following year in Alabama, and university desegregation was under way in all states.

The year 1963 saw the peak of the peaceful victories of the civil rights movement and the beginning of a new stage. Violent resistance sharply increased; in Birmingham, Alabama, police dogs were used against marchers, and four black girls were killed in a church bombing; in Jackson, Mississippi, Medgar Evers, an NAACP field secretary, was killed from ambush outside his home. Throughout the lower South, unpunished acts of white violence against the persons and property of blacks rose sharply. In June, the president proclaimed a state of moral crisis in the nation and committed the government more fully than at any time since Reconstruction to the achievement of equality. A new civil rights bill attacking discrimination in public accommodations was introduced in Congress as a major administration objective. In August, the nation seemed profoundly impressed by a peaceful march of a quarter of million people in Washington, under the leadership of Martin Luther King, Jr.

Superficially, it seemed that great progress was being made peacefully on this crucial front, and opportunities undoubtedly increased for many blacks, especially those with skills and education. Yet the economic gaps between most blacks and most whites were not lessened, the city ghettoes remained almost unaffected, and there were signs that some blacks were losing their patience with moderate leadership. It was also clear that a large and determined white minority was ready to oppose any real social equality for the black population.

KENNEDY AND THE WORLD

Perhaps the most important development of the 1960s was a deterioration of the opposing pacts formed by the United States and the Soviet Union with their respective allies in the early Cold War period. In 1960, as the Sino-Soviet split widened, the USSR withdrew technicians from China, and during the rest of the decade hostility between the two great communist nations escalated. From time to time, Soviet satellites in Eastern Europe increased their efforts for autonomy, and in the Soviet Union itself, intellectuals fought for freedom of expression. Though neither Communist party dictatorship in the USSR nor Soviet control of Eastern Europe was seriously threatened, Soviet freedom of action was more limited than at any time since World War II. The situation had obvious advantages for American policy. It also meant, however, that Russian leaders felt the need of some major success, either peaceful or military, to consolidate their leadership in a divided communist world.

The Western alliances put together under Truman and Eisenhower were no more secure than the Soviet's. Like his predecessors, Kennedy tried to promote European economic and military unification. With a stronger trans-Atlantic partnership in mind, he persuaded Congress to adopt the reciprocal trade law of 1962 that permitted tariff reductions of up to 50 percent with

European Common Market nations. France, under General Charles de Gaulle, insisted on maintaining an independent and highly nationalistic stance. In January 1963, De Gaulle blocked England's effort to enter the European Common Market. Insisting on a separate French nuclear force, he resisted European military unification and refused to join in efforts for nuclear disarmament. England, generally loyal to its special relationship with the United States despite many disagreements, became increasingly less able to play the role of Great Power, especially in the Far East. Japan, America's principal ally in that region, continued under U.S. protection to prosper without rearming. Without solid alliances, a stable balance of power, or a powerful international defense pact, Kennedy dealt with each crisis as it arose according to the means available.

In military terms, the means increased. Robert McNamara, the talented secretary of defense, successfully imposed modern administrative techniques and Kennedy policies on the massive military establishment. Whatever remained of Dulles's reliance on massive retaliation was scrapped in favor of a balanced development of nuclear, conventional, and guerrilla capabilities. The mistaken impression of Soviet military superiority, fostered by Kennedy's campaign emphasis on a nonexistent missile gap, gave way to a clear American lead in most areas of armament. Between 1960 and 1967, the number of American Inter-Continental Ballistic Missiles (ICBMs) quintupled; in McNamara's judgment the nation had "more than we require." Rocket development was further demonstrated by successes in putting astronauts into space. In the various theaters of foreign policy, both America's increased might and its inability to solve every international problem became clear.

Far more than its predecessors, the Kennedy administration turned its attention to the problems of the impoverished and unstable Third World. The Peace Corps was formed and recruited young Americans for service in regions that needed their efforts. With less success, the president tried to persuade Congress to provide massive aid for struggling, underdeveloped economies. A special effort to promote unity, economic development, and nonrevolutionary social change in Latin America was given the name of the "Alliance for Progress." Though only the barest beginning was made in the social and economic goals of the alliance, goodwill was increased. Willingness to tolerate diversity and neutrality led to some other successes, especially in relations with African states. A Chinese attack on Indian borders in 1962 led India to turn a friendlier face toward America.

One of America's closest neighbors, Cuba, remained on unfriendly terms. When Cuban guerrilla forces led by Fidel Castro ousted a pro-U.S. but reactionary dictator in 1959, many Americans welcomed the arrival of an apparently more democratic leader. But sympathy gave way to suspicion as the Cuban Revolution turned leftward. Within the administration, Vice President Nixon, convinced that Castro was a communist, advocated U.S. military intervention to topple him. President Eisenhower secretly authorized the CIA to train an invasion force of anti-Castro Cuban exiles. In April 1961, with some misgivings (and without an attempt to negotiate U.S.–Cuban differences), the new Democratic president approved this ill-advised act of American adventurism. Misled about the extent of support likely in Cuba, the administration provided logistical assistance but refused decisive military help. The resulting humiliating defeat at the Bay of Pigs increased Kennedy's suspicion of military adventure and expert military advice.

The truculent side of Khrushchev's changeable policy was shown at the West's most vulnerable point, Berlin. In a meeting with Kennedy in Vienna in June 1961, Khrushchev refused to give up his threat to negotiate a treaty with East Germany that would have the effect of ending the occupation rights of the Western Allies. Kennedy let it be known that the defense of Berlin was an American commitment even to the extent of nuclear war. To emphasize the point, the president increased draft quotas, asked Congress for additional military spending, and outlined a civil defense program including the construction of nuclear fallout shelters. The crisis climaxed in August 1961, when the East German government closed the border to the city's western sector and began the construction of a concrete-and-barbed-wire wall between East Germany and West Berlin. Because it stopped the flow of East Germans to the West, this barrier made the presence of a Western enclave within the communist world more tolerable to the Soviets. The Berlin tension gradually subsided, but the wall remained as a ghastly reminder of East-West division.

A more serious conflict with the Soviets developed in Cuba in 1962, where the Cold War seemed perilously close to turning hot. In August, American reconnaisance planes reported that the Soviet Union, contrary to repeated and specific assurances, was building in Cuba sites for short-range missiles (220 miles) capable of striking the southernmost reaches of the United States with nuclear warheads. Soviet and Cuban intentions are subject to debate. Kennedy linked this challenge to the Berlin crisis and interpreted it as an extension of Soviet nuclear capabilities. But his response was also colored by political considerations. Because he had been humiliated by the Bay of Pigs fiasco, and because the installations were made known on the eve of a congressional election, he felt compelled to act decisively. Some historians believe that he overreacted, that the missiles were defensive and designed to deter further U.S. intervention; in their view, continued American efforts to destabilize Castro's regime — including a plot with organized crime figures to have the Cuban leader assassinated — raised legitimate Cuban security concerns.

In a series of tense meetings, Kennedy and his advisers debated various responses ranging from pacific to belligerent. Kennedy chose neither extreme. On the one hand, the administration was unwilling to propose, under pressure, the reciprocal withdrawal of Soviet missiles from Cuba and American missiles from Italy and Turkey. (The latter bases, rated obsolete, were soon quietly withdrawn; missile-carrying submarines were regarded as less vulnerable.) On the other hand, Kennedy also rejected an immediate though limited airstrike recommended by his military advisers and others. Instead, he announced that he had ordered American warships to stop and search vessels coming to Cuba that might contain offensive weapons. In case this

MAP 11: THE UNITED STATES, THE CARIBBEAN, AND CUBA

proved insufficient, he ordered military concentrations preparatory to possible invasion of the island, which might mean a direct clash with Russian personnel at missile bases. Again, the president rejected the idea of a face-to-face negotiated settlement.

To Khrushchev, Kennedy publicly pledged not to invade Cuba if the installations were removed. The Soviet leader, who had earlier promised that the missiles would fly in Cuba's defense, accepted Kennedy's terms, and a dozen Soviet vessels turned back before encountering the American blockade. "We're eyeball to eyeball," Secretary of State Dean Rusk observed, "and I think the other fellow just blinked." For the moment, it seemed that American boldness and Russian prudence had produced not only a victory for Kennedy but a chance for peace. Shrewdly refraining from any tendency to gloat over its success, the administration stressed the mutual advantages of the Soviet-American disengagement. It had been the single most dangerous moment since World War II. It proved to be Khrushchev's Bay of Pigs and Kennedy's most politically popular hour.

Although the crisis ultimately spurred a Soviet effort to close the missile gap — this gap real and in the American favor — East-West tension lessened. A "hot-line" was installed between Washington and Moscow and arms-reduction talks were resumed. In 1958, as part of the last rapprochement, both powers had suspended nuclear testing pending disarmament negotiations. In the fall of 1961, during the last great Berlin crisis, the Soviets resumed testing, exploding the largest bombs yet. The United States quickly followed suit. In 1963, however, a complex and determined American diplomatic effort produced a treaty banning atmospheric, but not underground, tests. Ratified by the Senate despite conservative fears, this treaty was signed by the USSR, the United States, Britain, and many other countries, but not by France or China. Further gestures toward détente were promised, and in October the United States agreed to a large sale of wheat to the Soviet Union.

JFK IN VIETNAM

Kennedy's important though limited foreign policy successes were unfortunately not to be duplicated in Vietnam. Once a remote and peripheral concern of the United States, Vietnam rapidly became the scene of the nation's longest (1950–1975) and most unpopular war. During World War II, Ho Chi Minh's nationalist Viet Minh forces cooperated with the United States in the common struggle against the Japanese. In 1945, Ho modeled his country's Declaration of Independence after the American document, and thereafter repeatedly expressed his good will for the government and people of the United States. Roosevelt had affirmed that the United States would not assist in the re-establishment of colonial rule in Southeast Asia, but Truman refused Ho's appeals for military and economic assistance in the Vietnamese War of national liberation from the French (1945–1954). The reasons are numerous and complex, but the most important include: American eagerness to strengthen ties with its European Cold War partner and American reluctance to make common cause with Ho, founder of the Vietnamese Communist party. In 1950, following the "fall" of China and the invasion of South Korea, fear of further Communist gains in Asia (particularly in Japan and the Philippines) prompted Truman to recognize the French puppet regime. By 1954, American taxpayers were underwriting nearly 80 percent of the cost of France's colonial war.

In 1954, Eisenhower considered but finally refused unilateral American military intervention to save the collapsing French. Yet he, too, misunderstood the nationalist character of Ho's revolution. Reading East-West conflict into an indigenous and fundamentally anticolonial struggle, he described a non-communist Vietnam as vital to American security. Following Ho's victory over the French, American economic and military aid was shifted to the anticommunist but increasingly repressive dictatorship of Ngo Dinh Diem in Saigon. The CIA began secret "counter-insurgency" activities in North Vietnam. In 1956, the administration blocked the national elections mandated by the Geneva Conference to reunify Vietnam because, as Eisenhower later noted, "possibly 80 percent of the population would have voted for the Communist Ho Chi Minh."

Until 1960, Diem's enemies in the South received only sporadic assistance from Hanoi. In that year, insurgents with the support of Ho's government organized the National Liberation Front, political arm of the Vietcong (South Vietnamese Communists). Unwilling to permit a Communist victory, and convinced that Vietnam was "the keystone to the arch, the finger in the dike" of the Asian Cold War, Kennedy picked up where Eisenhower left off. Responding to the intensifying civil war in the South, he secretly increased the American military presence. By late 1963, U.S. aircraft were flying reconnaisance and support missions for South Vietnamese troops, and the nearly 17,000 U.S. "advisers" were unmistakably engaged in combat.

Increased American support, however, brought only frustration. Despite repeated Pentagon assurances that overwhelmingly favorable "kill ratios" and "body counts" assured a non-communist victory, the United States was not winning when Kennedy was assassinated on November 22, 1963. By that date, the unpopular Diem had been assassinated by his own generals. His government gave way to a succession of others, none more successful or popular. Subsequently, as the increasingly unpopular war ground on, the slain American president's aides argued that if Kennedy had lived to be re-elected, the United States would have been spared much of the agony of the escalated war under Lyndon Johnson. That contention is unprovable.

THE GREAT SOCIETY

The contrast between the elegant, rational, slightly aloof, and handsome Kennedy and his successor, Lyndon Baines Johnson, was great. Tense, ambitious, hard-driving, gregarious, and earthy, Johnson had risen to wealth and political power through the hard school of Texas politics. His enemies considered him unscrupulous and coarse. In the opening days of his administration, however, most Americans were reassured by his emphasis on familiar programs of domestic reform. Modeling his approach on that of Franklin Roosevelt and concentrating on domestic affairs — particularly on the problems of poverty — Johnson called his program the Great Society and made clear his intent to build a new and workable consensus, the first since New Deal days. While courting business and Congress, the new president hoped to retain the support of liberals and intellectuals. The administration's brightest hope was that the first wholly southern president since the Civil War would reconcile the South to the advancement of blacks. Committing himself to this cause more eloquently than to any other, Johnson succeeded in pushing through in 1964 Kennedy's Civil Rights bill, which included further support for blacks in voting rights, education, job opportunities, and public accommodations. A further massive tax reduction gave rise to record economic advance. The Economic Opportunity Act spelled out Kennedy's proposal for a "War on Poverty" in terms of job training, grants to cities, and other measures. As the election of 1964 approached, Johnson gave the impression of masterful success.

Conservative Republicans, restive since New Deal days with moderate candidates of the Eisenhower variety, nominated Senator Barry Goldwater of Arizona. Their convention had a highly organized anti-liberal fervor, which alarmed many moderate Republicans. Goldwater, a personally attractive if unduly forthright man, urged upon farmers an end to agricultural programs, proposed the sale of the TVA in Tennessee, and criticized Social Security to the elderly. In the campaign, he played into Democratic hands, permitting Johnson to portray him as a "trigger-happy" reactionary whose election would imperil the reform tradition and world peace. Even his campaign slogan — "In Your Heart, You Know He's Right" — backfired. In an obvious reference to the presidential hand on the nuclear button, Democrats retorted: "In Your Heart, You Know He Might." While the challenger denounced big government, labor unions, rising crime, and declining morals, Johnson promised a reassuring combination of moderate reform at home and restrained but steadfast resistance to aggression abroad. In the balloting, Johnson won all but six states and the biggest popular landslide (61 percent) since 1936.

With the increased Democratic majorities in Congress, the power of the conservative Republican-Southern Democrat coalition was broken for the first time since 1938. Demonstrating his practical political skill and experience, Johnson pushed through the "Congress of Fulfillment" a coordinated reform program. Laws passed in 1965 and 1966 centered on many concerns, old and new. Black equality was promoted by the Voting Rights Act, easily the most effective civil rights measure ever enacted. Johnson also appointed the first black cabinet member and the first black Supreme Court Justice, Thurgood Marshall. Kennedy's Medicare program of health insurance for the aged and Medicaid for the poor were approved, breaking a long taboo against federal support of medical care. Traditional sectarian opposition to federal aid to education was overcome, and the president, who was largely self-educated, took special pride in such measures as the Elementary and Secondary Education Act and the Higher Education Act. The complex problem of urban poverty was addressed through such innovations as rent subsidies (the Housing Act) and the Demonstration Cities program. Finally, Johnson also won congressional support for highway safety and anti-pollution programs and for two additional cabinet-level departments, Transportation and Housing and Urban Development. Not unjustly, the president claimed the most spectacular legislative record since Franklin Roosevelt's "hundred days" in 1933.

THE AGONY OF POWER

Despite domestic achievements, by the middle of the decade the United States, potentially a great society, was clearly a divided and confused one. In both foreign and domestic affairs, the Johnson administration inherited the unsolved problems and shifting balances of the last decades. In both spheres, old policies were pushed to new lengths. In both, increased commitments seemed, by 1965 or 1966, to bring increased frustration.

The disintegration of the international alliances continued to offer a strange mixture of menace and opportunity. By 1966, De Gaulle had announced France's withdrawal from the NATO military organization. China, at last a nuclear power but torn by domestic turmoil, was denouncing Russian revisionism as bitterly as it attacked American imperialism. Though the suddenly deposed Khrushchev was replaced by Leonid Brezhnev in October 1964, the United States and the USSR continued their rapprochement gingerly. Johnson was able, in the wake of Kennedy's test-ban treaty, to win congressional support for a consular treaty (establishing additional consulates in both the United States and the USSR). There was also a Soviet-American understanding not to place nuclear warheads into orbit, and additional cultural exchanges were arranged. In 1968 the two powers also signed a nonproliferation treaty, which was designed to prevent the further spread of nuclear weapons.

To both Great Powers, the restless and impoverished Third World seemed to present impossible problems. The Alliance for Progress failed to solve Latin America's economic or political problems, and in one instance the president reverted to older methods. In the Dominican Republic, where the liberal government was overthrown by a military coup in 1963, a revolt against the new military regime threatened civil war in 1965. Stating reasons ranging from protection of American lives to preventing a triumph of Castroism, Johnson sent 22,000 troops to the island. Fortunately a compromise among contending factions eventually produced a regime with some claim to legitimacy. Yet the Johnson action was widely denounced as a throwback to Theodore Roosevelt's gunboat diplomacy.

The problems of power were most tragically illustrated, however, in the interminable struggle in Vietnam. When Johnson took office, the prospect for an American solution could not have been bleaker. Diem's death was followed by a long period of political instability in the South; the National Liberation Front (NLF) had grown increasingly formidable, and the Viet Cong controlled nearly half of South Vietnam; North Vietnamese involvement in the struggle against the Saigon regime was mounting. In effect, the president had but two choices: escalation in pursuit of a military victory, or a negotiated compromise with Hanoi for a coalition government in Saigon. Although he campaigned as the peace candidate and promised not to send Americans to fight "Asian wars," Johnson found negotiation unacceptable and ultimately moved to "Americanize" the war against "international communism" in Indochina.

Determined to win the war, but wary of congressional interference and public criticism, the president moved cautiously until the controversial Tonkin Gulf incident. In August 1964, a U.S. destroyer cruising in the gulf in an area of recent South Vietnamese naval action, was attacked — once inside North Vietnamese territorial waters and, according to disputed evidence, a second time in international waters — by North Vietnamese PT boats. Ordering retaliatory action against enemy torpedo-boat bases, the administration requested and got from Congress (which knew nothing of American air raids against the North) blanket authorization for whatever further military action might prove necessary to repel attacks on American forces. The measures also authorized American assistance to Southeast Asian states that requested it. During the presidential campaign, Johnson emphasized the limited character of the reprisals; in the fall of 1964, he resisted pressure for U.S. bombing raids against the North. His critics soon charged, however, that the Senate had been duped into granting the "functional equivalent" of a declaration of war. The Tonkin resolution — whatever the circumstances of its passage and whatever Johnson's reason for introducing it — later provided crucial justification for the escalation of American involvement.

In February 1965, an attack on an American barracks in Pleiku became the pretext for systematic air raids on North Vietnam. "We seek no wider war," Johnson affirmed. But the new aerial offensive against the North, "Operation Rolling Thunder," shifted from transport to factories and fuel dumps and included buildings in the center of large cities. The raids were defended less in terms of specific reprisals and more as part of an effort to stop troop infiltration into the South or to force North Vietnam to negotiate by showing that victory was impossible. Partly in support of the intensified air offensive, American ground forces were massively increased. By 1968, more than one-half million U.S. troops were engaged in an effort to search for guerrillas and to destroy them throughout the country.

By 1967, it was clear that this massive military presence was not succeeding in its objectives. The American buildup was more than matched by increased enemy activity. Rolling Thunder had little effect on North Vietnamese supply lines, and infiltration of Northern troops increased. Repeated and complex suggestions of negotiations failed to promise solutions acceptable to the Johnson administration. The weak South Vietnamese government remained corrupt and unpopular, and the desertion of its troops was a continuing embarrassment. U.S. attempts to secure parts of the country for the promotion of agrarian reform were failing. Amid the mounting carnage of American "pacification" efforts and search-and-destroy missions — and particularly after the bloody My Lai massacre (March 1968) of unarmed peasants by an American unit — the administration's characterization of the war as a struggle between tyranny and freedom grew less credible.

At home, as the casualties increased (25,000 Americans had died in Vietnam by 1968) and the end seemed no nearer, the war was denounced more widely and more intensely than any American war since 1865. Opponents included powerful senators, much of the press, large sections of the liberal clergy, and a large number of fervent and articulate young people. On the left of the antiwar movement, some critics insisted that the Vietnam War was part of a long pattern of American aggression, that the administration had no intention of negotiating and desired permanent bases, and that the outcome would be war with China and possibly Russia. Other critics believed the war impossible to win, and incompatible either with the needs of domestic policy or the effort of worldwide stability. Still others were appalled by the very heavy bombing of both halves of Vietnam (by 1968, America had dropped a greater tonnage of bombs on Vietnam than had been dropped on Europe and Asia together in World War II), by the use of napalm and fragmentation bombs, by the forcible relocation of villages, and by the chemical destruction of crops and forests. The minimum demands of the growing antiwar movement were the end of bombing in the North, recognition that the NLF must play a part in the government of the South, and the scaling down of operations. Defenders of the administration, while insisting that they were willing to negotiate and denying any intention of carrying the war to the North, insisted that South Vietnam must be defended. They insisted that communist success in Vietnam would mean the spread of communist power through Southeast Asia, the collapse of American efforts everywhere to prevent the expansion of communism, especially through Chinese-style guerrilla wars, and immediately, bloody reprisals against government supporters in South Vietnam. The president argued that the failure to defeat Hanoi threatened the security of Hawaii and even San Francisco.

THE BLACK REVOLUTION

By 1967, the unsuccessful war in Vietnam was obviously only one of a number of pressing and divisive problems facing the United States. The most serious was the disaffection of the black minority. While both civil rights progress and violent resistance to it continued in the South, a series of cataclysmic events turned the nation's attention to the northern black ghettoes. In August 1965, a riot in Watts, a black section of Los Angeles, resulted in 34 deaths and 30 hours of looting and arson. For the next three years, scenes of burning buildings, helmeted troops, and even tanks moving down city streets became almost commonplace on American television screens. The worst disturbances took place in Newark (23 killed) and Detroit (43 killed) in July of 1967, but few major cities escaped violence altogether. In 1967 alone, there were 41 major disturbances.

A final wave of urban rioting followed the murder on April 4, 1968, of Martin Luther King, Jr., by a white man in Memphis, Tennessee. The leading black advocate of nonviolence, Dr. King better than any other American had articulated black aspiration and appealed to the nation's moral conscience. His death triggered a great outpouring of grief and riots in 125 cities.

The inflammatory rhetoric associated with black militance was scarcely less disquieting than the disorders themselves. Though most Afro-Americans, as opinion polls revealed, still believed in integration and longed for racial reconciliation, a growing minority subscribed to Black Power, not so much a doctrine as a cry of rage that could mean anything from bloc-voting and separate economic development to outright separatism. By 1966, "white liberal" had joined "Uncle Tom" as a term of black militant abuse. Strident cries of "Burn, Baby, Burn," "Off the Pigs," and "Kill Whitey" suggested that innercity blacks had come, in James Baldwin's words, "to hate the hater."

The civil rights movement, which had grown younger, blacker, and less patient with the pace of change, was torn by factional and racial strife. In 1966, both the Student Nonviolent Coordinating Committee (SNCC) and the Congress of Racial Equality (CORE) officially abandoned their philosophical traditions of biracialism and nonviolence. Such Marxist-oriented revolutionary movements as the paramilitary Black Panther party and the nationalist Republic of New Africa advocated the territorial separation of black from white. The themes of black chauvinism and retaliatory violence, once preached primarily by the Nation of Islam (Black Muslims), seemed increasingly attractive to young innercity blacks.

Whites feared that these developments portended race war. Conservatives cried that the "Negro Revolution" threatened to tear the nation apart, and many liberals were afraid that black activists, frustrated in their efforts to reform the American system, sought its destruction. Yet no important ghetto disturbances occurred after 1968, and despite militant rhetoric, those before that date had few revolutionary implications. Opinion polls confirmed that the great majority of black Americans wanted nothing more radical than a share of the good life. The principal victims of the convulsive long hot summers of the 1960s had been blacks themselves; destroyed property nearly always lay within the ghetto, and the dead and injured were mostly black. According to the National Advisory Commission on Civil Disorders report in February 1968, the riots were spontaneous upheavals, chiefly caused by white racism and the "explosive mixture" it fostered: police brutality, slum housing, poverty and welfare dependency, job discrimination and unemployment, and blighted opportunity. To counter the threat of a completely and permanently divided society, the commission recommended a sweeping program for additional jobs, education, housing, and "income supplementation."

The problem was more easily identified than solved. Many whites demanded not additional reforms but repression. Instead of a new commitment to equality, the white community in many cities increased its armament. The principal urban response seemed to be more sophisticated riot-control training for police. President Johnson, preoccupied by Vietnam and wary of a white backlash, ignored most of the Advisory Commission's recommendations and pressed only for the open housing law that he had been advocating since 1966. This measure, which became the Civil Rights Act of 1968, banned discrimination in the sale of some 80 percent of housing. It also imposed stringent penalities for incitement to riot.

Meanwhile, the momentum of reform had slowed. Disenchanted reformers noted that the War on Poverty had done more for landlords and construction companies than for the children of depressed rural areas or ghettoes. Many antipoverty programs had been hastily devised, oversold, and underfunded. Although much had been done to soften the burdens of the poor, the elderly, and the blacks, the nation's social problems seemed as intractable as ever. And President Johnson, having squandered his great consensus of 1964 on the nation's most unpopular war, found his domestic programs in neglect and his leadership in ruins by 1968.

OTHER PROTESTS

A parallel and in some ways remarkably similar social problem, sexual discrimination, was also thrust upon the national conscience in the 1960s. In 1963, a presidential commission reported widespread discrimination against women workers, who comprised more than a third of the nation's labor force. That same year, Betty Friedan's *The Feminine Mystique* forcefully attacked the socialization process whereby woman's role was defined exclusively as wife and mother. Neither publication attracted immediate widespread public attention, yet both were symptoms of the awakening of feminism from a slumber of four decades. Having won the vote, the women's movement, after nearly a century of vitality, had collapsed during the 1920s. It was reborn, however, amid the passions of the 1960s. Constituting 51 percent of the population, women were not a minority. But many feminists came to identify with other oppressed groups. Stirred by student protests and the civil rights and antiwar movements, women activists again addressed the problems of their sex. Although the resulting feminist resurgence seemed to take the nation by surprise, the grievances expressed were all too apparent. The Nineteenth Amendment had enfranchised women but it had not redefined their role in home and society. Nor had it opened the way to educational and employment equality. In the four decades since the suffrage amendment was ratified, women's position relative to men had in fact deteriorated in important areas. A smaller percentage of the nation's college students, both graduate and undergraduate, were women in 1960 than in 1920 or 1930. Well-intentioned but often arbitrary "protective legislation" denied them access to some desirable occupations; they had only limited access to managerial and executive positions; and they were generally denied equal pay for equal work.

To attack these injustices Friedan and several other women formed in 1966 the National Organization for Woman (NOW), a worthy successor to Susan B. Anthony's and Carrie Chapman Catt's NAWSA. NOW, which proved attractive primarily to middle-class white professional and business women, represented the moderate wing of the Women's Liberation movement. Often identified as the "feminist's NAACP," it waged a dignified program of public education and lobbied for more equitable state and local legislation. But younger activists, often those associated with the New Left, were generally critical of NOW and formed their own radical groups. Among these small and often factious units, the most notable was probably WITCH (at first Women's International Terrorist Conspiracy from Hell, but later sometimes called Women Infuriated at Taking Care of Hoodlums or Women Inspired to Commit Herstory), a tiny but shrill, loosely knit "nonorganization" that employed street theater to dramatize sexual injustice.

Whatever their persuasions, the new feminists, like their sisters a half-century earlier, faced the ridicule and hostility of tradition-minded men and women who either argued that woman's place was defined by biology or that sexual equality would destroy the institutions of marriage and family. There was some triumph as well as much abuse. At the most abstract level, sexual bigotry was not routed, but it retreated a little as women in growing numbers became sensitive to sexual issues. More particularly, governments, both state and federal, began to respond to this new sensitivity. Title VII of the 1964 Civil Rights Act forbade both sexual and racial job discrimination; HEW sponsored "affirmative action" programs for women as well as minorities; Congress enacted in 1972 an Equal Rights Amendment to the Constitution, which was not ratified by all the states; the Supreme Court in 1973 issued a remarkably liberal abortion ruling. To be sure, sexism, like racism, possessed subtleties that seemed to defy government solution. But the status of women had indisputably improved during the first decade of women's liberation.

A very different kind of protest in this age of change and unrest was that of the self-conscious youth culture. In 1964, a number of northern university students had gone to Mississippi as "summer soldiers" in the civil rights movement. The violence they encountered undermined their respect for authority, and the success of nonviolent methods suggested new kinds of power. Radicalized by the experience and disenchanted with the "sandbox politics" of student government, some students were prepared to oppose an "impersonal," "authoritarian," and "irrelevant" academic order.

The first major confrontation between collegiate rebels and administrators came in 1964 at the University of California at Berkeley, where the Free Speech Movement challenged campus restrictions on student political activity. Largely successful in securing its immediate objectives in Berkeley, the movement spread as a shrill but comparatively small minority of the nation's college students turned to social agitation and identified with such New Left organizations as Students for a Democratic Society (SDS), formed in 1962. Objectives varied from campus to campus, ranging from student participation in matters of governance and curriculum, to increased minority representation in student bodies and faculty, to the dissociation of universities from the military-industrial complex. Toward the end of the decade, as U.S. involvement in Southeast Asia escalated and student draft deferments were ended, grievances concentrated on the war that many college youths thought was an extension of a racist, imperialist, and militarized nation.

In some cases, student energies were benignly channeled into off-campus experiments, such as "free universities" or to the antiwar "teach-ins," which brought students and professors into extended discussions about the war. In others, explosive confrontations occurred between youths and the police. Campus ROTC and administration buildings became targets of student sit-ins and even arson. In 1968, after the murder of Dr. King, a strike led by the SDS forced temporary closure of Columbia University. The next year, gun-wielding black youths intimidated Cornell University administrators into concessions. Following the American invasion of Cambodia in 1970, student protest erupted on hundreds of campuses; in Ohio and Mississippi, authorities opened fire on campus demonstrators, killing a total of six and wounding more than a dozen others.

The youth movement also had a less overtly political side, one that led not to confrontation with authority but to withdrawal into personal experience. Many adults failed to distinguish between the radical activists of the New Left and the hippies, or flower children — and some youths experimented with both forms of rebellion. Both groups inhabited what came to be called the counterculture; both shared an affinity for casual sex, hallucinogenic drugs (most commonly "acid" or LSD), rock and roll, long hair, and pseudo-proletarian dress. But the true "freaks," as hippies called themselves, chose to "drop out" rather than to agitate. Drawing on the experience of post–World War I bohemians on both sides of the Atlantic and, more particularly, on that of the "beat generation" of the 1950s, the flower children rejected bourgeois values and the traditions of Western thought. Preferring emotion to reason, oriental mysticism to science, community to individualism, and self-fulfillment ("doing one's thing") to material success, they pursued an alternative life style in rural communes or urban "crash pads."

At the time, much was made of a generation gap between young and old. Many adults worried that the baby-boom cohort (then in late adolescence and early adulthood) had run amuck. In truth, however, the 1960s were notable for continuity as well as change, and many of the nation's young people were about as straight as their parents. Opinion polls revealed that the youth movement was a movement of *some* youth. Typically, the cultural and political rebels of the "tumultuous sixties" were the children of well-educated, white, middle-class parents and attended the more cosmopolitan and prestigious universities. Noncollege white youths, often resentful of their more affluent counterparts, frequently had little sympathy for black liberation, the peace movement, woman's rights, or public disorder. Even on the most politicized campuses, the student left was a distinct, if voluble, minority. In time, some cultural affectations and drugs of the youth revolution would become adopted widely, and not merely among the young. More fundamentally, the counterculture had a lasting impact on American attitudes toward such important matters as sex, marriage, work, leisure, career, and war. But the tumult of the sixties and the pervasiveness of youthful radicalism have been exaggerated.

THE WARREN COURT

More fundamental and perhaps more controversial challenges to the status quo came from an unexpected and usually conservative source, the Supreme Court. Under the leadership of Earl Warren (1953–1969), perhaps the most influential chief justice since John Marshall, the court became a major agency of social change in the 1950s and 1960s. Although not widely heralded as a legal scholar, Warren was a compassionate and practical jurist who presided during an era of wide-ranging judicial activism that delighted liberals and enraged conservatives.

Following the famous 1954 decision in *Brown* vs. *Board of Education*, the Warren Court extended its concerns with fairness, justice, and equal protection for all citizens in a series of landmark decisions. In the 1957 cases of *Yates* vs. *United States* and *Watkins* vs. *United States,* the court softened the excesses of post-McCarthy anti-communism. In the *Yates* decision, the court hobbled the repressive Smith Act (1940) and extended First Amendment guarantees of free speech to communists and other subversives by distinguishing between "advocacy . . . as mere abstract doctrine" and "advocacy which incites to illegal action." In *Watkins* the court curbed the much-abused investigatory powers of the House Un-American Activities Committee.

The court also pressed forward on school desegregation. In 1964 it declared that the time for "all deliberate speed" had passed; in 1969 it ordered recalcitrant white southern school administrators to begin desegregation "at once." In other cases the justices abolished segregation in public recreation, public transportation, and private business; they sanctioned the sit-in demonstrations of young blacks, arguing that state enforcement of trespass laws violated the Fourteenth Amendment. The court's liberal majority also used the "equal protection" clause of the same amendment to protect urban voters from rural overrepresentation. In a series of cases beginning with *Baker* vs. *Carr* (1962), the court ordered congressional and legislative reapportionment on the basis of "one man, one vote."

The judicial ideal of fairness was also apparent in a series of decisions (*Gideon* vs. *Wainwright*, 1963; *Escobedo* vs. *Illinois*, 1964; *Miranda* vs. *Arizona*, 1966) that reformed legal procedure by extending federal guarantees to criminal justice proceedings at the local and state levels. In the name of free speech, the court overturned laws against pornography and prohibited prayer and Bible reading in the public schools.

Although widely hailed by civil libertarians and social activists, these and other rulings provoked angry public dissent. Many worried that the court was "coddling" criminals; others feared that its rulings encouraged subversion and atheism. Extremists, led by the right-wing John Birch Society, demanded the impeachment of Earl Warren. In 1968, presidential candidate Richard M. Nixon campaigned on the promise to remake the court by appointing "strict constructionist" judges.

THE GREAT SOCIETY IN RETREAT

By 1968, Johnson's Great Society, like the equalitarian doctrine of the Warren Court, had collided with mounting popular anxiety and conservatism. Indeed, the Johnson administration was seemingly beleaguered on every front. At home, the disenchantment of the young was augmented by the rising frustration of the extreme right wing and of the substantial, but amorphous, group later identified by Richard Nixon and other conservatives as the "Silent Majority" (see Chapter 31). Outraged by student protest and black militance and confused by a rising chorus of complaints from such previously quiescent groups as Indians, homosexuals, welfare recipients, migrant workers, and women, these anxious "Middle Americans," particularly working-class whites, feared social and moral upheaval. Self-reliant, family-oriented, conventionally religious, and patriotic, they angrily responded to this new age of protest and permissiveness with demands for political change and "law and order."

Abroad, American problems seemed worse. In February 1968, the Viet Cong launched the Tet offensive that produced heavy fighting and widespread destruction in thirty South Vietnamese cities, including Saigon. Although the invaders suffered heavy losses and were driven back, the intense fighting completed the destruction of some friendly villages and forced the Americans to abandon much of the "pacified" countryside. The surprise attacks also dealt a staggering blow to Johnson's political prospects and to American expectations of military victory. Recognizing that four years of intensified commitment had not even secured the capital from invasion, Americans in growing numbers questioned administration policy, and the president himself denied Pentagon requests for more American ground troops. The peace movement gained new recruits.

Elsewhere in the world, Soviet-American relations remained tense. The eruption of war between Israel and the Soviet-backed Arabs threatened to produce a Great Power confrontation in June 1967. A smashing Israeli victory prevented immediate disaster, but American powerlessness in this crisis seemed to demonstrate the dangers of overcommitment in Vietnam. In January 1968 the U.S. spy ship *Pueblo* was captured by North Koreans off the Korean coast. By responding with negotiations rather than armed counteraction, the administration avoided further military engagement in the Far East, but not humiliation. Again, in the following August, the administration could do nothing but stand by while Soviet tanks crushed a budding movement toward political and intellectual freedom in Czechoslovakia.

Meanwhile, the leadership crisis deepened. Despite Johnson's reputation for political wizardry, his popularity polls declined sporadically from a high of 80 percent to a disastrous 35 percent in the fall of 1968. In 1966, Democratic election losses had reinstated the conservative Republican-Southern Democrat coalition in power in Congress. The new realities were shown by drastic cuts in foreign aid and in funds for such administration social programs as Medicare and open housing. By the time of the 1968 presidential campaign, presidential appointments (including that of a new Chief Justice) were being rejected and even the treaty for stopping the spread of nuclear weapons was stalled in the Senate.

Thus, as a new presidential election approached, the Johnson landslide of 1964 seemed distant indeed. By 1968, consensus had become division; even the spectacular Johnson prosperity seemed threatened by a sharp upturn in prices and a declining economic growth. In March, sensing the futility of his own candidacy and challenged from within the Democratic party by Senators Robert F. Kennedy and Eugene McCarthy (both of them "peace candidates"), the president ended the bombing of North Vietnam, urged a negotiated settlement, and declared he would not seek re-election. This apparent victory for the party's antiwar forces, however, was offset by the assassination of Robert Kennedy in June. McCarthy attracted many of Kennedy's supporters and arrived at the convention as the favorite among Democratic voters. But the delegates, after voting down a peace plank, nominated Vice President Hubert Humphrey, a veteran liberal, who despite private doubts about the war had loyally supported administration policies. In the streets outside the convention, angry and frustrated antiwar demonstrators, a few of whom hoped to disrupt the proceedings within, were clubbed by police while the world watched on television. The popular reaction reflected the growing polarization of American society: many citizens were shocked and outraged at police violence against the young, but many others applauded police containment of unruly dissidents. The bloody melee seemed all the more unseemly in contrast to the well-managed Republican convention. Amid apparent order and restraint, the convention nominated Richard Nixon and his obscure running mate, Spiro T. Agnew, a conservative favorite of the party's increasingly vital southern wing.

During the campaign, both Humphrey and Nixon stressed "law and order" and supported the negotiations then proceeding unproductively in Paris with the North Vietnamese. Humphrey belatedly tried to dissociate himself from Johnson's war policies. Nixon spoke vaguely of a secret plan to end the fighting. Faced with seemingly unattractive alternatives, many mainstream voters picked the least objectionable major party candidate. But a substantial number refused to support either. The articulate, but impotent, left wing either boycotted the election or cast protest ballots for symbolic radical candidates; the disaffected right, far more formidable, turned to American Independent party candidate George C. Wallace, an Alabama segregationist who developed remarkable support among blue-collar workers and noncollege youths.

The balloting was unusually close. Humphrey, struggling vainly to hold the crumbling Democratic coalition, commanded the Eastern cities and the minorities, especially blacks. But he lost the upper South and the election to Nixon, who swept the traditionally Republican strongholds of the Middle and Far West. Despite the shattering of the Johnson consensus of 1964 and an apparent shift to the right, there was little cause for jubilation in the GOP. By election day, early predictions of an easy Republican triumph had eroded to a hairline victory. Nixon's share (43.4 percent) of the total popular vote was smaller than that of any president since Wilson. For the first time since Zachary Taylor in 1848, a newly elected president faced an opposition Congress. Indisputably, a nation divided by war and tormented by fear of violence and race had repudiated the party in power. But the incoming administration faced seemingly insurmountable domestic and foreign problems without a popular mandate and without congressional support.

FOR FURTHER READING

William L. O'Neill's *Coming Apart* (1971) is a splendid "informal" history of the 1960s. Two first-rate books by members of Kennedy's staff are A. M. Schlesinger, Jr.'s *A Thousand Days* (1965) and T. C. Sorenson's *Kennedy* (1965). Bruce Miroff's *Pragmatic Illusions* (1976) is critical of the Kennedy leadership; Carl Brauer's *John F. Kennedy and the Second Reconstruction* and Herbert Parmet's *Jack* (1980) are more sympathetic. Kennedy's assassination is detailed in William Manchester, *Death of a President* (1967); and Tom Wicker's *JFK and LBJ* (1968) offers balanced judgments of both presidents. Hugh Sidey's *A Very Personal Presidency* (1968) is an essay on Johnson's leadership style; and Robert Caro's *The Path to Power* (1982) offers a detailed and very critical account of Johnson's early career. Johnson guardedly speaks for himself in *The Vantage Point* (1971). Rowland Evans and Robert Novak's *Lyndon B. Johnson* (1966) and Eric F. Goldman's *The Tragedy of Lyndon Johnson* (1968) are highly suggestive assessments; Doris Kerns in *Lyndon Johnson and the American Dream* (1976) provides a psychobiography. *The Great Society Reader* (Marvin E. Gettleman and David Mermelstein, eds., 1967) is highly partisan and should be supplemented by narrower monographs such as James T. Patterson's *America's Struggle Against Poverty* (1982). The judicial activism of the Supreme Court is assessed by John D. Weaver in *Warren: The Man, the Court, the Era* (1967); while Victor Navasky has dissected *Kennedy Justice* (1971). Benjamin Muse portrays *The American Negro Revolution* (1968); Malcolm X has written a moving *Autobiography* (1966); Alphonso Pinkney analyzes black nationalist movements in *Red, Black and Green* (1976); and John Hersey, in the *Algiers Motel Incident* (1968), has focused on a ghetto riot. Studies of other disaffected groups include William H. Chafe's *Women and Equality* (1977); Sara Evans's *Personal Politics: The Roots of Women's Liberation* (1979); Vine Deloria's *Custer Died for Your Sins: An Indian Manifesto* (1969); Alvin Josephy's *Red Power* (1972); Arnulfo D. Trejo, ed., *The Chicanos* (1979). Richard Maxwell Brown's *Strain of Violence* (1975) and Hugh Davis Graham and Ted R. Gurr's *Violence in America* (1969) contribute to an understanding of an unhappy American tradition. Kirkpatrick Sale sympathetically analyzes *SDS*

(1973); Irwin Unger's history of the New Left, *The Movement* (1974), is generally critical; and Theodore Roszak charts the *Making of a Counter Culture* (1969). One chilling Cold War drama is presented by both Herbert Dinerstein in *The Making of a Missile Crisis* (1976) and Robert F. Kennedy in *Thirteen Days* (1969). Important studies of the war in Southeast Asia include Frances Fitzgerald's *Fire in the Lake* (1972); George Herring's *America's Longest War* (1979); Guenter Lewy's *America in Vietnam* (1978); William Shawcross's *Sideshow: Kissinger, Nixon, and the Destruction of Cambodia* (1979); and Neil Sheehan, et al., *The Pentagon Papers* (1971).

TABLE 19.   SOUTHEAST ASIA, 1969–1975

1968	**November Richard M. Nixon** elected president.
1969	**Spring** Secret U.S. bombing of Cambodia begins.
	April Peak U.S. troop strength in Vietnam.
	August Phased troop withdrawal begins.
	October Vietnam mobilization demonstration.
	November Nixon announces "Vietnamization" policy.
1970	**April** U.S. and ARVN forces invade Cambodia.
	May Campus disorders; Kent State killings; "hard hat" rally in support of war.
1971	**January–March** United States supports ARVN "incursion" into Laos.
	June Pentagon Papers leaked to press.
1972	**Spring** Haiphong Harbor mined; Hanoi bombed.
	October Kissinger announces that "peace is at hand."
	November Nixon re-elected.
	December "Christmas Bombing" of North Vietnam.
1973	**January** Paris accords end U.S. involvement in Vietnam.
	March Last U.S. combat troops leave Vietnam.
	August Bombing of Cambodia halted.
1974	Nixon resigns; **Gerald R. Ford** becomes president.
1975	**March–April** Congress denies further military aid.
	April Khmer Rouge take Phnom-Penh; Vietcong seize Saigon.
	May *Mayaguez* incident.

31

★ ★ ★ ★ ★ ★

Crises of Confidence,
1970–1980

OF DECADES (IMMEDIATELY) PAST

In a memorable inaugural address, John F. Kennedy had challenged Americans to "ask not what your country can do for you — ask what you can do for your country." A dozen years later, in an apparent evocation of that challenge, Richard M. Nixon at his own second inauguration in January 1973 urged Americans to "ask — not just what will government do for me, but what can I do for myself." However similar, the phrases carried very different meanings. The differences reflected the contrasting personal styles and (rather less starkly contrasting) social philosophies of these two chief executives, and marked the decade of change and turmoil that had intervened. But the two inaugural admonitions may also suggest, in ways unintended by either president, the differing tempers of the decades upon which they left their marks.

The 1960s are likely to be recorded in the book of popular thought as a time when American public figures were assassinated with alarming frequency; when campus ROTC buildings and inner-city ghettos went up in smoke; when disruptive racial confrontations and violent student demonstrations overshadowed all other issues of national concern; when the "love generation," the unkempt children of the middle class, withdrew to a workless counterculture of sex, drugs, and rock and roll. But the 1960s were not merely years of rebellion and dissent. The Age of Protest was also a period of social concern and moral commitment, during which the United States addressed some of its more pressing social ills. To be sure, the millennial aspirations of the decade's social planners and political activists now seem naive. Too often the problems they addressed defied solution. Civil rights legislation and affirmative action programs did not, and perhaps could not,

MAP 12: SOUTHEAST ASIA AND THE VIETNAM WAR

C H I N A

• Mengzi • Guixian

Cao Bang • • Nanning

• Lao Cai

• Pingxiang

Thai Nguyen Loc Binh

Black R. Red R.

• Dien Bien Phu • Zhanjiang

BURMA

Hanoi

Haiphong

Communist—Pathet Lao victory, 1975 Nam Dinh • Harbor mined, 1972

Mekong R. • Thanh Hoa

• Luang Prabang Gulf of Tonkin

PLAIN OF JARS

⊕ Maddox incident, 1964

HAINAN

• Nan NORTH VIETNAM

L • Vinh U.S. Seventh Fleet

A Mu Gia Pass operations during

Vientiane O the war

S Ca R.

Udon Thani • Demilitarized Zone

Nakhon Phanom Demarcation Line, July 1954

• Phitsanulok Khe Sanh Quang Tri

Sépone • A Chau SOUTH

• Khon Kaen Lang Vei Hué

Mekong R. Kham Duc • Da Nang

T H A I L A N D • My Lai

CHINA

Ubon Ratchathani Chu Lai • Quang Ngai

■ Ta Khli

• Rachasima SEA

• Dak To

■ Don Muang Ban San Keo Kontum

Pleiku An Khe

• Bangkok • Duc Co • Qui Nhon

CENTRAL

HIGHLANDS • Tuy Hoa

K A M P U C H E A

(CAMBODIA) • Ban Me Thuot

• Sattahip

Pursat • Tonle Sap • Nha Trang

Kompong Cham U.S. invasion, 1970 • Dalat • Cam Ranh Bay

Bu Dop

Phnom Penh • SOUTH VIETNAM

Communist—Khmer Rouge Vietnamese invasion, 1978

Gulf of Siam victory, 1975

⊕ W.H.S. Cholon • Bien Hoa

Mayaguez Chau Doc Tan Son Nhut • Long Binh

incident, 1975 Saigon

Vinh Long My Tho • Vung Tau

Can Tho Viet Cong victory and

• Ben Tre U.S. withdrawal, 1975

Mekong Delta

• Ca Mau ──────▶ Ho Chi Minh Trail

CA MAU PENINSULA ══════▷ Boat-People Refugees, 1975 —?

✵ Major battles of the Tet Offensive,

January 1968

| 0 | 100 | 200 miles |

| 0 | 100 200 | 300 kilometers | ■ Major U.S. bases during the war

produce a color- and gender-blind society. The War on Poverty proved to be much less than "unconditional" and the dizzying welter of agencies and programs it enlisted did not, as Lyndon Johnson hoped, "throttle want" in an otherwise affluent society. Although organizations as disparate as the National Organization for Women, the National Farm Workers' Association, and the American Indian Movement articulated minority grievances, women, Chicanos, and Indians along with blacks found that the benefits of American justice and opportunity remained unequally distributed. The failures of the 1960s, however, have been unduly emphasized. Although the "sensibility of the sixties" may have faded, the decade stands as one of the great ages of American reform, a time of achievements in such areas as school desegregation, women's and minority rights, education, environmental and consumer protection, health and welfare. Nor should it be forgotten that because of the social activism of the passionate visionaries of the 1960s, the burdens of class, race, and sex are less oppressive today than ever before.

In the 1970s, however, retrenchment — not reform — was the watchword. The faltering of the liberal Democratic coalition brought Nixon and Gerald Ford to the office held by Kennedy and Johnson. Although neither was an inflexible idealogue, these conservative Republican chief executives, like the "Middle Americans" they presumed to represent, had little taste for social experimentation. Whatever else it would be called, the period following Nixon's inauguration in January 1969 would not be known as a season of reform.

The peace movement also collapsed in the 1970s. Despite the widespread popular outrage occasioned by the American invasions of Cambodia (1970) and Laos (1971), the antiwar movement lost its momentum when Nixon ended the draft and began phased troop withdrawals. More than half a million American soldiers were brought home from South Vietnam between the elections of 1968 and 1972. In the spring of 1970 student demonstrators on 448 campuses were either on strike or had closed down their institutions. Several years later, as the war ended and the Selective Service System gave way to an all-volunteer army, the focus of student concern was more often the grade-point average than international peace.

The student left, including the Students for a Democratic Society (SDS) and its offshoot, the Youth International Party (Yippie), also abruptly disappeared with the war that had done so much to nourish it. Its leaders, the youthful rebels who set out to destroy "the establishment" in the 1960s, sometimes tried to join it in the 1970s. "Last year, Jerry Rubin came here and told us to pull this rotten system up by the roots," one puzzled undergraduate at the University of Rochester reported in 1971. "This year, he came here and told us to register to vote in the primary." Older if not always wiser, some radical youth leaders of the 1960s turned from the politics of confrontation to what Yippie spokesman Rubin called the "inner revolution of the '70s." Rubin himself experimented with "a smorgasbord course in New Consciousness," which included seemingly everything from Gestalt therapy, bioenergetics, and est to jogging, health foods, yoga, and acupuncture. Following this exhausting therapeutic regimen, he wrote a new book, *Growing (Up) at Thirty-Seven* (1976), and became a Wall Street securities analyst. His Yippie colleague, Abbie Hoffman, author of the 1968 publication *Revolution for the Hell of It*, went underground for a time to avoid imprisonment on drug charges and then dropped out of politics. Tom Hayden, founder of the SDS and always a thoughtful New Left activist, ran unsuccessfully for the U.S. Senate but was later elected to the California state assembly; his codefendant in the "Chicago Eight" conspiracy trial, Panther party leader Bobby Seal, tried and failed to be elected mayor of Oakland, California. Others turned to Oriental mysticism, among them Hayden's former SDS associate, Rennie Davis, who bought a Mercedes and became the disciple of teenage guru Maharaj Ji. Still others joined former Panther official Eldridge Cleaver, former Nixon hatchet man Charles Colson, and President James Earl Carter as born-again Christians. Of course, a great many "old revolutionaries" of the 1960s remained true to their radical ideals. But American youth in the 1970s was more committed to individual development than to social reform.

The decade of the 1970s had its popular movements, of course, but even protest often assumed conservative forms. Singer Anita Bryant led a crusade against civil rights for homosexuals. Resentful whites, convinced that the minority-rights campaign had gone too far, challenged affirmative action on grounds of "reverse discrimination." Many applauded when the Supreme Court's ambiguous *Bakke* ruling (1978) restricted the use of quotas to achieve racial balance in college-admissions programs. In 1978, conservative Republican Howard Jarvis won voter support for California's Proposition 13, which slashed property taxes by 57 percent, severely limited state social services, and launched a nationwide tax revolt. A "Right-to-Life" coalition of Roman Catholics, evangelical Protestants, and other conservatives sought an anti-abortion amendment; opponents of the welfare state endeavored to make federal budget deficits unconstitutional; and a militant and well-financed gun lobby, led by the National Rifle Association, worked to offset public support for handgun control.

The conservatism of the decade also slowed the advance of the women's rights movement. Despite such achievements as Title VII of the Civil Rights Act of 1964, which forbade sexual discrimination in the workplace, and the Equal Credit Opportunity Act (1974), which promised equal access to bank loans and credit cards, the disadvantages of womanhood remained all too numerous. In the decade after 1970, the percentage of women entering the labor market was at a substantially higher rate than that of men. By 1980, 42 percent of all American workers were female; more than half of all married women and 90 percent of female college graduates worked outside the home. In one of the most important social and economic developments of the century, the two-career family had become the American norm. But women, like blacks and Hispanics, were heavily concentrated in poorly paid, entry-level jobs. Although an increasing number found management positions in government and industry, many more continued to work in clerical, secretarial, and other "sexually segregated" occupations. In 1980, the median wage for women was 60 percent of that for men. Added to changing family patterns and a sharply rising divorce rate, these wage disparities were particularly onerous. During the 1970s single-parent households increased by nearly 80 percent, and most of them were headed by women. The persistence of gender-related wage and occupational discrimination ensured that a great many of these new American families were poor.

Another and not unrelated problem was the development of an antifeminist backlash, much of it inspired by tradition-minded women. Organizations of conservative women — Fascinating Womanhood and Total Woman — emerged late in the decade to challenge the objectives of the women's liberation movement. Styling themselves "pro-family" and "anti-libber," they opposed the Equal Rights Amendment (ERA) — first introduced in Congress in 1923 — on the questionable grounds that it would foster unisex restrooms, conscription of women, and homosexuality. Effectively countering the pro-ERA feminist lobby led by the National Organization for Women, the right-wing Republican activist Phyllis Schlafly organized a national "Stop ERA" movement, which blocked this endeavor to outlaw economic or social discrimination based on sex.

In 1979, many of these "anti's" — anti-feminist, anti-busing, anti-gay, anti-abortion, anti-intellectual, anti-communist — united under the banner of the Moral Majority, a fervid band of "New Right Christians" dedicated to Americanism and a more righteous political order. Led by Jerry Falwell, a radio-TV evangelist, the Moral Majority plunged into a series of right-wing causes, issued morality ratings for elected officials, and worked to defeat liberal Democrats in Congress. Although its political influence may be overrated, the organization played an important role in the conservative election victories of 1980 and counted among its supporters such influential politicians as Ronald Reagan and Senator Jesse Helms, the North Carolina fundamentalist who once spoke for the segregationist Citizens' Councils.

Such were the crusades of the seventies. To one degree or another, all were legitimate expressions of the concerns of broad categories of a diverse body politic. But collectively they seemed to reflect the cramped spirit of an age that was less hopeful, less expansive, and less generous than the one before.

THE "ME DECADE" — THE AGE OF NO CONFIDENCE

The apparently divergent contours of the 1960s and 1970s could also be charted in ways that transcended the merely political. As noted elsewhere in this volume, the historian's tendency to periodize, to make the past intelligible to the present by organizing it into manageable blocks of time, has its hazards. History, it seems worth repeating, is an all but seamless fabric; its developments are notable more often for continuity than for change. At close range, what appears distinctive in human conduct and institutions more often than not loses its particularity when viewed from a longer perspective. Still, the temptation to find peculiar meaning in current events is irresistible.

The 1970s were not half over before self-styled "new journalist" Tom Wolfe labeled it the "Me Decade." Wolfe, who won an enthusiastic readership with such "pop analyses" of the 1960s scene as his *Pump House Gang* (1968) and the *The Electric Kool-Aid Acid Test* (1968), found in the 1970s a new "alchemical dream" that promised not to make base metals into gold but to remake oneself. The spirit of the 1970s, he averred, was most clearly seen in the "Me movements," in est, Arica, and Scientology; in encounter sessions, assertiveness training, Oriental meditation groups, and charismatic Christianity; in the new national passion for "changing one's personality — remaking, remodeling, elevating, and polishing one's very self . . . (Me!)"

In a lighter vein, political humorist Russell Baker, the Peter Finley Dunne of his generation, deplored "the growing public absorption in the hedonism of public pleasure and private consumption — the hunt for the ideal restaurant, the perfect head of lettuce, the totally satisfying relationship." Articles in *Esquire, New Yorker,* and *Harper's* diagnosed the narcissistic preoccupation of the 1970s. In *The Culture of Narcissism* (1978), the most fully developed cultural analysis of the politically quiescent and socially passive 1970s, the historian Christopher Lasch similarly argued that "Americans have retreated to purely personal preoccupations." After the political turmoil and social dissidence of the recent past, "people have convinced themselves," Lasch observed, "that what matters is psychic self-improvement: getting in touch with their feelings, eating health foods, taking lessons in ballet or belly dancing, immersing themselves in the wisdom of the East, jogging, learning how to 'relate,' overcoming the 'fear of pleasure.' " In the judgment of some contemporary observers, Americans of the 1970s had turned from the War on Poverty and the peace movement, from political passion and social commitment, to join Jerry Rubin in a "journey into myself," to self-discovery, psychic growth and intimate encounters — to what Lasch called "strategies of narcissistic survival."

Inevitably, commentators found it easier to describe than to explain the apparently different sensibilities of the two decades immediately past. Few doubted, however, the importance of demography. The youth culture of the 1960s was, by all accounts, a by-product of the postwar baby boom. For reasons not yet satisfactorily explained, the period immediately following World War II was one of unprecedented population growth in the United States. Between 1948 and 1953 the number of births rose by nearly 50 percent. By the mid-1950s the boom crested. By 1960, again for reasons not fully understood, the total number of births began to drop sharply. By the mid-1970s the "population bomb" was defused and the nation approached what demographers called ZPG (zero population growth).

But the baby-boom generation was not so easily dispensed with. A disproportionate bulge in the nation's population curve, it passed through the 14- to 24-year-old age category in the 1960s. (In 1960 the center of population gravity in the United States was the 35 to 40 age group; by 1965, the center had shifted to age 17.) In a less demanding age, in one less vexed by issues of race and war, the social impact of this extraordinary cohort might have been very different. But the postwar generation reached late adolescence and early adulthood at a critical moment in American history, and it gave that decade of youthful rebellion its special character. By the 1970s, a decade of falling birth rates had pushed the center of population gravity upward. By 1980, 11 percent of the population was over 65 (compared to 4 percent in 1900). Inexorably, the youth of the 1960s reached the dread age of 30. Population dynamics do not in themselves determine social behavior, but they can help define shifting styles in the recent past. One of the counterculture's most talked-about books was Charles Reich's *The Greening of America;* in 1970 when that publication appeared, the rebellious youth culture, harbinger of what Reich hoped would be "Consciousness III," was already subsiding. In the decade that followed, America was not so much greening as graying.

The character of the "Me Decade" was also linked to what the historian Henry Steele Commager called the "Age of No Confidence." Lasch's subtitle — "American Life in an Age of Diminishing Expectations" — suggested, and other social analysts generally agreed, that the culture of narcissism, the new ethic of self-preservation, reflected the erosion of the optimism of the 1950s and 1960s. In 1941, Henry Luce, publisher of *Time, Life,* and *Fortune,* proclaimed the advent of the "American Century," an age in which "the most powerful and vital nation" would go unchallenged in a world it would dominate "for such purposes" and by "such means" as it alone saw fit. In fact, throughout the nearly four centuries of their New World experience, Americans had shared the exuberant faith of Puritan leader John Winthrop that theirs was a "Citty Upon a Hill" with "the eies of all people Uppon us." With Thomas Jefferson, they believed that they were the chosen people of a "New Israel." This sense of American exceptionalism, which suggested that the nation stood somehow apart from the tawdry stream of human history, survived and was embellished by the Second World War. Among the world's great nations, the United States alone had emerged from the most terrible of wars not only unscathed but with its wealth and power enhanced.

But the American Century lasted only a generation. As the 1960s ended, traditional presumptions of American omnicompetence and omnipotence were in tatters. Heretofore confident of their nation's role as both global police officer and moral preceptor, Americans now faced defeat in Vietnam and declining influence around the world. Never doubting the strength of the "almighty dollar" or the seemingly perpetual expansion of their gross national product, they soon were flooded by economic ills — unchecked inflation, economic stagnation, declining productivity rates, staggering trade deficits, and a sharply devalued dollar. Following the Arab oil boycott of 1973 came a creeping awareness that the United States was dangerously dependent on uncertain, rapidly depleting, and ruinously expensive foreign energy supplies. As the energy crisis of the 1970s unfolded, the American people — who with roughly 6 percent of the world's people produced about one-third of its goods and consumed more than one-third of its petroleum — slowly and imperfectly came to understand what the impending exhaustion of nonrenewable natural resources could mean to an industrial society and its economy.

The unsettling news of the 1970s, then, was that the United States, too, lived in a world of limits — limited world influence, limited economic growth, limited natural resources, and limited expectations for a better future. At least since the Enlightenment, the spirit of Western humanity has been elevated by faith in progress, the assumption that human society was, if not perfectable, at least infinitely meliorable. Despite the evidence to the contrary, Western democracies in general and the American nation in particular enjoyed a sense of limitless possibilities. In the last century that optimism was repeatedly tested by thinkers from Charles Darwin to Oswald Spengler. More concretely, the horrors of two world wars, the spread of totalitarianism, the Nazi holocaust, the threat of nuclear destruction, the contagion of world lawlessness and terrorism — all suggested that whatever its state of grace, humanity's course was not inevitably upward.

In the face of such dangers and uncertainties, the sanguine Western spirit sagged noticeably. Even the Americans, those seemingly incurable optimists, began to feel this malaise in the 1970s and 1980s. With the end of the American Century at hand, with the American Dream of unlimited abundance subject to doubt, the American people began uneasily to discard comfortable myths about their own virtue and uniqueness.

By definition, contemporary historical writing is shortsighted. The instant analyses of our times will be challenged by those who enjoy greater perspective. Future writers may well find unsuspected social purpose in the "Me" age. Very likely the configurations of the "Culture of Narcissism" and the "Age of No Confidence" will seem overdrawn. For the moment, Thomas Jefferson's "chosen people," the 226 million inhabitants of the "Citty Upon a Hill," appeared to be engaged in the disquieting task of joining the human race.

NIXON AND THE (FIRST)
NEW FEDERALISM

Of the four men who served as presidents since 1969, Richard Milhous Nixon alone seemed to have both national and international political expertise. A veteran of both houses of Congress, vice president for two terms and well versed in American politics, and a widely traveled student of foreign affairs, he brought experience and intellect to the White House Oval Office. Doubts about his political methods and personal character, however, haunted his presidency. Reserved and formal, he was one of the most isolated presidents in American history. He was defensive and suspicious of the news media and rarely held press conferences. Intense, hardworking, but uncomfortable in the public eye, he maintained a low executive profile and spent much of his time at Camp David, the presidential retreat, or at his private estates in California and Florida. Nixon chose conservative and reasonably competent cabinet officers but, with the exception of Attorney General John Mitchell, generally denied them access to the Oval Office. Although he delegated power and responsibility freely, he did so, not to the cabinet but to intensely loyal subordinates led by presidential assistants H. Robert Haldeman and John D. Ehrlichman. Called the "Disneyland Mafia" and "The Germans," even by White House staffers, these men had few contacts with the parties or Congress and had little experience in public affairs. Jealously protective of Nixon's time and energies, they erected a "Berlin Wall" that was rarely penetrated even by cabinet members, top Republican officials, or congressional leaders. The president preferred to operate, as one of his speech writers noted, in a "soundproof, shockproof bubble."

Before assuming office, Nixon revealed that foreign affairs would be his principal concern: "I've always thought this country could run itself domestically without a president." True to his word, he gave international issues, particularly the Vietnam War, priority throughout his first term. But one domestic legacy of the Johnson administration, a runaway economy, required much presidential attention. Having promised the nation both "guns and butter," Johnson had refused to seek a tax increase to finance the rapidly escalating Southeast Asian war. By 1968 the result was a raging inflation that threatened not only the dollar's value, but the nation's role as a Great Power and the U.S. quality of life.

Nixon's free-market response to this crisis proved inadequate. By tightening the money supply (through higher interest rates) and balancing the budget, the Republican president hoped to curb inflation without economic controls or even wage-price guidelines. The ineffectual result was called "Nixonomics." Economists coined a new term, *stagflation,* to describe the disastrous combination of sharply rising living costs and recession. Under strong public pressure, the administration reversed itself in August 1971. Now proclaiming himself a Keynesian (after liberal British economist John Maynard Keynes), Nixon briefly froze prices and wages, adopted budgetary deficits (the largest in peacetime history), and then pursued a fitful course of "schizoid economics" — moving from stringent controls to voluntary restraints, to a second price freeze and renewed controls.

Although a temporary respite from stagflation in 1972 deprived the Democrats of an election issue, economic problems reached crisis proportions early in Nixon's second term. By mid-1973, as the president imposed his second price freeze in 15 months and prepared to reinstitute stringent price controls, corporate profits and wages were soaring, the stock market was in a prolonged slump, and consumer costs, especially for food, were spiraling at a rate unequaled since the early post–World War II period. By that date, the administration had already twice devalued the dollar in a desperate attempt to offset mounting trade deficits by improving the competitive position of American goods in foreign markets. In large part, the administration's erratic economic policies were rooted in the president's own stalwart Republicanism. Despite his use of economic activism, he remained to the end a devoted free marketeer.

That same traditional conservatism also placed him at odds with the liberal social programs of his Democratic predecessors. Again, there was confusion at first and much inconsistency in word and deed. Convinced that many Great Society programs were unwise and unworkable, Nion proposed to decentralize authority and emphasize local solutions to local problems. But acting upon the advice of Daniel Patrick Moynihan, his urban affairs adviser, he delayed immediate action. A "neoconservative" (ex-liberal) Democrat who had served in the administrations of both Kennedy and Johnson, Moynihan persuaded Nixon that wholesale dismantlement of the Great Society programs would further divide a nation torn by an unpopular war, a rising crime rate, and domestic unrest. To nearly everyone's astonishment, bills authorizing extension of antipoverty programs — including such conservative targets as Job Corps and Model Cities — won presidential support and were enacted by Congress. In August 1969, Nixon shocked his party's right-wing by advocating a Family Assistance Payments (FAP) plan to provide every American family with a guaranteed annual income of at least $1,600. Although the administration's policies often enraged environmentalists, Nixon also created the Environmental Protection Agency in 1970 and signed (though he had not supported) the Clean Air Act, Water Quality Improvement Act, and the Resource Recovery Act. In January 1971 the president proclaimed a "New American Revolution . . . as profound, as far-reaching, as exciting as that first revolution 200 years ago." The watchword of his administration, Nixon said, was reform.

Whatever his watchword, the president's personal instincts and political philosophy favored retrenchment and consolidation, not innovation and reform. Having drifted uncertainly in its first two years, the administration moved resolutely toward the "New Federalism" and the conservative policies and programs that would "reverse the flow of power and resources from the states and communities to Washington." In October 1972, under heavy pressure from the administration, Congress enacted a "revenue sharing" measure to return to local government over a five-year period $30.2 billion in federal monies. Revenue sharing was not a windfall, however, as the nation's hard-pressed city officials readily understood. The administration's first-term domestic energies had been largely devoted to beating back appropriation bills for social programs. When that failed, Nixon used his veto (19 times during the Ninety-Second Congress alone); when his vetoes were overridden, he simply (and unconstitutionally) "impounded" or refused to spend congressionally authorized funds. In his budget proposals for fiscal 1974, the frugal Republican chief executive slashed previously budgeted federal grants for social services and community development. The crisis of the cities, he said, had passed.

The Nixon administration's conservatism, although emerging slowly in legislative areas, was immediately apparent in areas outside the control of a Democratic Congress. Fulfilling a campaign promise to appoint a no-nonsense attorney general, Nixon named John Mitchell, his campaign manager and former law partner. Gruff and taciturn, Mitchell served — until his resignation to manage Nixon's re-election campaign in 1972 — as the stern symbol of a law-and-order administration. With one eye fixed on the crime rate and another on the mood of the electorate (particularly Wallace's 13 percent), he sponsored a controversial "no-knock" crime law for predominantly black Washington, D.C., advocated preventive detention and stop-and-frisk laws, claimed an unrestricted government right to eavesdrop electronically on suspected "security risks," and dealt harshly with antiwar demonstrators and other political dissidents.

Fear of crime was but one facet of a pervasive national malaise that had emerged gradually in the late 1960s as the nation's most salient political issue. However troubled by the stalemate in Vietnam, the American people seemed more deeply disturbed by such domestic ills as drug abuse, racial disorder, and violent protest. Identified originally as the Wallace "backlash" but later more accurately described as the "Social Issue," this widespread dysphoria portended, some analysts believed, a fundamental national political realignment. Indeed, White House strategists viewed the Social Issue as the cement for a majority Republican coalition of the unyoung, the unpoor, and the unblack. In the first test of that strategy, the midterm elections of 1970, the results were inconclusive. However much they disliked "scroungy student dissenters," "pusillanimous pussyfooters," and the "effete corps of impudent snobs," the voters themselves seemed as concerned with runaway inflation as with the Social Issue. The Democrats retained control of Congress.

In the administration's design for a new Republican coalition, the conservative white voters of the South were of central importance. Increasingly disenchanted by the liberal, pro-black policies of the national Democratic party, white Southerners admired Nixon more than any recent president. He did not sweep the region in 1968, but he dominated the upper South and, without Wallace in the running, could easily have carried every southern state except Texas. To an administration that took pride in playing political hard ball, it seemed only logical to absorb the Wallace vote by openly courting the troubled white South.

This "southern strategy," of course, ran counter to Afro-American aspirations. Despite the race chauvinism of youthful black militants and a growing black emphasis on separate economic and cultural development, the great majority of Afro-Americans still hoped for assimilation in a colorblind society. Black fears, aroused by Nixon's attacks on forced integration and busing, were not allayed by his pre-inaugural promise to do "more for the Negro" than any other president. Few were surprised when he reversed his predecessors' policy of executive engagement in the civil rights struggle. In 1969, for the first time since World War II, the Justice Department intervened on behalf of white defendants in school desegregation cases. Attorney General Mitchell relaxed government equal rights compliance standards and shifted the burden of civil rights enforcement to the courts. Though the administration exploited and even nurtured the white backlash, the civil rights achievements of the past seemed secure. Over Nixon's opposition, the Democratic Congress extended the Voting Rights Act of 1965. In 1969 the Supreme Court refused to delay school desegregation in Mississippi; in 1972 it ruled in favor of busing to achieve racially balanced classrooms. The South, despite the southern strategy, became the nation's most desegregated region, and segregated northern inner-city schools came under judicial attack. Nixon's campaign promise to promote "black capitalism" proved empty, but he supported the extension of the Civil Rights Commission, opposed federal tax-exemptions for all-white academies, and advocated labor union desegregation. Ironically, then, the Nixon record on civil rights, though modest, was better than either the president or his critics would admit.

In his judicial appointments, Nixon broke with the policies of his immediate predecessors. Harshly critical of liberal judicial activism, the Republican president sought to remake the Supreme Court in his own conservative image. Although he failed in two attempts to appoint conservative Southerners with segregationist records to the Supreme Court, he filled four court vacancies with judicial conservatives. Joined by one and sometimes two of the other five justices, the Nixon appointees (perhaps only one of whom was a genuine "strict constructionist") were expected to reverse nearly two decades of Warren Court liberal activism. Once again, however, there was more continuity than seemed apparent. The decisions of the reconstituted court neither expanded nor eroded basic civil liberties and rights. Contrary to White House wishes, it ruled in favor of abortion and against state aid to parochial education. Its principal departures from early Supreme Court rulings came in a tougher attitude toward criminals and pornography. But not until the mid-1980s would the Court move sharply rightward.

TOWARD A GENERATION OF PEACE

The caution and ambivalence that so often marked Nixon's domestic policies found no parallel in his bold handling of international affairs. Promising a "full generation of peace" through negotiation, not confrontation, he moved quickly to normalize relations with the Peoples' Republic of China and the Soviet Union. In both cases, détente was complicated by the president's reputation as an intractable cold warrior. A vigorous Red-hunter during his congressional career, he had often found his political opponents "soft" on communism. Though initially viewed by Kremlin leaders as the most belligerent in a long line of anti-communist presidents, he proved more flexible than any of his post–World War II predecessors in his dealings with communist nations. Placing ideology aside, he pursued a policy of realism based on the ancient maxim that nations have no permanent friends or enemies, only permanent interests. In this exercise in *Realpolitik*, Nixon was assisted by Henry Kissinger, a former Harvard professor, who served as director of the National Security Council, and was perhaps the most remarkable foreign policy adviser ever to serve the White House. Kissinger did not formally become head of the Department of State until 1973, but he was the nation's chief diplomat throughout the first term.

The most spectacular examples of the new realism in American diplomacy came in 1972. In February, while a nation of television viewers watched via satellite, the president journeyed to Beijing (Peking) to lay the groundwork for a resumption of Chinese-American relations. Although denied recognition by the United States and its Western allies since the triumph of Mao Zedong in 1949, mainland China was a major power armed with nuclear weapons and populated by one-fifth of the world's people. In 1971 the Peoples' Republic was admitted to the United Nations with American support, and, over ineffectual American opposition, Jiang's Nationalist regime was ousted. In a second internationally televised summit meeting, Nixon became the first president since Franklin Roosevelt to set foot on Soviet soil when he conferred in Moscow in May 1972 with Soviet party leader Leonid Brezhnev. A year later, a second Nixon-Brezhnev meeting occurred in Washington amid rising hopes of a permanent thaw in the Cold War. Seasoned diplomatic observers cautioned that other summits had been followed by deteriorating relations, and ultraconservatives, Vice President Agnew among them, were alarmed by the open camaraderie between the nation's chief executive and the leaders of its postwar adversaries. But the president declared that 1972 had been a year of unparalleled "achievement for peace," and most Americans believed him.

The summits were followed by substantive agreements. As Nixon's second term began, China and the United States had not exchanged formal diplomatic recognition, but relations between the two nations were vastly improved and a cultural and economic exchange was begun. The first phase of the Strategic Arms Limitations Talks (SALT) with the Soviets placed short-term (five years) ceilings on offensive nuclear weapons, including ICBMs (intercontinental ballistic missiles) and submarine-based missiles, and limited each country to two ABM (antiballistic missile) sites. These were significant agreements although they were weakened by the failure to control the number of warheads each missile could carry. The new technology of MIRVed warheads (multiple independently targetable re-entry vehicles) allowed the escalation of the arms race to continue. The United States and the Soviet Union also signed cooperative agreements on trade, cancer research, and space exploration, and began negotiating a "Mutual and Balanced Force Reduction" for Europe.

Soviet-American rapprochement, however, was tenuous. Divergent East-West interests in the Middle East and Africa threatened renewed tension. In the first major test of détente, the Yom Kippur war of 1973, revenge-minded Egyptians attacked Israel to recover territories lost in 1967. The Russians aided the Egyptians and the Americans supplied the Israelis, but a larger international crisis was avoided when the big powers forced a cease fire. No long-range solution resulted, however, and the strategic location and oil riches of the Middle East made it a likely setting for continued East-West rivalry.

Soviet interests also posed a threat to American ambitions for an independent but pro-Western black Africa. The collapse of Portuguese colonialism in Angola and Mozambique and black restiveness under minority white rule in Rhodesia and South Africa piqued the interests of both major powers. These and other international developments suggested that to Nixon and

Kissinger, local issues in Asia, Africa, and the Middle East held little importance by themselves. Rather, superpower relationships were the administration's passion.

In 1972 the administration's most pressing problems remained in Vietnam. Elected on a campaign pledge to end the war and win the peace by a "secret plan," Nixon sought an early conclusion to the fighting through negotiations in Paris with the North Vietnamese. When these talks, underway since the autumn of 1968, proved unproductive, the president shifted to a policy of "Vietnamization." Designed to "de-Americanize" the war by transferring American combat responsibility in Vietnam to South Vietnamese (ARVN) soldiers, the policy reversed a decade of accelerating troop strength by gradually withdrawing American forces. Although the success of Vietnamization and the future of the wobbly Saigon regime remained in doubt, troop withdrawals continued throughout the first term. From a peak strength of 550,000 in April 1969, the number of American soldiers fell to 27,000 in early 1973; American annual combat deaths dropped from a 1968 high of 14,592 to only 300 in 1972.

As American involvement in Vietnam declined, the war was carried to other theaters in Southeast Asia. In secret missions unknown to even congressional leaders and the Secretary of the Air Force, American aircraft bombed communist "sanctuaries" inside Cambodia throughout most of 1969 and well into the spring of 1970. On April 30, 1970, U.S. and ARVN soldiers invaded Cambodia; the following winter ARVN troops with American air support moved into Laos. Although defended by the administration as vital to American withdrawal, these limited but much criticized "incursions" provoked domestic disorders. In May, on campuses across the country, students picketed and struck, and at riot-torn Kent State University, four of them were killed by Ohio national guardsmen. The bloodletting at Kent, soon followed by a similar though unrelated tragedy at all-black Jackson State College in Mississippi, brought a sense of renewed urgency to the peace movement. But a substantial majority of the voters remained steadfast in support of the president who promised to shorten the war by widening it.

In the end, it was negotiation, not Vietnamization, that brought American troops home. Although Kissinger returned from Paris in October 1972 to announce that "peace is at hand," the war carnage continued for three months. During the Christmas season, when it appeared that negotiations had stalled, the president dispatched B-52s to rain bombs in unprecedented tonnage on Hanoi and Haiphong. At last, however, late in January 1973, the longest war in U.S. history ended. The Paris Accords, signed by the United States, North and South Vietnam, and the National Liberation Front, provided for a supervised cease-fire, complete American withdrawal, and a prisoner exchange. While the nation celebrated "peace with honor," the U.S. air war over Cambodia continued. Not until mid-August 1973, after Congress terminated funds for all military operations in Southeast Asia, did Nixon end the bombing sorties against the enemies of Lon Nol's corrupt military regime in Phnom Penh, the Cambodian capital. With Congress and the public unwilling to continue to support the ineffective Indochinese anti-communist governments, Nixon's successor, Gerald Ford, proved incapable of delivering promised military support to Cambodia and South Vietnam. In April 1975, Cambodia fell to Khmer Rouge troops. Later that month, the South Vietnamese regime also surrendered to communist insurgents. Following a hasty evacuation of American personnel and Vietnamese children from Saigon, the long American nightmare in Southeast Asia ended. The toll had been awesome: 56,000 American combat dead; uncounted hundreds of thousands of Asian casualties; and some $350 billion in direct American war costs and veteran benefits.

"WHITE HOUSE HORRORS"

The administration's foreign policy successes offset early Republican fears of a one-term Nixon presidency. The president's popularity had slumped markedly following the midterm elections of 1970. Early in 1971, opinion pollsters revealed, he trailed Senator Edmund S. Muskie of Maine in public esteem. Popular enthusiasm for Nixon's peace initiatives abroad and favorable developments at home, however, soon brought renewed hopes. During the early months of 1972, the good news from Beijing and Moscow was matched by a dramatic, though temporary, economic upswing that brought new jobs and stabilized prices. Soon thereafter, Muskie's bid for the Democratic nomination was crippled by a feeble showing in the hotly contested Democratic primaries; in May, Wallace's threat to Nixon's southern support was eliminated when the Alabamian was critically wounded in an assassination attempt. Then in July an army of enthusiastic and idealistic amateurs capitalized on recent Democratic convention reforms and nominated Senator George McGovern. A liberal South Dakotan, McGovern rallied supporters through his issues of immediate peace in Vietnam, reduced military spending, and sweeping tax and welfare reforms. He was branded by Republicans and conservative Democrats as the candidate of "amnesty, acid, and abortion." His efforts to brand the Nixon administration as the "most corrupt in American history" proved ineffectual. On election day, he led the Democrats to their worst defeat in half a century.

Only half the eligible voters (some 55 percent) turned out, but Nixon won an electoral (521 to 17) and popular (60.7 percent) vote landslide. Except for Lyndon Johnson's triumph of 1964, no president had ever polled a larger popular majority; except for Franklin Roosevelt's record-shattering sweep of 1936, no president had ever won more electoral votes. Still, Nixon's was a personal rather than a party victory; ticket-splitting voters returned solid Democratic majorities to both houses of Congress.

But if the mandate of 1972 was unclear, Richard Nixon's second-term intentions were not. Having built a structure of peace through détente abroad, he turned to restructuring the nation's domestic priorities; he diffused federal responsibilities for local problems and decreased federal spending for "visionary" and "unworkable" social services. By eliminating such programs as Model Cities, Job Corps, Community Action, and Neighborhood Youth, the goverment could hope not only to ease mounting inflationary and tax pressures, Nixon said, but to free additional monies for revenue-sharing grants to hard-pressed cities and states.

This "New Federalism" proved no more appealing to the 93rd Congress than it had to the 92nd. Lawmakers from both parties were angered by apparent executive usurpations of legislative prerogatives. In the tradition of strong chief executives, Nixon, despite his self-styled strict construction-ism, had governed in the grand manner. Without either the advice or con-sent of Congress, he had initiated the invasion of Cambodia and Laos, the mining of Haiphong Harbor, and the resumption of saturation bombing of Hanoi. He had invoked executive privilege to shield White House policy makers from congressional inquiry and had impounded funds slated by Con-gress for programs that he opposed. Although precedents for such extraor-dinary assertions of presidential authority were numerous, aroused congres-sional leaders began urging redress of an imbalance of power. At stake, many believed, was the governmental doctrine of checks and balances itself.

The overriding issue of Nixon's second term, however, was the abuse, not the accretion, of executive power. During the presidential campaign of 1972, two Nixon campaign aides were arrested for their roles in a conspiracy to burglarize and plant illegal wire taps in Democratic National Committee headquarters in Washington's Watergate Building. Although Democrats cried "political espionage," the White House denied executive involvement, and Nixon dismissed the incident as a "third-rate burglary attempt." Vice President Spiro T. Agnew — who would resign when it became known that he had accepted bribes from contractors — even suggested that the Demo-crats had burgled their own National Committee.

The voters, for the most part, showed little interest, and in November the unseemly affair was buried in the Nixon victory landslide. Or so it seemed until early in 1973, when congressional investigators, aided by a courageous federal judge and a vigorous press, began exposing White House crimes and scandals that shocked the nation and raised profoundly disturb-ing questions about Nixon's fitness for leadership. Almost daily throughout the spring and summer, evidence of official misconduct and lawlessness mounted. By autumn, most of what Attorney General Mitchell later called the "White House horrors" were fully in view. Nixon's popularity collapsed, and for the first time in more than a century, there was serious talk in Con-gress of the impeachment of a president.

At the heart of the Nixon scandals lay, of course, the Watergate break-in and subsequent efforts by highly placed administration officials to limit the investigation and conceal or destroy evidence. But there were also allega-tions that the White House, or its Committee for the Re-Election of the President, engaged in: (1) unethical and illegal campaign practices ranging from "dirty tricks" against Democratic hopefuls to the extortion of illegal contributions from corporations and interest groups desiring government favors; (2) efforts to politicize such nominally independent and traditionally nonpartisan government agencies as the Federal Bureau of Investigation (FBI) and the Internal Revenue Service; and (3) illegal and wide-ranging domestic security and intelligence gathering operations. Additionally, there were charges that Nixon's income and property taxes were not in order, that his estates in California and Florida were acquired under questionable circumstances, and that federal funds (totaling nearly $10 million) spent on improvements for these private dwellings often had little to do with presidential security. Quite apart from the scandal, allegations of constitutional abuses included the misuse of impoundment and executive privileges; the secret and unauthorized air war against Cambodia; and the continued conduct of the war in Southeast Asia after the repeal of the Gulf of Tonkin Resolution. To some of Nixon's harshest critics, these too were impeachable offenses.

Initially the White House tried to ignore the uproar; then it issued a series of general denials of executive wrongdoing. But each presidential statement raised more questions than it answered. At first Nixon refused even to permit his aides to testify before the Select Senate Committee on Presidential Campaign Activities. Under mounting congressional pressure, he reversed this position but refused investigators access to secret White House tape recordings of selected presidential conversations and telephone calls. When these recordings were subpoenaed by the Justice Department's independent special prosecutor, the president fought compliance through two federal courts, promising obedience only to a "definitive" ruling of the Supreme Court. After months of negotiation and litigation, Nixon agreed to turn over the disputed material — but not before he had fired the special prosecutor and forced the resignation of the Attorney General and Deputy Attorney General, and not before Congress moved toward his impeachment. To the nation's astonishment, however, the surrendered tapes did not contain conversations presumed by investigators to be most relevant to the inquiry. The president's lawyers attributed these critical gaps in the evidence to equipment failure and secretarial error. Evidence rapidly accumulated, however, to prove the obvious: Nixon, though apparently not implicated in the burglary itself, was engaged in a conspiracy to obstruct justice by concealing evidence.

In July 1974 a unanimous Supreme Court, acting upon a second special prosecutor's request, ordered the White House to surrender other recordings of 64 key presidential conversations. Following the release of this incriminating material, the House Judiciary Committee voted to recommend three articles of impeachment to the House of Representatives. Charged with obstruction of justice, abuse of power, and contempt for constitutional procedures on a scale without parallel in American history, Nixon resigned on August 9 rather than face impeachment. Still denying criminal action, he acknowledged that the loss of public confidence rendered him incapable of leadership. Returned to private life, the first American chief executive to resign in disgrace continued to assert that he had been victimized by the zeal of his friends and the malice of his enemies. Nixon was later pardoned by his successor, but 25 administration officials, including his attorney general and two top White House assistants, were sent to prison. Four Nixon cabinet officers were named in criminal cases.

FORD'S INTERLUDE

And thus Gerald Ford became the thirty-eighth president. In every respect, his ascent was as incredible as Nixon's fall. A veteran congressman from Michigan and former House minority leader whose highest political ambition was to be speaker, Ford had been nominated vice president after Spiro Agnew's resignation from that office in 1973. Ford became the first vice president to assume office under the procedures outlined in the Twenty-Fifth Amendment and the first nonelected president. He had, as he said, "received the vote of no one."

Decent, open, and gregarious, Ford restored some measure of public confidence in the integrity of the presidency. But he failed to provide convincing leadership, and a broad segment of the press and public wondered openly if he was qualified to be president. His imprudent decision to pardon Nixon, without an admission of guilt from the former president or a full disclosure of his misdeeds, stirred controversy and reopened the wounds of Watergate. Some critics who remembered Ford's earlier efforts to derail the congressional Watergate investigation and his later promise not to pardon Nixon, cried "corrupt bargain." Others believed that unconditional immunity from prosecution for Nixon should be accompanied by equal presidential compassion for Vietnam-era draft evaders. Ford provided a program of conditional amnesty, however, that required two years of alternate government service for the youthful dissenters.

The conclusion of the Watergate tragedy brought to the fore long-neglected international and domestic problems. Despite administration predictions and a temporary upturn of the business cycle in 1972, the United States in 1974 suffered its worst recession in four decades. A "stagflated" economy of high unemployment and high inflation was further aggravated by a continuing petroleum shortage that promised soaring energy costs and greater dependence on uncertain foreign supply. There were scandals in the FBI and CIA (Central Intelligence Agency), ranging from revelations of burglary and illegal surveillance to foreign coups d'état and assassination plots. Abroad, there were crises seemingly without number: a continuing and volatile Arab-Israeli standoff, ominous Soviet ambitions in the Middle East and sub-Saharan Africa, the final collapse of America's Southeast Asian allies, a Marxist-oriented revolution in Portugal, a transfer of power in post-Franco Spain, near-anarchy and the growth of communist strength in Italy, and the diminishing influence and growing isolation of the United States in the UN General Assembly.

In responding to these disquieting problems, Ford rarely veered from Nixon's course. More conservative and less flexible than Nixon, he vetoed more legislation in one year than Herbert Hoover did in four. More solicitous toward corporations than to civil rights, he pursued traditional Republican monetary and fiscal policies, warned against overly stringent controls on either intelligence agencies or private enterprise, and continued to support both the principle of détente and unprecedented peacetime defense spending. In matters of style and personality, Ford differed markedly from

Nixon, but his policies and programs were very nearly the same. He was, most Americans seemed to believe, a likeable mediocrity.

During Senate confirmation hearings in 1974, then Vice President–designate Ford disavowed any ambition to be president. Upon Nixon's resignation, however, Ford succeeded to that office, and though few thought his chances good, he sought election in 1976. Even White House officials viewed him as an underdog. Personally popular but not widely hailed for his executive talents, Ford seemed to lack the traditional advantages of incumbency. He had served half of Nixon's second term, but he had not developed a national or even a statewide constituency. Michigan's Fifth District contained the largest electorate he had ever faced at one time. His early campaign organization was remarkably inept; the candidate himself seemed curiously "unpresidential" in his electioneering.

When compared to his party's weaknesses, Ford's difficulties appeared minor. Although the Republican party had won four of the past seven presidential elections, it had dominated Congress only twice since 1932. A minority party since the Great Depression, it could now claim the allegiance of only 22 percent of the electorate. Only 19 of the nation's 50 state governors were Republicans. In control of the White House since 1969, the party had delivered peace but not prosperity nor economic stability. Its claim to be the law-and-order party had been mocked by the misdeeds of a Republican president, his vice president, and two attorneys general. Republican unity was threatened, moreover, by the party's increasingly influential right wing. Led by former Governor Ronald Reagan of California, the arch-conservatives demonstrated surprising strength in the primaries and dictated a platform that repudiated many of Ford's policies and very nearly blocked his nomination.

In the opposition camp, a profusion of candidates (variously labeled as conservatives, hawks, liberals, populists, and progressives) entered the hotly contested Democratic primaries, while former nominees George McGovern and Hubert H. Humphrey stood by expectantly. No obvious favorite emerged, but voter indifference eliminated a dozen competitors by convention time, leaving a single practical choice: Jimmy Carter, a retired naval officer, engineer, peanut farmer, and former governor of Georgia.

After a colorless campaign, the voters' alternatives seemed to lie between one candidate who could not shake his reputation as a political "bumbler" and another who made much of the fact that he was not a politician at all. The lackluster election produced a lower voter turnout than any recent presidential race. Carter carried the South and enough large midwestern and eastern states to win electoral (294) and popular (51 percent) majorities. In congressional and gubernatorial races, the electorate again clearly preferred Democratic candidates.

OUTSIDER IN WASHINGTON

President James Earl Carter, Jr., preferred to be called Jimmy. A self-proclaimed "outsider" in Washington, his governmental experience was limited

to one term each as state senator and governor of Georgia. In a nation disenchanted with the "imperial presidency," Carter's inexperience was at first
a political asset. In the presidential campaign he shrewdly capitalized on
Watergate. From the Oval Office he urged Americans to "trust me" and
cultivated an image of righteous candor: "I'll never lie to you." In the spirit
of Jefferson, that other gentleman farmer from the South, he took pains to
demonstrate that he, too, had the common touch. The pomp and ceremony
so characteristic of Nixon's presidency were ostentatiously abandoned. Following inaugural ceremonies at the Capitol, he refused the presidential lim-
ousine and walked down Pennsylvania Avenue to the White House hand-in-
hand with the First Lady. In his first televised address, a "fireside chat," he
appeared in a cardigan and open-collared shirt. He wore denims and polo
shirts at congressional picnics, briefly banished the musical flourishes of
"Hail to the Chief" at official functions, and conferred frequently with the
press. He attended town meetings in out-of-the-way places and stayed overnight in the homes of ordinary Americans. He even sent his eight-year-old
daughter to an inner-city public school. In time, as the memory of Watergate
receded, such self-conscious symbolism came to seem gratuitous. Gradually,
a less accessible, less informal chief executive emerged, sometimes to the
strains of "Hail to the Chief." This least pretentious of all recent presidents,
however, must be credited for his effort to strip the presidency of its more
imperial forms.

However engaging his personal style, Carter's popular support was small.
During his second year in office, his approval rating fell to 40 percent. By
1979 it plummeted to 26 percent, marking him as less popular than Nixon
at his lowest point. Aside from the self-evident fact that Carter, like Ford,
inspired little popular confidence, there was no single explanation for his
rapid descent from public favor. Some thought him to be the victim of his
own demystification of the presidency; some said he was a weak swimmer
out of his depth. Others thought him the legatee of the peoples' mistrust of
Johnson and Nixon; a few believed that he came to be president at a time
when the nation's problems were insoluble, when its bloated bureaucracy
and its unruly political insitutions were unmanageable.

By all accounts, Carter was an earnest, intelligent, hardworking president
who lacked neither courage nor character. To provide the practical experience he and his staff so obviously lacked, he appointed several old Washington hands, including such members of the foreign policy establishment as
Secretary of State Cyrus Vance and Secretary of Defense Harold Brown, and
such seasoned bureaucrats as Health, Education, and Welfare Secretary Joseph Califano and Energy Secretary James Schlesinger. However, his tangible achievements were few. He did appoint more women and blacks to
high office than any other president, and he managed to trim a costly
congressional pork barrel for dam and water projects and to win support for
new Departments of Education and Energy. But his detailed and technically
sound proposals for long overdue tax, welfare, and civil service reforms, his
bill to create a consumer protection agency, and his hospital-cost containment measure got nowhere. His energy bill, the centerpiece of his domestic

program, encountered withering fire from the oil and gas lobby. By shifting the measure's emphasis from conservation to development and from consumer compensation to investment incentives, Congress satisfied the demands of powerful private interests, but it passed a bill that was anything but the "moral equivalent of war" promised by a frustrated president. In its final form, the energy bill provided appreciable reductions in neither of the two most critical areas: domestic consumption and foreign dependence.

In other areas of the economy the administration's record was worse — the worst, it was said, since Herbert Hoover. During the campaign, Carter identified recession as the nation's foremost domestic problem. In his term an assortment of ills identified with a troubled economy continued unabated: unemployment (particularly for black teenagers but also for nonwhites generally); declining investment, savings, and productivity levels; stagnated or declining after-tax earnings; and mounting trade deficits. But it was high and variable inflation — which in early 1980 threatened to reach an annual rate of 20 percent — that proved to be the curse of the 1970s and Carter's greatest political liability. Spurred by sharply rising food, fuel, housing, and transportation costs, consumer prices doubled between 1967 and 1978. Between 1973 and 1978, the cost of automobiles jumped 72 percent and new homes 67 percent; in 1979 gasoline prices rose 60 percent.

Carter's approach to the crisis of double-digit inflation was hesitant, belated, and fully as conservative as his Republican predecessors. Convinced that mandatory "wage and price controls have never worked in peacetime," he did not find a workable alternative. In 1978 he proposed voluntary guidelines (7 percent) and created a Council on Wage and Price Stability to monitor the results. This was not strong medicine and the patient got worse. The Consumer Price Index rose 13.3 percent in 1979; early the following year both inflation and interest rates topped 18 percent. In March 1980, midway into the presidential primaries, Carter proposed to balance the budget through drastic spending cuts and imposed a modest federal gasoline consumption tax and new restraints on consumer credit. Such halfway measures promised no immediate relief. Short of fundamental structural changes in the economy, many economists believed a deep recession to be the most effective way to slow the rising wage-price spiral.

CARTER AND HUMAN RIGHTS

In foreign affairs the Georgia president often proceeded more imaginatively. From the outset he indicated that his administration would be less devoted to traditional balance-of-power geopolitics than to human rights. Practical considerations, however, often undercut this policy. Despite a decade-long thaw in the Cold War, conflicting Soviet-American interests in Africa, Asia, the Middle East, and Latin America often seemed to dictate continued U.S. support for repressive anti-communist regimes. Thus, following the Soviet invasion of Afghanistan in December 1979, Carter offered military aid to, and alliance with Pakistan dictator Mohammad Zia ul-Haq. Similarly, the administration's support for Russian "prisoners of conscience" sometimes clashed with the president's wish to promote détente and a Soviet-American arms reduction agreement. Despite the unattractive trade-offs apparently required by world politics, Carter more than any other chief executive since Franklin Roosevelt tried to practice the human rights doctrine that the nation preached.

Other foreign policy successes included an act of singularly bold and personal diplomacy. Carter brought together Egypt's President Anwar Sadat and Israel's Prime Minister Menachem Begin for direct negotiations that resulted in the historic Camp David accords. Although hopes for a full resolution of the Middle East crisis were not realized, Carter's initiative marked the first real break-through in Arab-Israeli relations since the October War of 1973. He also completed the normalization of relations with the People's Republic of China, and over the opposition of Ronald Reagan and other conservatives, he negotiated the gradual return of the Panama Canal to Panamanian authority.

Administration efforts to win early confirmation of the SALT II agreement were less successful. The SALT process, begun by Nixon and Kissinger in the heyday of détente, was a confusing issue to the average American who had little understanding of modern nuclear defense systems. Generally favored by a people who wanted peace, the process was nonetheless complicated by a pervasive American mistrust of the Soviet Union and by a growing fear that the United States was no longer militarily superior to its principal Cold War adversary. Some arms experts opposed SALT II on the grounds that its limits were too high and that it would accelerate rather than slow the race for strategic advantage. But others argued that the Carter administration had been outbargained by the sharp traders of the Kremlin. On balance, the treaty seemed to promise some measure of arms stability at a time when the Soviets had the edge in ICBMs and submarine missles and the United States had a substantial lead in long-range strategic bombers and nuclear warheads.

Arguments of comparative advantage, however, quickly became moot. Troubled from the outset by Soviet interests in the affairs of such third-world nations as Ethiopia, South Yemen, and Angola — and in late 1979, by the discovery of a Soviet combat brigade in Cuba — the SALT II treaty ratification process was derailed by the Soviet occupation of its hapless Islamic neighbor to the South, Afghanistan. To be sure, the Afghans, through a succession of pro-Soviet governments, had been closely allied to the USSR for a decade or more. But this was the first Soviet military action since World War II outside the Warsaw Pact countries. Given the political and religious turmoil then sweeping much of the Islamic crescent, given the proximity of the oil fields in Iran, given traditional Russian designs on the warm waters of the Persian Gulf, the Carter administration could not have ignored this latest example of Soviet aggression. With Cold War fevers rising, the administration indefinitely delayed consideration of SALT II. The president also announced an American boycott of the 1980 Summer Olympics in Moscow and an embargo of American grain and high technology exports to the USSR.

The seizure of U.S. diplomatic personnel by fanatically anti-American militants in Teheran roused the nation's martial spirit. Once praised by Carter as an "island of stability," the oil-rich kingdom of Iran, with its repressive and staunchly pro-American Shah, was toppled by religious and cultural fundamentalists bent on the creation of an Islamic republic. In November 1979, with the apparent support of the revolution's elderly spiritual leader, the austere and (to Westerners) inscrutable Ayatollah Ruhollah Khomeini, youthful militants stormed the American Embassy taking some 65 hostages and demanding the return of the Shah then temporarily in exile in the United States.

The administration's response to this violation of international conventions was restrained. Dismissing immediate military action as counterproductive, it applied economic and international pressure, but did not at first sever diplomatic relations. In time the embassy's black and women employees were released. Despite the censure of a nearly unanimous world community, the constructive intervention of the United Nations and the World Court, and the urgings of duly constituted but impotent secular officials of Iran, the militants and their patron, the aging Ayatollah, refused further compromise and kept more than 50 Americans in captivity. Having apparently exhausted all practical remedies, the president risked a military rescue mission in May 1980 that ended before it began with death for eight American commandos, due to equipment failure. After this aborted mission, the United States remained a frustrated giant. For Jimmy Carter, who had often questioned the Cold War expedient that brought American aid to counterrevolutionary regimes no matter how autocratic, the situation was surely ironical. In an American election year, in a Near Eastern theocracy halfway round the world, sentiment raged against the "American devils" who had propped up the Shah, trained SAVAK, his dread secret police, and supplied the arms he sometimes turned on his own people. To be sure, Carter had stood by the Shah after it was clear that most Iranians did not. But it was a cruel fate that forced this champion of human rights to reap the bitter harvest of a policy he had so eloquently disavowed. To ensure maximum political damage to the president, the Iranians released the hostages on Ronald Reagan's inauguration day, 14 months after their capture.

As Carter began his re-election campaign, he seemed destined to be the first elected president since Hoover to be denied a second term. Having promised the moon in 1976, he had to run on his own uninspiring record in 1980. Republican, independent, and Democratic voters dismissed him as ineffectual. Members of his own party launched a "Dump Carter" movement. Nevertheless, he denied the challenge of his Democratic rivals, among them California Governor Jerry Brown and Massachusetts Senator Edward M. Kennedy. Among the Republicans, seasoned campaign watchers believed that such relative moderates as Senator Howard Baker of Tennessee and former CIA Director George Bush of Connecticut were more "electable" than the aging (69-years-old), rigidly conservative frontrunner, Ronald Reagan. But the attractive Californian was the favorite of party stalwarts and easily won a first-ballot nomination. Progressive Republican Congressman John Anderson of Illinois defected to become a third-party candidate.

Scarcely half of the electorate voted; among those who did, 51 percent preferred Reagan. The Democrats retained control of the House, but the Republicans for the first time since 1952 seized the Senate. Among the Democratic casualties were several leading Senate liberals — including George McGovern — targeted for defeat by Protestant fundamentalists and other "New Right" political action groups. Analysts generally agreed that Reagan had benefitted heavily from the issues of inflation and hostages in Iran and an election-eve debate with Carter. Also, the voting pendulum seemed to be moving to the right, as a declining birthrate and longer life expectancies produced an older electorate and major population shifts increased clout to the politically conservative Sun-Belt states of the South and West. A genuine mandate is a rarity in American politics, and only time would tell if the election of 1980, like that of 1936, marked a major partisan realignment. Liberals, finding comfort in the low voter turnout, noted that only one in four adult Americans voted for Reagan in 1980, but the new president could legitimately claim a landslide. He was elected, he seemed to believe, to roll back the Soviet threat and dismantle the welfare state.

CONFLICTING HISTORICAL VIEWPOINTS: NO. 16

Is the Presidency Too Powerful?

Soon after the ratification of the Constitution, Thomas Jefferson advised his friend and protégé, James Madison, that "the tyranny of the legislature is really the danger most to be feared and will continue to be so for many years to come. The tyranny of the executive power will come in its turn, but at a more distant period." Some two centuries later, following the extraordinary assertions of presidential power by Lyndon Johnson and Richard Nixon, a growing number of scholars believed that Jefferson's "more distant period" was at hand. In recent decades, they argued, the presidency had been unduly exalted; the presidents had grown too aloof, too arrogant, too neglectful of congressional prerogatives. In this view, the system of constitutional checks and balances devised by the founders no longer effectively restrained executive authority. In the words of one political scientist, the man in the Oval Office had been elevated from "Servant to Sun King."

The Vietnam War and the Watergate scandals were the most flagrant and frequently cited examples of a runaway presidency. Yet most scholars agreed that Johnson's wholesale escalation of the undeclared war in Southeast Asia, Nixon's secret bombing of Cambodia, or even John Mitchell's "White House horrors" were not so much aberrations as a culmination of the twentieth-century tendency toward presidential aggrandizement. The roots of the activist presidency could be traced to the bold examples of such assertive chief executives as Andrew Jackson and Abraham Lincoln — and more recently to Theodore Roosevelt and Woodrow Wilson, the first of the so-called "modern presidents." But closer in time and in importance was the growth of presidential power since the New Deal. In a period of almost uninterrupted crises, stretching from the Depression of the 1930s to the threat of nuclear destruction in the 1960s, executive authority in such critical areas as the economy and foreign policy had expanded enormously.

*Until the intrusions of Vietnam and Watergate, scholars generally agreed that these developments were both inevitable and constitutional. In an increasingly complex and threatening world, they concluded, the nation's welfare and security required a strong president. The legislative process was properly deliberative and inherently slow. Only the president enjoyed the capacity for centralized leadership; only he possessed the control of information and communication demanded by a modern nation in a troubled world. This view, noted the political scientist Thomas E. Cronin (*Congressional Record, *October 5, 1956), became "textbook orthodoxy." It was forcefully advocated by such eminent students of American government as Clinton Rossiter (*The American Presidency, *1956), Lewis W. Koenig (*The Chief Executive, *1964), and James MacGregor Burns (*Presidential Government, *1965). Perhaps the most influential spokesman for executive domination was Richard E. Neustadt, whose* Presidential Power *(1960) characterized the president as the "Great Initiator" of both domestic and foreign policy and the "Final Arbiter" in matters of war. The standard in its field for nearly a decade, this popular book has been aptly called "a latter-day version of Machiavelli's* Prince," *a primer for chief executives who would maximize their power.*

*Amid the disillusionments of war and scandal, however, this expansive view fell rapidly into scholarly disfavor. Even without the example of Watergate, Neustadt (*Alliance Politics, *1970) became more cautious in his claims for presidential power. Alarmed by the president's seemingly unchecked capacity to wage war, some writers called the office a "Frankenstein monster"; an increasing number expressed fear that the ship of state had listed dangerously to its presidential side. Almost overnight a new scholarly consensus emerged; even many former aggrandizers became critics of executive authority. Among the most provocative of these was the historian Arthur M. Schlesinger, Jr., whose widely read* Imperial Presidency *(1973) elegantly lamented the development in the office of the American president of "the most absolute monarch (with the possible exception of Mao Zedong of China) among the great powers of the world." Although in earlier works Schlesinger had, by his own admission, contributed to the "rise of the presidential mystique," he now attacked the "cult" of presidential activism and argued for a return to a "properly balanced" system of executive restraint and legislative responsibility.*

And so the pendulum swings. Taken together, these sharply diverging schools of presidential analysis — the one dominant in the 1960s, the other emerging full-blown in the 1970s — provide as neat an example of the importance of perspective to the interpretative process as the student is likely to find. With the Nixon excesses so near to mind, scholars who once lauded Theodore Roosevelt for his sweeping theory of executive "stewardship" or faulted Dwight Eisenhower for his unseemly "Whiggery" fell under the spell of the two-centuries-old mandate for separated powers. Similarly, in the aftermath of Vietnam, historians and political scientists who once praised Franklin Roosevelt and Harry Truman for their bold foreign policy initiatives became critical of executive usurpations in the areas of war and treaty making. Whither revisionism? Only time can tell. But president watchers seem momentarily confused about executive power. During the apparent paralysis of the later Carter years, many wondered if American institutions, and particularly the presidency, could effectively address late twentieth-century problems. More recently, during the American military build-up in Central America, others worried that presidential initiative might once again involve the country in a war that neither Congress nor the public wanted.

FOR FURTHER READING

Those who would chart the social contours of the very recent past should begin with newspapers and periodicals. Other suggestive and widely varying points of departure include: Jerry Rubin's *Growing (Up) at Thirty-Seven* (1976) and Christopher Lasch, *The Culture of Narcissism* (1978) — both mentioned in the text; M. Rossman's *New Age Blues* (1979); Tom Wolfe's *Mauve Gloves & Madmen, Clutter & Vine* (1976); Jim Hougan's *Decadence* (1975); and P. Dolan and E. Quinn, eds., *Sense of the Seventies* (1978).

A multitude of books cover the Nixon era. Rowland Evans and Robert Novak have written *Nixon in the White House* (1971), and Jules Witcover in *The Resurrection of Richard Nixon* (1970), Garry Wills in *Nixon Agonistes* (1971), and Fawn Brodie in *Richard Nixon* (1980) examine the man, his personality, and his politics. Nixon tells his own story in *RN* (1978). Watergate books include John Dean's *Blind Ambition* (1976), Leon Jaworski's *The Right and the Power* (1976), and Bob Woodward and Carl Bernstein's *All the President's Men* (1976). Kevin Phillips suggestively analyzes Nixon's election strategy in *The Emerging Republican Majority* (1969); Richard Scammon and Ben Wattenberg portray the popular mood in *The Real Majority* (1970); and George Tindall, in *The Disruption of the Solid South* (1972), places the southern strategy in historical perspective. Accounts of the Nixon-Kissinger foreign policy include: Kissinger's important autobiography, *White House Years* (1979); Marvin and Bernard Kalb, *Kissinger* (1974); Seymour Hersh, *The Price of Power* (1983); and William Shawcross, *Sideshow: Kissinger, Nixon and the Destruction of Cambodia* (1978).

In the post-Nixon era, Jerry Hartmann's *Palace Politics* (1980) is an inside account of Ford's years, but see also Ford's own *A Time to Heal* (1980). Carter's memoir, *Keeping Faith* (1982) is disappointing and should be supplemented with W. L. Miller's *Yankee from Georgia* (1978), Betty Glad's *Jimmy Carter* (1980), and Bruce Mazlish and Edwin Diamond's psychobiographical *Jimmy Carter* (1979). Memoirs by notable insiders include Rosalyn Carter's *First Lady from Plains* (1984) and Zbigniew Brzezinski's *Power and Principle* (1983).

32

★ ★ ★ ★ ★ ★

New Directions: Federal Policy in the 1980s

PERHAPS more than any other American president, Ronald Wilson Reagan presents a paradox. A divorced, former actor and self-styled king of Hollywood's Grade B movies, he entered the White House as the symbol of traditional family values and the critic of a permissive society. A sincere admirer of Franklin Roosevelt, Reagan as a Republican presidential candidate draped himself in FDR's mantle, even as he carried the banner of the resurgent anti–New Deal right. By his own admission he had been "a near-hopeless hemophilic liberal" during his acting days. After World War II, he helped form California's branch of the liberal Americans for Democratic Action. He remained a registered Democrat until 1962. During the 1950s, however, while touring the nation as a representative of General Electric, he moved sharply to the right. By 1964 he was a Goldwater partisan, and when the conservative Arizonian's presidential hopes perished in the Johnson landslide of that year, Reagan emerged as the most effective evangel of the New Right. In 1966 he was elected to the first of two terms as governor of California.

THE NEW FEDERALISM REDUX

Reagan charmed the press and public with his undisguised pleasure in being president and his self-deprecating style. Any apprehensions about his age were soon dissolved by his demonstrated courage and fast recovery from an assassination attempt during his first months in office. Although his political experience was limited to two terms as California's governor, he quickly proved himself to be a masterful legislative tactician with impressive support on both sides of the congressional aisle. A seasoned television and radio performer, his skillful public appearances won him a reputation as "the great communicator." Critics noted, however, that he preferred set speeches to press conferences, that he was most effective when delivering well-rehearsed lines, and that his off-the-cuff remarks often required clarification by White House staffers. Some doubted that he possessed the intellectual capacity and expertise required by the office. Even presidential aides conceded that he took little interest in detailed analysis of complex issues. During his re-election bid in 1984, the *New Republic,* the most prestigious liberal journal, pondered the delicate "Ignoramus Issue" and reported the widespread view among political observers that "Reagan is the most ignorant President anyone can recall." These doubts were not widely shared by the voters, who found their president, even when they did not share his uncompromising ideology, the most likeable chief executive since Eisenhower.

Much of Reagan's appeal could be traced to his uncomplicated vision of the American destiny. A buoyant man who preached the simple virtues, he brought to Washington a sense of purpose that contrasted sharply with the disconsolate drift of the post-Watergate period. While Carter had spoken of a national malaise — "a crisis of confidence . . . that is threatening the very fabric of America" — Reagan exuded a refreshing optimism. In an age of disminishing expectations, he spoke of the "rebirth of confidence and hope and progress." His appeal lay not in the depth of his understanding of national and international issues but in his confident evocation of an "era of renewal," of unbounded growth and unrivaled power.

The U.S. domestic maladies, the president believed, were attributable to the disease of "big, never-mind-the-cost government." To promote recovery, he borrowed Nixon's slogan, the New Federalism, and prescribed massive doses of laissez faire and what conservative economists called "supply-side economics." Although the Republicans spoke of a new beginning and many praised the administration's "bold departure" in domestic economic policy, Reagan's New Federalism of the 1980s recalled Calvin Coolidge's New Era of the 1920s. Supply-side policy, as the administration's budget director conceded, found its most direct antecedent in the "trickle-down" policies of Andrew Mellon. In practice, if not precisely in theory, the supply-siders promised that the administration could reduce taxes, increase military spending, and balance the budget, all at the same time. Tax cuts that favored business and the wealthy, the Reaganites reasoned, would promote prosperity and increase federal revenues by encouraging capital investments. Deregulation would stimulate productivity by freeing both labor and capital from federal meddling. The elimination of social programs for all but the "truly deserving needy" would foster a more self-reliant citizenry and bring government receipts and expenditures into balance for the first time since 1969. Together, the president predicted, these initiatives would provide full employment without inflation, frugal government without social distress, military strength without economic pain.

Dubbed "Reaganomics" by the press, the administration's proposals received mixed reviews. Conservatives, sharing the president's distaste for progressive taxes, social services, and intrusive government, were enthusiastic. Consumer advocates and environmentalists, on the other hand, feared a decline in the quality of American life; and liberals protested that the Reagan revolution portended a new age of opulence for the rich and austerity for the poor. Other critics, including many Wall Street analysts, were skeptical that free-market Republicanism could balance the budget of a government that tried to buy more arms with less revenue. In the end, however, the supply-siders and the free marketeers had their way.

During 1981 the Reagan taxation and spending measures moved through the conservative 97th Congress with a speed that invited comparison to the legislative triumphs of Franklin Roosevelt and Lyndon Johnson. In the largest tax reduction in history, income taxes were cut, across the board, by 25 percent over a three-year period; military outlays were sharply increased; expenditures were slashed for welfare payments, food stamps, student aid, cancer research, school lunches, job training, and other social purposes. (Subsidies for such powerful interest groups as tobacco and dairy farmers, on the other hand, escaped the axe; the administration sponsored Payment in Kind, a per-acre farm subsidy of most benefit to the biggest growers.) Free-market enthusiasts, opposed on principle to government regulation or planning, were assigned to regulatory, environmental, and consumer-protection agencies. Opponents of collective bargaining were appointed to the National Labor Relations Board; the Civil Rights Commission was packed with conservatives who shared Reagan's opposition to such federal remedies for discrimination as affirmative action programs, court-ordered busing, and legal services for the poor.

Conservative setbacks took place, as well as successes, and administration support in the House slipped considerably in the election of 1982. Reagan failed to win congressional support for reduced Social Security benefits. The administration's heavy-handed deregulators, particularly in the Environmental Protection Agency and the Department of the Interior, provoked a backlash that brought new vitality to the environmental movement and renewed public support for consumer- and worker-safety regulations. Single-issue crusaders, moreover, felt betrayed by presidential neglect of New Right social policy. Reagan was applauded by many conservatives as the most "pro-gun" president and for his opposition to the ERA and his support for tax-credits for all-white private schools. But his half-hearted support for school prayer, anti-abortion, and anti-busing amendments embittered the Moral Majority. When he appointed Sandra Day O'Connor to the Supreme Court, the Moral Majority again expressed outrage, alleging that the first woman justice (however conservative) was "soft" on abortion.

The results of the Reagan economic program were not encouraging in the short term. Although inflation declined appreciably, apparently in response to stabilizing world oil and food prices, the American unemployment rate approached 11 percent (the highest since 1940). By 1982, with bankruptcies and interest rates soaring and the stock and bond markets in disarray, the nation was in full-scale recession, the worst since the 1930s. The resulting revenue shortfall pushed annual deficits and the cumulative national debt to new and alarming heights. The president repeated his commitment to a balanced budget and attempted to use the deficit to force larger reductions in social programs. But he also vowed to continue the fiscal policies of low taxes and high military expenditures that compounded the budget crisis. In 1983–1984 the administration could also point to an upturn in the economy and a reduction in unemployment. Meanwhile, despite Reaganite fulminations against big government, federal expenditures as a share of the GNP grew from 21 percent in 1980 to an unprecedented 24 percent in 1984.

REAGAN'S FOREIGN POLICY

Reagan's foreign policy was also implacably conservative. Reviving the apocalyptic rhetoric of the early Cold War years, he identified the Soviet Union as "the evil empire." The United States, he believed, had learned too much from the disastrous Vietnam War and too little from the appeasement of Hitler at Munich. It had "starved" its military and permitted the USSR to gain a "definite margin" of nuclear superiority. Falling to "Number Two in military power" during the 1970s, the United States risked "nuclear blackmail."

Moderates in both parties deplored Reagan's intemperate anti-Sovietism, and three former presidents and most military authorities disputed his assessment of relative Soviet-American might. But the commander-in-chief once again generally had his way with Congress. With military outlays increasing up to 12 percent annually, the administration projected a $1.6 trillion defense budget for 1984–1988, much of it for a controversial new generation of nuclear hardware. In the 1960s and 1970s, the nation's defense establishment had sought security in a stable world order with a policy of essential military parity between the Superpowers. The intent of the Reagan administration's huge defense expenditures seemed to be to push the arms race beyond "strategic sufficiency" into a new era of unchallenged American military primacy.

The Reagan hard line was mirrored by increasing Soviet bellicosity, as both sides pronounced an end to détente. The American grain embargo was lifted (a campaign pledge to farmers), but prospects for additional arms limitation agreements dimmed when the administration announced that further negotiations must be linked to Soviet "good behavior." Salt II, withdrawn from Senate consideration by Carter in 1979, was discarded in 1981. In 1983 Reagan, citing recent missile implacements in the western USSR, deployed American missiles (under NATO auspices) in Western Europe. The Kremlin responded by placing additional rockets in Eastern Europe, by suspending all arms discussions then underway, and by boycotting the 1984 Summer Olympic Games in Los Angeles, along with other Eastern bloc nations.

Under mounting pressure from world opinion, both sides expressed renewed interest in nuclear reductions, but neither appeared ready to negotiate on terms acceptable to the other. A crisis in Eastern Europe passed without major East-West incident when the Soviet-dominated Polish government crushed a liberal movement (led by the trade union Solidarity) with martial law rather than risk a Soviet invasion. Again, in September 1983, tension mounted when the Soviets inexplicably shot down an off-course Korean commercial airliner, which was inside Russian air space. This incident sparked a new round of recriminations and fed a universal fear of nuclear exchange by accident or miscalculation.

The danger of a major war seemed particularly acute in the Third World. Distinguishing between regimes that were merely "authoritarian" (or right wing) and those that were "totalitarian" (left wing), Reagan renounced Carter's human rights policy and returned to one of alliance with anti-communist governments, however repressive. The most controversial application of this policy came in Central America, where the U.S. military presence was markedly increased to preclude "more Cubas" and to frustrate perceived Soviet ambitions. The administration sent military advisers and arms to support a brutal military dictatorship in El Salvador, trained and equipped right-wing insurgents to overthrow a leftist regime in Nicaragua, and sent U.S. marines to the Caribbean island of Grenada to topple a revolutionary government. Reagan's critics, many of them Republicans, faulted his propensity for military, as opposed to economic or diplomatic, solutions. In 1984 a presidential commission chaired by Henry Kissinger recommended a Marshall Plan for this long-neglected region. Yet few White House observers expected a change of course. Despite mounting congressional opposition to Reagan's big-stick interventionism — and the president's repeated promise not to commit combat troops — many feared that Central America was rapidly becoming the American Southeast Asia of the 1980s.

Amid these confusions, the national attention shifted to the presidential election of 1984. Reagan and his vice president, George Bush, were enthusiastically renominated by the most conservative Republican convention in modern times. The Democrats selected Walter Mondale, the liberal former vice president as their presidential nominee, and his running mate, Geraldine Ferraro of New York, a congressional representative and the first woman to be nominated by either major party for the vice presidency. Both presidential candidates affirmed that the election offered voters a clear-cut choice between conflicting visions of the American future. Although skeptics noted that the campaign itself turned more often on personalities than issues, the conservative mood of the mid 1980s clearly favored Reagan. In November the likeable Republican president, if not precisely his domestic or foreign policies, won an impressive vote of confidence. The Reagan-Bush ticket carried 59 percent of the popular vote and every state except Minnesota (Mondale's home state) and the District of Columbia.

FOR FURTHER READING

Again the student's attention is directed toward newspapers and periodicals, the best windows through which to view current events. Early accounts of Reagan and the resurgent right include: Peter Steinfels's *The Neo-Conservatives* (1980); Alan Crawford's *Thunder on the Right* (1980); Lou Cannon's *Reagan* (1982); Robert Dallek's *Ronald Reagan: The Politics of Symbolism*

(1984); and Strobe Talbott, *The Russians and Reagan* (1984). The president's own writings include a memoir, *Where's the Rest of Me?* (1965), and his recent campaign tract, *Abortion and the Conscience of the Nation* (1984). The first inside account of the Reagan administration is the mildly critical *Caveat* (1984) by former Secretary of State Alexander Haig.

INDEX